THE NEW CIVIL RIGHTS RESEARCH

To my loving wife Ruth and our warm and fuzzy "kits" Daphne, Stanley and Misty
BFS

To my husband Eric, my love, my life
LBN

The New Civil Rights Research

A Constitutive Approach

BENJAMIN FLEURY-STEINER
University of Delaware, USA

LAURA BETH NIELSEN
Northwestern University and The American Bar Foundation, USA

Routledge
Taylor & Francis Group

LONDON AND NEW YORK

First published 2006 by Ashgate Publishing

Reissued 2019 by Routledge
2 Park Square, Milton Park, Abingdon, Oxon OX14 4RN
52 Vanderbilt Avenue, New York, NY 10017

Routledge is an imprint of the Taylor & Francis Group, an informa business

Publisher's Note
The publisher has gone to great lengths to ensure the quality of this reprint but points out that some imperfections in the original copies may be apparent.

Disclaimer
The publisher has made every effort to trace copyright holders and welcomes correspondence from those they have been unable to contact.

Typeset by Saxon Graphics Ltd, Derby

A Library of Congress record exists under LC control number:

ISBN 13: 978-0-8153-9802-8 (hbk)
ISBN 13: 978-1-138-62112-1 (pbk)
ISBN 13: 978-0-429-06063-2 (ebk)

Contents

List of Contributors

Catherine R. Albiston, University of California-Berkeley School of Law

Hadar Aviram, Faculty of Law, Tel Aviv University

Frank Rudy Cooper, Suffolk University Law School

Benjamin Fleury-Steiner, University of Delaware

Elizabeth A. Hoffmann, Purdue University

Jessica Hodge, University of Delaware

Idit Kostiner, Faculty of Law, Tel Aviv University

Anna-Maria Marshall, University of Illinois at Urbana-Champaign

Michael McCann, University of Washington

Laura Beth Nielsen, Northwestern University and the American Bar Foundation

Jérôme Pélisse, University of Reims

Kimberly D. Richman, University of San Francisco

Judith Taylor, University of Toronto

Preface

On Legal Rights Consciousness:
A Challenging Analytical Tradition

MICHAEL McCANN

This volume gives voice to a new generation of sociolegal scholars committed to innovative scholarship on the subject of ordinary legal consciousness about civil rights. Their projects represent important contributions to a now well-established tradition in sociolegal study. The following prefatory essay has been included to outline some of the most prominent conceptual and empirical features of this scholarly tradition. My chapter title's reference to a "challenging analytical tradition" is purposely ambiguous. On the one hand, studies of legal consciousness have openly challenged and transgressed a variety of premises central to older traditions of "realist" scholarship on law *and* society. This spirit of innovation is evidenced in claims throughout this book to provide accounts that are post-realist, post-behavioral, post-positive, non-instrumental, and the like. On the other hand, the study of legal consciousness itself has been fraught with its own intrinsic conceptual, theoretical, and empirical challenges. This essay will catalogue some of these puzzles with which contemporary intellectuals, including those authors in this collection, have had to grapple. My modest goal is to help clarify more than to resolve the complexities, contradictions, and conundrums at stake in the inquiries facing scholars. Put another way, the aim here is to map out the distinctive but demanding conceptual terrain on which scholars have constructed their research rather than to prescribe the best way to navigate through the more treacherous zones of that complex landscape.[1]

I begin by briefly tracing the historical context of this developing topography, for present challenges in part reflect the multifaceted legacy of earlier research from which attention to legal consciousness arose. I then outline key concepts at stake in studies of legal consciousness; this will provide something like the conceptual nomenclature, or key, for the map. The last and longest section outlines a half dozen or so of the puzzles that bewilder scholars trying to find their way through the roughest terrain on the map.

---

[1] I point out that other scholars have provided excellent surveys of the terrain at various stages of its development – McCann and March (1996), Engel (1998), Marshall and Barclay (2003), and of course the introduction to this volume by Fleury-Steiner and Nielsen.

Precursors and Intellectual Context

The study of legal rights consciousness developed in response to a variety of different research agendas in sociolegal research.[2] One important antecedent from the 1960s and early 1970s was research regarding "legal needs." A variety of scholars observed that persons of low status and income are treated unequally by judges and other actors in the civil legal system. Among the reasons for this differential, discriminatory treatment was the fact that poor people did not view themselves as, or adopt the subjectivity of, fully-fledged rights-bearing citizens. As Carlin, Howard, and Messinger (1967) put it, many people in the population lack "legal competence." The authors' contentions that many lack a recognition of their due rights and a confident willingness to claim such rights in many circumstances provided insights developed later by many scholars of legal consciousness. Levine and Preston found much the same lack of awareness about rights among low-income people in their 1970 study. They attributed both a lack of relevant legal knowledge and a general sense of "powerlessness" or resignation that subjects felt in dealing with their circumstances. A later American Bar Foundation survey sampling "perceptions" of American citizens provided further support for this insight. The study, led by Barbara Curran (1977), found that persons of lower status viewed lawyers and the legal system less positively than did more affluent citizens. The findings emphasized that both social class and personal experience were major factors shaping perceptions about law as well as that those perceptions varied with different types of everyday problems and situations. At the same time, this study also illustrated the limitations of traditional mass survey instruments in capturing the contingencies and nuances of citizen perceptions about law or "legal consciousness."

By far the most important and direct influence on the development of studies regarding legal consciousness, however, has been scholarship focusing on "disputing processes." This included classic studies in diverse contexts by legal anthropologists Llewyllen and Hoebel in the 1940s, Gluckman in the 1950s and 1960s, and Abel (1973), Galanter (1974), Felstiner (1974), Jacob (1969), and, especially, Nader (1969) in the 1960s and 1970s. These studies were followed by a host of projects specifically within the US during the 1970s and 1980s that provided models of inquiry for later scholarship on legal consciousness. This scholarship generally offered frameworks grounded in carefully contextualized qualitative case studies of legal practice "in action," decentered the role of lawyers and judges as legal actors, and began to shift attention toward the legal "meanings" that attended and informed routine legal practice among "ordinary" citizens (see Engel 1998:124–26). The shift from behavior to meaning was equally apparent in quantitative survey research that developed out of the disputing paradigm. For example, the classic essay by Miller and Sarat reporting survey data from the Civil Litigation Research Project was clearly framed as a realist study of patterns in disputing behavior, conceptualized in terms of the famous disputing pyramid (1980–81). However, the essay began by questioning assumptions about an "adversary legal culture" and the alleged pervasiveness of

---

[2] David Engel's classic essay (1998) addresses the "antecedents" to legal consciousness research at greater length in his essay. My discussion here draws from, adds to, but little improves on his terrific essay.

"rights claiming" in the US, and it ended with a call for new types of inquiry into "the generation of injurious experiences and grievance perception" (p. 883).

The shift in attention toward legal meaning, knowledge, and subjectivity was influenced and reinforced by a variety of other developments as well. Lawrence Friedman (1989), Stewart Macaulay (1987), and others began to write about legal culture. Their conception of culture referred initially to the values, beliefs, and attitudes that provide coherence to social life; the approach drew on behavioral social science but clearly highlighted concern for meaning, especially in relation to society-wide norms, values, and categories of understanding. At the same time, influential neo-Marxist sociologists like Alan Hunt (1985), Douglas Hay (1975), and Stuart Hall (1978), as well as the legions of "critical legal scholars" (Kairys 1982) in US law schools, shifted attention to ideological analysis of law. The former scholars connected official legal discourse to broader issues of shifts in mass political culture and social understanding, aiming to develop a more complex and less deterministic analysis of how the concept of ideology is useful in linking studies of law to social class and hegemonic order. Much of the study by CLS scholars in the US focused on official, judicially constructed case law, but it likewise linked legal ideology to questions of power and hegemony, including to arguments over the concept of "false consciousness," further focusing attention on questions of meaning and power. These engagements were paralleled in the same era by the increasing attention to Foucault's theories that decentered "knowledge/power," emphasizing how disciplinary power circulates throughout society and the role of "discourse" in constituting social relations generally. Cultural anthropologists integrated all these various lines of thinking into new, more dynamic understandings of culture as pluralistic traditions of constitutive knowledge (see Merry 1988). The scholarship of Jean and John Comaraff regarding colonial and post-colonial politics in particular was significant in rethinking legal culture and hegemony. Likewise, critical legal studies generated other Crits engaged in critical race (Matsuda 1987; Crenshaw 1988; Williams 1991) and gender (see Bartlett and Kennedy 1991) theory. These latter scholars challenged not only important premises and conclusions of the critics, but again focused attention on the everyday relationships, practices, and discourses that figure in reproducing and challenging hierarchy. Critical race theorists in particular focused attention on narratives as both an object and method of analysis regarding legal meaning and power.

Finally, influential studies of "legal mobilization" grew amidst all of these other developments. Some strands of legal mobilization theory were developed in decidedly behavioral directions (Black 1976) but, much like closely related studies of disputing processes, other scholars pushed legal mobilization analysis in more interpretive directions, attending to matters of perception, language, and understanding as well as behavior. For example, Stuart Scheingold's classic *The Politics of Rights* (1974) focused attention on images and ideologies of law in American society, on both the "myths of rights" and the mobilization of rights talk as a resource in struggles for social change. Frances Kahn Zemans' classic 1983 essay on the topic defined legal mobilization itself as the transformation of a desire into a claim of right, which itself is influenced by citizens' understandings and perceptions. Studies of individual legal mobilization were paralleled by an explosion of study into collective action around rights. My own 1994 study *Rights at Work* made legal discourse, understanding, and intersubjective meaning a focus, and dedicated the longest chapter to the subject of "legal consciousness" of working women involved in struggles to raise wages. Legal rights consciousness provided a topic for inquiry into legal meaning and an angle for expanding analysis regarding the impacts of legal mobilization activity. A host of scholars have continued to study legal mobilization and legal consciousness together in a variety of fascinating ways (Silverstein 1996; Marshall 2003).

Scholarship specifically addressing the developing conception of "everyday legal consciousness" began to emerge in the 1980s. The new literature reflected all of the influences listed above, but also struggled to distinguish its own unique conceptual framework, empirical approach, and contributions in various ways. For example, a special issue of the *Law & Society Review* in 1988 (and a parallel issue of *Legal Studies Forum* in the same year) organized by the influential Amherst seminar identified legal "ideology" *in* society as its focus but linked this to studies of popular consciousness, legal culture, legal discourse, and legal meaning. Important books by Greenhouse (1989), Merry (1990), Yngvesson (1993), Greenhouse, Engel and Yngvesson (1994), Sarat and Felstiner (1995), and Ewick and Silbey (1998) during the 1990s propelled the study of everyday disputing and legal consciousness into prominence as a cutting edge area of sociolegal inquiry. From the start, insights gleaned from disputing analysis and legal mobilization frameworks have been integral to study of legal consciousness, even while scholars have labored to challenge, transcend, or revise elements of the former enterprises (see Brigham 2000). Understanding these earlier intellectual pursuits and debates that engaged, enraged, and energized scholars studying legal consciousness is very important in appreciating both the challenges the project poses to older traditions and the challenges that bedevil the project itself still.

Key Premises and Contributions of Scholarship on Legal Consciousness

The catalogue of studies regarding legal consciousness over the last two decades is long, and the scholarship is hardly unitary in its core premises, principles, and project design. Nevertheless, it is worth identifying some general features that most scholars would agree distinguish this research agenda.

We can begin with the basic *reorientation to imagining law itself* that is central to studies of ordinary legal consciousness. In short, most such scholars focus on law as forms of knowledge that saturate intersubjective social life in various ways and degrees. Whether conceptualized in terms of discourse, ideology, narratives, or "schemas," legal knowledge is envisioned as part of the cultural repertoire or "toolkit" through which citizen subjects understand and negotiate their social activity. Legal knowledge includes but is hardly limited to rules; it contains the full array of linguistic, discursive, and conceptual conventions that facilitate human thought and action. Scholars thus identify legal consciousness as the ongoing activity of meaning-making employing the knowledge and logics, the vocabulary and styles of reasoning, that we associate with "the legal." Legal consciousness is not a static "thing," but rather is a dynamic process of cognition facilitated by legal knowledge accumulated through social experience. In short, legal consciousness is the cognitive activity through which legal understandings, expectations, aspirations, strategies, and choices are developed. As Ewick and Silbey write:

We conceive of consciousness as part of a reciprocal process in which the meanings given by individuals to their world, and law and legal institutions as part of that world, become repeated, patterned and stabilized, and those institutionalized structures become part of the meaning systems employed by individuals (1992:741).

It follows that legal knowledge and consciousness are understood to be inherently *indeterminate*. In other words, the discourses and logics at work in legal consciousness are fluid, flexible, dynamic, and subject to multiple constructions and repeated reconstruction. One aspect of this indeterminacy derives from the intrinsically open-ended character of legal language and logics. "Culture always contains within it polyvalent, potentially contradictory meanings, images, actions" (Comaroff and Comaroff 1992:27; Sarat 1990:375). Another source of indeterminacy is the multiplicity of law itself – the fact that what we label as discrete "legal systems" usually comprise plural legal traditions. Official state law in most complex societies is a mélange of different legal forms (civil, common, administrative, constitutional, etc.) that concurrently govern various regions of social life. The result is that, in most societies, law is a mosaic of interconnected and even hybrid traditions constantly in development, contested, clashing, and contorted by differently situated social actors and groups (see Merry 1988). Moreover, the various normative logics and discourses that we associate with law are inherently contingent, which is to say that they are shaped by a variety of extra-legal factors. These influences may include extra-legal normative and interpretive traditions (morality, custom, religion) and discursive logics (science, markets, professionalism, etc.) that regularly interact with legal conventions in practical understanding, decision-making, and activity. Finally, specific acts of legal cognition, speaking, and doing tend to vary with particular places, spaces, and situations. As such, legal consciousness may vary dramatically in different situations for even the same individuals. Indeed, "a person may express, through words or actions, a multifaceted, contradictory, and variable legal consciousness," posits Susan Silbey (1992:46). If each person is constituted by multiple selves, as post-modern theorists insist, it is hardly surprising that legal consciousness is plural, dynamic, complex.

All of these factors underline the importance of the *contexts* in which subjectivity is formed and expressed. Indeed, contextual factors are widely considered to be very important topics of analysis by sociolegal scholars interested in legal consciousness and practice. Analytical focus thus should on the "situated, bounded, local place and time ... The play of law in the everyday world is stratified and culturally specific," write Sarat and Kearns (1993:4, 9). How does legal consciousness interact with other norms and logics? How does the specific institutional setting, the character of relationships, the situation or position of individuals, the nature of the problem or dispute at stake, and the larger social environment affect the workings of subjects? These are questions that studies of legal consciousness routinely raise. Such analyses of context have most often been undertaken through narrative forms, whether by simple descriptions of particular situations (Merry 1990; Ewick and Silbey 1998) or more in-depth ethnographic focus on communities (Greenhouse et al. 1994).

Although legal knowledge is indeterminate, contingent, and context-specific, scholars insist that it matters a great deal, that legal knowledge, following Foucault, conveys power through its workings in subjects' consciousness. The conventional ways that interpretive scholars capture this dynamic is by referring to law's *constitutive* power. In this view, legal discourses, logics, and language – the raw material processed by legal consciousness – may not rigidly determine what subjects think, but they do shape the capacity for understanding social reality, imagining options, and choosing among them. We can recognize both prefigurative and instrumental dimensions to how legal knowledge conditions legal consciousness. Legal knowledge prefigures or shapes subjectivity in that it provides a preexisting lens for experiencing meaning, for "seeing" and thinking, for constructing and imagining in culturally "sensible" ways. But subjects also actively use legal knowledge instrumentally as a "toolkit" of cultural resources (Swidler 1986), sorting and reconstructing from among variously acquired legal tools to understand social relations, to frame options, to assess relational or material consequences of various options, to formulate what is right and wrong, etc. In both senses, legal consciousness thus is viewed in terms of practical activity; it develops from a combination of learned practices and practical experience, and continues to develop through ongoing social engagement. Not surprisingly, scholarly studies often refer to legal consciousness as matters of both "thinking" and "doing," which are inherently interrelated.[3] And all this closely connects the study of legal consciousness to the study of subjectivity. Studies of legal consciousness often focus specifically on "rights-bearing subjects" in modern social contexts, although this is often a little-developed background assumption more than an explicitly formulated project.

It is relevant to interject here a point that is, it seems, widely assumed but rarely articulated. Simply put, "'consciousness' does not refer only to the conscious thought processes of the self" (Engel 1998:116). Consciousness refers to cognitive processes that are *both* unconscious and conscious. Subjects are conscious in that active thinking takes place through, and is facilitated by, legal consciousness; subjects are aware of the world through the reference points provided by the learned language, logics, and lessons of experience that inhabit consciousness. At the same time, we are often quite limited in our awareness about the prefigurative lens that unconsciously shapes our vision of things, enabling us to "see" certain aspects of reality while obscuring or displacing other dimensions from attention. However, even that boundary between thinking through the dynamic lens of consciousness and thinking critically about the limits of our consciousness itself tends to be indeterminate, dynamic, often in flux. Scholarship tends to be intrigued by and attentive to such matters of relative subject reflexivity, although confident conclusions are almost always speculative and inconclusive.

Understood in the above ways, legal knowledge most obviously permeates the practical consciousness of people routinely participating within official institutional contexts such as courts, lawyers' offices, and police stations. Analysis of legal constructions by official actors in these institutional contexts plays a role in many studies of legal consciousness. But the thrust of most recent studies has instead aimed to *decenter official law and legal institutions,* focusing instead on legal thinking and acting by non-officials outside of formal legal institutions.[4] This is where the

---

[3] Merry 1990:5: "the way that people understand and use the law." See Ewick and Silbey (1998:46) "Legal consciousness is produced and revealed in what people *do* as well as what they *say.*"

[4] Studies of prisoners by Fleury-Steiner in this volume and of the welfare poor by a number of scholars (Sarat 1990; Gilliom 2001; White 1990) in some senses are all about legal consciousness within institutional settings. But the focus on the gaze of legal control in which subject mobilization of law is so constrained makes these subjects and their contexts fascinating areas of inquiry.

trademark emphasis on the "ordinary," "everyday," or "commonplace" figures prominently. These terms variously refer to certain types of *people*, stressing non-elites and especially lower income or lower status individuals; of *institutional contexts*, which include workplaces, homes, neighborhoods, community centers, public spaces, and the like; and of *relationships or disputes*, such as routine, low-profile disputes among neighbors over noise or rowdy kids, among family members, between employers and employees, among employees, and the like. There is some debate in this regard whether the primary aim of interpretive sociolegal study should still be to look specifically for law, but largely outside of official legal institutions, or whether "law first" should even be a priority in studying social life (see Levine and Mellema 2001). Many scholars have followed Sarat and Kearns in focusing study on those "events or practices that seem on the face of things, removed from law," leaving it for more in-depth analysis to determine whether law figures prominently into particular dimensions of social life or not (Sarat and Kearns 1993:55).

It is worth underlining that in most cases, this decentering project tends to make individuals the primary units of analysis. The bulk of research on legal consciousness, including even studies of collective legal mobilization, focuses on loosely structured narrative interviews with ordinary people about their lives. Much attention is given to the volunteered linguistic and conceptual terms that subjects use in making sense of their relational worlds as well as to observation of their actions – again, to what people both say and do. Moreover, one of the most fundamental and challenging contributions of sociolegal scholars is to insist that the forms of thinking and doing by ordinary citizens in everyday life often constitute law as much as does the activity of legal officials. To quote Ewick and Silbey again, "The ways in which the law is experienced and understood by ordinary citizens as they choose to invoke the law, to avoid it, or to resist it, is an essential part of the life of the law" (1992:737). At the same time, most empirical research emphasizes that law is routinely constructed by ordinary citizens in ways that substantially depart from, and even challenge or resist, constructions by legal officials such as judges, police, or administrators. Ewick and Silbey coined the word "legality" to refer to the wide range of constructed legal meanings only loosely tethered to official law in any social context (1998:22). Legal consciousness is the "participation in this process of constructing legality" (1998:45).

An important implication of these understandings is a radical expansion of what counts as law, or the legal, or legality. This perspective has been most concisely captured by Austin Sarat's pithy phrase, quoted from an interviewee, that "the law is all over." By this, Sarat was not claiming that every social context was fully and equally saturated by legality, but rather that legal forms of meaning thrive variably among subjects in many places and spaces throughout society, often far from direct, regular involvement by state officials who traditionally have been the focus of realist behavioral research. Exploring social meanings and practices in these disparate social sites and relationships is the focus of most scholarship on legal consciousness.

Finally, it is worth noting that scholars who study legal consciousness tend to be highly interested in issues of unequal power and the failures of law to produce social justice. In particular, interpretive sociolegal scholars – many influenced by neo-Marxist, Foucaultian, feminist, and critical race theory – frequently explore the ways in which everyday legal consciousness sustains, contests, and resists hegemonic social power. Virtually all scholars in this tradition are interested in demonstrating the ways that intersubjective legal norms, knowledge, and logic as manifest in subject consciousness contribute to the aggregation of forces that sustain social order and induce acquiescence from the citizenry. At the same time, legal mobilization scholars tend to focus on the ways that legal norms, aspirations, and strategies can sometimes be appropriated to challenge the existing social order. Even in such cases, however, legal sense limits the "number of available interpretations for assigning meaning to things and events within any situation or setting" (Silbey 1992:46; McCann 1994), and legal officials utilize force to back up their constructions policing the boundaries of permissible legal meaning. Consequently, other scholars instead focus on the everyday resistances of individuals, on the evasions, dodges, and ruses that subjects undertake to deflect the most oppressive impacts of the dominant legal order (Gilliom 2001) and survive "outside" the law.

Challenges, Complexities, and Conundrums: A Quick Review

It should hardly be surprising that an interpretive enterprise which draws on a host of disparate intellectual traditions to reconceptualize law in bold new terms and to expand radically the range of inquiry into that subject tends to be highly complex, contested, and riddled with conceptual conundrums. Indeed, the most challenging aspects of the inquiry – defined in both senses I have identified – no doubt work to make legal consciousness research so intriguing for many scholars. The remaining pages of this essay very briefly outline just some of the lingering tensions, puzzles, debates, and questions for researchers in this tradition. As noted earlier, my aim is less to resolve these issues than to highlight the questions, debates, and options that confront scholars.

Mapping Legal Consciousness

Several points about the difficult project of identifying and mapping legal consciousness are worth noting. *The first concerns the relationship previously noted between* "constitutive" *and* "instrumental" *ways of understanding legal consciousness.* On the one hand, many scholars, including several in this book, tend to identify constitutive and instrumental understandings as different, even opposed. Most scholars who frame issues in this dichotomous way claim to be endorsing a constitutive over an instrumental understanding. The general reasoning here seems to be that instrumental perspectives treat legal norms as independent of subjects, as exogenous resources that are manipulated by autonomous individuals whose subjectivity, and consciousness, remain little altered by legal activity. On the other hand, some scholars, and especially those inclined to studies of legal mobilization, tend to view the dichotomy between constitutive and instrumental perspectives as misleading and myopic. It is commonplace for scholars to "take sides" in this debate, although elaboration on the points at stake is rare.

It strikes me that there are at least two types of misconceptions or confusion that sustain this divergence in views. For one thing, those who reject the dichotomy tend to agree wholeheartedly with adherents of the dichotomous view that specific instrumental approaches that treat law as merely exogenous resources to be manipulated by autonomous subjects, such as is common in rational choice and other realist behavioral models, are limited and unsatisfying. The difference is that some opponents of the dichotomy do not reject instrumentalism per se, but instead insist on reconceptualizing instrumental activity in different ways that are consistent with, and essential, to understanding law's constitutive power. Their point is that legal knowledge and consciousness are inherently practical; legal logics are meaningful because they make sense and prove "useful' in instrumental activity – formulating expectations of others' actions; naming and framing harms; constructing aspirations for changing relations; trying to change other people's ways of naming, blaming, and claiming; and the like. Most citizen engagements with legal logics are not abstract and pointless, after all, but are enacted in circumstances in which people seek to protect or advance their own or others' interests or status. Even arguments over legal interpretation around a kitchen table, in a tavern, or in a seminar have some generally instrumental motivation, even if it is simply to win a debate. In short, our acts of "saying and doing" are at least in part instrumental to some end.

But such scholars likewise recognize that both the ends and means of such instrumental action is prefigured by accumulated learning and experience as subjects, and that each new enactment itself reconstructs the subject. In short, those scholars who reject the blanket dichotomy tend to appropriate and redefine instrumental activity in terms that make sense about legally constituted subjects. Such scholars tend to want to sustain the emphasis on instrumental dimensions to emphasize the active, dynamic, ever-changing processes and practical domain of subjectivity, and hence of legal consciousness. The cost of excluding instrumental concerns, they aver, is the tendency to overdetermine or oversimplify the constitutive power of learned legal knowledge on subjectivity. In sum, the stark dichotomy of instrumental and constitutive understandings seems accurate about some distinctions in scholarship, but it also often obscures linkages among subtle varieties of constitutive analysis.

A second misconception similarly sustains the debate. This issue involves less the conceptualization of human subjectivity than the researcher's posture toward studying legal consciousness in practice. Those scholars who oppose instrumentalism to constitutive analysis often seem most concerned about how questions of "effectiveness," outcomes, and impact of legally constituted action can impede focus on matters of "meaning," of understanding the "sense" at stake, regardless of whether it "works" in effecting change, empowerment, and the like. The focus, they suggest, should be on "how" social actors are constituted by and act through law rather then "why" they act in particular ways or to what effect, on meaning rather than behavioral outcomes. Instrumental analysis throttles intellectual inquiry and threatens to snare critical scholars, however unwittingly, in the web of elite policy-making designs (Sarat and Silbey 1988).

Other legal consciousness scholars see the issues differently, but only slightly so. They tend to address legal consciousness as a repository of effects as well as sources of legal activity, as products as well as producers of legality. If activity constitutes subjects, these scholars reason, then inquiry into effects of legal activity on subjectivity should enhance rather than impede studies of changing consciousness. For example, my own study of legal mobilization by grassroots women workers challenging unequal wages probed the changing consciousness of women that attended rights-claiming activity over time (1994). My interviews documented that many women were transformed from a meager, fragmented cognitive engagement with rights to a more substantial, expansive, and confident rights consciousness through the politics of practical struggle. The content, coherence, and centrality of their legal consciousness was enhanced greatly, which is very relevant to assessing how law "mattered" at multiple levels. My agenda, like that of other scholars, was at once to make legal consciousness a topic of study in itself and to expand how we think about social change, which can be evidenced in reconstructions of identity, of connections to others, and of subjectivity (see also Silverstein 1996).

Scholars working in this latter tradition often join the other group in criticizing the limits of narrow instrumentalism characterized by much realist, policy-oriented, behavioral scholarship, but at the same time they retain the linkage between legal consciousness and change, legality and "effectivity" (Hunt 1985), in ways more aligned with focus on constituted legal subjects. Again, they affirm the clear tension between constitutive analysis and certain types of instrumental study,[5] while emphasizing continuity between legal consciousness research and other, more complex, less causally linear, and behavioral ways of thinking about "impact" (see McCann 1996). Scholars who emphasize the intersection of concerns especially emphasize how such matters are important for examining the multiple dimensions of power at work in social life. All in all, the apparent disagreements among scholars about "instrumental" analysis often are grounded in misperception or simplistic attribution. The fact that behavioral models of both agency and policy impact exemplifying one version of instrumentalism are invoked by some legal mobilization scholars no doubt often sustains some of the imprecision or misconceptions at stake, driving a bit of a lamentable wedge between interpretive scholars interested in legal consciousness.

Yet another basic puzzle arises often in studies of legal consciousness, a point often pressed by critics of the entire enterprise and troubling to students first introduced to interpretive socio-legal study. *In short, the second puzzle is that, if legality is inherently indeterminate, contingent, and only loosely tethered to official law, how do we define the boundary between law, or legality, and that which is not law?* Do we, for example, accept the most boundless implications of Sarat's line that "the law is all over."? And since he himself has cautioned against presuming that law saturates every space and relationship (1993), how do we mark the limits or absence of the legal? Just how long and substantial are the tethers of official law that make socially constructed meaning sensible as "legality?" This is especially vexing in contemporary mass mediated societies where the "juridico-entertainment complex" saturates so much of life with legal images, narratives, and referents. If law saturates everything, and legality is boundless, does the category have any meaning or analytical value (see Mezey 2001:153)?

---

[5] One reason why recent scholars have distanced themselves from legal mobilization studies is that a few scholars in the latter camp once pursued a traditionally realist, behavioral, and positivist variation of the model that tends to be highly instrumental in both senses discussed here. Others in the legal mobilization tradition, however, emphasize interpretive, post-realist understandings of constituted subjects and imagine instrumental activity in more relational terms. Scholars who reject or seek to go beyond legal mobilization analysis often overlook or minimize these deep differences.

These are fascinating questions but, in my view, it is wrong to expect great answers in response.[6] Indeed, the questions themselves can be understood as forms of what Wittgenstein identified as conceptual puzzlement, contradiction, and paradox intrinsic to the specific language "games" of interpretive sociolegal analysis (see Pitkin 1972:85–98). That is, the puzzles follow from the limits of the conceptual tools that we have developed, and they cannot be answered very well in terms of that logic. Specifically, it strikes me that the problem of defining boundaries to the concept of law is an implication of precisely the goal of expanding the concept itself, of looking for law's power in places that traditionally have been overlooked, of looking for law "all over" in legal consciousness. That a boundary-shattering enterprise results in imprecision about drawing anew the boundaries of the topic should hardly be surprising.

If one accepts this premise, the most useful response is to inquire as to how and how much the question about conceptual perimeters matters for the goals of the inquiry. There is no doubt that the study of everyday legal consciousness forfeits some specificity and certainty about law as the object of study. But so what? The interpretive project itself began with extensive critiques about what ostensibly more parsimonious, precise, positive conceptions of law omitted from study and understanding, about how such pretenses to precision are quite illusory, and how much we gain by recognizing the complex, expansive, dynamic, and significant – if indeterminate – dimensions of legality in the exchange. In short, the questions of conceptual definition matter only if they address what we want to know and what we are willing to sacrifice in return, which ultimately is a matter of intellectual taste. Scholars inclined to study legal consciousness tend to be excited and edified by seeing more aspects of law in more places, while others find the reveling in "indeterminacy" frustrating. Such is the fate of humans to struggle diversely with limited conceptual capacities and different values. But recognizing this fact of unalterable puzzlement also underlines at least two basic points: first, that the case for studies of legal consciousness must be made in terms of the quality of new, expanded understandings that they produce; and, second, that the indeterminacy of legal consciousness studies places a premium on constructing conceptual clarity to the greatest degree where it is possible. Defining the boundaries of legality is simply not an area where we should expect much in that latter regard.

At the same time, however, establishing the linkage of ordinary constructions and meanings of law, or legality, to officially approved legal constructs does have important analytical implications for studies of legal consciousness.[7] Simply put, how can we ascribe to and assess law's contributions to "hegemony," or to domination, or even to social order if we cannot draw clear connections between elements of subject consciousness and what we can confidently identify as their "legal" sources? Without specifying and elaborating the substantial tether between legality and officially recognized law or legal norms, claims about law's constitutive power in

---

[6] These questions provide one reason to speculate why Foucault defined the "juridical" in traditionally narrow, state-centered, even quasi-positive ways, while developing a broad field of inquiry into disciplinary practices and mechanisms, which legal consciousness scholars tend to bring back as legality into sociolegal inquiry.

[7] I thank Scott Barclay for pushing me to recognize the very important points developed in this paragraph.

cultural life will be largely empty, vague, unconvincing. Scholarship exploring the plurality of legal meanings that citizens construct can well demonstrate law's indeterminacy and contingency, but this plurality also aims to demonstrate law's capacity to shape, influence, invite, or colonize – to establish the oft-recognized "shadow" cast over – citizen cognition and action. The danger of the decentering project undertaken by many recent scholars is that it eviscerates this connection between indeterminate meanings and the powerful norms articulated and enforced by official institutions that sustain and circumscribe meaning-making by citizens. Such projects risk losing touch with the collective, intersubjective aspects of legal norms from which citizens draw to make sense of social life. Hence, while defining the boundaries between the legal and extra-legal can be a difficult, elusive enterprise, there are real stakes for understanding and analysis in making the effort. That is, I think, why many legal mobilization studies exploring citizen contests over constructed legal meanings begin with, or at least include, a review of official legal constructions by courts and other bodies charged with policing the boundaries of legal meaning. By connecting individual legal meanings with sources of authoritative institutions, the power and reach of law is more fully demonstrated.

Finally, I add one other related observation regarding inquiry into two rather different levels or modes or legal consciousness. David Engel once noted, in an important essay, that studies often fail to clarify the important distinction between general "perceptions or images of law and legal institutions" and specific expressions of "legal aptitude, knowledge, or competence" that are identified in citizens' legal consciousness (1998:119). I and a co-author have written in similar terms about distinctions regarding how subjects think *about* law in general and, by contrast, how they act or think *through* a particular set of legal conventions or logics (McCann and March 1994). The first inquiry focuses on how subjects relate to law overall as a phenomenon or system, while the second refers to particular constructions of meaning within or apart from established legal conventions.

Of course, these different dimensions of legal consciousness are often related. If one thinks that a legal system tends to be accessible and just, one is probably more likely to engage the world through logics, conventions, and strategies associated with law. If one views law as immutable, inaccessible, and yet unavoidable, one is likely to submit to law more passively, although this posture could support both great ignorance of law (too esoteric) or detailed familiarity (need to know it to obey). If one instead views law as mostly a mask for oppressive power, one is likely to maneuver around and against more than through law. And so on. These two dimensions of legal consciousness are, moreover, related to the study of legal ideology, which has shadowed interpretive study of everyday legality from the start. The focus on legal knowledge of the first type, regarding law generally, tells us much regarding ideologies *about* the law, regarding how people think about the law per se in the larger scheme of things. Is law good or bad, accessible or remote, a tool of the powerful or the powerless, a force for or against justice? The focus on legal reasoning through law or legality, by contrast, provides us with a purchase on the particular points of intersections between discrete legal logics or practices and those broader ideological values, norms, and discursive logics that circulate throughout society.

These distinctions are relevant to understanding the promises and limits of different scholarly approaches to legal consciousness. The first generation of studies regarding legal consciousness tended to be primarily of the second, latter type, examining how legal logics and categories that comprise legal consciousness sustain or challenge broader ideological currents within the dominant society. Hence, Merry (1990) studied how the legal consciousness of working-class subjects expressed the aspirations and constraints of American "individualism." Sarat (1990) examined how the welfare poor must struggle with images of low worth and dependence in a society that trumpets opportunity, achievement, and independence. McCann (1994) examined how working women struggled with legal concepts of equal worth, opportunity, merit, markets, and the like, at once reconstructing legal language to challenge dominant norms and yet ultimately succumbing to the constraining power of the latter enforced by the state and powerful social groups. These studies tended to treat law both as a window into broader ideological formations and as a force sustaining their discursive power and institutional enforcement.

The important and powerful work of Ewick and Silbey (1992, 1998) marked a transition in focus. While retaining some connection to the concept of ideology, their analysis of "schemas" reflected a shift in attention to how subjects related to law itself at a broader level. Their now-famous tripartite categorization of *above the law, before the law, and against the law* captures general understandings about law generally, like those noted above and cited often in the following pages. This conceptual analysis of general schemas marked an advance in thinking about how citizens imagine and relate to law generally, about ideologies specific to law. But it also signaled a move away from the previous types of inquiry as to how law sustains, reproduces, and facilitates contestation of broader ideological norms in society – including in the US case, for example, such norms as individual responsibility, equal opportunity, limited government authority, free markets, retributive justice, etc. My point is not to critique either agenda, for each is important. Rather, I simply highlight that the trajectories and challenges for these conceptions are different, as are the implications for what each type of scholarship does and not tell us about law, power, and justice. At the same time, there is no reason why scholarship cannot pursue these separate projects jointly. To some degree, a variety of studies – Greenhouse et al. (1994) and McCann (1994) in earlier works, and more recently in studies by Engel and Munger (2003) and Neilsen (2004) – have successfully integrated ideological analysis of legal consciousness at both levels.

Choosing Subjects, Mapping Contexts: Is Comparison Possible?

Studies of legal consciousness claim to document and analyze ordinary legal practice in the specific contexts of everyday life. This aspiration may seem quite straightforward, but the project has been rather less fully and evenly developed than often is claimed. Several points are worth brief attention.

First, the focus on "ordinary" people, practices, and relationships has, somewhat paradoxically, involved a narrowing as well as expansion of sociolegal research. The category of "ordinary," I noted above, is best understood in terms of what is *not* included from traditional research. In short, the category of "ordinary" people excludes legal officials such as judges and legal elites like lawyers; everyday disputing is that which takes place mostly outside of courtrooms, police stations, and lawyers' offices. Those subjects who are studied include mostly lower-income middle and working class, poor, or minority citizens; the relationships, practices, and disputes that are highlighted usually take place in, and rarely spill beyond, workplaces, homes, neighborhoods, churches, schools, and public streets. It is notable that much is left unstudied by this agenda, however. What about the legal consciousness of the affluent, of the rich and famous, of the corporate elite? What about these subjects' legal practices, relationships, and disputes? Are not the understandings and practices of powerful actors not part of everyday, ordinary life, including the life of law? And should they not be especially important topics for those scholars interested in differences of law's workings as a form of power, related to other dimensions of hierarchical power? Should we not care about everyday constructions of law at these levels of influence?

Some scholars have instead expressed a preference for categorizing study as from the "bottom up," which more clearly connotes a focus on understanding the legal consciousness of less powerful people in society, of those least clearly advantaged or empowered by law. However, this label has been assailed for exhibiting a structuralist tendency to re-center law in hierarchical official institutions. In any case, the point here is not to develop a better label but to identify the limits of the prevailing agenda to date. In particular, such constraints on who and what is studied arguably impede the possibilities of broadly comparative study. Would not studies of legal consciousness among the welfare poor and lower-income citizens take on new meaning if we could compare and contrast them to the documented legal understandings and practices of the wealthy and powerful?[8] Would not the specificity of legal understandings by defiant workers become clearer if we studied the employers, the managers, and the owners of production as well?[9] Would not studying a wider array of subjects contribute more to understanding and demonstrating the role of legality in sustaining, and occasionally contesting, the gaps between haves and have-nots? In this regard, revisiting some of the earliest studies predating attention to legal consciousness – Curran's study comparing attitudes to law among different groups; Macauley's study of business norms and practices, and so on – might be a source of widening and deepening the scope of study along these lines.

These omissions in the selection of subjects are paralleled by another type of narrowing in post-structural interpretive studies of legal consciousness – that involving the specific contexts of practical legal saying and doing. It is worth repeating that students of legal consciousness tend to reject radically individuated understandings of autonomous selves, and instead emphasize the ways in which thinking selves are constituted. Such scholars emphasize how consciousness develops out of participation in intersubjective ways of life, institutionalized routines, and common cultural practices. Legal consciousness is, Merry wrote long ago, "embedded in the practical constitution of everyday life, part and parcel of the process whereby the subject is constituted by external sociocultural forms" (1990:5). And it is this ongoing interdependence between selves and sociocultural forms that distinguishes interest in

---

[8] Somewhat ironically, powerful elites – especially white males in corporate roles – form a sort of stigmatized "other" in bottom-up studies of everyday legal life. Contrasts between the "haves" and "have-nots" are often vaguely suggested or implied, but rarely are actual legal understandings and practices (the manifestations of consciousness) of powerful subjects directly, systematically studied.

[9] I humbly note that I have been troubled by this question ever since I conducted the research for my book *Rights at Work* (1994).

the deeper, more complex workings of "consciousness" from traditional behavioral study of attitudes and opinions. Since consciousness is constructed out of context-specific life experiences and cultural practices, it is hardly surprising that studies of legal consciousness emphasize the particulars of context in which people and their activities are situated. For the most part, social context is described through narratives about individuals and the settings of events. Sometimes these narratives are long and detailed, but usually they are relatively brief and unsystematic efforts limited to making sense of specific events or disputes.

While context-specificity is emphasized as a general commitment, however, what is specific and important about context is often given a perfunctory, almost arbitrary nod in actual empirical study. Discussions of context frequently involve little more than random discussion about surface features of the physical space and a few identifying characteristics of the subjects in question. Case studies are primarily minimalist vignettes, more snapshots or quick action videos of events than systematic, multidimensional analysis of important features in social relationships. The result is to shortchange inquiry into how consciousness is shaped by specific contexts, and even more so the effort to develop general conceptual frameworks for analyzing contexts in ways that make comparative study possible. Indeed, very few studies of legal consciousness explicitly develop and illustrate systematic searches for the interrelated elements that might define adequate contextual analysis. The issue at stake is not the need to develop capacities for positive theorizing and prediction about the causal relation of consciousness and context. The very premise that consciousness is complex and indeterminate defies such positivist pretenses (see McCann 1996). However, more systematic efforts to analyze key aspects of context and subject situation might prove useful in making sense of the common sense displayed by subjects regarding legality, in understanding how and why some understandings tend to trump other potentially reasonable ways of thinking, in identifying what is truly specific to some contexts and not to others. More systematic analysis of context would advance thinking regarding the constitution of selves and consciousness.

Two specific types of omissions from contextual analysis in particular are common place. *One is the palpable reluctance to situate subjects in terms of traditional theories of relational hierarchy.* Studies of legal consciousness routinely use categories of race, gender, and class to distinguish particular subjects, to identify various inequalities or disadvantages of those subjects, or to comment about law's contributions to sustaining (or challenging) injustice. Some of the most important contributions of sociolegal study involve explorations into how variously situated individual subjects construct the terms of meaningful *difference* – among various individuals and groups, among different types of relations and problems, among values and strategies, among the markers of identity. But very rarely are concepts of class, race, and gender developed independently as scholarly tools for analyzing the hierarchical institutionalized patterns of relationship among subjects, whether at work, in homes, in communities, in the street, etc. In this regard, contemporary interpretive studies tend to abandon the long, rich legacies of structural analysis, including neo-Marxist, feminist, and critical race theorizing that has labored to transcend the deterministic elements of older structural traditions.

Instead, the interpretive thrust of much recent inquiry has focused almost entirely on the subjective experiences narrated by the subjects under study. Thus gender, race, or class seem to be relevant if explicitly voiced by subjects, but rarely do analysts draw at length on social theorizing about relational power to compare and contrast subject narratives in terms of the institutionalized patterns of hierarchical power in which subjects are enmeshed.[10] This inclination not only leads scholars to abandon much of their traditional intellectual role, but it significantly limits the potential for analyzing social contexts, for exploring the interplay of agency and structure that traditionally is posited to produce subjectivity. In short, the laudable commitments to understanding subject consciousness in non-deterministic, responsive, and respectful ways often work to truncate the contributions of sociolegal scholarship.

Some important exceptions to this generalization are worth noting, however. Critical race scholarship has compellingly employed and contributed to sophisticated theorizing about the deep structures of racial hierarchy and marginalization. Much of this theory has been relatively traditional in its analytical style (Crenshaw 1988), while other contributions have developed more diffusely, even poetically through narrative presentations (Williams 1991). Likewise, much scholarship on legal mobilization (McCann 1994) has emphasized the importance of systematic analysis of contexts in general and structural dimensions of race, class, gender, and the like in particular, although the balance of structural and interpretive analysis has been subject to some criticism as well (Seron and Munger 1996).

Engel and Munger's important volume *Rights of Inclusion* (2003) represents a very different and innovative approach to the challenge. On the one hand, their effort to trace the development of legal consciousness through in-depth, interview-based personal biographies of disabled persons seems like the most extreme example of individualized, decontextualized study. On the other hand, however, the authors organize their findings from these personal stories into highly sophisticated discussions regarding how relational categories of difference – race, class, gender – play out in people's lives. The systematic analyses of how persons with disabilities make sense of their circumstances is greatly enriched by independent analysis of class relations in workplaces and markets, of gender relations and women's experience, and of race relations. The result is one of the most intriguing and successful efforts to analyze the dynamic development of individual experience and identity in contemporary stratified society. It is a thoroughly post-structural mode of revitalizing, rather than abandoning, structural analysis of power.

Finally, it is worth noting the continuing tradition of study into the role of law in colonial and post-colonial social contexts. For example, Sally Engle Merry's formidable *Colonizing Hawai'i* (2000) provides a rich, well contextualized historical analysis of macro-political struggles and everyday disputing by workers and women that features sophisticated theorizing about race, class, and gender. Her subsequent studies of how liberal legality have at once undermined traditional forms of native

---

[10] As Seron and Munger argue, "social difference – race, class, gender, or sexual preference – is explained entirely through the words, meanings, and language used by actors ... Interpretive explanations of difference are theoretically severed from any analysis of ongoing patterns of society outside the framework by which meaning is created for the actors being considered" (1996:195). Seron and Munger provide an expansive, compelling discussion about the general points I try to develop here and elsewhere (see McCann and March 1996). In some ways, this inattention to deep structural conflicts continues tendencies manifest in studies of dispute processing, which have importantly influenced study of legal consciousness. See Abel (1973).

Hawaiian women's power *and* provided new resources for contesting male violence demonstrates again the possibilities of sophisticated, non-deterministic analysis of structural power (Merry 2001). All of these studies noted above provide models worth consideration for further explorations of systematic contextual analysis.

Yet another limitation of much inquiry into legal consciousness is the relative inattention to broader society-wide dimensions of collective life – what often is referred to as "macro-contextual factors" – that shape subjectivity and practical activity. Most study of everyday legal practice and legal consciousness addresses context in terms of influences that are spatially proximate to the individual subjects. A living room, street scene, neighborhood, or workplace might receive some description, as might some characteristics of immediate family members, co-workers, or neighbors of subjects under study. But too rarely is attention devoted to more distant and broad sources of cultural knowledge production and influence, to wider "communities of meaning" that reproduce the patterns of discursive logic and narrative from which legal consciousness and subjectivity is constructed (Engel 1998). No doubt this reflects the recent commitment to decentering legal analysis, to focusing on micro-contexts and what Foucault labeled the "capillary sites of power". But it also arguably misses an opportunity to explore context by connecting with the rich traditions of analyzing popular or mass legal culture and ideology that have generated many important insights about the production of legal knowledge.[11]

Both the diversity and power of efforts to make connections between micro, mezzo, and macro-cultural levels can be illustrated by several examples. One classic example from the "early days" of legal consciousness is the book compiled by Carol Greenhouse, Barbara Yngvesson, and David Engel, *Law and Community in Three American Towns*. The three authors' marvelous case studies, individually and together, locate individuals within densely mapped communities where the terms and categories of belonging are socially produced and reinforced in a variety of ways across many institutional sites and levels. Courts mattered, but so did police, lawyers, insurance agents, politicians, and local leaders of all types as well as ordinary citizens in producing and enforcing collective norms. Individual legal consciousness is related to group constructions of difference between insiders and outsiders, between culturally approved actions and those that are disapproved, and between how certain groups do or do not become linked to such stigmatized activity. This book defines one approach to contextual analysis that offsets the more fragmentary individualized accounts that frequent scholarship on the subject.

These authors, all anthropologists, are very careful to restrict their claims about communal construction of legality to the specific small-town contexts that they study. However, Haltom and McCann (2004) have recently explored how similar moralistic logics of difference that stigmatize adversarial rights claiming are produced and reproduced through the national news and entertainment media, by what Reed calls the "juridico-entertainment complex" (1999). This is important, for while legal consciousness surely develops out of individual practical experience, it can hardly remain unaffected by the ceaseless parade of news stories, TV shows, movies, and

---

[11] "... How and when does the circulation of narrative come to form a pattern that is more broadly recognizable as cultural practice? What are the mechanisms of mass public transmission?" asks Naomi Mezey (2001:161).

other spectacles of entertainment-oriented simulacra about cops and criminals, lawyers and clients, judges and juries, and ordinary people variously tangled in and resistant to the webs of law that bind modern society. What could be a more "commonplace" and "everyday" site of legal meaning construction than such mass cultural participation? Haltom and McCann do not focus on how individuals process mass-produced knowledge, but they make a systematic effort to point the way to potential for linkages between studies of macro-level processes and of legal consciousness among individual subjects.

Likewise, Austin Sarat, a pioneer in studies of legal consciousness, has shifted much of his research agenda to representations of law in popular culture and their implications for both public attitudes and the deeper formation of legal consciousness. For example, his classic book on the death penalty, *When the State Kills*, links popular movies to public understanding and misunderstanding about capital punishment. Ben Fleury-Steiner, an editor of this book, likewise has produced much research that links mass cultural production of legal "folk knowledge" to his studies of individual legal consciousness (2002). And Laura Beth Nielsen, the other editor of this book, has found fascinating ways to integrate studies of individual consciousness with attention to mass culture (2000, 2004). Her most recent studies of disputing over gender discrimination have explicitly studied mass media representations as part of the larger research agenda (Nielsen and Beim 2004).

The point illustrated by these examples is not that studies of mass cultural production of legality are more important than, and should replace, studies of individual legal consciousness. Nor is the message that every case study of legal consciousness among selected subjects should be attended by systematic study of mass cultural production. The latter would be asking far too much, and would demand an agenda that is unrealistic and unwieldy. Rather, the point is that studies of individual consciousness and of mass legal culture can very productively enrich and inform one another, deepening the analysis of the social context in which subjectivity and legality are produced. As argued earlier, such connections are critical to making the case about the reach of law's power, not to mention its role in sustaining hegemony and order. And it is from the dynamic dialectic of research linking these different levels of study that we might expect some of the most exciting scholarship about the production and workings of legal consciousness to develop in the future.

Conclusion: Between Past and Future

This essay has largely looked backward from this volume toward the past. My aim has been to describe and to analyze the complex projects of mapping legal consciousness that preceded the essays in the coming pages. For the most part I have labored more to identify and to clarify complexity and contestation than to recommend the proper intellectual course of action. The authors in this volume have responded to this legacy of past scholarship in their own different ways, pushing forward studies of everyday life among new subjects in divers places, following a variety of different routes in their explorations, avoiding different bumps and variously choosing to meet others head on. It has been my hope that recognizing the complexities at stake increases appreciation for the variety and innovation in these fascinating studies. I invite readers to join me in learning from this latest series of contributions to the tradition.

References

Abel, R.L. (1973) "A Comparative Theory of Dispute Institutions in Society." *Law & Society Review* 8(2):217–347.

Abercrombie, N., Hill, S. and Turner, B.S. (1980) *The Dominant Ideology Thesis*. Boston: Allen & Unwin.

Bartlett, K., and Kennedy, R. (eds) (1991) *Feminist Legal Theory: Readings in Law and Gender*. Boulder, CO: Westview Press.

Barzilai, G. (2003) *Communities and Law: Politics and Cultures of Legal Identities*. Ann Arbor: University of Michigan Press.

Bell, D. (1987) *And We Are Not Saved: The Elusive Quest for Racial Justice*. New York: Basic Books.

Black, D. (1976) *The Behavior of Law*. New York: Academic Press.

Bourdieu, P. (1987) "The Force of Law: Toward a Sociology of the Juridical Field." 38 *Hastings Law Journal* 805.

Brigham, J. (1987) "Rights, Rage, and Remedy: Forms of Law in Political Discourse." *Studies in American Political Development* 2:303–317. New Haven: Yale University Press.

—— (2000) *The Constitution of Interests: Beyond the Politics of Rights*. New York: New York University Press.

—— and Harrington, C.B. (1989) "Realism and Its Consequences: An Inquiry into Contemporary Sociolegal Research." 17 *International Journal of the Sociology of Law* 41.

Bumiller, K. (1988) *The Civil Rights Society: The Social Construction of Victims*. Baltimore: Johns Hopkins University Press.

Carlin, J.E., Howard, J. and Messinger, S.L. (1967) *Civil Justice and the Poor: Issues for Sociological Research*. New York: Russell Sage Foundation.

Cocks, J. (1989) *The Oppositional Imagination: Feminism, Critique, and Political Theory*. London: Routledge.

Comaroff, John, and Comaroff, Jean (1992) *Ethnography and the Historical Imagination*. Boulder, CO: Westview Press.

Conley, J.M., and O'Barr, W. (1990) *Rules versus Relationships: The Ethnography of Legal Discourse*. Chicago: University of Chicago Press.

Crenshaw, K.W. (1988) "Race, Reform, and Retrenchment: Transformation and Legitimation in Antidiscrimination Law." 101 *Harvard Law Review* 1331.

Curran, B.(1977) *The Legal Needs of the Public: The Final Report of a National Survey*. Chicago: American Bar Foundation.

de Certeau, M. (1984) *The Practice of Everyday Life,* trans. Steven T. Randall. Berkeley: University of California Press.

Delgado, R. (1987) "The Ethereal Scholar: Does Critical Legal Studies Have What Minorities Want?" 22 *Harvard Civil Rights–Civil Liberties Law Review* 301.

—— et al. (1985) "Fairness and Formality: Minimizing the Risk of Prejudice In Alternative Dispute Resolution." 85 *Wisconsin Law Review* 1359.

Edelman, L.B., Erlanger, H.S., and Lande, J. (1993) "Internal Dispute Resolution: The Transformation of Civil Rights in the Workplace." *Law & Society Review* 27(3):497–534.

Engel, D. (1984) "The Oven Bird's Song: Insiders, Outsiders, and Personal Injury in an American Community." 18 *Law and Society Review* 549.

—— (1998) "How Does Law Matter in the Constitution of Legal Consciousness?" in B. Garth and A. Sarat (eds) *How Does Law Matter?* Evanston, IL: Northwestern University Press.

—— and Munger, F. (2003) *Rights of Inclusion: Law and Identity in the Life Stories of Americans with Disabilities*. Chicago: University of Chicago Press.

Ewick, P., and Silbey, S. (1992) "Conformity, Contestation, and Resistance: An Account of Legal Consciousness." 26 *New England Law Review* 731.

—— (1998) *The Common Place of Law: Stories from Everyday Life*. Chicago: University of Chicago Press.

Felstiner, W.L.F. (1974) "Influences of Social Organization on Dispute Processing." *Law and Society Review* 9:63.

Felstiner, W., Abel, R., and Sarat, A. (1980–81) "The Emergence and Transformation of Disputes – Naming, Blaming, and Claiming …" *Law and Society Review* 15:631–655.

Fleury-Steiner, B. (2002) "Narratives of the Death Sentence: Toward a Theory of Legal Narrativity." *Law and Society Review* 36:549–576.

Foucault, M. (1978) *The History of Sexuality, Volume 1: An Introduction*, trans. Robert Hurley. New York: Pantheon.

—— (1980) *Power/Knowledge: Selected Interviews and Other Writings, 1972–1977* (ed.) C. Gordon. New York: Pantheon.

Friedman, L. (1989) "Law, Lawyers, and Popular Culture." *Yale Law Journal* 98:1579.

Galanter, M. (1983) "The Radiating Effects of Courts", in K.D. Boyum and L. Mather (eds), *Empirical Theories of Courts*. New York: Longman. pp. 117–142.

—— (1974) "Why the 'Haves' Come Out Ahead: Speculations on the Limits of Legal Change." 9 *Law and Society Review* 95.

Gaventa, J. (1980) *Power and Powerlessness: Quiescence and Rebellion in an Appalachian Valley*. Urbana, IL: University of Illinois Press.

Genovese, E.D. (1976) *Roll, Jordan, Roll*. New York: Pantheon Books.

Gilliom, J. (2001) *Overseers of the Poor: Surveillance, Resistance, and the Limits of Privacy*. Chicago: University of Chicago Press.

Glendon, M.A. (1991) *Rights Talk: The Impoverishment of Political Discourse*. New York: The Free Press.

Gluckman, M. (1955) *The Judicial Process among the Barotse of Northern Rhodesia*. Manchester: Manchester University Press.

Gramsci, A. (1971) *Selections from the Prison Notebooks* (ed.) Q. Hoare and G. Nowell Smith. New York: International Publishers.

Greenhouse, C.J. (1989) *Praying for Justice: Faith, Order, and Community in an American Town*. Ithaca, NY: Cornell University Press.

——, Engel, D.M., and Yngvesson, B. (1994) *Law and Community in Three American Towns*. Ithaca, NY: Cornell University Press.

Hall, S. et al. (1978) *Policing the Crisis: Mugging, the State, and Law and Order*. London: Macmillan.

Haltom, W., and McCann, M. (2004) *Distorting the Law: Politics, Media, and the Litigation Crisis*. Chicago: University of Chicago Press.

Harrington, C., and Yngvesson, B. (1990) "Interpretive Sociolegal Research." 15 *Law and Social Inquiry* 135.

Hay, D. et al. (eds) (1975) *Albion's Fatal Tree: Crime and Society in Eighteenth Century England*. New York: Pantheon.

Hunt, A. (1985) "The Ideology of Law: Advances and Problems in Recent Applications of the Concept of Ideology to the Analysis of Law." *Law & Society Review* 19(1):11–37.

—— (1990) "Rights and Social Movements: Counter-Hegemonic Strategies." 17 *Journal of Law and Society* 309.

Jacob, H. (1969) *Debtors in Court*. Chicago: Rand McNally.

Kairys, D. (ed.) (1982) *The Politics of Law: A Progressive Critique*. New York: Pantheon.

Kritzer, H.M., Vidmar, N., and Bogart, W.A. (1991) "To Confront or Not to Confront: Measuring Claiming Rates in Discrimination Grievances." *Law and Society Review* 25: 878–887.

Levine, K., and Mellema, V. (2001) "Strategizing the Street: How Law Matters in the Lives of Women in the Street-Level Drug Economy." *Law & Social Inquiry*. 26(1):169–207.

Levine, F., and Preston, E. (1970) "Community Reorientation Among Low Income Groups." *Wisconsin Law Review* 1970:80–113.

Macauley, S. (1963) "Non-Contractual Relations in Business: A Preliminary Study." *American Sociological Review* 28:55–69.

—— (1987) "Images of Law in Everyday Life: The Lessons of School, Entertainment, and Spectator Sports." *Law & Society Review* 21:185.

—— (1989) "Popular Legal Culture: An Introduction." 98 *Yale Law Journal* 1545.

McCann, M.W. (1993) "Resistance, Reconstruction, and Romance in Legal Scholarship." 26 *Law and Society Review* 733.

—— (1994) *Rights at Work: Pay Equity Reform and the Politics of Legal Mobilization.* Chicago: University of Chicago Press.

—— (1996) "Causal versus Constitutive Explanations: Or On the Difficulty of Being So Positive ..." *Law and Social Inquiry*, v. 21, no. 2, 457–482.

——, and March, T. (1996) "Law and Everyday Forms of Resistance: A Socio-Political Assessment." *Studies in Law, Politics, and Society* 15.

Marshall, A-M. (2003) "Injustice Frames, Legality, and the Everyday Construction of Sexual Harassment." *Law and Social Inquiry* 28(3):659–690.

Marshall, A-M., and Barclay, S. (2003) "Introduction: In Their Own Words: How Ordinary People Construct the Legal World." *Law & Social Inquiry* 28(3):617–628.

Mascia-Lees, F.E., Sharpe, P., and Cohen, C.B. (1989) "The Postmodernist Turn in Anthropology: Cautions from a Feminist Perspective." *Signs* 15(1):7–33.

Mather, L., and Yngvesson, B. (1980–81) "Language, Audience, and the Transformation of Disputes." 15 *Law and Society Review* 775.

Matsuda, M. (1987) "Looking to the Bottom: Critical Legal Studies and Reparations." 22 *Harvard Civil Rights–Civil Liberties Law Review* 323.

Merry, S.E. (1985) "Concepts of Law and Justice Among Working-Class Americans: Ideology as Culture." IX *Legal Studies Forum* 59.

—— (1988) "Legal Pluralism." 22 *Law and Society Review* 868.

—— (1990) *Getting Justice and Getting Even: Legal Consciousness Among Working Class Americans.* Chicago: University of Chicago Press.

—— (2000) *Colonizing Hawai'i: The Cultural Power of Law.* Princeton: Princeton University Press.

—— (2001) "Rights, Religion, and Community: Approaches to Violence Against Women in the Context of Globalization." *Law and Society Review* 35:1301–1350.

Mezey, N. (2001) "Out of the Ordinary: Law, Power, Culture, and the Commonplace." *Law & Social Inquiry* **26**(1):145–168.

Miller, R., and Sarat, A. (1980–81) "Grievances, Claims, and Disputes: Assessing the Adversary Cultures." *Law and Society Review* 15(3–4):525–566.

Nader, L. (1969) *Law in Culture and Society.* New York: Academic Press.

Nielsen, L.B. (2000) "Situating Legal Consciousness: Experiences and Attitudes of Ordinary Citizens about Law and Street Harassment." *Law and Society Review* 34:201–236.

—— (2004) *License to Harass: Law, Hierarchy, and Offensive Public Speech.* Princeton: Princeton University Press.

——, and Beim, A. (2004) "Media Misrepresentation: Title VII, Print Media, and Public Perceptions of Discrimination Litigation." *Stanford Law and Policy Review,* 15:101–130.

Pitkin, H.F. (1972) *Wittgenstein and Justice.* Berkeley: University of California Press.

Reed, D.S.(1999) "A New Constitutional Regime: The Juridico-Entertainment Complex." Paper presented at the Law & Society Association Annual Meeting, Chicago, IL.

Sarat, A. (1985) "Legal Effectiveness and Social Studies of Law." IX *Legal Studies Forum* 23.

—— (1988) "The 'New Formalism' in Disputing and Dispute Processing." 21 *Law and Society Review* 695.

—— (1990) "'... The Law is All Over': Power, Resistance and the Legal Consciousness of the Welfare Poor." 2 *Yale Journal of Law and the Humanities* 343.

—— and Silbey, S. (1988) "The Pull of the Policy Audience." 10 *Law and Policy* 97.

—— and Felstiner, W.L.F. (1989) "Lawyers and Legal Consciousness: Law Talk in the Divorce Lawyer's Office." 98 *Yale Law Journal* 1663.

—— and Felstiner, W.L.F. (1995) *Divorce Lawyers and their Clients: Power and Meaning in the Legal Process*. Oxford: Oxford University Press.

—— and Kearns, T.R. (eds) (1993) *Law in Everyday Life*. Ann Arbor: University of Michigan Press.

Scheingold, S.A. (1974) *The Politics of Rights: Lawyers, Public Policy, and Social Change*. New Haven: Yale University Press.

Seron, C., and Munger, F. (1996) "Law and Inequality: Race, Gender ... and, of course, Class." *Annual Review of Sociology*, 22(1):187–212.

Silbey, S.S. (1985) "Ideals and Practices in the Study of Law." IX *Legal Studies Forum* 7.

—— (1992) "Making a Place for Cultural Analyses of Law." 17 *Law & Social Inquiry* 39.

—— and Sarat, A. (1987) "Critical Traditions in Law and Society Research." 21 *Law & Society Review* 167.

Silverstein, H. (1996) *Unleashing Rights: Law, Meaning, and the Animal Rights Movement*. University of Michigan Press.

Steiner, B.D., Bowers, W.J., and Sarat, A. (1999) "Folk Knowledge as Legal Action: Death Penalty Judgments and the Tenet of Early Release in a Culture of Mistrust and Punitiveness." *Law & Society Review* 33:461–506.

Swidler, A. (1986) "Culture in Action: Symbols and Strategies." 51 *American Sociological Review* 273.

Thompson, E.P. (1975) *Whigs and Hunters: The Origin of the Black Act*. New York: Pantheon.

White, L. (1990) "Subordination, Rhetorical Survival Skills, and Sunday Shoes: Notes on the Nearing of Mrs. G." 38 *Buffalo Law Review* 1.

Williams, P. (1991) *The Alchemy of Race and Rights*. Cambridge: Harvard University Press.

Williams, R. (1977) *Marxism and Literature*. Oxford: Oxford University Press.

Yngvesson, B. (1989) "Inventing Law in Local Settings: Rethinking Popular Culture." 98 *Yale Law Journal* 1689.

—— (1993) *Virtuous Citizens, Disruptive Subjects: Order and Complaint in a New England Court*. New York: Routledge.

Zemans, F.K. (1983) "Legal Mobilization: The Neglected Role of the Law in the Political System." *American Political Science Review* 77:690–703.

Introduction

A Constitutive Perspective of Rights

BENJAMIN FLEURY-STEINER AND LAURA BETH NIELSEN

with
Catherine R. Albiston, Hadar Aviram, Frank Rudy Cooper, Kaaryn
Gustafson, Jessica Hodge, Elizabeth A. Hoffmann, Idit Kostiner, Anna-
Maria Marshall, Jérôme Pélisse, Kimberly D. Richman and Judith Taylor

The fiftieth anniversary of the Supreme Court's historic decision to strike down school segregation as unconstitutional in *Brown v. Board of Education* provides an especially important opportunity to bring together studies that shed light on questions begged by *Brown* and other landmark civil rights cases: What role does the law play in fostering social change? Can new rights guaranteed under law influence widespread and often taken-for-granted cultural belief systems and thus ensure that minorities are afforded the same privileges as members of the majority? Following the Civil Rights Movement of the 1960s, there have been several influential books that have explored these questions from a sociolegal perspective (Rosenberg 1991; Scheingold 1974). *The New Civil Rights Research* differs from these early studies in one very important respect. This collection explicitly avoids a focus on an objective evaluation of the "effectiveness" of rights. Specifically, the research collected in this book builds on and goes beyond a legal mobilization approach to rights (McCann 1994; Silverstein 1996), as it places in the center of the analysis people's understandings of rights.

In so doing, *The New Civil Rights Research* privileges the everyday stories, experiences, interactions, and rhetoric of disadvantaged individuals, social activists, and ordinary people. This volume brings together a diverse array of studies that employ a more cultural perspective of rights. Some of the contexts explored are more traditional in nature (employment discrimination, educational justice, welfare rights, etc.), while others search for law's role and meaning in very different settings such as the street.

The chapters in this book take a fresh – indeed, a *new* – approach to exploring this vitally important question. Rather than focusing on rights from the *top-down* – that is, how judicial decisions impact social change – the approach taken by the contributors to the *New Civil Rights Research* focuses on law from the *bottom up*. How do individuals *experience* their legal rights in action?

What are Civil Rights?

In the US, civil rights (as traditionally conceived) are constitutional or statutory guarantees of various protections from unfavorable or harmful treatment by private individuals or state actors. In the past 15 years, civil rights in the US have been growing. There are increasing statutory protections for individuals in the workplace (for example, the Civil Rights Act, 1991; The Americans with Disabilities Act, 1990; and the Family and Medical Leave Act, 1993), and court-created common law causes of action (such as sexual harassment). At the same time, there has been a tremendous increase in the volume of civil rights cases filed for abuses in the workplace (Litras 2000, 2002; Nielsen and Nelson 2005), in prisons (Litras 2000, 2002) and housing (Litras 2000, 2002), to name but a few.

In the US, civil rights guarantees typically are enforced in the courts. In other words, a person or group of people who believe that their rights have been violated threaten to or actually file a lawsuit, which resolves the matter. Violations are costly for violators and, in theory, lead to changes in the behavior of third parties who alter their policies and practices to avoid violating individuals' civil rights and paying civil damages. This mechanism of civil rights enforcement is, what Burke calls a "litigious policy" (Burke 2002). In other words, in the US, at least, we rely on the threat of litigation, litigation itself, and the outcomes of litigation as the mechanisms by which civil rights are guaranteed. In other less litigious countries, such as Israel (see Aviram this volume) and France (see Pélisse this volume), rights guarantees under law may be far more a matter of entitlement, as is especially the case of conscientious objectors in Israel, political values and nationalism.

The "litigious policy" model of civil rights enforcement in the US centers on the identification of a specific problem. For example, in the case of workplace racial discrimination, well-meaning, intelligent people think about and enact a law which gives rise to rights (for example, Title VII of the Civil Rights Act of 1964). Individuals engage typically in private lawsuits, which eventually, through precedent, create a system of rules and incentives to change behavior and achieve the desired outcome.

There is, of course, variation in procedure among different laws. For example, for many forms of employment discrimination, Title VII established a federal regulatory agency, the Equal Employment and Opportunity Council (EEOC), through which potential plaintiffs must proceed prior to filing a lawsuit. In some very rare cases, the EEOC might represent individuals in a lawsuit against an employer. In contrast, consider prisoners' rights. In these cases, individuals often enter a class when one entity is depriving multiple, similarly situated individuals their rights by adopting a particular practice or procedure. Despite these variations, the private right of action is the primary mechanism by which law is thought to affect social change. All sorts of legal problems rely on private rights of action that require citizens to use the law to enact the policy changes they seek.

Scholars of law and society, law and public policy, and the sociology of law study the relationship between social problems, law, and outcomes to attempt to understand how effective law is with regard to creating the desired outcomes. Scholars study and describe how the law is mobilized (meaning used or not used), how the law is enacted (meaning where and how it is deployed), and how the law is or is not enforced (comparing the law-on-the-books to law-in-action). From these studies, we attempt to understand the conditions that constitute successes and failures both for our own understanding of law as a social institution, but also to inform policymakers and legislators so that they can pass laws that lead more directly to the kind of policies they seek.

To return to the example of employment discrimination, crudely formulated, the question shared by scholars, policymakers, and ordinary citizens is: Has Title VII reduced employment discrimination? We may disagree over the proper measure. For example, some believe that reduced employment discrimination should be measured by a declining or non-existent wage gap. Others think the appropriate indicator of workplace equality is that white women, people of color, and people with disabilities are now represented in top management. But does "represented" mean in proportion to their representation in society, in the industry, or in the company? Whatever the outcome measure we choose, sociolegal scholars traditionally have analyzed law and social change by asking: Is law working to have the kind of impact we seek and how could it be made more effective?

Limits of the "Crude Model" of Law as a Catalyst for Social Change

The questions begged by the "crude model" of law as a catalyst for social change exclude a variety of crucial elements for understanding the role of law in producing social change. Given the model's explicit reliance on individuals to be aware of their rights, to mobilize them formally and informally, and to engage in litigation, we must better understand *how and where the individual fits* into the model. The processes that make mobilization more complex – ordinary citizens' understandings of rights, their willingness and ability to mobilize formally or informally, and finally their willingness and ability to litigate a legal claim – the process of "naming, blaming, and claiming" is explained in clear detail elsewhere (Felstiner, Abel and Sarat 1980).

The importance of the individual must not obscure the ways in which the individual is embedded in organizational and institutional contexts. Indeed, context affects both their ability to understand law and their capacity to mobilize it. As such, it is of crucial importance for scholars of law and social change to have a set of tools that allows them to examine the role of the individual in thinking about and mobilizing law for social change. These analytical tools must allow us to be attendant to the organizational and institutional contexts in which laws operate. Attentiveness to the individual, the social processes, the organizational constraints and the institutional burdens placed on the individual requires scholars of law and social change to rely on a set of theoretically developed empirical tools.

Legal Consciousness

Scholars of legal consciousness have made important advances in the development of such a set of tools. By advancing both theoretical and methodological innovations and by adapting standard social science methods to the study of legality, legal consciousness scholars have made great strides in advancing our understanding of the law-in-action. Drawing on ethnographic and narrative analyses of everyday disputes, contemporary studies of legal consciousness show that how individuals experience law in their ordinary lives is of central importance for understanding law's influence on societal change (Bumiller 1988; Ewick and Silbey 1992, 1998;

Hull 2003; McCann 1994, 1999; McCann and March 1996; Merry 1990b; Sarat 1990; Yngvesson 1985, 1988). Scholars of legal consciousness use the analysis of, among other locations, the neighborhoods (Ewick and Silbey 1998), jury rooms (Fleury-Steiner 2002), welfare offices (Sarat 1990), workplaces (Albiston 2000, 2005; Bumiller 1988; Hoffmann 2003; McCann 1994), marriage rituals (Hull 2003), court houses (Yngvesson 1988), and public places (Nielsen 2000) in which legality is enacted, to study how law is understood and acted upon by ordinary citizens.

This research, while focused on law, demonstrates that law is only *one* – albeit an important – source of symbolic and cultural influence in the social practices that give meaning to everyday events (Merry 1990; Ewick and Silbey 1998; Nielsen 2000). Legality is among the rules and interpretative frameworks "that operate to define and pattern social life" (Ewick and Silbey 1998:43; Sewell 1992):

> Through its organization, society provides us with specific opportunities for thought and action. Through language, society furnishes images of what those opportunities and resources are: how the world works, what is possible and what is not. These schemas ... include cultural codes, vocabularies of motive, logics, hierarchies of values and conventions, as well as the binary oppositions that make up a society's "fundamental tools of thought" (Ewick and Silbey 1998, 39–40, quoting Sewell 1992).

This conception goes beyond treating law (or any other social or cultural organization or institution) as merely a source of authority that dictates action. Rather, this conception recognizes the *interplay* between individuals and law, which is fluid, and influenced by any variety of factors. Thus, individuals are influenced by and enact schema at once. Ewick and Silbey explain: "At the same time that schemas and resources shape social relations, they must also be continually produced and worked on – invoked and deployed – by individual and group actors" (Ewick and Silbey 1998:43). Thus, consciousness of law is reflected in both people's understandings of their rights *as well as* their efforts to enact those rights.

Law is one such schema. Like other societal schemas, legality imposes constraints on the meanings available for particular experiences, but it is by no means fixed, static or inflexible. Rather, the study of legality using a legal consciousness perspective recognizes the myriad factors that can affect how an individual understands his or her rights, what they do about those rights, and even if they believe they enjoy a right. The formal law can affect ordinary citizens' legal consciousness through its repeated enactment by individuals and groups (Ewick and Silbey 1998; Sewell 1992), but so can informal practices and procedures that embody legality. Legal consciousness can be multiple; meaning an individual can have one attitude toward laws of a particular variety (say, murder) versus another area of law (say, tax fraud). Legal consciousness can be contradictory; meaning an individual may have explicit double standards. Legal consciousness also embodies legal *un*consciousness; meaning that it is important to understand what types of problems ordinary citizens do not view as ones that are appropriate for the law to handle. Legal consciousness (and other schema) is "transposable" or generalizeable to many different situations; meaning that attitudes about and understandings of law can come from experiences with law and legal actors that one might not think of as connected. For example, a bad experience with a lawyer may taint how an individual thinks of judges or politicians. The possibility of legal and social change emerges in the interaction between flexible schemas and the creative potential of human agency which generates alternative arrangements in the workplace, the family, and the community. At the same time, and importantly, this interaction may also reinforce such arrangements.

A key work in the development of legal consciousness has been Ewick and Silbey's *The Common Place of Law* (1998). In this work, Ewick and Silbey argue that legal consciousness is a framework of attitudes and practices stemming from cultural resources. Through the analysis of dozens of interviews, they observe three main "schemas" of relation to the law: "before the law", "against the law" and "with the law." These schema are complex, but simply understood. An individual, at any time can be "before the law" (standing as an object on which the law operates), "with the law" (meaning that the individual relates to the law instrumentally, gaming the system and using it to get what he or she seeks), or "against the law" (meaning they resist the law, either formally or informally). When one is against the law, one may be fighting to change the law, voicing one's objection to legal interference with one's life, and, on occasion, being cynical as to the possibility of positive change through legal channels. The "with the law" schema puts people in a position of using the law to their own advantage, playing the system to better their personal situations.

Whether Ewick and Silbey's interviewees chose to locate themselves "before" "with" or "against" the law in a certain situation, the legal realm was meaningful to their everyday experience, and an important share of their meaning-making was done through applying these cultural resources in their daily lives, enterprises and problems (Ewick and Silbey 2000). Similarly, Sarat's work on the welfare poor (1990:343) reached the conclusion that, in the life course of his interviewees, the law was an overpowering and ever-existing presence – it was "all over" them in a variety of contexts. Their responses to the omnipresence of law were submissive or resistant (perhaps, similar to Ewick and Silbey's "before" and "against" schemas), but they were certainly dialoguing with law throughout their life struggles and problems. This power of the law was also evident in Merry's work on conflict-resolution for working class New Englanders (1990). Merry's subjects were empowered by the possibility of bringing their disputes to court, but later found themselves overpowered by its presence.

These theoretical breakthroughs about how law as a cultural force gives shape to individuals' understanding of and decisions about life and law was accompanied by methodological innovation as well. Scholars of legal consciousness built on the legal needs studies of the 1970s (Curran 1977) which sought to document the unmet legal needs of ordinary citizens in order to ask a broader set of questions about when ordinary citizens do *not* turn to the law. Classic studies focused on simple lack of resources – when an individual could not afford to hire an attorney – but these new studies sought to understand what was at stake socially and culturally in the decision not to invoke the law either formally or informally. These studies demonstrated that people often were simply unaware of their rights (Sarat 1990), unwilling to be labeled a "victim" to enforce those rights (Bumiller 1988), thought that law was not the appropriate mechanism for dealing with disputes that could be handled another way (Ewick and Silbey 1998), or found that the law transformed their disputes into something nearly unrecognizable even to the involved parties (Yngvesson 1988).

In addition to an examination of where the law is not, scholars of legal consciousness began to conceive of their work as the study of some set of social problems to explore how, if at all, law plays into the ordinary citizens' understanding of law's appropriate role in rectifying such problems. This meant not introducing the concept of law early in an interview or participant/observation session in order to allow the respondents to demonstrate the salience of law in any given situation. Thus, Ewick and Silbey ask about "neighborhood problems" and inquire what, if anything the respondent did about the problem allowing respondents' answers to indicate the primacy (or not) of law in their analysis of how to solve a particular problem.

Legal consciousness is an appealing concept for the study of civil rights in its expansive nature. It invites us to explore how people experience rights. The flexibility of legal consciousness theory enables the researcher to focus on *the impact of setting* – that is to say, an important contribution of this approach is the possibility and value of examining the importance of law outside the traditional boundaries of the formal legal institution. And, indeed, legal consciousness work gives voices to people who are largely voiceless in sociolegal scholarship.

Legal consciousness raises an interesting question for the study of civil rights: how is legal consciousness shaped by the interaction between identity, legal discourses, and other institutionalized systems of meaning? In other words, the dynamic process through which individuals construct their understanding of law can be understood as a contest over meaning, in which their identities interact with legal discourses and alternative discourses constructing consciousness. Civil rights reforms both reflect and produce struggles between legal discourses and other social discourses because legal reforms often challenge existing social arrangements, taken-for-granted meanings (Engel and Munger 1996; Krieger 2000), and hierarchies of power and privilege. Note that this approach to legal consciousness treats law as a resource for resistance rather than an institution to be resisted (cf. Sarat 1990). In this way, adapting legal consciousness to the study of civil rights builds on other, more macro-level studies that view law as a discursive resource for bringing about social change (McCann 1994; Scheingold 1974).

Understanding how competing discourses shape legal consciousness is important for understanding both the dynamic of social change and possible sources of resistance to social change. Legal consciousness theory suggests that legal change may bring about social change by destabilizing existing meanings and de-legitimizing accepted practices. In this view, opportunities for destabilizing meanings arise when actors respond to conflicting or overlapping schemas, sometimes by transporting systems of meaning from one context to another (Sewell 1992). Legal reforms provide new discourses for reframing the meaning of social events and destabilizing existing meanings. But just as actors can draw on new legal discourses to destabilize existing meanings, actors may also draw on existing discourses to undermine legal reforms. In other words, established discourses can be resources for resisting social change through legal reform, and these discourses can shape actions to be consistent with existing social structure.

To Mobilize or Not to Mobilize?

The study of legal consciousness has been and continues to be intimately tied to questions of mobilization (Marshall and Barclay 2003; McCann 1994; Rosenberg

1991). More than "simply a summary of a person's attitudes and opinions about law" (Marshall and Barclay 2003), legal consciousness explores "how legal concepts influence the goals, options, choices, and problems of ordinary individuals" (Marshall and Barclay 2003:617). The focus of the study of legal mobilization primarily has been, "when and how will people mobilize law to solve their problems?" with an emphasis on when they do use the law.

Nonetheless, scholars long have recognized that there are a multitude of reasons that ordinary people do *not* turn to the law to solve their problems. Ordinary citizens may be unaware that they have a legal remedy for the problems they suffer (Marshall 2003, 2005), they may think that other informal solutions are preferable for a variety of reasons (Albiston 2000; Engel 1993; Ewick and Silbey 1998), or they may simply not have the financial resources required to pursue a legal remedy (Curran 1977). Understanding at a more fundamental level *why* ordinary citizens use or fail to use the law is thus a fundamental concern to scholars of the New Civil Rights Research.

The constitutive approach to the study of law employed by the scholars in this volume treats formal legal complaints as only one, albeit an important one, measure of legal mobilization.[1] By probing respondents in depth about their problems, researchers have come to see not just how ordinary citizens think about and understand law, but also how they mobilize law in a multitude of settings including the workplace (Albiston 2000; Hoffmann 2003; Marshall 2003, 2005; McCann 1994), the neighborhood (Ewick and Silbey 1998), the family (Hull 2003), and the street (Levine and Mellema 2001; Nielsen 2000, 2004). How ordinary citizens understand the particular problem they face and the law's role (or lack of role) in solving it is a situational accomplishment that is dependent on the symbolic, organizational, institutional, and spatial factors that are unique to each setting.

The chapters in this book uncover and elaborate myriad complex ways that law is used informally to structure debates (for example, Cooper, this volume, chapter 7), provide motivation for political organizing (for example, Fleury-Steiner and Hodge, this volume, chapter 8), or otherwise influence outcomes short of formal legal

---

[1] As we demonstrated earlier in this introduction, in the context of civil rights, law is enacted in an effort to make some sort of social change. For example, we hope that Title VII reduces the amount of workplace discrimination faced by members of disadvantaged minorities. Similarly, we hope that the Americans with Disabilities Act reduces barriers to full social participation faced by people with disabilities. Can law affect the changes we seek if it is invoked in informal ways? If there is no court filing or formal complaint to the EEOC, was the law mobilized? If the employer violating the law resolves the dispute only to the satisfaction of one worker but continues to discriminate against those who remain ignorant of their rights, is law affecting social change? We will have different answers to the questions, "what is mobilization?" and "what constitutes law affecting social change?" If we think social change only occurs when a full-blown social movement emerges, many of the actions documented by the authors in this volume will not qualify as law affecting social change. At the other extreme, if we say law is "working" because we see evidence that it is changing what people believe they are entitled to without them actually getting what they are entitled to, our theory of law and social change is bankrupt as well. This volume does not propose an answer to these debates. Normative questions such as what constitutes mobilization and what constitutes law's "successful" intervention in a problematic situation, while certainly worth debating, are not the focus of this volume. Rather, the chapters in this volume contribute to the debate by exploring how the law sits, comfortably or uncomfortably, with other systems of rules and behaviors in a variety of settings. This empirical evidence does however help us better understand these debates.

complaint (for example, Albiston, this volume, chapter 3). In so doing, we learn about the power of law beyond its formal institutional capacity.

Situating Legal Consciousness and Identity

How do preexisting power relations add to an understanding of the struggle for rights on the ground? To what extent do social class, gender, sexuality, education, disability, and race identity play a role in shaping people's experiences with law? Nielsen's research on citizens' experiences with street harassment goes a long way in demonstrating the importance of *situating* individual's legal consciousness – what Nielsen calls a theory of "situated legal consciousness":

> Studies of legal consciousness that elaborate typologies of legal consciousness demonstrate variation in that consciousness ... but how do we account for these variations? The data herein go beyond describing general orientations toward the law to trace the factors that influence how people arrive at their general position vis-à-vis the law, demonstrating that people make connections from their past experiences – good or bad – which arise in part from the social position they occupy – and that these experiences shape their understandings of law. Thus, the social location of subjects, and the experiences that arise from that location, are a vital part of our understanding of legal consciousness. From this study we that being a member of a traditionally disadvantaged group has a significant effect on an individual's orientation to the law (Nielsen 2000:1087).

In addition to understanding how people of different statuses have different experiences with the law, a constitutive perspective of rights must also pay particular attention to the ways identity informs people's many experiences in the context of law. From this perspective, Fleury-Steiner's (2002) research on jurors' experiences in death penalty cases elucidates what he calls a theory of "legal narrativity":

> A theory of legal narrativity posits "that it is through narrativity that we come to know, understand, and make sense of the social world, and it is through narratives and narrativity that we constitute our social identities" (Sommers and Gibson 1994:58). From this perspective, legal consciousness is understood by elucidating both the stories that give meaning to actors' identities and in turn how such identities give meaning to "law" ... In addition to focusing on "variation across group when examining legal consciousness" (Nielsen 2001:1088), a focus on narrativity moves beyond an analysis of law as a single isolated phenomenon occurring across or among isolated social groups. In this way, events are made episodic ... [Law] [is] both constituting [of] and constituted by multiple identities (Fleury-Steiner 2002:573).

Engel and Munger's (2003) recent book *Rights of Inclusion* goes even further in demonstrating the centrality of identity to a constitutive approach to the study of civil rights. Their study of the impact of the *Americans with Disabilities Act* (ADA) on ordinary citizens opens a window into the importance of family, race, class, gender identity and the nature of an individual's disability for understanding the effects of rights on the ground. Specifically, Engel and Munger's study of the life story narratives of Americans with disabilities reveal the subtle ways that "who" a person is has on their consciousness as rights-bearing individuals. They bring identity into the equation of legal consciousness in an innovative way by interviewing people with disabilities multiple times to explore how legal consciousness and identity change and interact in the course of their lives. This insight about the importance of identity will have an impact on how we understand and explain the contingency of legal consciousness. Moreover, Engel and Munger's approach highlights the need for the study of and attention to other forms of narrative information as well. For example, how rights are realized for prisoners or women in the workplace also requires a complete understanding of the institutional contexts in which these individuals are embedded.

Like Engel and Munger, the authors of the chapters that comprise this collection are attentive to the often subtle ways in which identity constitutes rights consciousness on the ground. These essays demonstrate, however, that attention not only must be paid to biographical details but also to a number of other potentially critical factors – including, if not especially, organizational and institutional context. As Edelman (1990) – reporting on findings from her seminal study of the effects of Title VII civil rights laws on 52 organizations – observed with regards to the problematic ways that new legal rights afforded to workers may go unrealized in the context of the actual ways organizations govern themselves:

> [E]mployment rights do not simply mirror law and public policy. The complexity of the organizational reaction to environmental changes means that formal structures that become institutionalized may be relatively unaffected by – or at least slow to respond to – a subsequent loss of public or legal support ... It is important to recognize that the formalization of due process rights does not guarantee substantive justice in the workplace (Edelman 1990:1436).

Taken as a whole, *The New Civil Rights Research*, we believe, demonstrates convincingly the need for civil rights researchers to be expansive and attentive to the multitude of important details revealed in people's stories of their experiences. Without this flexibility on the part of the researcher, we believe the very complex phenomenon of rights articulated in people's stories will be silenced; thus denying the possibilities for social and legal change.

Overview of the Book

The chapters presented in this book bring together some of the most innovative and important research on civil rights law and legality. Along with other very recent books that document the complexities of rights among Americans with disabilities (Krieger 2003; Engel and Munger 2003) and gays and lesbians (Goldberg-Hiller 2002), *The New Civil Rights Research* makes a fascinating and diverse contribution to the field. Drawing on narratives of individuals from a variety of contexts, the material in this collection allows for rich and contextualized understandings of what happens when law interacts with other competing systems or forms of social organization. By privileging the real-world, lived experiences of those most influenced by rights, the collection moves beyond the typically polarizing debates "for or against" rights.

Part I of the volume explores issues that make up ordinary people's everyday lives – work, school, family, and health. Each of the chapters in this section explores the new civil rights at issue not as one unconnected facet of an individual's life or daily activity but rather with an explicit focus on how life is experienced with relation to inclusion in mainstream organizations and institutions that shape everyday life. Moving beyond a formal legal model in which rights can be deployed and fundamentally alter power relations by sheer force of law, the authors explore the complicated ways that rights are negotiated with respect to existing structures, organizations, and institutions. Analysis with attention to existing hierarchies allows for a nuanced and systematic understanding of how the culture of rights works in the contexts in which rights are invoked.

In Chapter 1, "'That's Right': Truth, Justice, and the Legal Consciousness of Educational Activists," Idit Kostiner explores the effectiveness and effects of civil rights law passed in the wake of *Brown v. Board of Education* for attaining educational reform. Kostiner's chapter goes beyond the "for-and-against-rights" debate by studying the role of rights in education as it is reflected in everyday consciousness. Drawing on in-depth interviews with 30 educational justice activists in the San Francisco Bay Area, Kostiner suggests that activists' subjective – as opposed to formal legal – understandings constitute the objective reality of rights and their role in educational reform.

In Chapter 2, "Who Manages Feminist-Inspired Reform? An In-Depth Look at Title IX Coordinators," Judith Taylor's analysis of the consciousness and commitments of six Title IX coordinators who served in the same public agency over a 20-year period demonstrates how laws inspired by the civil rights movement are practised on the ground. Moreover, she demonstrates the diverse ways in which those involved understand their mandates and the organizational and political milieus within which they work. By presenting a constitutive perspective on post-civil rights educational reforms, Taylor's findings complicate one-dimensional tropes about bureaucrats, and signal why feminist movement adherents might be served by looking more closely at the work Title IX coordinators do.

In Chapter 3, "Legal Consciousness and Workplace Rights," Catherine Albiston's study of the Family and Medical Leave Act (FMLA) draws together two strands of social constructivist theories, one from the law and society tradition and the other from sociological understandings of work and family. First, Albiston reviews how the institutionalized features of work historically were constructed in opposition to gender and came to exclude care. Second, through qualitative interviews with workers who negotiated contested leaves in the workplace, Albiston examines how social institutions, culture, and social interactions shape the process of asserting these rights. Albiston finds that employers' resistance to leave and respondents' understandings of their situations are shaped by institutionalized conceptions of work and care. Family wage ideology continues to give meaning to taking time off from work, despite the protections of the law, and legal rights remain embedded within deeply held belief systems, institutionalized work practices, and relations of power. Albiston also finds, however, that the FMLA's legal norms make the tensions between work and gender more visible, allowing workers to challenge institutionalized work practices that exclude care.

In Chapter 4, "LGBT Family Rights, Legal Consciousness, and the Dilemma of Difference," Kimberly D. Richman explores the dilemma of difference in gay rights-related legal consciousness – specifically, the variation and diversity of LGBT rights consciousness around family law issues, the perceived role of law in the lives of gay and lesbian parents, their beliefs about the meaning of gay rights, and the implications of these differences. She draws on data from a study of gay and lesbian parents' custody and adoption cases over the last 50 years and 36 in-depth interviews with LGBT parents, lawyers, and family court judges from across the United States. She finds that, contrary to assumptions of homogeneity in this common category of discrimination by both opponents and proponents, gay and lesbian parents have vastly different notions of what "gay family rights' should look like and how they should be achieved, and struggle with conflicting issues of ideology and strategy in enacting and exercising these rights. She argues that recognition of these differences, while complicating the concept of gay rights, is necessary for a nuanced and truly constitutive understanding of LGBT legal consciousness.

Chapter 5, "Consciousness in Context: Employees' Views of Sexual Harassment Grievance Procedures," by Anna-Maria Marshall, is the first of two chapters on sexual harassment in the workplace. Marshall's interviews with 25 female staff members and administrators at a Midwestern university shows how rights are mediated by powerful forces that can sometimes limit their value to ordinary people fighting injustice in their daily lives. Specifically, she finds that the women she interviewed adopted a skeptical position with respect to sexual harassment policies in their working environments. While they were familiar with the policies and the expansive protection offered on paper, women were also aware of supervisors' narrow interpretations when implementing the policies. They viewed the grievance procedure as an adversarial process, designed to protect the employer from liability rather than to protect their rights. As a result, they relied on the procedure in only very narrow circumstances, preferring to lump their problems or engage in self-help. As a result, rights fell into disuse and became relatively ineffective at dismantling inequality.

Part II presents right practices in more problematic, highly contested contexts. While again careful to reveal the complexities of rights in the lives of those studied, Part II of the book shows the serious and often disquieting challenges present in contemporary American civil rights law and society.

In Chapter 6, "On-the-Job Sexual Harassment: How Labels Enable Men to Discriminate through Sexual Harassment and Exclusion," Elizabeth A. Hoffmann presents a study of "token" women workers in a medium-sized taxicab company, which produces a nuanced critique of sexual harassment law in practice. Specifically, Hoffmann shows how the male cab drivers in her study apply conceptual labels to their women co-workers and treat each differently based on her assigned label. Through the use of these labels, the narratives of the women in Hoffmann's study reveal how male co-workers' legal consciousness encompassed an understanding of sexual harassment law that permitted them to harass some women at the company, while ignoring other women workers. Accordingly, Hoffmann shows how this pervasive sexual harassment fosters a culture of exclusion for both the harassed and non-harassed women taxicab drivers; both are given limited access to the more powerful members of the company, the male managers, as well as losing out on mentoring opportunities.

In Chapter 7, "The 'Seesaw Effect' From Racial Profiling to Depolicing: Toward a Critical Cultural Theory," Frank Rudy Cooper explores the consequences of recent Supreme Court fourth amendment jurisprudence on law enforcement and public safety in the African-American community. Drawing on a case study of the politicolegal consciousness of race, politics, and law enforcement in New York City before, during, and after the election of Mayor Rudolph Giuliani, Cooper explicates a shift from extreme racial profiling to depolicing in such events as the police's failure to prevent mass sexual assaults during the city's Puerto Rican Day parade of 2000.

In Chapter 8, "Keeping Rights Alive: The Struggle for HIV Infected Prisoners," Benjamin Fleury-Steiner and Jessica Hodge explore how the recent retrenchment of a prisoner's right to adequate medical treatment is experienced by those who advocate on behalf of HIV infected prisoners. Fleury-Steiner and Hodge focus on the experiences of 25 such advocates from across the US. Specifically, they find that the world of HIV infected prisoner rights advocates is largely an uphill battle fought against a Prison Industrial Complex that is neither willing nor equipped to address their clients' many needs. However, rather than simply complain about the law's limitations to ensure HIV infected prisoner rights, Fleury-Steiner and Hodge's respondents are found to subvert a system they see as inherently stacked against them.

Part III presents studies that open up new possibilities for a constitutive perspective of civil rights. Specifically, each of the three contributors to Part III demonstrates how attention to subtle dimensions of experience – emotions, silence, time, and place – may have profound implications for understanding the ways rights are experienced within a variety of contexts.

In Chapter 9, "When the Saints Go Marching In: Legal Consciousness and Prison Experiences of Conscientious Objectors to Military Service in Israel," Hadar Aviram considers the behavior of conscientious objectors to military reserve service in the recent Israeli-Palestinian crisis from a constitutive perspective. Through interviews with imprisoned objectors, Aviram explores how her respondents *cope* with their imprisonment. That is to say, she explores the ways that objectors relate to other prisoners, the prison system, and the law in general. Findings suggest that conscientious objectors interact with the law, and its manifestation in prison, by perceiving themselves and their imprisonment to be "above the law." Despite the prevalence of this extra-legal schema, the interviewees occasionally turn to intra-legal schemas as well. Shifting in and out of the legal realm according to setting, the objectors' in Aviram's study are found to employ coping mechanisms that enable them to enhance their range of responses to the law, including liberation from it.

In Chapter 10, "Time, Legal Consciousness, and Power: The Case of France's 35-Hour Workweek Laws,' Jérôme Pélisse explores the relationships between legal consciousness and social inequalities through the analysis of the implementation of recent laws reducing work time in France. While previous analyses of these laws demonstrate how job status and gender have pervasively made their application increasingly unequal, Pélisse shows how "time" is a key narrative for understanding how workplace inequalities are experienced by workers. Specifically, his analysis of the varieties of time in workers' stories demonstrates how their legal consciousness is linked to resources, constraints and power relations that are peculiar to their workplaces. Pélisse's analysis of time has important implications for futures studies – specifically, his findings demonstrate the importance of attention to how the implementation of supposedly progressive laws may be made problematic by the subtle and pervasive ways social inequalities pervade the workplace.

In Chapter 11, "The Power of 'Place': Public Space and Rights Consciousness," Laura Beth Nielsen draws on empirical evidence from an ongoing study of offensive street speech to explore the locations in which such interactions occur and the role of those locations in constructing people's experiences of those interactions. Nielsen's data open new doors for future research – namely, that the law is implicated in the expectations people have about appropriate behavior in certain locations and that identity also is centrally implicated in how ordinary people understand rights. Thus, future studies must pay attention to conceptions about how law, space, and identity work together to affect how individuals understand and construct their "rights."

References

Albiston, C.R. (2000) "Legal Consciousness and the Mobilization of Civil Rights: Negotiating Family and Medical Leave Rights in the Workplace." Paper presented at the Law and Society Association Annual Meeting, Miami, FL.

—— (2001) "The Institutional Context of Civil Rights: Mobilizing the Family and Medical Leave Act in the Courts and in the Workplace."

Bumiller, K. (1988) *The Civil Rights Society: The Social Construction of Victims*. Baltimore: Johns Hopkins University Press.

Burke, T.F. (2002) *Lawyers, Lawsuits, and Legal Rights*. Berkeley: University of California Press.

Curran, B.A. (1977) *The Legal Needs of the Public: The Final Report of a National Survey*. Chicago: American Bar Foundation.

Ewick, P. and Silbey, S. (1992) "Conformity, Contestation, and Resistance: An Account of Legal Consciousness." *New England Law Review* 26:731–749.

—— (1998) *The Common Place of Law: Stories From Everyday Life*. Chicago: University of Chicago Press.

Felstiner, W., Abel, R. and Sarat, A. (1980) "The Emergence and Transformation of Disputes: Naming, Blaming, and Claiming." *Law and Society Review* 15:631–655.

Fleury-Steiner, B. (2002) "Narratives of the Death Sentence: Toward a Theory of Legal Narrativity." *Law and Society Review* 36:549–576.

Hoffmann, E.A. (2003) "Legal Consciousness and Dispute Resolution: Different Disputing Behavior at Two Similar Taxicab Companies." *Law & Social Inquiry* 27.

Hull, K.E. (2003) "The Cultural Power of Law and the Cultural Enactment of Legality: The Case of Same-Sex Marriage." *Law and Social Inquiry*.

Litras, M.F.X. (2000) "Civil Rights Complaints in U.S. District Courts 1990–98." US Department of Justice, Bureau of Justice Statistics (Federal Justice Statistics Program, NCJ 173427).

—— (2002) "Civil Rights Complaints in U.S. District Courts 2000." US Department of Justice, Bureau of Justice Statistics (Federal Justice Statistics Program, NCJ 193979).

McCann, M.W. (1994) *Rights at Work: Pay Equity Reform and the Politics of Legal Mobilizations*. Chicago: University of Chicago Press.

—— (1999) "Review of 'The Common Place of Law: Stories from Everyday Life,' by P. Ewick and S.S. Silbey." *American Journal of Sociology* 105:238–240.

McCann, M.W. and March, T. (1996) "Law and Everyday Forms of Resistance: A Socio-Political Assessment." *Studies in Law, Politics, and Society* 15.

Merry, S.E. (1990) *Getting Justice and Getting Even: Legal Consciousness among Working Class Americans*. Chicago: University of Chicago Press.

Nielsen, L.B. (2000) "Situating Legal Consciousness: Experiences and Attitudes of Ordinary Citizens about Law and Street Harassment." *Law and Society Review* 34:201–236.

Nielsen, L.B. (2004) *Licence to Harass: Law, Hierarchy, and Offensive Public Speech.* Princeton: Princeton University Press.

Nielsen, L.B. and Nelson, R.L. (2005) "Scaling the Pyramid: A Sociolegal Model of Employment Discrimination Litigation." in L.B. Nielsen and R.L. Nelson (eds) *Legal and Social Scientific Perspectives on Employment Discrimination.* Dordrecht, The Netherlands, Springer.

Rosenberg, G.N. (1991) *The Hollow Hope: Can Courts Bring About Social Change?* Chicago: University of Chicago Press.

Sarat, A. (1990) "The Law is All Over: Power, Resistance, and the Legal Consciousness of the Welfare Poor." *Yale Journal of Law and Humanities* 2.

Scheingold, S. (1974) *The Politics of Rights: Lawyers, Public Policy, and Political Change.* New Haven, CT: Yale University Press.

Silverstein, H. (1996) *Unleashing Rights: Law, Meaning, and the Animal Rights Movement.* Ann Arbor: University of Michigan Press.

Yngvesson, B. (1985) "Law, Private Governance, and Continuing Relationships." *Wisconsin Law Review* 1985:623–646.

—— (1988) "Making Law at the Doorway: The Clerk, the Court, and the Construction of Community in a New England Town." *Law and Society Review* 22:409–448.

PART I
RIGHTS IN PRACTICE

Chapter 1

"That's Right": Truth, Justice, and the Legal Consciousness of Educational Activists

IDIT KOSTINER

The role of civil rights law in promoting educational justice is complex and controversial. Since the famous 1954 decision in *Brown v. Board of Education* academics and activists have been debating the effectiveness and effects of civil rights law in attaining educational reform (Sarat 1997). The purpose of this chapter is to go beyond the "for-and-against-rights" debate and to study the role of rights in education as it is reflected in everyday consciousness. Instead of objectively assessing the effects of rights on educational justice, I focus on the subjective understandings of those who struggle for educational justice. Drawing on legal consciousness theory (Ewick and Silbey 1998; Kostiner 2003), I suggest that those subjective understandings constitute the objective reality of rights and their role in educational reform.

Based on this theoretical rationale, I have conducted in-depth interviews with 30 educational justice activists in the San Francisco Bay Area. These interviews allow me to analyze the various ways in which activists understand the relationships between rights and education. At face value, activists' understandings seem chaotic. A closer look, however, reveals that activists justify or criticize the role of rights in education based on three schemas or "modes of evaluation" (Boltanski and Thévenot 1987, 1991, 1999). I refer to these schemas as instrumental, political, and cultural. In the instrumental schema, activists emphasize the need of disadvantaged students to have concrete resources such as access to quality education, funding, decent learning conditions, and trained teachers. In the political schema, activists view educational injustice as rooted in unequal power relations, and therefore they focus on empowerment of disadvantaged groups and on guaranteeing the power of those groups to make decisions with regard to their own education. In the cultural schema, activists view educational injustice as a result of stereotypical and biased assumptions that both students and educators share, assumptions that are often unconscious and taken for granted. Their goal, in this last schema, is to expose those assumptions and promote respect for other cultures.

Each schema provides activists with a particular rhetoric, which allows them to assess the role of civil rights law in attaining educational reform. Under each schema, activists may justify or criticize civil rights law, but their mode of evaluation is different in each schema. Interestingly, the schemas are not reducible to individual actors but are rather found in the narratives of all activists. The same activist may evaluate rights based on one schema and then, in a different part of the interview, shift to another schema. The multiplicity and coexistence of schemas create a complex net of justifications and counter-justifications with respect to the role of civil rights law in education. This complexity is often ignored by sociolegal scholars, who provide conflicting accounts on the role of rights in education based on unified, preconceived definitions of rights and of educational justice. My analysis of activists' legal consciousness suggests that the various academic accounts exist in popular consciousness. While none of them can alone account for the reality of rights and their role in education, each of them is part of the available cultural repertoire for assessing civil rights. Operating together, they all constitute the reality of rights and their role in attaining educational justice.

From Brown to the 21st Century: Debating the Role of Rights in Education

The United State Supreme Court decision in *Brown v. Board of Education* gave rise to extensive academic debate on the role that civil rights law should and could play in promoting justice and equality in education (Davis 1997; Friedman 1997; Kateb 1997). In the years that followed *Brown*, liberal legal scholars celebrated the judicial activism of the Warren Court and expressed their belief in the ability of courts, and especially the Supreme Court, to correct "most of the flaws in American society" (Kalman 1996:43). They viewed the Warren Court and its judicial activism as evidence of the capacity of law to bring about progressive social reform in general, and in the area of education in particular. As Owen Fiss has put it:

> In the 1950s, America was not a pretty sight. Blacks were systematically disenfranchised and excluded ... These were the challenges that the Warren Court took up and spoke to in a forceful manner. The result was a program of constitutional reform almost revolutionary in its aspiration and, now and then, in its achievements ... [T]he truth of the matter is that it was the Warren Court that spurred the great changes to follow, and inspired and protected those who sought to implement them (Fiss 1991:1118; see also Auerbach 1980; Bachmann 1984–85).

Thus, liberal legal academics view *Brown* as "a revolutionary statement of race relations law" (Carter 1968:237). They consider it a decision that "profoundly affected national thinking and has served as the principle ideological engine" of the civil rights movement (Greenberg 1968:1522). They argue that *Brown*

> ... [m]ay be the most important political, social, and legal event in America's twentieth century history. Its greatness lay in the enormity of the injustice it condemned, in the entrenched sentiment it challenged, in the immensity of law it both created and overthrew (Wilkinson 1979:6).

Most importantly, for legal liberal advocates and academics *Brown* serves as a sign that law (and therefore "we") could play an important part in building a better society (Glendon 1994:155).

Critical Legal Scholars (CLS) reacted against this appraisal of *Brown* and of the Court in general. For CLS not only is civil rights law not a useful tool for promoting educational justice, but it was actually "a mechanism for creating and legitimating configurations of economic and political power" (Singer 1984:5). CLS view civil rights law as an ideological construct that supported existing power relations by creating an appearance of social reality that is inevitable and just. As opposed to liberal legal scholars who celebrated progressive judicial activism, such as the Court decision in *Brown*, for Critical Legal Scholars such activism was not socially transformative. It emphasized individual over group empowerment, legitimated power arrangements, and served as a pressure valve permitting social injustice (Kalman 1996:86; see also Gable 1984; Gable and Kennedy 1984).

In his assessment of antidiscrimination law, Freeman (1990) argues that instead of promoting social equality, antidiscrimination law served to legitimize the persistence of racial inequality. Freeman suggests that, "in the long run, the Court offers a vision of America that normalizes the existing patterns of inequality and hierarchy" (1990:123). He argues that legal reforms that grew out of the civil rights movement were highly limited by the ideological constraints of the law. According to Freeman, the framework of antidiscrimination and formal individualistic equal opportunity that was adopted by the courts denied the existence of a class structure in American society, and by so doing helped to sustain this structure. The legal liberal framework, he argues, served not only to rationalize but also to celebrate inequality (see also Tushnet 1984; Perry 2001).

Some minority legal scholars have found the CLS critique to be too categorical and inattentive to the role that legal rights play in the everyday lives of racial minorities. They argue that the source of racial domination in the US was not the hegemonic power of liberal legal ideology, but rather the pervasiveness of racism (Crenshaw 1988). Despite the mystifying effects of civil rights, they maintain, rights fulfill a useful function in the lives of those who were historically excluded and oppressed (Crenshaw 1988:1357–58; see also Williams 1987, 1988; Delgado 1987; Matsuda 1987; Milner 1989; Minow 1987). Thus, the idealistic notion of rights promoted by liberal legal academics gave raise to the skeptic and critical approach of Critical Legal Scholars who emphasized the mystifying effects of rights. This general dismissal of rights led, in turn, to a counter-reaction of minority legal scholars who found rights, despite their hegemonic nature, to be important, in practical ways for historically disadvantaged groups.

A similar pattern of appraisal, critique, and counter critique of the role of rights in education can be seen in the writings of social scientists who study *empirically* the effects of rights on educational reform. One of the most famous accounts in this regard is Rosenberg's study *The Hollow Hope* (1991). Reacting against the belief of social reformers in the courts as an engine for change, Rosenberg investigates the actual consequences of much celebrated Supreme Court decisions, among them the *Brown* decision. He concludes that, despite the fame and glory that was attached to this case in academic writing and in popular consciousness, a thorough exploration of its *actual effects* revealed its failure to produce any significant educational reform. Based on various data sources Rosenberg finds that the *Brown* decision did not have any significant impact on the actual integration of public schools in the South. Schools in the South, he argues, continued to be highly segregated during the ten years that followed the Court decision. Only in 1964 when Congress has joined the battle field and enacted the Civil Rights Act (1964), did change start to occur. Since that year, public schools in the South became more and more integrated. According to Rosenberg, these facts demonstrate the inability of courts and of litigation tactics, to bring about meaningful social change. It is only through the acts of the other branches of government that such change could be produced. His evidence on other civil rights cases reveal similar findings. Despite much investment in litigation campaigns and despite the responsiveness of federal courts to the claims raised by activists, those campaigns did not produce much change in practice. The courts, Rosenberg concludes, are mostly impotent in promoting significant social reform. The *Brown* decision in fact, represents the ineffectiveness of rights litigation. As he puts it:

> The use of the courts in the civil rights movement is considered the paradigm of a successful strategy for social change ... Yet, a closer examination reveals that before Congress and the executive branch acted, courts had virtually *no direct effect* on ending discrimination in the key fields of education, voting, transportation, accommodations and public places, and housing. Courageous and praiseworthy decisions were rendered, and nothing changed. Only when Congress and the executive branch acted in tandem with the courts did change occur in these fields. In terms of judicial effects, then, *Brown* and its progeny stand for the proposition that courts are impotent to produce significant social reform. *Brown* is a paradigm, but for precisely the opposite view (1991:70–71).[1]

McCann (1992) has reacted against this categorical dismissal of rights and litigation as strategies for social reform. He suggests substituting Rosenberg's court-centered approach with a dispute-centered approach. Shifting the focus from judges to nonjudicial actors and from the direct effects of court decisions to the indirect effects of legal processes, McCann's model offers a different perspective for assessing the effects of *Brown*. He suggests that *Brown* was crucial for the evolving leadership role of the NAACP (National Association for the Advancement of Colored People) among the black community. It raised the hopes of southern blacks by demonstrating that the southern white power was vulnerable and it enabled the NAACP to rally the black masses behind its program.

Thus, legal tactics, in McCann's bottom-up model, are only one component in a larger strategic plan of a social movement. Yet it is by no means an insignificant component. For McCann "[L]egal action was just one of many factors that played a role, but this hardly means that litigation and major court victories were an inconsequential dimension of the struggle" (1992:737; see also McCann 1994, 1998; Hunt 1992; Silverstein 1996; McCann and Silverstein 1998; Paris 2001).

Thus, while legal academics are engaged with a theoretical debate over the utility of rights in bringing about social justice, social scientists are similarly occupied with conflicting accounts of the effects of rights strategy on social reform. As I stated in the introduction, in this chapter I wish to shift the focus from the objective analysis of the effects of rights into the subjective experiences (or the legal consciousness) of the subjects of rights. Focusing on the specific question of the role of rights in promoting educational justice, I study the legal consciousness of activists for educational justice. In the next section, I describe and justify the methods that I used for collecting and analyzing data in this study.

---

[1] For other judicial impact studies see Becker and Feeley (1973); Cannon and Johnson (1999).

Methodology

I conducted in-depth personal interviews with 30 activists for educational justice in the San Francisco Bay Area during 1999–2003. While activists are not the only actors whose consciousness constructs the role of rights in educational justice, I have decided to focus on activists as people who not only think of educational justice, but also act for its attainment. The concept of educational justice and the role that civil rights law plays in it is salient in the everyday life of educational activists. As such, they provide a "pure case" (Luker 1984) for studying the meaning-making process in this specific context.

I selected activists through newspaper articles, web-search, and snowball sampling. Some of my interviewees were activists who devoted most of their time and energy to struggles for school reform. Others worked for organizations that combined advocacy for school reform with other fields, like employment discrimination, police brutality, environmental justice, etc. Activists in my sample consist of a diverse group of individual in terms of their gender, race, and age. The following table lists their basic demographic characteristics.

Table 1.1 Sample demographics

Gender	Race	Age
Men (11)	Black (7)	20–29 (10)
Women (19)	White (11)	30–39 (11)
	Asian (5)	40–49 (3)
	Latino (7)	50+ (5)

Interviews lasted between one and two hours and were tape-recorded and transcribed. Each interview was an open-ended discussion on activism for educational reform and on the various strategies that are employed, or could be employed for attaining this goal. The topic of civil rights law was not introduced to interviewees directly until later stages in the interview. My goal was to examine the extent to which activists brought up this topic independently. I took care not to impose specific definitions of rights or of educational justice, preferring to derive such definitions from activists' own narratives.

A crucial point in my analysis of interview transcripts is related to the unit of analysis. Because I am interested in consciousness as a collective phenomenon, my unit of analysis is not the individual activist. Instead of approaching my interview transcripts as 30 separated texts that needed to be compared to one another, I refer to them as one unified text, that includes within it various schemas, cultural codes, and modes of evaluation. Thus, my unit of analysis is the cultural schemas that are contained in activists' legal consciousness. Individual activists, through their language, are only carriers of this collective phenomenon. Following this logic, I refrain from assuming that an activist has one coherent opinion about rights and their role in education. Rather, I explore the various types of rhetoric that each activist invokes while justifying or criticizing the role of rights in education. In the reminder of this chapter, I present this range of rhetorical modes and comment on their broader implications.

Talk of Rights: Activists' Evaluations of the Role of Law in Education

As stated above, through my analysis of activists consciousness I have located three central modes that activists invoke to evaluate the role of civil rights law in education. Each mode of evaluation (or schema) assumes a different way of understanding the causes for educational injustice. Thus, under each schema activists view differently the available strategies for eliminating such causes, among which, is the strategy of civil rights law. In this part of the chapter, I describe the ways in which activists view educational injustice under each schema, and then demonstrate how they invoke the various schemas to assess the role of rights in education.

The Instrumental Schema

In the instrumental schema, activists view educational injustice as deprivation of specific resources from disadvantaged students. Because they place the actual needs of students in the center of the discussion, they view the goal of activism as serving those needs, either directly or through policy advocacy. They maintain that the main cause of educational injustice is the lack of concrete resources. Peggy Siegel is a grade school teacher in Berkeley and is also an activist for educational justice. When I ask her what she saw as the main problem in education, she answers in the following manner:

> I'd say ... really the main problem is lack of resources. I work with poor students, we get people from all different levels of society and somehow we're supposed to level the playing field ... You're supposed to take kids who are coming from poverty, have drug addicted parents, all these things, and somehow bring them to the same level as someone who comes from a household where there's so much support for education, tutoring, and all this other stuff. So if you want us to do that ... we just need so many more resources. You know, even working in Berkeley which is a district that isn't so bad, I come home with these stories and Steve [my husband] is just horrified at the stories of how little we have to work with, how little resource there is.

As this quote suggests, the instrumental schema involves practical types of justifications: "People have needs and to help them we need more resources." Activists view justice in practical terms and tend to believe that money is important. As they emphasize the need to have money, they also criticize those who downplay the importance of money. The following quotes demonstrate this point:

> People say you can't solve all education problems by throwing money at them. I say it could be nice to try. Let's do it first and then decide (Kirsten Rosenberg, Activist Academics United).

> A lot of people say, "Oh, just throwing money at the problem won't help it." Well, in a lot of cases it will! [laugh] (Peggy Siegel, Berkeley grade school teacher).

However, the instrumental schema is not limited to material problems or material demands. Activists in this schema acknowledge the fact that people may have non-material needs and they present such needs in specific, concrete and measurable ways. A good example is the demand for a multicultural curriculum. Activists in the instrumental schema justify this demand, suggesting that students of color *need* to have a multicultural curriculum in order to succeed in school and in future life. They maintain that because current curricula do not reflect the experiences of students of color, these students are alienated from school's institutions, which often leads to their failure or even to their dropping out of school. Consider the following quote:

> You know, not seeing themselves represented in the curriculum could mean them dropping out of community or schools. A lot of times that is the difference with a lot of students of color (David Watanabe, Youth for Change).

The Role of Civil Rights in the Instrumental Schema

When activists invoke the instrumental schema they assess the role of civil rights law based on its capacity to provide the concrete needs of disadvantaged students in schools. Based on this criterion, activists often justify the use of rights strategy and litigation, suggesting that by using such strategy the immediate and specific needs of disadvantaged students might be satisfied. In the following example, Carla Ferrera, a Latina activist for educational reform, maintains that rights litigation, may enable her to help immigrants who were deprived of their rights to send their children to public schools. As she puts it:

> I think the laws change real situations for real people. Specifically, I don't think that if I could bring Prop[osition] 187 to the Supreme Court anybody in the state is going to change their mind about Prop[osition] 187, but that woman who lives next door is going to be able to take her kid to school the next week (Carla Ferrera, Social Concerns).

Based on similar rhetoric of needs, Laurie Johns, a teacher and a school activist, justifies her advocacy against police involvement in schools. She describes a case in which one of her students, who is African–American, was badly treated by the police. As Laurie Johns explains, this case got her involved in a campaign for regulation of police power in schools.

> I got involved with that because I had a student who I felt had an unfair and pretty terrible interaction with the cops at school, and ended up jailed and in youth guidance center for like three weeks for an offence in the classroom that was really not warranted that she be in YGC for as long as she was, and she was out of school for like two months ... So I got involved with that just because it was a pretty compelling story about why *there needed to be some regulation* on the role that the police were playing in the schools. And so I spoke at a couple of school board meetings about it, and wrote something about it.

However, the instrumental schema is invoked not only to praise rights but also to criticize rights. One of the main critiques that activists make against rights is related to the gap between the promise of rights on the books and their lack of implementation in reality. The following quote exemplifies this type of "instrumental critique of rights."

> My whole experience of growing up is that depending on the income level of where you live will determine the quality of school that you have. I mean, if you come from a poor community, you're not going to have books. And you're going to be using really old books, and you're not going to have any classes that actually get you into college. I mean it's not even very subtle. In the school I went to I had to go to community college in order to get in through the special action ... because I didn't have a lot of classes that were required. I think if you grow up in a poor community – *it may in those books look like everything's equal, but in reality, how it ends up playing out, it's very different* (Xiomara Silva, Social Concerns).

Other activists attribute the lack of implementation of legal rights to the bureaucratic gap that exists between legal rights and everyday practice. The following quote demonstrates this argument.

> If you look at desegregation laws, so schools are now desegregated, but then you have magnet programs that track all the students, and that's exactly what I went to ... So I would say, it's almost still separate but equal. It didn't really change. Because we were getting more money, more resources, more everything, and the kids from the neighborhood weren't getting any of it. So essentially there were laws, but they were always circumvented by everybody, and that's what we still find (Ruby Garcia, Social Concerns).

Another "instrumental" critique of rights is related to the costs that are involved with the implementation of rights. In justifying a decision to avoid litigation strategies, activists often point to the high costs that are associated with those strategies. The following quote demonstrates this point.

> It's very expensive to do litigation. Very expensive and very intensive. And it takes years, and you know, really hundreds of thousands if not millions of dollars to properly litigate a major case. So who has the capacity to do that? It's very limited to a few of the people (Glen Stevens, Social Concerns).

Another instrumental justification that activists invoke against litigation strategies is related to the length of *time* that is often involved in such processes. As activists in the instrumental schema tends to value short-term strategies that bring about immediate results, they often criticize litigation for the length of time that is involved with it. The following quote demonstrates this critique.

> I think it [litigation] is a very selective kind of option. Because the infrastructure isn't really set up to give people relief in a short enough time that you actually feel like you've won something. The courts are able to drag that out for years, and people have to go on with their lives (Kirsten Rosenberg, Activist Academics United).

In sum, in the instrumental schema civil rights law is often evaluated positively based on its capacity to provide concrete and immediate changes in the lives of students. Yet for the very same reason, civil rights law is criticized under this schema for its imperfections and failure to fulfill its promises.

The Political Schema

Contrary to the instrumental focus on students' needs, when activists invoke the political schema their main focus is on the oppression of minority students and on the way in which the educational system perpetuates this oppression. Activists' main concern is to empower minority students and parents, so they are able to lead their own struggles, and fight for their own needs. They maintain that the educational system systematically deprives minorities of their needs in order to ensure that they remain in disadvantaged positions. They argue that schools in minority communities are intentionally deprived of resources in order for their students to maintain their subordinate position. In this way, the educational system perpetuates the power structure. The following quotes illustrate how activists use such rhetoric of power and domination to account for educational injustices.

> I think that people are pretty aware that shitty schools are a reflection of neighborhoods that have no investment in them, and that they'll perpetuate themselves, they'll keep people in the neighborhood, and I think that it's an unspoken thing that basically that's the intention of why schools are shitty. If people wanted to figure out how to run a good school, it's not that hard. There are examples of great schools all around. There's no interest in having effective schools (Edward Chung, Third World Alliance).

> At every phase of US development, essentially, public education has provided business with the set of employees that they needed ... Why businesses are willing to pay taxes for it, is because it forms the labor pool, and saves them the trouble of doing the training. And that is why I think, in the current period, because there is an entire group of people that business ... considers essentially superfluous to the labor market, they don't really care if ... they ever enter the labor markets ... This is this whole set of people that because business doesn't care, you see literally no education ... Because it's not in the interest of capitalism ... Basically I think that business would be very happy with ... a three-tier system. Rolls Royce Education, basic literacy, and nothing (Kirsten Rosenberg, Activist Academics United).

According to the political schema, schools in communities of color lack resources because dominant groups in society wish them to remain in this position. Therefore, activists maintain, the way to solve this problem is to ensure that poor communities and communities of color have the power to make decisions about their own lives. The strategy, then, is not to advocate for the various resources that minorities lack. Rather, it is to confront the root cause of their problems, that is, their lack of social and political power. The following quote illustrates this point:

> The main problem is that people who have kids in the public schools don't have power in the political process and that is reflected in a whole other set of problems. That's the root of the problem. If you understand why they don't have a political power then you understand the real problem and out of that basic problem comes a basic lack of resources within the school ... Resources are allocated according to race and class (Elli Smith, Youth For Change).

While in the instrumental schema activists justify the struggle over school curriculum based on the rhetoric of needs, in the political schema they justify the same struggle by invoking the rhetoric of power. They maintain that the reason for their struggle against mainstream school textbooks is not related to the *content* of the books, but rather to the question of who has the *power to decide* what this content would be. Communities of color, activists maintain, should have the power to make decisions with regard to their own education instead of being subject to decisions made by the white, middle-class school establishment. Bernard Roseman of Activist Academics United describes a textbook battle that took place in Oakland in 1991. He explains that despite the fact that the author of the textbook – a white middle-class history professor – tried to create a multicultural textbook, the textbook was rejected by the Oakland community. In Roseman's view the issue that gave rise to the Oakland textbook struggle was an issue of power and control. Consider his words:

> A professor of history from UCLA, who was supposedly a liberal, wrote these guidelines, or textbook guidelines ... He hadn't a clue as to what was going on. He came down to a citizens' meeting and he was dumbfounded. I could see it in his face. That you had people from a multicultural community, who are Native Americans, who are Spanish, who are angry. And he'd say, "You know, I've been active in the civil rights movement, I'm a good guy, how could you ..." He never really understood that the issue had to do with *who has the power to make the choices*. He didn't understand that. He thought it just had to do with what was in there [in the textbook] ... He never really grasped that the issue has to do with *power, who has the power to make the decisions*.

The Role of Civil Rights in the Political Schema

When activists invoke the political schema they assess the value of civil rights law based on its relationships to power. This mode of evaluation often leads to a highly critical assessment of rights, viewing them as obscuring social injustices and preventing social movements. Activists often suggest that prior to the enactment of civil rights laws it was easier to mobilize individuals in minority communities, as these individuals were facing overt state-sponsored discrimination. Today, activists maintain, discrimination and injustices still exist, but their covert nature makes it harder to mobilize people against them. Consider the following quote:

> I hate to be a cynic, but in a way I feel like this [the enactment of civil rights laws] has stolen the thunder from any kind of movement. Like I can't point at that sign and say, "Because of that sign I'm going to go organize, and all the people of color, or all the community." I feel like they [civil rights laws] are a safety valve, where some people of color can do well in society but most people of color cannot get ahead or succeed. And now there's a way that people can say, "Oh look, it's not because of race, you're just not trying hard enough, because look, that's a black man and he's on the Supreme Court or that's a black woman and she's doing this and she's doing that." So for me, those laws are a safety valve. And it's really taken the anger and power behind any kind of movement to really change things (Carla Ferrera, Social Concerns).

When activists invoke the political schema, they believe that the main problem that minorities face is lack of power, which results from racial and economic oppression. This problem, they argue, cannot be addressed by principles of equal access and equal opportunities. Consider the following quote:

There was a whole framework that thirty and forty years ago was very relevant to understanding how racial justice could be achieved, which is mainly that there's obviously state sponsored institutionalized segregation, and one could talk about access and discrimination as the central problems facing people of color. Sort of access to higher education, access to jobs ... The liberal civil rights stuff wasn't a critique of the way the economy works in general. It was much more about people marginalized getting access. And I think that realized some really critical things ... But on the other hand, it didn't change some of the fundamental structuring of the economy. In many ways, that's worsened. So now it's like we're struggling for a way to understand the way in which racism works in this country today. Because the dominant framework and paradigm has been through "discrimination," "access," "equal treatment," and "equal rights," but not about the ways in which, you know, the economy [works] ... So that's what I think the main challenge is: figuring out how we can understand what is racism, how does racism work in this country? (Edward Chung, Third World Alliance).

Thus, in the political schema, activists criticize the discourse of "rights," "equal access" and "antidiscrimination." They view this discourse as distracting attention from the real cause of social injustice; that is, from a systematic economic stratification that constantly places people of color at the bottom of the educational system and later on at the bottom of the workforce ladder. Anna Castro of the Oakland Citizens Union talks about her father, who was a civil rights activist in the 1960s. When I ask her about her own activism and whether she also considers herself an activist for civil rights, she responds by saying: "I think the struggle is for social justice; people don't really call it civil rights now." Thus, activists distinguish the current period from the civil rights movement, arguing that civil rights language is anachronistic and does not fit the needs of the hour.

Some activists maintain that the language of rights and antidiscrimination that used to serve the goals of the Left in the past is used today by the Right to resist progressive policies. They mention the way in which the Right is using rights language to oppose affirmative action programs, by presenting them as reverse discrimination. In the following quote, David Watanabe of Youth for Change talks about the backlash reaction against the initiative to diversity the reading list in the San Francisco School District. This reaction, he maintains, relied on the language of rights and antidiscrimination. In his words:

Shortly, like the day after [we] proposed the resolution, the media jumped on it. The front page of the *Examiner* was "all white books out." Something really divisive that didn't exemplify or present the resolution's substance. [It] touched on the kind of mainstream backlash of affirmative action ... And it really touched on saying, "This was like discriminating against white people or white history or white literature."

Nevertheless, while employing the political schema, activists often acknowledge that because rights are so closely associated with power, they cannot be ignored by those who are trying to increase the power of people. Following this logic, several activists use the political schema to make positive assessments of the role of civil rights campaigns in the struggle of social movements. They refer to situations in which organizing legal campaigns was useful for empowering people in minority communities, for having their voices heard and for making them more involved in decisions that affect their own lives.

Laurie Johns, a teacher and an activist, justifies her participation in school board campaigns by explaining that such campaigns enable minority parents to make their voices heard, to take control over their lives and over the lives of their children, and thus to be mobilized and empowered. In her words:

> All of these organizing attempts around these campaigns bring parents to school board meetings and show the board that it's not just white parents who are going to come and advocate for their issues. That people can mobilize parents of color to come, and kids of color to come. You know, I think that's important. And so whether it's immediately affecting the schools, long term I think it's going to have an effect (Laurie Johns, San Francisco middle-school teacher).

Legal campaigns are seen as useful in the political schema when they are able to gather a large number of individuals and especially when they are able to bring together people from different ethnic groups, as well as people who work on various social issues. Consider the following quote:

> The board meeting that was set to be voted on, you know, amazing community support came out in favor of it. Diverse community groups from the African-American community to the Asian-American community to, you know, just the whole range from teachers, parents, to students themselves, came out in support of multicultural education (David Watanabe, Youth for Change).

To sum up, activists in the political schema are critical about civil rights due to their association with power and domination. Yet, for this very reason they often justify the strategic use of rights for political mobilization. Since rights are powerful, they cannot be ignored by those who seek to change the balance of power. After all, as Alan Hunt has already put it, "all struggles commence on old grounds" (1990).

The Cultural Schema

Activists in the cultural schema view the cause of injustice as rooted in people's thoughts. They believe that the main obstacle for attaining justice in education is the biased and disrespectful ways in which people think of others (and sometimes of themselves). The following quote demonstrates this point.

> Q: What do you think is the biggest problem of people of color in the United States?
>
> A: The biggest problem? I think the lack of cultural acceptance by other individuals and a lot of stereotyping. I think that's usually the biggest barrier that people have in terms of trying to advance themselves, not just in education, but also in the workplace, and also in society ... I think that's the biggest challenge. Because if that were to go away, then people would be able to have more economic opportunities, and not always be in poverty. I think that's the biggest [problem]. Because everything else, it's sort of just a domino effect (Jennifer Huang, Asians for Diversity).

While focusing on thoughts and ideas, activists in the cultural schema do not ignore the actual needs of individuals. However, based on their own experience, they maintain that the satisfaction of those needs cannot solve social problems. Beth

Handler, an activist in Social Concerns, who used to be a mental health worker in schools, describes how she worked in schools where all the concrete changes that needed to be done were done, and yet the injustices suffered by students of color did not change. As she explains, this experience led to her realization that the source of the problem is not the lack of actual resources, but rather the existence of systematic racism in schools. In her words:

> It makes me so sad when I hear about these schools where the buildings are totally falling apart, and there are no books for the kids and stuff. And I have never worked in a school like that. I have worked in schools where they had the basics. In terms of the buildings and the books, and where the teachers were very well trained and ... everything that we say should be done is being done. And it's still not enough. It's still not working. So then you look at *"Well, what's left?"*, that's when you really start to try and reach out and touch *racism* in a way that's beyond the – you know, "Is there the same amount of money going to that school as to this school?" "Do they have their basic supplies?" "Are the teachers trained?" – some of the really easy things, which unfortunately, a lot of places are still dealing with. *But even when you get past all that*, there're some other issues. And those are the issues that I think we're focusing on [racism in schools] (Beth Handler, Social Concerns).

In the cultural schema, activists believe that educational injustice is primarily a result of teachers' prejudices and biases towards minority students. They maintain that public school teachers, who are disproportionately white, share – consciously or not – stereotypical and biased way of thinking about minority students, which in turn, affects the way they treat those students. Therefore, when activists invoke the cultural schema, they often mention the need to *train teachers* in order to make them less biased. Consider the following quote:

> A common complaint among both parents and students is that many times the teachers are not culturally competent ... Some teachers tend to stereotype students. They see a Chinese student and they feel like "Oh, Chinese students are really good, I don't have to pay that much attention to them, because they'll be fine." And then the other side of the spectrum is Pacific Islander students, Samoan students; "Oh, she's Samoan, she's going to be a trouble maker," or "She's not going to do well." So it's like having that kind of perception already *embedded in your head* before you even get to know the student. So it's a matter of *training teachers* that there are certain things that are sensitive to the culture, but at the same time, you should be treating each student individually, and not using these stereotypes to sort of *set barriers between student and teacher* (Jennifer Huang, Asians for Diversity).

The demand to diversify the school curriculum can help to distinguish the cultural schema from the previous two schemas. While in the instrumental and political schemas activists justify multicultural curriculum based on the rhetoric of needs or power, in the cultural schema, activists maintain that school curriculum should be multicultural simply because this is the only *true* curriculum. In their view, every person in society – not only people of color – needs to have a multicultural education because the *true* nature of our society involves the existence of different cultures, languages and traditions. In a multicultural society – like the American society – a monocultural curriculum is simply *false*. Such a false curriculum promotes ignorance with regard to other cultures, which in turn, promotes, racism and cultural disrespect.

According to activists in the cultural schema, a curriculum that is not multicultural cannot prepare students for living in the world, which is increasingly multicultural. Consider the following quote.

Q: How do you justify the need for multicultural education?

A: Well, I think that's pretty simple. We educate our kids to prepare them for the world, and the country, for the work force. And San Francisco is such a diverse [city], full of different cultures. And so I think it [multicultural education] is an excellent way to learn about each other, and to work as a team. Because that's what's going to happen. You're going to have to be able to *understand, respect* each other, work as a team when you grow up. You know, *that's what life is all about.* What better way to do it than when you're in school to prepare them for that? (Jennifer Huang, Asians for Diversity).

The Role of Civil Rights in the Cultural Schema

In the cultural schema, activists usually view civil rights as inapplicable for meaningful social change. A central idea in the cultural schema is that a meaningful change requires free will, and that attempts to force change can only lead to superficial changes that cannot be sustained. While assessing the value of the civil rights laws of the 1960s, Ruby Garcia argues that many people did not accept the ideas behind those laws and complied with them only out of fear of sanction. Such compliance, in her view, led people to manipulate the laws in ways that empty those laws of their content. In her words:

It's almost like it's there for show. It didn't change the mindset of the people who had the power. They did it because they were forced to almost, but not everybody accepted it … And that's what we still find. I think part of it is because there wasn't a conscious effort of an education movement that really said, "Okay, now we need to work on changing the attitudes of this country." It's never happened (Ruby Garcia, Social Concerns).

For Ruby Garcia, civil rights laws are "there for show" because they attempted to coerce people to change their behavior. Without an educational effort to change people's "mindset," compliance was superficial or even completely absent. Instead of forcing people to change, she believes that people should be educated in ways that would make them appreciate the changes, and change out of their own free will. While invoking the cultural schema, activists view this coercive aspect of the law as futile for educational reform. The following quote illustrates this point:

I feel like you can actually have laws to pressure people, but ultimately you have to have people working in the grass roots level that are helping people change in terms of their *thoughts* in terms of how [they view] race, how they *view* education. People have to *believe* that there is inequality, and *agree* to that. Otherwise, I think people will not change (Xiomara Silva, Social Concerns).

However, activists in the cultural schema also make positive assessments of rights. This is especially when they talk about the "symbolic effects" of rights. They suggest that the symbolic aspect of legal right may be a source of inspiration. For example, the passage of a school board resolution mandating a multicultural curriculum implies the statement that "we as a society" value the writings of authors of color. Such a statement may lead people of color to gain more pride in their culture and therefore may provide a certain contribution to the goal of increasing respect for minority cultures, as Beth Handler explains in the following quote:

> I think it has a lot of symbolic importance. What is in the textbook, or what is in the curriculum says what is important. What is important about history, what's important about literature ... Because people can argue that how a teacher teaches is more important than what they teach, and that might be true, but there's a symbolic statement that's made by what the curriculum's about. What we as a society, what schools and institutions think is important (Beth Handler, Social Concerns).

The way to attain educational justice in the cultural schema is to promote truth. This is also the rationale for mandating multicultural education. It is needed because it represents the truth. Based on this rationale, civil rights law is often seen as inadequate. When I ask Kirsten Rosenberg whether there is any legal basis for demanding multicultural education, she refers to federal civil rights law and explains why, in her opinion, this law is inadequate in this context. In her view, using civil rights law in the context of multicultural education relies on the assumption that *only* students of color need to have multicultural education. This assumption contradicts the basic belief in the cultural schema, according to which, multicultural education is needed by *all* members of society, simply because it reflects the *truth*. In her words:

> There is federal law about every student having equal access to education ... In order to have an equal access kind of argument, though, you're sort of making the underlying assumption, and I'm not sure you want to, that it's *only* children of color who need multicultural education. When in fact what is *true* is that in a multicultural society, or in fact to be an educated person in any society, *everybody needs that*. And so then you have a problem with the law (Kirsten Rosenberg, Activist Academics United).

Because activists view multicultural education as the only true education, presenting this "true education" as "a civil right" of one group against another misses what is most important about multicultural education. In other words, injustice, under the cultural schema, is seen less as violation of civil rights and more as deviation from the truth.

Beth Handler talks enthusiastically about the important of multicultural education, and about the various strategies that her organization is using to promote multicultural education. But when I ask her whether there is a legal right for multicultural education, she reacts with surprise, as if the question does not fit the flow of the story. The connection between multicultural education and legal rights that was implied in my question seemed unnatural to her and she feels that she needs to think about it some more.

> I think it's hard. I haven't thought about it before. I'd have to really think about it. My answer is yes, but justification I would have to think about ... It's really hard to think legally and what it means (Beth Handler, Social Concerns).

After giving it some thought, Beth Handler finds an interesting way to connect between rights and multicultural education, as she says:

> But the other thing that comes to mind – *do we have the right to lie?* You know, getting away with a monocultural curriculum? Do *we* have a *right* to do that?

Instead of saying that minority students have a right to have their culture represented in the curriculum (which in turn imposes an obligation on the schools or on the state), Beth Handler argues that "we" (society?) do *not* have a right to *lie* (to ourselves? to others?). Since she views the current monocultural curriculum as false or as "a lie," she thinks that we have no right to continue having it in schools. Following this line of thought she suggests that:

> If the curriculum is being mandated, it should be *accurate*, which means multicultural. I mean, I think yes. I think if curriculum's being mandated, yes, there is a *right* it should be mandated *correctly* …

Both Kirsten Rosenberg in the previous quote and Beth Handler in the above quote think that multicultural education is justified because it is the only *true* education. But the two activists share a different understanding of "rights." Kirsten Rosenberg refers to federal civil rights law that guarantees equal access. She rejects the use of this law arguing that such use implies the wrong idea that *only* minorities need multicultural education. Contrary to this understanding of rights, Beth Handler talks about rights in the abstract, arguing that "we do not have a right to lie." It is as if she talks about rights not from a perspective of positive law but rather from a natural law perspective. This perspective allows her to say that there is a right that the truth is taught, without referring to any specific positive law. Moreover, as opposed to Kirsten Rosenberg, Beth Handler does not invoke this understanding of rights to justify or to criticize the actual *use* of legal strategies. Rather, she employs this "natural law" type of understanding to suggest that the changes that her organization is promoting are not only "just," but are also "legally right."

To sum up, where the legal is equated with what is generally right, rights and justice are seen as related in the cultural schema. Yet as opposed to the previous two schemas, this relation is not a relation of two separate beings, where rights are a means for justice (or for injustice). Rather, rights, in their natural sense, and justice are one being. This being is not the means but rather the end. It is the goal that activists, while invoking the cultural schema, aspire for.

Conclusions: Civil Rights in Everyday Consciousness

I have argued that educational activists constitute a "pure case" (Luker 1984) that represents the collective consciousness, or the available "tool kit" (Swidler 1986) for evaluating the relationship between educational justice and civil rights law. My analysis of interviews suggests that such consciousness is complex, consisting of multiple schemas and modes of evaluation. This multiplicity is a result of the diversity of meanings that we assign to "educational justice" on one hand and to "civil rights" on the other hand. Paradoxically, this multiplicity of understandings and the contradictions between them reproduces the centrality of rights in our thinking of educational justice. This is primarily due to the coexistence of the instrumental and political schemas in our repertoire.

In the instrumental schema rights are judged based on their capacity to satisfy individuals' needs. They are seen as important tools for attaining this goal. Yet, they are also criticized for their imperfections and for their failure to fulfill their promise due to various constraints. The political schema represents the opposite assessment of rights. Through the lens of social power, it suggests that not only that rights cannot promote change, they actually prevent change by sustaining the power structure. While this account seems to oppose the instrumental schema, it actually shares with it a vision of rights as a means to an end. Through the cynical eye of the political schema, rights are seen as a tool for sustaining the hegemony of those in power. Therefore, based on this association between rights and power, activists who employ the political schema are also able to justify the use of law as a counter-hegemonic strategy.

In the cultural schema we have seen a similar dichotomy. Rights are perceived as both harmful (because of their coercive character), and as useful (because of their symbolic nature). Nevertheless, within the cultural schema we have also seen a different approach to rights. In this schema, activists refer to rights not only from a positive law perspective but also from a natural law perspective. In those moments the right is no longer a means for attaining justice but rather it is justice. It becomes an end in itself. The lawful, the just, and the truthful become one entity which is represented in the word "right."[2]

The constant appraisal and rejection of rights, then, seems to be a result of the illusionary perception of rights as means to an end. The ongoing shifting between instrumental and political perceptions of justice contributes to the reproduction of this illusion. Yet, if we look at rights as something that is not only legal or just but also true – we might be able to see that those rights are nothing more than our own self.

References

Arvey, R.D., and Cavanagh, M.A. (1995) "Using Surveys to Assess the Prevalence of Sexual Harassment: Some Methodological Problems." *Journal of Social Issues* 51:39–52.

Auerbach, C. (1980) "The Relations of Legal Systems to Social Change," *Wisconsin Law Review* 1227.

Bachmann, S. (1984–85) "Lawyers, Law, And Social Change," *New York University Review* of *Law and Social Change* 13:1.

Becker, T.L. and Feeley, M.M. (eds) (1973) *The Impact of Supreme Court Decisions* (2nd ed.). New York: Oxford University Press.

Bisom-Rapp, S. (1999) "Bulletproofing the Workplace: Symbol and Substance in Employment Discrimination Law Practice." *Florida State University Law Review* 26:959.

---

[2] In the Oxford dictionary a "right" is "something that one may do or have by law" (the lawful), but it is also "that which is good" (the just) and "that which is true" (the truthful). The English language tells us that the legal, the just, and the truthful can merge into one. The consciousness of activists offers a similar merging in the moments in which the law is seen as natural and justice is seen as truth.

Boltanski, L., and Thévenot, L. (1987) *Les économies de la grandeur*, Paris: Presses Universitaires de France.
—— (1991) *De la justification. Les économies de la grandeur*, Paris: Gallimard.
—— (1999) "The Sociology of Critical Capacity." *European Journal of Social Theory* 2(3):359–377.
Brown v. Board of Education 347 U.S. 483 (1954).
Cannon, B.C., and Johnson, C.A. (1999) *Judicial Policies: Implementation and Impact* (2nd edn). Washington DC: Congressional Quarterly Press.
Carter, R. L. (1968). "The Warren Court and Desgregation", Michigan Law Review 67:237.
Casper, J. (1970) "The Supreme Court and National Policy Making." *American Political Science Review* 70:50–63.
Crenshaw, K. (1988) "Race, Reform and Retrenchment: Transformation and Legislation in Antidiscrimination Law," *Harvard Law Review* 101:1131–1387.
Davis, P.C. (1997) "Performing Interpretation: A Legacy of Civil Rights Lawyering in Brown v. Board of Education" in A. Sarat (ed.) *Race, Law and Culture: Reflection on Brown v. Board of Education*. Oxford: Oxford University Press.
Delgado, R. (1987) "The Ethereal Scholars: Does Critical Legal Studies Have What Minorities Want?" *Harvard Civil Rights–Civil Liberties Law Review* 22:301–322.
Ewick, P., and Silbey, S.S. (1998) *The Common Place of Law: Stories from Everyday Life*. Chicago: University of Chicago Press.
Fiss, O. (1991) "A Life Lived Twice." 100 *Yale Law Journal* 100:1117.
Freeman, A. (1990) "Antidiscrimination Law: The View from 1989" in D. Kairys (ed.) *The Politics of Law: A Progressive Critique*, pp. 121–150. New York: Pantheon.
Friedman, L. (1997) "*Brown* in Context" in A. Sarat (ed.) *Race, Law and Culture: Reflection on Brown v. Board of Education*. Oxford: Oxford University Press.
Gable, P. (1984) "The Phenomenology of Rights Consciousness and the Pact of Withdrawn Selves." *Texas Law Review* 62:1563–1599.
Gable, P., and Kennedy, D. (1984) "Roll Over Beethoven." *Stanford Law Review* 36:1–55.
Glendon, M.A. (1994) *A Nation Under Lawyers: How the Crisis in the Legal Profession Is Transforming American Society*. New York: Farrar, Straus and Giroux.
Greenberg, J. (1968) "The Supreme Court, Civil Rights and Civil Disobedience." *Yale Law Journal* 77:1520.
Hunt, A. (1990) "Rights and Social Movements: Counter Hegemonic Strategies." *Journal of Law and Society* 17:309–328.
Kalman, L. (1996) *The Strange Career of Legal Liberalism*. Yale University Press.
Kateb, G. (1997) "Brown and the Harm of Legal Segregation" in A. Sarat (ed.) *Race, Law and Culture: Reflection on Brown v. Board of Education*. Oxford: Oxford University Press.
Kostiner, I. (2003) "Evaluating legality: Toward a cultural approach to the study of law and social change." *Law & Society Review*: 37: 323–368.
Luker, K. (1984) *Abortion and the Politics of Motherhood*. Berkeley: University of California Press.
McCann, M.W. (1992) "Reform Litigation on Trial." *Law and Social Inquiry* 17:715–744.
—— (1994) *Rights at Work: Pay Equity Reform and the Politics of Legal Mobilization*. Chicago: University of Chicago Press.
—— (1998) "How does Law Matter for Social Movements" in G. Bryant and A. Sarat (eds) *How Does Law Matter?* Evanston, IL: Northwestern University Press.
—— and Silverstein, H. (1998). "Rethinking Law's 'Allurements': A Relational Analysis of Social Movement Lawyers in the United States." In *Cause Lawyering: Political Commitments and Professional Responsibilities*. A. Sarat and S. Scheingold (eds). New York: Oxford University Press.
Matsuda, M. (1987) "Looking to the Bottom: Critical Legal Studies and Reparations." *Harvard Civil Rights–Civil Liberties Law Review* 22:323–399.

Milner, N. (1989) "The Denigration of Rights and the Persistence of Rights Talk: A Cultural Portrait." *Law and Social Inquiry* 14:765–787.

Minow, M. (1987) "Interpreting Rights: An Essay for Robert Cover." *Yale Law Review* 96: 1860.

Paris, M. (2001) "Legal Mobilization and the Politics of Reform: Lessons from School Finance in Kentucky, 1984–1995" *Law and Social Inquiry* 26:631–684.

Perry, B. (2001) *In the Name of Hate: Understanding Hate Crimes.* New York, NY: Routledge.

Rosenberg, G.N. (1991) *The Hollow Hope: Can Courts Bring About Social Change?* Chicago: University of Chicago Press.

Sarat, A. (1997) "The Continuing Contest about Race in American Law and Culture: On Reading the Meaning of *Brown*" in A. Sarat (ed.) *Race, Law and Culture: Reflection on Brown v. Board of Education.* Oxford: Oxford University Press.

Silverstein, H. (1996). *Unleashing Rights: Law, Meaning and the Animal Rights Movement.* Ann Arbor: University of Michigan Press.

Singer, J. (1984) "The Player and the Cards: Nihilism and Legal Theory." *Yale Law Journal* 94:1.

Swidler, A. (1986) "Culture in Action: Symbols and Strategies." *American Sociological Review* 51:273–286.

Tushnet, M. (1984) "An Essay on Rights." *Texas Law Review* 62:1363–1403.

Wilkinson, H.J. III (1979) *From Brown to Alexander: The Supreme Court and School Integration, 1954–1978.* New York: Oxford University Press.

Williams, P. (1987) "Alchemical Notes: Reconstructing Ideals from Deconstructed Rights." *Harvard Civil Rights–Civil Liberties Law Review* 22:410–433.

—— (1991) *The Alchemy of Race and Rights: Diary of A Law Professor.* Cambridge, MA: Harvard University Press.

Chapter 2

Who Manages Feminist-Inspired Reform? An In-Depth Look at Title IX Coordinators in the United States[1]

JUDITH TAYLOR

In 1972, the US Congress enacted Title IX of the Educational Amendments Act prohibiting sex discrimination in education. Title IX, one of the first major legal steps taken in the United States to guarantee students equal educational opportunities without regard to their sex, was inspired by similar statutes concerning equal opportunity and race enacted eight years previously. Title IX is considered one of the most enduring contributions of the US women's movement (Ferree and Hess 1994). In 2002, US President George Bush's administration established a blue ribbon commission to review the law, and many feminists presumed the commission would recommend it be dismantled. However, the commission affirmed the federal commitment to the legislation, promising new funds and educational outreach programs to bolster it (Strauss 2003).

Specifically, Title IX stipulates that educational institutions denying equal opportunity by sex will be deprived of federal funding. Some of the first areas subject to Title IX reform included admissions policies and practices, academic programs and activities, course offerings, athletics, counseling, and employment (Lindgren and Taub 1988; McGee Bailey 1992; Stromquist 1997). However, because this legislation was sufficiently broad and vague, requiring considerable time to work out the regulations and educate thousands of relevant institutions, its effects were not felt immediately, nor have they been uniform.

Research on organizational change indicates that organizations often develop their own systems and definitions of compliance after such laws are passed, irrespective of the kinds of regulatory measures in place (Dobbin et al. 1993; Edelman 1992). Such was the case with Title IX. Before the courts determined the meaning of equity in measurable terms, school districts and other educational institutions funded wholly or partly with federal funds began appointing coordinators of Title IX to introduce policies, educate staff, and protect them from legal liability. Legal liability is a legitimate fear for school districts. In the case of Title IX, parents across the United States have increasingly pursued equity in athletics for their daughters by

[1] This chapter first appeared in *Gender & Society*, Vol. 19 No. 3, June 2005, and is reproduced by kind permission of the publisher.

filing lawsuits (Pennington 2004). Resistance to Title IX among educators and administrators – due to either general opposition to change or a specific opposition to feminism – has been formidable. The tasks of protecting the organization from lawsuits and contending with ideological resistance to equity make the job of a Title IX coordinator challenging.

Several questions can be asked about these coordinators. One question that will have to be asked is whether they have been effective, but neither the state nor feminist organizations have reached consensus on a definition of effectiveness. There are several questions that can precede this one. Who are the individuals who have been working in this capacity? How are they hired? What kind of allegiances and relevant experience do they have? What do their job responsibilities entail? To whom are they responsible? How much latitude do they have to interpret laws and create policies? During a period of two years, I conducted extensive interviews and field research in one of the largest school districts in the United States to answer these questions. Herein, I present findings concerning the political consciousness and organizational behavior of Title IX coordinators employed consecutively from 1983 to 2003 in one school district. In closely examining the work and political consciousness of Title IX officers charged with implementing gender equity law, I illustrate the dynamic way in which laws are brought to life by different people charged with implementing them and the way these individuals' political consciousness can change in the process of doing this work.

While this study involves the impact of feminist activism, the findings I present are relevant for thinking about any movement that inspires the creation of new forms of governance. This research answers the call made to study "implementation politics" or the non-mass protest phase of reform in which society actually implements the changes movements advocate (McCann 1998). Movement proponents and scholars often view laws and policies as signs of movement success without looking at what happens to them after their passage (Burstein 1991). In addition, my research corresponds to Mayer Zald's (2000) appeal to broaden the social movement research agenda by studying "ideologically structured action" in a variety of institutional settings, including bureaucratic agencies. Using a group of Title IX coordinators as an illustrative case, I offer a grounded account of the individuals responsible for manifesting social movement ideals.

This elaborated, exploratory case study generated two propositions that should be taken into account in thinking about "equity coordinators" or the people charged with implementing law inspired by women's movements: (1) Gender equity coordinators have considerable autonomy in defining compliance, and (2) while they tend not to be feminist identified when hired, gender equity coordinators can develop or strengthen their feminist consciousness in the course of their work. In other words, the experience of working as an arbiter of gender equity law can inspire adherence and deepen commitment to it. These propositions indicate a dialectical relationship between the state and its agents, each influencing the other, and the dynamism social movement-related laws can have even after the height of the movement passes. This article is organized into three sections. First, I review research and discussion on the topic of creating feminist change from within the state. Second, I introduce my research method and findings on the subject based on two years of interviews and observation. In the Discussion, I indicate the significance of paying more attention to organizational life and government administrators as a means of better understanding the impact of a state-focused, reform-based, social change agenda that has been so central to feminist and other contemporary movements.

Can Feminist Work be Done Within the State?

Feminist theory, particularly that emanating from the Marxist Left in the 1970s and 1980s, saw the state more as a mechanism for the maintenance of women's subordination than as a potential vehicle for the attainment of rights and freedoms (Hart 1992; Pringle and Watson 1998). Doctrinaire assessments characterized it as profoundly patriarchal and thus unfit for feminist engagement (Allen 1990; MacKinnon 1983). Similarly, feminists warned of the ways in which bureaucracy as a system strips public policies of the politics that inspired them and is an obstacle to gender justice (Eisenstein 1975; Ferguson 1984).

Yet as Lynne Haney (1996) usefully pointed out, these arguments did not keep feminist scholars from seeing the value in conducting research on a range of state-centered processes. Nor did it keep feminist activists from continuing to join government agencies with the intention of creating social change. Haney's research on two state-sponsored youth programs in California illustrates possible reasons. The state, she found, is not a monolith and is variously represented by a host of state workers, each with his or her own approach and commitments. In other words, a range of practices and programs exist because government structures employ many different individuals who, despite organizational norms and intransigence, find it possible to enact their own conception of equity.

This finding is consonant with the findings of social scientists studying "femocrats," feminists working in the upper echelons of government to create social change. Studies on this population of women reveal that while working from within can be frustrating because of the lack of sufficient power and resources, particular cohorts of feminists concerned with women's empowerment still consider it a worthwhile endeavor (for the Australian context, see Bulbeck 1997; Deacon 1989; Eisenstein 1995, 1996; for South Africa, see Goetz 1998; Seidman 1999, 2001; for Uganda, see Goetz 1998; for the United Nations, see Booth 1998; for Latin America, see Alvarez 1990; Waylen 1996; for Italy, see Bilotta 1991; for the Netherlands, see Swiebel 1988; for Canada, see Black 1993; Daenzer 1997; Findlay 1997; and for the United Kingdom, see Chappell 2002). The diversity of experiences encountered by women contributing to the femocratic project, or developing an approach to state feminism, supports Nira Yuval-Davis and Floya Anthias's theoretical assertion that while the state is primarily interested in control, it is "neither unitary in its practices, its intentions nor its effects" (1989, 5). This fluidity indicates that the state is more "a site of struggle" than a simple transmitter (Waylen 1996) and is not inherently masculine (Hart 1992).

The absence of the term "femocrat" in US parlance and research is notable but should not be taken as a sign of the absence of feminists in US governance structures. In her study of the Minimum Wage Board in the District of Columbia (1918–1923), Vivien Hart (1992) found that progressive era reformers created feminist change as employees of the state, despite limited resources and hostility from employers.

Contemporary studies of women attempting to transform the US Army from within their ranks (Fainsod Katzenstein 1990, 1998) and of urban social service workers in New York City concerned with welfare transmission (Naples 1998) illustrate the ways in which non-elite women in the United States have also successfully worked to empower women from within "male-stream" institutions that have historically controlled or excluded them.

These studies led me to believe I would find feminists in the school district bureaucracy I studied who joined the district specifically to implement gender equity law. However, with a few exceptions, I did not find women who joined the school district administrative ranks with the idea of creating social change within them. Contemporary research on US affirmative action and civil rights officers in public organizations (positions comparable to Title IX officers) might have enabled me to predict this. This group of administrators is diverse in background and political commitments and not likely to be radical crusaders (Edelman 1992; Edelman et al. 1991). Those pursuing an activist agenda are in the minority. This research indicates the significance of looking not just at the work of state agents but also at how their political consciousness informs their work.

In their survey of judges in Florida, Martin, Reynolds, and Keith (2002) found that women respondents had more of a feminist consciousness and that this consciousness informed their decisions in court. They employed Ethel Klein's (1984) definition of feminist consciousness as the belief that systematic gender discrimination exists and is wrong and that collective action is required to undermine it. While Martin, Reynolds, and Keith call feminist consciousness a "political achievement," the process by which judges achieved this consciousness is not a focus of their study. Its absence, therefore, gives the impression that political consciousness is static rather than evolving, that individuals enter jobs with a particular political take on the world that endures throughout their careers. In this research, therefore, I pay close attention to the dynamic relationship between job experiences and consciousness, illustrating in particular the ways in which the former can deepen the latter.

Method

This article is culled from a larger study of the process by which social movement ideas become organizational realities in a large school district bureaucracy in the United States, herein called Urban School District. I selected Urban School District because I wanted to focus on a bureaucracy with obvious power and consequences, and similarities with other large government agencies, but with relatively little status and visibility.

The larger study consisted of one year of participant observation, two surveys of administrators, content analysis of district-related records and materials, newspaper articles, and 52 structured interviews conducted from 1999 to 2001. This number does not reflect the several follow-up e-mail exchanges and phone conversations I used to clarify points in transcribed interviews and learn of any new developments. Those interviewed included past and current district administrators located in several different movement-related units (for example, school desegregation, gay and lesbian youth outreach, disability services, gender equity, the human relations commission), administrators outside of these offices, current and former school board members, teachers, students, and Parent Teacher Association members. Also interviewed were community activists and employees in other city-, county-, and state-level bureaucracies to learn their understandings of and interactions with Urban School District and the offices within it of concern to me. Data also come from 10 hours of participant observation each week in district headquarters for a period of one academic year in which I shadowed employees and attended public meetings.

The district's office of gender equity was one of three social movement-related offices in which I conducted intensive research. This office was established in 1980, eight years after the passage of Title IX, and still exists. The data primarily drawn on for this article include in-depth interviews lasting from between two and four hours with each of the six women who coordinated gender equity during a 20-year period, 10 other administrators related to this office in either a support or a supervisory capacity, two employees working in other city-level agencies, one professional equity consultant, and five activists from local feminist social movement organizations. In addition, I make use of the personal papers, meeting notes, clipping files, and journals of the gender equity coordinators and those of grassroots activists who lobbied them. I also draw on relevant materials from the school board secretariat archives and two local newspapers. All names of informants have been changed for the purposes of this article. Principal informants reviewed interview transcripts to ensure their comfort level with the information they provided. At that time, all interview content with which they were not comfortable was excluded from coding and analysis. Regrettably, this included discussion of the racial and ethnic identities of the officers and its possible pertinence in understanding how they were received in the bureaucracy at large.

This project's research questions, propositions, and conclusions are formed around three levels of analysis: a school district, offices or departments within that district, and district employees in and around those agencies. My treatment and particular framing of these subjects are informed by feminist, organizational, and social movement research and theories and by my own suppositions and claims (Ragin 1992). Focusing on one case enabled me to explore the character of the organization and its leadership, culture, and evolving relationship to social movements and the reform they inspire. Herein, I do not make claims to know how all school districts, let alone large public bureaucracies, respond to contemporary social movements.

Case studies are often thought to be "bounded" units, the study of which can be significant on its own without comparison to other cases (Stake 1994: 236). In fact, much sociological knowledge is derived from single-site case studies (Walton 1992). At minimum, case studies can disprove generalities, corroborate existing findings, raise new questions, and suggest new avenues for research (Goodwin and Horowitz 2002; Lieberson 1992; Reinharz 1992). In this article, I present propositions generated from this case study concerning the autonomy equity coordinators have to define their mandates and the way in which doing compliance work can affect their political consciousness.

Political Consciousness and Gender Equity Work

In the mid-1970s, a couple of years after the passage of Title IX, Urban School District assigned a high-ranking white man in its management systems office the task of administering the law. Feminist activists working on issues of gender equity in the district wrote letters and spoke at school board meetings demanding that a separate coordinator be hired who would devote substantive time and attention to implementing the law. Some of their letters explicitly asked that the coordinator be a woman, engaged in local women's movement organizing, with gender equity experience.

Following these sustained demands, the district created a designated Title IX coordinator position in 1978 and has consistently hired women to fill it since then. This coordinator position evolved in name (sex equity officer, gender equity commissioner, Title IX specialist, compliance coordinator) and location (in the district general counsel's office or the evaluation and assessments department). For a time, it splintered into two positions and then returned to one. This lack of fixity reflects shifts in organizational expectations, fluid personnel practices, and cultural or political trends.

Equity offices in both public and private organizations are often staffed by people who belong to the group for whom equity is purportedly being sought (Collins 1993). While all the Title IX coordinators were women, they varied greatly in their commitment to feminism and their experience with equity work. For the purposes of this analysis, I defined feminists as those who identified as such, had links to feminist organizations and grassroots networks, and had a record of promoting women's and girls' empowerment.

At the time of hiring, four of the six women did not identify, publicly or otherwise, as feminists. Of those, three became feminist identified in the course of their work, and one did not. Two women were feminist identified prior to being hired, one liberal and the other radical, and their political commitments grew in intensity as a result of being equity coordinators. It is significant to note that the first three women hired as Title IX coordinators were not feminist identified at the time of hiring, illustrating a possible initial organizational interest in hiring "team players" (Edelman et al. 1991) who would put organizational concerns ahead of feminist principles. This interest seemed to wane in the 1990s as reflected in the more explicitly feminist backgrounds of the hires in this era.

The Title IX coordinators I interviewed confessed to applying for or accepting the Title IX coordinator position because they wanted to join administrative ranks, earn more money, exercise more authority, experience more autonomy, or try something new. Only one said she applied for the job to make a difference for women and girls. So how did the others come to share this sentiment? Through the course of interviews, I identified three ways by which they developed or concretized an explicitly feminist and oppositional consciousness (Mansbridge and Morris 2001). They include (1) witnessing unequal treatment and hearing women's grievances, (2) experiencing boredom or frustration with organizational stasis, and (3) feeling isolated, stereotyped, and discriminated against as a result of being a Title IX coordinator.

Exposure to Inequality

Helen Fong, the first Title IX coordinator at Urban School District, never applied for the position. In 1983, she met a senior male administrator at the district while doing research on school desegregation for a graduate class in policy studies; soon thereafter, he contacted Fong and offered her the job. Initially, Fong was apprehensive because she sensed the ratio of pay to workload would not be a good one and she lacked a background in gender equity. Recalling that at the time, she frequently called herself "apolitical," Fong figured she was a bad fit for the job. However, she also recalled being an "opportunist" who wanted a significant career with access to powerful connections in municipal governance. These interests led her to accept the job offer.

Fong described herself as having "hit the ground running," determined to show that she took the demands of her position and responsibilities seriously. She set herself the task of learning everything about Title IX she could, backwards and forwards, until she felt competent to speak on the issues. Of the sex equity committee members, Fong said, "I think they thought I was slick, that I could talk the talk and walk the walk but that there was something missing. And there was. My heart wasn't in it. I was spinning my wheels, I had some discomfort, and I knew I was not the right person for the job." Fong's discomfort and embarrassment grew with time. She was most disturbed by the district's response to a group of women teachers and administrators seeking a systematic review of hiring and advancement decisions. Having reviewed their case, Fong agreed that the district's personnel practices consistently favored men for administrative advancement. Her efforts to bring their case to the attention of the affirmative action officer were unfruitful, and the superintendent dismissed her recommendations and forbade her further involvement because the problem fell outside her job responsibilities. Fong found his response "shockingly unsympathetic" and attributed her feminist awakening to the anger and injustice she felt on reading his letter. She said of this moment, "I just kept thinking, Why me? Why do I have to be a part of this? And then I thought, I am going to leave. But I am going to doing something about [this] first." Fong approached a woman school board member who also was not feminist identified and presented the case to her. In a school board meeting, the board member made an impassioned speech about inequality in hiring practices. Newspapers reported her as saying, "I feel very strongly about this. I didn't start out being a feminist, but I sure as hell am going to be one now." Their continued teamwork led eventually to a landmark consent decree that required the district to markedly increase the number of women in administrative positions during the next five years. While Fong did eventually leave the district for law school and equity work on the state level, she stayed for another three years. She said of her shift in political consciousness, "You know, I grew up feeling entitled. I would put down other women who said they didn't make it because of discrimination because I made it, and I rationalized that they didn't try hard enough. I found out it was otherwise."

Fong attributed the development of her feminism to witnessing (rather than experiencing) injustices she found personally and morally problematic. While she remembers administrators' derogatorily referring to her as "the Title IX girl," trying to intimidate and humiliate her, and hoarding the resources necessary to do her job competently, she understands these as contributing rather than catalyzing factors in its development. Subsequent Title IX coordinators, however, found the sexism they experienced more central to the development or intensification of their feminist politics than did Fong.

Fear of Feminism

All the Title IX coordinators who worked at Urban School District during a 20-year period reported that most administrators and teachers expected them to be militant feminists. Several discussed the body language senior-level school administrators exhibited in their initial meeting before any words had been exchanged, most commonly eye rolling, audible exhalation, finger or toe tapping, leg bouncing, exaggerated yawns, loud whispers to colleagues, and groaning. In addition, coordinators reported hearing countless speeches of a personal nature concerning "the problem with feminism" or cautionary tales about the adverse outcomes of Title IX initiatives. For example, several skeptics made the argument that co-ed sports teams would increase girls' injuries and decrease boys' endurance and strength. Others expressed the belief that most sexual harassment claims are found to be fatuous on investigation.

While all coordinators acknowledged they knew when they applied for the job that it was highly politicized and inspired opposition, the initially non-feminist among them believed their lack of feminist credentials and warm dispositions would ease opposition. Hiring committees encouraged them to believe so by expressing appreciation for their lukewarm approach to feminism. However, once they became Title IX coordinators, gossip about them as bitter and tough minded circulated despite their stated efforts to institute a friendly, non-threatening approach to equity compliance.

Brenda Pastori became the Title IX coordinator in 1984, despite concerns similar to Fong's that she lacked the necessary credentials for the position. Pastori entered the school district bureaucracy working in the office of adult education. When a colleague suggested she apply for the position, she remembers responding, "I'm not a bra burner. I'm not a fighter like that. I won't be nailed to the cross." While Pastori liked seeing girls succeed, she was not interested in incurring personal damage in the process of helping them.

Colleagues' sustained encouragement led Pastori to apply for the position despite her trepidation. Given the steep competition for the position and a short list of 40 applicants, many of whom had extensive related experience, Pastori made the tactical decision to promote herself as a safe, apolitical candidate. In a final interview, the superintendent asked her why she wanted the job. She recalled telling the hiring committee she thought the district needed a good mediator and that she had the personality of a healer capable of building bridges and soothing ruffled feathers. When asked if she was a feminist, she reported replying, "No, I'm a humanist." Pastori got the job and attributed her success to these answers. As coordinator, Pastori recalled rarely referencing feminism or civil rights but rather making use of American credos such as "I was brought up to believe everyone should have equal opportunity." Initially, Pastori felt successful at disarming men made skittish by feminism and social change. She utilized what she called "maternal behavior" in both the schools and the bureaucracy to heighten their receptivity. For example, Pastori brought home-baked cookies to staff training sessions on gender equity. In an effort to ease fears that she was foisting feminist change on the schools, Pastori endeavored to make suggestions rather than institute directives. Rather than ask school principals why they did not have any girls' sports teams yet, Pastori would query, "What would be the benefit of girls' sports participation?" Her tactic was to befriend her audiences by performing recognizable, gender-normative behavior. She humored them, laughing at their jokes, inquiring about their families, hoping to make them feel she really cared about them. One former director of a high school athletics program said of Pastori's performance, "It was a kinder, gentler inquisition." Pastori explained her approach in the following way: "The thing about doing gender equity work in the schools is that you have to get used to being treated with a cold attitude. That's why I had to do that song and dance, [the gist of] which was, 'I'm not here to beat you over the head.' Only then would they begin to warm up."

Despite Pastori's efforts to alleviate fears of feminism, she still endured hostility. She puzzled that in an organization rife with gossipy communication networks, word of her good work did not seem to precede her. As she made her way through a district of roughly 500 schools, her goodwill and patience frayed. Pastori remembers embracing feminism one day when she was making a presentation to high-level administrators about equity in occupational training. She tells the story of her interaction with one male administrator there this way: "He said, 'My wife and I have four children, and she has never worked a day in her life.' And I said, 'She has four children and is married to you? I bet she has worked every day of her life.'"

While Pastori had not initially planned to humiliate her opposition, doing so became part of her behavioral repertoire over time as she wearied of negative treatment and lack of positive reinforcement. Despite the initial care she took to appear congenial, she earned a reputation for being "full blown and political." Expectations of oppositional politics inspired Pastori to claim a feminist identity. This dynamic reflects an organizational (or social-psychological) inability to distinguish people from the positions they hold. Nearing retirement after decades of service in the district, Pastori concluded that she could not have evaded the reputation as a hard-line feminist even if she had "done nothing more than chat in the hallways."

Evading the Expectation to Do Nothing

All of the Title IX coordinators expressed the feeling that they were expected to make the district appear gender equitable without instituting changes. All but one expressed the desire to apply herself and her skills as a means of feeling efficacious, making feminist change, or appearing worthy of advancement. In addition, the majority reported feeling spurred on by stories of their predecessors' incompetence or intransigence. Breaking the cycle, each thought, meant perfecting a balance between effectual and amiable.

Karen Stevens started working for Urban School District in the 1970s and began coordinating Title IX in the 1990s. Stevens traces her interest in feminism and her involvement in her local chapter of the National Organization of Women to her experience of being a single mother after her divorce. When she interviewed for the position of Title IX coordinator, Stevens did not believe she hid her feminist ideals from the hiring committee, nor did she think that doing so would improve her candidacy.

As coordinator, Stevens became increasingly frustrated by the lack of sufficient resources to do her job. This feeling was exacerbated by her hunch that Title IX monies intended for her office were not reaching her. Amendments to the state education code during one academic year signaled the allocation of more money for compliance education and investigation, but Stevens felt the increase was insufficient. For the first couple years, Stevens played by the rules and took pride in her ability to implement change on a miniscule budget. She reflected, "I built up this [office] on a shoestring." Rather than voice her need for better resources, Stevens used what she called "chits" (metaphorical tickets for favors) with senior colleagues she had helped or with whom she had built credibility.

In 1998, an administrator in the state department of education suggested she attend a conference sponsored by the National Coalition for Sex Equity in Education, an organization for educational equity officers. But because Stevens coordinated Title IX from within the general counsel's office and it would not fund out-of-state travel, she could not attend. Her efforts to receive special dispensation failed.

Stevens remembers that as "the bottom line." It was embarrassing to her that while she held more power than many National Coalition for Sex Equity in Education members, she did not have the opportunity to participate. Incensed by district inflexibility and fearful that remaining compliant was contingent on attending the meeting, she went to the superintendent's office and negotiated a separation of her budget from the general counsel's. In addition to enabling her to attend the conference, her new budgetary power reflected a change in allegiance. Stevens shifted her accountability from the district as an employer to equity as a cause and Title IX as a law. In addition, Stevens's commitment to social change intensified. The conversations she had at the conference lent legitimacy to her impatience with district intransigence. She recalled saying to her staff on her return, "This legislation has been around for decades. It's time to start going beyond the minimum, not just comply." Over time, her peer and reference group shifted from coworkers in the district to a broad Internet- and phone-based community of gender equity compliance administrators, activists, and academics. The organizations Stevens joined, subscribed to, and took direction from included the Ms. Foundation, the National Women's History Foundation, the New York State Association for Women in Administration (State University of New York–Albany), the Wellesley Center for Research on Women, the American Association of University Women, and Girls Inc. In the end, what fueled a deepening commitment to feminist ends was not witnessing injustice but being subject to policies that she felt diminished her professional status and her autonomy as an equity coordinator.

These Title IX coordinators' descriptions of the moments that led them to develop or enhance their identifications as feminists reflect the complexity of political consciousness. Experiencing sex discrimination is just one of several catalyzing experiences. Others, such as witnessing discrimination or experiencing frustrating or disrespectful working conditions, can propel individuals to adopt and enact a new set of politics.

How to Define Title IX? Let Me Count the Ways

Title IX coordinators working at Urban School District during a 20-year period had sufficient autonomy to define their mandates and promote programs they believed forwarded the goal of gender equity. This finding corroborates similar findings concerning affirmative action officers (Edelman et al. 1991). Similarly, I found that coordinators' political consciousness, specifically their relationship to organized feminism, influenced how they defined their job responsibilities. Also critical in shaping their agendas were available resources, past work experiences, personal interests, gender equity advocacy organizations (particularly university and nongovernmental organizations), networks to which they belonged within or outside the school district, state- and national-level regulatory bodies, and larger structural and political trends that emerged while they were in the position. One coordinator spent the bulk of her time on employee equity, even though Title IX is concerned with student equity. She explained this inconsistency with an argument about how to produce social change. Creating gender equity among the students, she believed, would not be possible without first changing the administration. She said, "If all the big positions are held by men, gender equity in the schools cannot happen." Her replacement had a different focus and philosophy. She saw herself as a conduit to the community and so worked on issues brought to her by parents. Some of the issues she worked on included giving girls' sports teams equal time on the fields, helping immigrant girls attain citizenship so they would not marry older American men, and developing dropout prevention programs for pregnant and teen mothers. In what follows, I focus on two coordinators in particular whose commitments stand in starkest contrast to indicate the wide range of approaches taken.

Working without Guidance and Vision

Carmen Roth began working at Urban School District in the 1970s as an educational psychologist in a suburban high school. Eventually, she was promoted to an administrative position overseeing classroom integration of disabled students. In 1985, she heard about the Title IX coordinator position through unofficial channels, and the superintendent's office hired her not long after. Roth was pleased to be able to move to the highest level of the district headquarters, to a set of offices directly below the superintendent's. She recalled on her first day as coordinator being led to her new office and shown several stacks of paper on top of the desk. She recalled her supervisor's pointing to them and saying, "Acclimate yourself to the law and policies."

Roth loved her new job because she believed it exposed her to smart, powerful people and enabled her to do important work. Said Roth, "It was like being part of a tiny think tank that produced policy. There were only a few people, but their decisions had big consequences. I was suddenly privy to everything, and it was very exciting." She received a recommendation from her boss to produce and implement a complaint procedure for student grievances. Until that time, no clear mechanisms existed through which students and parents could contest inequitable treatment. After struggling unsuccessfully to develop a system, Roth hired an equity consultant from outside the district to develop materials and policies. Without adequate publicity, however, the system went unused. Roth said, "I received virtually no complaints, but there was a procedure in place." Roth's statement may be read as reflecting a primary concern not with effecting change but with creating technical, legal compliance necessary to avoid district liability.

Roth also attended meetings of the district committee on gender equity, many of whose members grew resentful of her. Committee members who dubbed her "do nothing" and "obstructionist" believed her selection as coordinator to be an accurate indication of the district's commitment to gender equity. Roth, in contrast, felt a professional obligation not to be a vehicle for feminists' political aims. She said of this tension, "It wasn't easy because I was seen as a barrier. Being a bureaucrat, I couldn't work as quickly as they would have liked." After five years, the district restructured (as it often did), and Roth's new supervisor gave her notice. Roth attributed her dismissal to differences in personality rather than job performance.

It is not possible to determine whether Roth's interpretation of Title IX contributed to her dismissal, but the timing of the termination suggests she was a casualty of organizational dynamics because she was terminated in a major organizational downsizing rather than as a result of an independent performance review.

Bringing Activism to the Bureaucracy

In 1989, Deb Kerry sought and obtained a position as Title IX coordinator in Urban School District because she wanted to take a hiatus from a Ph.D. program in education that did not provide her with enough opportunities for involvement in what she called "the real world." Kerry, a self-described "outside agitator" active with the women's movement for more than 20 years, was not afraid to upset district sensibilities because she did not see herself as primarily accountable to it. Kerry understood her success as dependent on imagining she was working within a community-based organization rather than the district bureaucracy. Doing so enabled her to more freely design programs and plans of action and manage intimidating people within the organization who expressed disapproval of her activist style.

Her prior experience as an organizer greatly informed her approach to gender equity in terms of substance, strategy, and mind frame. When asked about the feasibility of creating change in such a large organization, she said, "I was in the women's movement in 1969, so size really wasn't an impediment; it wasn't intimidating. But it felt like a setup. I knew the people and the issues. If you're committed to the issues, the size won't matter. You could get scared, or you could do the right thing. Even if it was simply symbolic, the symbol itself was important."

While at first Kerry was committed to working with fellow district administrators, she soon found them both too resistant to feminist politics and territorial about job responsibilities. Said Kerry, "I just kept saying, 'There is so much work to be done! How come we can't just share it?' " In developing programs, she received complaints from administrators in vocational education, sports and recreation, and social services who believed she was infringing on their duties.

Kerry's chief goals were twofold: to make Title IX and gender equity accessible and relevant to communities of color that had become the majority populations in Urban School District and to use it to challenge traditional gender norms of behavior. Her focus on physical education extended beyond equal use of school facilities for girls and boys. She instituted programs that actively encouraged young girls to play sports rather than sit and talk during break periods and sought corporate donations of sports equipment for girls to use at home. Rather than simply ensure that girls had access to industrial arts classes, she developed educational programs that enabled them to interact with successful women in the trades. Similarly, she created scholarships for girls interested in attending math, science, or technology conferences. While her predecessors focused on helping pregnant students obtain general education diplomas, Kerry sought to reintegrate them into the school system after they gave birth so they could complete the same courses as their peers.

Kerry used her connections with feminist social movement organizations outside the district to define her mandate. Her connections with staff at Planned Parenthood, the most prominent organization for birth control provision and advocacy in the United States, led her to see sex education as relevant to Title IX and to facilitate revisions of the sex education program. Although having her inspiration and allies outside the organization made her work lonely, it also may have made her more successful.

Said one school board member of Kerry's performance, "[Deb] could do a lot precisely because she wasn't a part of the system."

Not feeling "of" the system also enabled Kerry to imagine ways of circumventing administrative control and budgetary constraints. When district supervisors denied her funds for programs or additional supplies, she sought community donations, corporate sponsorship, and federal grants. When denied additional support staff, Kerry developed an internship program that culminated in a trip for all of them to the International Women's Conference in Beijing. Kerry also found success in using press releases strategically to garner public attention when the school board or superintendent's office would not support her initiatives and spoke on morning television news programs about her work.

Unlike Carmen Roth, Deb Kerry was not primarily concerned with district compliance and conformity with federal mandates. Rather, she viewed gender equity law as a vehicle for feminist social change initiatives. While Kerry did develop accounting mechanisms to try to measure sexual harassment complaints and the numbers of girls and boys enrolled in math and science courses, she did not privilege these efforts in her discussion of her work. As these divergent cases illustrate, gender equity coordinators at Urban School District had significant autonomy to define their mandates and contributions.

Discussion

The voices and reflections of Title IX coordinators responsible for instituting gender equity in one large urban bureaucracy contribute to a more complex understanding of the people charged with instituting gender equity within organizations. The research presented here supports existing findings that coordinators of civil rights laws in the United States have considerable autonomy to develop their own agendas and approaches to the work within their own organizations (Edelman et al. 1991). Contrary to lingering understandings of state structures as inhospitable to feminist politics and individual agency, most women in this study used their positions as coordinators of gender equity law to remedy curricular, programmatic, and recreational inequities in schools as they saw fit. This fact complicates rather than diminishes findings about the ways state and corporate bodies create roles for activists as a means of co-opting or silencing them (Moss Kanter 1977; Pfeffer 1981).

This research corroborates research indicating the significance of political consciousness in determining job performance (Martin, Reynolds, and Keith 2002). The ways in which individuals interpret laws and professional obligations and form occupational goals are predicated on the condition of their political consciousness. To feel a sense of urgency and an obligation to be a conscientious advocate, one must cognitively connect social inequality to the movements and activism that call attention to it (Jasper 1997; Melucci 1996). Without this connection to the bigger picture of social change, administrators may be more likely to try to appease disadvantaged communities without doing anything tangible for them and to conservatively interpret their responsibilities.

How is this kind of movement consciousness reached? In their study of legal professionals, Martin, Reynolds, and Keith (2002) argued that women are more likely than men to develop a feminist consciousness because they are personally subject to discrimination as women. However, the women in this study gave more complex reasons for the enhancement or development of their feminist identification. Lacking sufficient resources to do their jobs, witnessing discrimination against other women, enduring administrative incompetence, and experiencing hostility and disrespect as women hired to implement gender equity led these five women to see themselves as agents of feminism. There are many paths to feminist consciousness in addition to personal experience with discrimination as a woman.

Another overlooked aspect of the study of femocrats and feminist consciousness is that these political identities and commitments can develop in the course of professional work, as it did for women in this study. Legislation can politicize those hired to implement it. Even when employees are hired specifically because they do not have allegiances to feminism, these allegiances can develop in the context of doing gender equity work. It is significant to note that the reverse does not seem to be true: None of the women in this study experienced a lessening of political commitment to feminism as equity coordinators, despite experiencing hostility, disrespect, stereotyping, and isolation.

On a final note, this case study indicates that local-level bureaucracies can be important sites for feminists seeking to create social change. Rather than write equity officers off as dupes or sellouts, activists might critically engage them in an effort to create shifts in allegiance and political commitments and find new allies previously ignored. Individuals in these positions can vary greatly in their interests and intentions and should be evaluated individually and over time, keeping in mind the question of what is possible given the larger political milieu in which they are working. Whether movement adherents want their ideals to be interpreted and applied in such an individual way is something worthy of more in-depth consideration and discussion.

References

Allen, J. (1990). "Does feminism need a theory of the state?" In *Playing the State*, edited by S. Watson. London: Verso.

Alvarez, S. (1990). *Engendering Democracy in Brazil: Women's Movements in Transition Politics*. Princeton, NJ: Princeton University Press.

Bilotta, B. (1991). "Women in bureaucracy in Italy in the 80s". *Sociologia del Diritto* 18:103–33.

Black, N. (1993). "The Canadian women's movement: The second wave". In *Changing Patterns: Women in Canada*, edited by S. Burt, L. Code, and L. Dorney. Toronto, Canada: McClelland and Stewart.

Booth, K. (1998). "National mother, global whore, and transnational femocrats: The politics of AIDS and the construction of women at the World Health Organization". *Feminist Studies* 24:115–39.

Bulbeck, C. (1997). *Living Feminism: The Impact of the Women's Movement on Three Generations of Australian Women.* Cambridge: Cambridge University Press.

Burstein, P. (1991). "Legal mobilization as a social movement tactic: The struggle for equal employment opportunity". *American Journal of Sociology* 96:1201–25.

Chappell, L. (2002). "The 'Femocrat' strategy: Expanding the repertoire of feminist activists". *Parliamentary Affairs* 55:85–98.

Collins, S. (1993). "Blacks on the bubble: The vulnerability of Black executives in white corporations". *Sociological Quarterly* 34:429–47.

Daenzer, P. (1997). "Challenging diversity: Black women and social welfare". In *Women and the Canadian Welfare State: Challenges and Change*, edited by P.M. Evans and G.R.Wekerle. Toronto, Canada: University of Toronto Press.

Deacon, D. (1989). *Managing gender: The state, the new middle class, and women workers, 1830–1930.* Melbourne, Australia: Oxford University Press.

Dobbin, F., Sutton, J.R., Meyer J.W., and Scott, R. (1993). "Equal opportunity law and the construction of internal labor markets". *American Journal of Sociology* 99:396–427.

Edelman, L.B., Patterson, S., Chambliss, E., and Erlanger, H.S. (1991). "Legal ambiguity and the politics of compliance: Affirmative action officers' dilemma". *Law and Policy* 13:73–97.

Edelman, L. B. (1992). "Legal ambiguity and symbolic structures: Organizational mediation of civil rights law". *American Journal of Sociology* 97:1531–76.

Eisenstein, H. (1995). "The Australian femocratic experiment: A feminist case for bureaucracy". In *Feminist Organizations: Harvest of the New Women's Movement*, edited by M. Marx Ferree and P. Yancey Martin. Philadelphia: Temple University Press.

—— (1996). *Inside Agitators: Australian Femocrats and the State*. Philadelphia: Temple University Press.

Eisenstein, Z. (1975). *Capitalist Patriarchy and the Case for Socialist Feminism*. New York: MonthlyReview Press.

Fainsod Katzenstein, Mary. (1990). "Feminism within American institutions: Unobtrusive mobilization in the 1980s". *Signs: Journal of Women in Culture and Society* 16:27–54.

—— (1998). *Faithful and Fearless: Feminist Protest Inside the Church and Military*. Princeton, NJ: Princeton University Press.

Ferguson, K.E. (1984). *The Feminist Case Against Bureaucracy*. Philadelphia: Temple University Press.

Ferree, Myra Marx, and Beth B. Hess. (1994). *Controversy and Coalition: The New feminist movement across three decades of change*. New York: Twayne.

Findlay, S. (1997). "Institutionalizing feminist politics: Learning from the struggles for equal pay in Ontario". In *Women and the Canadian Welfare State: Challenges and Change*, edited by P.M. Evans and G.R. Wekerle. Toronto, Canada: University of Toronto Press.

Goetz, A.M. (1998). "Women in politics and gender equity in policy: South Africa and Uganda". *Review of African Political Economy* 25:241–62.

Goodwin, J. and R. Horowitz. (2002). "Introduction: The methodological strengths and dilemmas of qualitative sociology". *Qualitative Sociology* 25:33–47.

Haney, L. (1996). "Homeboys, babies, men in suits: The state and the reproduction of male dominance". *American Journal of Sociology* 61:759–78.

Hart, V. (1992). "Feminism and bureaucracy: The minimum wage experiment in the District of Columbia". *Journal of American Studies* 26:1–22.

Jasper, J. (1997). *The Art of Moral Protest: Culture, biography, and creativity in social movements*. Chicago: University of Chicago Press.

Klein, E. (1984). *Gender Politics: From Consciousness to Mass Politics*. Cambridge, MA: Harvard University Press.

Lieberson, S. (1992). "Small N's and big conclusions: An examination of the reasoning in comparative studies based on a small number of cases". In *What is a Case? Exploring the Foundations of Social Inquiry*, edited by C. Ragin and H. Becker. Cambridge: Cambridge University Press.

Lindgren, R., and N. Taub. (1988). *The Law of Sex Discrimination*. St. Paul, MN: West.

MacKinnon, C. (1983). "Feminism, Marxism, Method and the State: Toward a Feminist Jurisprudence". *Signs: Journal of Women in Culture and Society* 8:635–58.

Mansbridge, J., and Morris, A., eds. (2001). *Oppositional Consciousness: The Subjective Roots of Social Protest*. Chicago: University of Chicago Press.

Martin, P., Reynolds, J., and Keith, S. (2002). (Gender bias and feminist consciousness among judges and attorneys: A standpoint theory analysis". *Signs: Journal of Women in Culture and Society* 27:665–701.

McCann, M. W. (1998). "Social movements and the mobilization of law". In *Social movements and American political institutions*, edited by A.N. Costain and A. McFarland. Lanham, MD: Rowman and Littlefield.

McGee Bailey, S. (1992). *The AAUW report: How schools are shortchanging girls: A study of major findings on girls and education*. Washington, DC: AAUW Educational Foundation.

Melucci, A. (1996). *Challenging Codes: Collective Action in the Information Age*. Cambridge: Cambridge University Press.

Moss Kanter, R. (1977). *Men and Women of the Corporation*. New York: Basic Books.

Naples, N. (1998). *Grassroots Warriors: Activist Mothering, Community Work, and the War on Poverty*. New York: Routledge.

Pennington, B. (2004). "Title IX trickles down to girls of generation Z". *The New York Times*, 29 June.

Pfeffer, J. (1981). *Power in Organizations*. Boston: Pitman.

Pringle, R.and Watson, S. (1998). "'Women's interests' and the post-structuralist state". In *Feminism and Politics*, edited by Anne Phillips. New York: Oxford University Press.

Ragin, C. (1992) "'Casing' and the process of social inquiry". In *What is a Case? Exploring the Foundations of Social Inquiry*, edited by Charles R. and H. Becker. Cambridge: Cambridge University Press.

Reinharz, S. (1992). *Feminist Methods in Social Research*. Oxford: Oxford University Press.

Seidman, G. (1999). "Gendered citizenship: South Africa's democratic transition and the construction of a gendered state". *Gender & Society* 13:287–307.

—— (2001). "'Strategic' challenges to gender inequality: The South African Gender Commission". *Ethnography* 2:219–41.

Stake, R.E. (1994). "Case studies". In *Handbook of Qualitative Research*, edited by Denzin N.K. and Y.S. Lincoln. Thousand Oaks, CA: Sage.

Strauss, V. (2003). "Administration opts not to make changes to Title IX". *Washington Post*, 11 July. Available from washingtonpost.com.

Stromquist, N.P. (1997). "Gender policies in American education: Reflections on federal legislation and action". In *Feminist Critical Policy Analysis I: A Perspective from Primary and Secondary Schooling*, edited by C. Marshall. London: Falmer.

Swiebel, J. (1988). "The gender of bureaucracy: Reflections on policy-making for women". *Politics* 8:14–19.

Walton, J. (1992). "Making the theoretical case". In *What is a Case? Exploring the Foundations of Social Inquiry*, edited by C. Ragin and H. Becker. Cambridge: Cambridge University Press.

Waylen, G. (1996). "Democratization, feminism and the state in Chile: The establishment of SERNAM". In *Women and the State: International Perspectives*, edited by S.M. Rai and G. Leivesley. Bristol, PA: Taylor and Francis.

Yuval-Davis, N. and Anthias, F. (1989). "Introduction". In *Woman-Nation-State*, edited by Yuval-Davis, N. and Anthias, F. London: Macmillan.

Zald, M. N. (2000). "Ideologically structured action: An enlarged agenda for social movement research". *Mobilization* 5:1–16.

Chapter 3

Legal Consciousness and Workplace Rights

CATHERINE R. ALBISTON[1]

Introduction

Sociolegal scholars have long been interested in how law interacts with other institutions and systems of meaning in particular social settings. Empirical research shows that law often competes with alternative normative frameworks for understanding social interactions (Edelman, Erlanger and Lande 1993; Ellickson 1991; Heimer 1999; Macaulay 1963). Nevertheless, although systems of meaning other than law matter, law is not irrelevant. Law is a cultural resource upon which actors may draw to make sense of their social experiences, and to influence the behavior of others (Lempert 1976, 1998). In many instances, law and other social institutions act in concert to give meaning to social life.

Law may be most likely to clash with other social institutions when new rights attempt to change long-standing social practices. For example, civil rights laws often challenge existing social arrangements that evoke strong normative commitments. In this context, rights provide one cultural discourse or schema for understanding social events, but other institutions also provide competing discourses. Actors often draw on legal discourse to construct their understanding of social events, a dynamic process that sociolegal scholars refer to as "legal consciousness," but other systems of meaning contribute to consciousness as well. As a result, civil rights claims can become a location for negotiating contested meanings and for either undermining or reinforcing existing social institutions.

This chapter asks how legal rights interact with other social institutions to shape legal consciousness in workplace negotiations over employment rights. It examines how actors come to understand and think about their rights in the context of a particular civil rights statute, the Family and Medical Leave Act of 1993 (FMLA). More particularly, this study focuses on how legal discourse interacts with institutionalized discourses about work, gender, and disability to shape workers' legal consciousness in disputes over leave. The analysis that follows shows that

[1] Assistant Professor of Law, Boalt Hall School of Law. I wish to acknowledge the generous support provided for this research by the National Science Foundation, # SES-0001905, and by the Sloan Foundation through the Center for Working Families at the University of California, Berkeley. The views expressed here are those of the author and not necessarily those of the National Science Foundation, the Center for Working Families, or the Sloan Foundation. An earlier analysis of some of these data appears in *Law & Society Review*, 39:11–50 (2005).

although deeply entrenched understandings of work, gender, and disability can create resistance to FMLA rights, workers also draw on legal discourse about leave to challenge those entrenched understandings and potentially to bring about social change.

The following sections develop this thesis in more detail. The first section introduces the concept of legal consciousness and connects this concept to broader sociological theory. The next section analyzes the competing discourses created by law and by institutionalized understandings of work, gender, and disability, all of which play out in workplace negotiations over family and medical leave. The following sections then report data from interviews with workers who negotiated leaves in the workplace. Finally, the chapter concludes by suggesting how alternative discourses about work and law interact in ways that both undermine and reinforce existing relations of inequality.

Legal Consciousness and the Construction of Meaning

Although the term "legal consciousness" has been defined many ways, definitions tend to converge around two elements. First, scholars focus on the dynamic process through which people draw on law as a discourse to make sense of their experiences, and, conversely, how those experiences inform their understanding of law (Ewick and Silbey 1998; Merry 1990). Second, the concept "legal consciousness" also takes into account how law gives meaning to social life by shaping our taken-for-granted understandings of the social world (Merry 1990). In other words, legal consciousness is the dynamic process through which actors draw on legal discourse to construct their understanding of and relation to the social world, but that process takes place within a social context already structured in part by law itself (Engel 1998; Ewick and Silbey 1992, 1998; Merry 1990; Sarat 1990).

As this definition suggests, legal consciousness is contingent upon, and therefore likely to vary with, one's experiences, social position, and the social context. For example, legal consciousness may vary across gender, race, and class (Ewick and Silbey 1998; Hirsch 1993; Merry 1990; Nielsen 2000; Sarat 1990). Also, legal consciousness is not a stable, unchanging characteristic of individuals. Instead, it is socially contingent. It is likely to vary across social location, and to be contingent upon the relationships within which actors are embedded (Ewick and Silbey 1998). One might also expect legal consciousness to vary across topic or subject matter, perhaps in ways that interact with social location and social status.

Legal consciousness research is part of a broader sociological literature on cognition and social construction that examines how actors draw on cultural systems of meaning to make sense of the social world and to construct the social institutions that shape that world. In this literature, these cultural systems of meaning are also called "discourses" or "schemas" (Ewick and Silbey 1998; Merry 1990; Sewell 1992). From this perspective, consciousness is part of a process of institutionalization through which the meanings individuals give to particular social interactions become taken for granted and objectified (Berger and Luckman 1967; Ewick and Silbey 1998). Social structure is made up of institutionalized discourses or schemas and the material practices associated with these systems of meaning (Giddens 1984; Scott

1995; Sewell 1992). As actors draw upon established schemas to make sense of the social world, they also discursively reproduce social structure (Bourdieu 1977; Sewell 1992). In other words, once institutionalized, cultural systems of meaning constrain consciousness and shape action to conform to and to reproduce existing social structure.

Law, in this view, can be seen as an institutionalized discourse that gives meaning to social life and reproduces social structure. For example, law helps define and legitimate the patterns and categories of social life so that they seem natural, normal, and inevitable (Sarat and Kearns 1993). Law provides both frame and context; actors may evoke law to give meaning to social events, but they do so within a social milieu already constructed by law (Ewick and Silbey 1998). This is not to say that because law constructs social life it is determinative. Rather, law is one of many available schemas through which actors make sense of the social world. As Swidler (1986:273) puts it, law is part of the cultural "'tool kit' of symbols, stories, rituals and world views [that] people may use in varying degrees and configurations to solve different kinds of problems."

Although law is one system of meaning that structures consciousness, it is not the only one, nor is it always dominant. For example, empirical studies show that law can be displaced or transformed by informal norms in particular communities (Ellickson 1991; Macaulay 1963), or by alternative systems of meaning that arise from organizational cultures and context (Edelman, Erlanger and Lande 1993; Heimer 1999). In other words, cultural schemas that are contradictory to law can also give meaning to social events and structure social interactions. Social constructivist approaches assume that although structural constraints shape consciousness, actors still have some agency in choosing among competing schemas to interpret a given situation (Sewell 1992). Nevertheless, some discourses may be more dominant than others, particularly if those discourses are part of historically entrenched and long-standing social institutions. Power can also affect which discourses are communicated and which are silenced.

This social constructivist understanding of legal consciousness, and of consciousness more generally, raises an interesting question: how is legal consciousness shaped by the interaction between legal discourses and other institutionalized systems of meaning? In other words, the dynamic process through which individuals construct their understanding of law can be understood as a contest over meaning, in which legal discourses and alternative discourses together construct consciousness. Civil rights reforms in particular are likely to produce a struggle between legal discourses and other social discourses because legal reforms often challenge existing social arrangements and taken-for-granted meanings (Engel and Munger 1996; Krieger 2000). Note that this approach to legal consciousness treats law as a resource for resistance rather than an institution to be resisted (cf. Sarat 1990). In this way, this approach builds on other, more macro-level studies that view law as a discursive resource for bringing about social change (McCann 1994; Scheingold 1974).

Understanding how competing discourses shape legal consciousness is important for understanding both the dynamic of social change and possible sources of resistance to social change. Social constructivist perspectives suggest that legal change may bring about social change by destabilizing existing meanings and delegitimizing accepted practices. In this view, opportunities for destablizing meanings arise when actors respond to conflicting or overlapping schemas, sometimes by transporting systems of meaning from one context to another (Sewell 1992). Legal reforms provide new discourses for reframing the meaning of social events and distabilizing existing meanings. But just as actors can draw on new legal discourses to destablizing existing meanings, actors may also draw on existing discourses to undermine legal reforms. In other words, established discourses can be resources for resisting social change through legal reform, and these discourses can shape actions to be consistent with existing social structure.

Competing Discourses: Law and Other Social Institutions

How do competing legal and cultural discourses shape legal consciousness in the context of a particular civil rights statute, the Family and Medical Leave Act of 1993? To answer this question, first it is useful to sketch the provisions of this new law. The FMLA provides some workers with a legal right to unpaid, job-protected leave for caring for family or for serious illnesses.[2] The FMLA requires covered employers to provide up to 12 weeks of unpaid leave per year to certain workers who need time off for family or medical crises.[3] Workers may also use FMLA leave for pregnancy disability, and both men and women may take FMLA parental leave to care for a new child in their family.[4] The statute protects workers who use FMLA leave from retaliatory harassment, termination, and discrimination.[5] It also requires employers to provide FMLA leave even if they do not allow time off for any other reason. In other words, the statute creates an entitlement to leave because it allows employers no discretion to deny qualified workers leave.

The legal reforms of the FMLA provide a fertile area for studying the interaction of legal discourse with other systems of meaning because these new rights fundamentally challenge deeply held beliefs about what work and being a good worker mean. For example, this new law chips away at employers' unilateral control over the time requirements and scheduling of work. It also challenges gendered family wage ideology about appropriate caretakers for "private" family matters because it requires work to accommodate family on a gender-neutral basis. And by protecting the jobs of workers who are temporarily unable to work due to illness or injury, this law undermines conceptions of "disability" and "work" as mutually exclusive categories. Accordingly, the law not only creates a right for workers, but also generates a new discourse that undermines the taken-for-granted practices, expectations, and material conditions that make up work as a social institution. In this way the law opens up new ways of thinking about and organizing the relationships among work, gender, and disability, and creates an opportunity for social change.

Although the FMLA challenges deeply entrenched beliefs about the nature of work and its relationship to gender and disability, these systems of meaning do not

---

[2] Not all workers are covered by the FMLA. Workers who have worked for their employers for less than one year are not eligible for FMLA leave. In addition, workers who work for companies with less than 50 employees are not covered by the FMLA. 29 U.S.C. § 2611.

[3] 29 U.S.C. § 2612.

[4] Ibid.

[5] 29 U.S.C. § 2614, 2615.

disappear overnight when the law takes effect. Moreover, the FMLA creates a private right of action that workers must negotiate individually within a social context where these meanings persist. How do both law and other systems of meaning shape the legal consciousness of workers who negotiate these rights in the workplace? When workplace conflict over leave arises, how do workers resolve the tension between legal discourses and institutionalized expectations and practices regarding work, gender, and disability? Do the experiences and legal consciousness of workers vary with characteristics such as gender? How do the cultural meanings that compete with law vary with the reason workers take leave – for example, are the discourses associated with parental leave different than those associated with disability leave? Answering these questions requires a deeper understanding of the legal and non-legal discourses in play in FMLA negotiations, which I develop in the following sections.

Legal Discourse

The legal reforms of the FMLA create a new interpretive frame for leave from work for family or medical reasons. In this discourse, work and at least some family responsibilities are compatible. Work can accommodate care obligations in crises situations, and the normative worker may have care responsibilities regardless of gender. For example, the law allows leave on a gender-neutral basis for parental leave, and to provide care for a child, parent, or spouse with a serious health condition. In addition, motherhood and work are nominally compatible in this discourse; women may take up to 12 weeks of job-protected leave for pregnancy disability and maternity leave. By prohibiting discrimination against workers who use leave, the law not only requires work to accommodate care obligations, but also prohibits employers from valuing workers differently based on their choices to use family or medical leave.[6]

The legal discourse of the FMLA also constructs work and disability as compatible in some instances. By allowing workers to take time off to receive treatment for or recover from temporary disabilities, the FMLA blurs the rigid line between work and disability. Rather than defining "disability" as the complete inability to work, the FMLA allows leave for a "serious health condition" that might only require, for example, intermittent leave for treatment.[7] Workers may, in some instances, take FMLA leave to reduce their work hours. This right allows them to accommodate an illness or injury by taking leave only intermittently rather than exiting the workplace completely. Accordingly, legal discourse legitimates the status of workers who take medical leave, and allows them to legitimately claim to be too sick to work a standard work schedule without giving up their claim to the status of "worker."

The legal discourse of the FMLA treats leaves not as special favors or deviations from the norm granted only at employers' discretion, but as entitlements. FMLA rights

---

[6] Of course, there are many ordinary, everyday care obligations that are not covered by the FMLA. Accordingly, it is important not to overstate the protections this new statute provides. Nevertheless, mandatory leave is a radical departure from prior employment rights based on formal equality because mandatory leave requires changes in established work practices that tend to disadvantage women and people with disabilities.

[7] 29 U.S.C. § 2612(b)(1).

represent an implicit assumption that the normative worker may have children, be needed to care for others, or suffer from a serious illness or injury sometime in his/her working career. The FMLA presumes that work can and should accommodate these events that are part of everyday life, and that filling these roles and maintaining the status of worker is not inconsistent or impossible. In this way, the law reframes the meaning of "work" and the status of "worker" to accommodate these common life events.

Other Discourses that Construct Work, Gender, and Disability

Legal discourse competes with alternative interpretive frameworks that reflect cultural conceptions of work. Work is a social institution that consists of deeply held beliefs, implicit expectations, and established practices that are so taken for granted that they are seldom questioned. For example, asked to imagine "work," our mental image is likely to include certain practices or features even if our own experience or that of others we know differs. Those features include labor for a wage or salary; permanent, uninterrupted year-round work; and a standard 40-hour work week on a five-day schedule. In addition, we generally expect employers to control both work schedules and the organization of the labor process, although historically, productive activities have been organized in other ways (Montgomery 1987; McEvoy 1998).

Of course, many jobs deviate from this standard, but we mark those deviations by referencing (and thus reinforcing) the institutional norm. That is, we speak of "part-time" work or "night shifts," "working at home" or "working for oneself." This standard is so taken for granted that employers need not specify that advertised positions conform to the standard. In contrast, advertisements for positions that deviate from this standard usually say so explicitly by specifying, for example, "part-time work."

"Work" includes a set of cultural meanings associated with these institutional practices. For example, in American society, work is closely associated with virtue, independence, and citizenship (Foner 1995; Glenn 2002; Weber 1930). Work lies at the intersection of American ideologies about the market, the meritocracy, and economic independence as a safeguard against tyranny (Fraser and Gordon 1994; Lipset 1996; Weber 1930). Work is not just a valued activity, but also a moral obligation; able-bodied individuals who are unemployed are seen as shirking an obligation to work (Glenn 2002; Kerber 1998; Lipset 1996; Shklar 1991). Thus, while work is valued, not working without justification is viewed as immoral voluntary idleness and a personal moral failing (Lipset 1996).

The material practices and cultural meanings of work operate together to define what work and being a good worker mean. Particularly salient for FMLA rights is how time is a normative marker of good workers, so that workers who fail to meet institutionalized time standards are devalued as less committed, valuable, and competent. For example, in modern work organizations where productivity can be hard to measure, hours worked have come to define the ideal worker. Those who meet the full-time standard are valued most, and part-time workers are devalued (Fried 1998; Hochschild 1997; Schor 1992; Williams 2000). Attendance and time invested in work, rather than other measures of productivity, are the primary markers of a "good" worker (Hochschild 1997; Schor 1992; Thompson 1967). The converse is also true; even a productive worker can be labeled as a "bad" worker for missing work, and breaks in employment can signal a lack of commitment to work.

Institutionalized practices and the cultural meanings embodied in those practices often protect existing relations of power and inequality, and the institution of work is no exception. Feminist and disability scholars have long recognized how work's institutionalized features incorporate an implicitly gendered and able-bodied norm. For example, a full-time, year-round uninterrupted work schedule does not accommodate childbirth or caretaking responsibilities for others, nor does it easily accommodate disabilities that require temporary absences for treatment or recovery. Because work's features are so taken for granted, however, the barriers they create appear to arise from the personal circumstances of women or people with disabilities, and not from the structure of work itself (MacKinnon 1989; Oliver 1990). Thus, caring for sick family members or children are "private" matters irrelevant to employers, and requests for workplace accommodations are "special treatment" for those who do not fit the able-bodied standard. Because institutionalized work features seem natural and normal, their role in recreating inequality is not easily perceived nor does it seem realistic to believe that they can be changed.

Although they seem "natural," stable, and unchanging, institutions like work are the product and embodiment of history (Berger and Luckman 1967). For example, institutionalized work practices reflect early twentieth-century family wage ideology that constructs the normative worker as a male breadwinner with a stay-at-home wife who cares for home and family (Folbre 1991; Fraser and Gordon 1994; Glenn 2002; Okin 1989; Pateman 1988). This ideology helped to justify marginalizing women in the labor market by presuming working women were the secondary earner in their family, or were working just for "pin money" until they married and had children (Frank and Lipner 1988). Although women have now gained formal legal access to the workplace, work's institutionalized features continue to be structured around ideal workers who are unencumbered by family responsibilities (Hochschild 1997; MacKinnon 1989; Okin 1989; Pateman 1988; Williams 2000). Moreover, the historical legacy of family wage ideology is normative as well as structural. Family wage ideology still influences how employers and others think about both working women and work itself (Hochschild 1997; Williams 2000).

Along the same lines, disability scholars have traced how, over time, work and disability came to have mutually exclusive meanings that are constitutive of each other (Oliver 1990; Stone 1984). Historically, the category "disability" emerged in part to determine who is employable and thus not deserving of charitable support that might undermine the incentive to work (Stone 1984). Legally, the definition of "disability" often has been construed narrowly to mean no residual working capacity to enforce this moral obligation to work. For example, social welfare legislation explicitly defines "disability" as the inability to work, rather than in terms of specific impairments.[8] One legacy of constructing disability in this way has been that claims

---

[8] The Social Security Act, 42 U.S.C. § 1382c(a)(3), defines disability for the purposes of supplemental income replacement as follows:

[A]n individual shall be determined to be under a disability only if his physical or mental impairment or impairments are of such severity that he is not only unable to do his previous work but cannot, considering his age, education, and work experience, engage in any other kind of substantial gainful work which exists in the national economy, regardless of whether such work exists in the immediate area in which he lives, or whether a specific job vacancy exists for him, or whether he would be hired if he applied for work.

of disability in the workplace can raise suspicions of shirking (Drimmer 1993). In other words, if the meanings of "work" and "disability" are fundamentally incompatible, one cannot legitimately claim to be both a worker and disabled.

The FMLA attempts to change some of these institutionalized work practices, but these rights are embedded within the interrelated meanings of work, gender, and disability. These systems of meaning can shape how workers understand and think about their rights, and how others respond to their use of leave. When conflict over leave arises, workers draw on these different and sometimes conflicting cultural frames to make sense of their situations and to think about their options. In addition, other actors draw on these frames when they talk with workers about their rights. As a result, institutionalized expectations about work, gender, and disability, as well as legal discourse, can shape workers' legal consciousness. The following sections draw on interviews with workers who negotiated leaves to illustrate how workers reconcile legal discourse with the alternative discourses that give meaning to their situation.

Method and Data

Studying legal consciousness in the context of out-of-court disputes can be difficult, as most employers are unwilling to allow researchers to interview their employees about conflict over legal rights. Indeed, it can be difficult to find workers who experienced conflict over rights but did not take their disputes to court because these disputes do not produce court records. To solve this problem, this project located respondents through a state-wide telephone information line in California run by a nonprofit organization that gives informal legal assistance to workers. Attempts were made to contact the universe of individuals who called the information line with questions about family and medical leave during a one-year period. Twenty-four of the 35 individuals in this group agreed to be interviewed, yielding a response rate of almost 70 percent.[9] The characteristics of the interviewees are summarized in Table 3.1.

The interviews, which typically lasted about 45 minutes, were tape-recorded and transcribed. The data were then analyzed using NUD*IST, a qualitative analysis software program that allows researchers to identify and code themes as they emerge from the transcripts. The analysis identified common themes in workers' experiences, including the factors that they considered in deciding whether to mobilize their rights and the problems they experienced taking leave. Like many qualitative studies, this analysis involved multiple readings of the interview transcripts to identify common themes as they emerged from the transcripts. For example, in this study, although I initially focused on consciousness about rights, themes about "gender", "slackers", and the meaning of "time" emerged from the transcript to shape the analysis in new ways. I then went back more systematically to code each instance of the themes that emerged from these interviews, and to look for patterns among those themes. This process is greatly simplified by NUD*IST which allows researchers to highlight text segments associated with a theme, to sort and index these segments by theme, and to analyze patterns in these data. Although the small sample size here requires caution in drawing generalizations, this approach has the potential to reveal considerable nuance and detail about the mobilization process.

---

[9] Four individuals could not be contacted after multiple attempts, four individuals refused to be interviewed, one number had been disconnected, and two numbers were incorrect.

Table 3.1 Demographic characteristics of interviewees

ID	Gender	Ethnicity	Age range	Marital status	Education	Family income	Leave reason	Job tenure	Job title
1001	Female	White	50–64	married	college grad	30K–50K	multiple-pg*	26	administrative assistant
1002	Male	White	35–49	divorced	high school	<20K	own condition	4	production associate
1003	Female	White	50–64	widowed	some college	30K–50K	own condition	5	station agent
1004	Female	White	25–34	married	some college	50K–75K	multiple-pg	8	customer service rep
1005	Female	White	65+	divorced	some college	50K–75K	sick child	10	case manager
1006	Female	Hispanic	35–49	married	college grad	75K+	own condition	16	medical assistant
1007	Female	White	50–64	married	college grad	75K+	own condition	3	comptroller
1008	Female	White	25–34	live w/ partner	some college	30K–50K	own condition	3	manager/ troubleshooter
1009	Female	Hispanic	35–49	married	some college	75K+	multiple	16	reservation manager
1010	Male	Asian	25–34	married	some college	75K+	new child	10	x-ray technician
1011	Female	White	18–24	separated	some college	<20K	pregnancy	7 months	electronic component merchandiser
1012	Male	Hispanic	35–49	married	high school	30K–50K	spouse	5	laborer
1013	Female	Hispanic	25–34	married	some college	<20K	multiple-pg	2	human resources assistant
1014	Female	Black	25–34	live w/ partner	some college	50K–75K	multiple-pg	8	deli clerk
1015	Female	White	18–24	married	some college	30K–50K	multiple-pg	2	hostess
1016	Male	Hispanic	25–34	married	some college	75K+	new child	1	car washer
1017	Female	Black	25–34	widowed	some college	50K–75K	pregnancy	1.5	courtesy clerk
1018	Female	White	35–49	separated	some college	50K–75K	sick child	7	file manager
1019	Female	White	35–49	live w/ partner	some college	30K–50K	own condition	3	account clerk/ senior clerk
1020	Female	White	35–49	married	graduate school	75K+	multiple-pg	4	vice president/ account supervisor
1021	Female	Other	25–34	live w/ partner	some college	20K–30K	own condition	2.5	service representative
1022	Male	White	25–34	married	graduate school	75K+	spouse	2	Pilot
1023	Female	Asian	25–34	married	some college	30K–50K	multiple-pg	8	key associate
1024	Female	White	35–49	married	some college	50K–75K	multiple-pg	10	bakery clerk

* "Multiple-pg" designates a leave taken for pregnancy and other reasons, such as recovering from a pregnancy-related illness after childbirth, or parental leave after childbirth.

Some limitations of these data bear mentioning here. As this study focuses on how workers who were aware of their leave rights negotiated their leaves in the workplace, the subjects are not and were not intended to be a random sample of the population of potential leave users. Instead, this study focuses on the experiences of workers who anticipated or experienced some difficulty in obtaining leave. Accordingly, these data do not identify how frequently problems with the FMLA arise, or about differences between workers who experience problems and those who do not. Also, workers who did not know they had legal rights or who took leave with no difficulty probably did not call the information line. This is an inherent methodological difficulty of studying the process through which people come to understand their rights; for example, it is difficult to identify individuals who may have suffered a legal wrong but failed to recognize it (Felstiner, Abel, and Sarat 1981).

Although these limitations apply, these qualitative data are useful because they complement other ethnographic and quantitative studies of family and medical leave (Commission on Leave 1996; Fried 1998; Gerstel and McGonagle 1999; Hochschild 1997). For example, these data add to quantitative research about patterns of leave-taking in general (see, for example, Gerstel and McGonagle 1999) because they access cognitive processes that contribute to choices about leave and rights. Similarly, this project differs from recent ethnographic studies of leave-taking and corporate culture within a single organization (see, for example, Fried 1998; Hochschild 1997), because it uses respondents as informants about diverse work settings to identify patterns that bridge multiple workers and workplaces. This approach helps identify common patterns *across* workplaces and *across* organizational boundaries that show how institutionalized practices and expectations regarding work can shape consciousness about rights.

Discussion

The process of negotiating FMLA rights is to some extent idiosyncratic and variable. It depends on the individual's particular conflict over leave, the social setting in which he/she negotiates rights, and the characteristics of the individuals themselves. Nevertheless, themes emerged from these interviews that suggest that cultural meanings and social structures other than law shape legal consciousness in systematic ways across individuals. These themes suggest how negotiations over leave rights can become a venue for recreating and reproducing the social patterns the FMLA was intended to change. At the same time, however, workers also draw on legal discourse to undermine institutionalized understandings of work, gender, and disability, and to articulate new ways of understanding the meaning of leave. The following sections draw on data from workers' interviews to illustrate how workers reconcile legal discourse about leave with alternative discourses that construct work as incompatible with disability or family obligations.

Competing Discourses and the Social Meaning of "Family Leave"

Most workers in this study who took leave for pregnancy-related disabilities or to care for family members encountered a discourse that constructed their leave in terms of family wage ideology. Family wage ideology presumes that the normative worker is a male breadwinner with a wife at home to care for family concerns (Fraser and Gordon 1994; Williams 2000). Although the central premise of family wage discourse is this gendered division of labor, both women and men whose work patterns meet the breadwinner norm have generally been able to claim the status of ideal worker (Williams 2000). Once the need for leave arises and family responsibilities become visible at work, however, the gendered discourses associated with the social institution of work tend to come into play.

Most women in this study who took family leave reported that leave changed perceptions of them at work, and seemed to signal that they were no longer committed to their job. Virtually all female respondents had no difficulty initially going out on family leave, but when they sought to return to their jobs they encountered both resistance and perceptions that they were less reliable and committed to their work. Their experiences suggest that family wage discourse, which labels women as at best the secondary worker in the family (and whose primary responsibility is caring for others) constructed the meaning of their leave.

The experience of a respondent who took leave for a difficult pregnancy and to recover from having twins illustrates this process of meaning construction. Even though this respondent had worked for her employer for 16 years before she needed leave, her employer assumed she would not return to work, and cancelled her health insurance while she was in the hospital. She also learned that her boss told her co-workers that she did not need her job because her husband could support her. "[T]hey were saying, 'Well she doesn't need to get paid,' my boss was saying. 'She has money – her husband is a doctor.'" Although a friend who was a lawyer told her that she would have a strong legal claim if she was fired when she attempted to return to work, she feared that involuntarily losing her job would hurt her prospects for finding future employment. She knew that her employer had fired other long-term employees who needed leave, and she decided to quit. When she left, however, she wanted to avoid a confrontation with her employer, and so she told her supervisor she could not return to work because she lacked childcare.

This respondent's experience illustrates how competing meanings of taking leave can play out in the process of negotiating FMLA rights. Family wage discourse informs her employer's response to her request for leave. Despite her 16 years of service, her employer presumes her employment is secondary to that of her husband, and therefore she does not "need" her job. Her employer attempts to legitimate letting her go by mobilizing a cultural discourse that women (particularly mothers) are and should be economically dependent upon their spouses. Legal discourse also contributes to her understanding of her situation, however. Her lawyer friend emphasizes that she would have a good legal claim if she is fired when she attempts to return to work. Her doctor also tells her that cancelling her health insurance is illegal. In addition, she draws on legal discourse herself by expressing outrage that her employer has ignored legal requirements regarding family leave.

This respondent must resolve the conflicting discourses of law and family wage ideology within a context already structured by power, gender, and taken-for-granted expectations about work. Her problems with leave arise in part because gendered constructions of work as incompatible with family responsibilities give meaning to her use of leave, undermining legal discourses that treat work and family as compatible. Family wage discourse helps to obscure how her employer's power to harm her chances for future employment shapes her decision. And even though she interprets her situation in terms of the law, she draws on other cultural discourses to avoid conflict by giving a culturally acceptable reason to quit: lack of childcare. As a result, the family wage schema seems to frame her situation as a mother who decides to stay home and care for her children because her husband will support her. In this way, the gendered inequalities embodied in the institution of work are recreated, and legal constructions of the situation are simultaneously undermined and obscured.

Legal discourse also competes with family wage ideologies when men attempt to take leave, but family wage discourse constructed the meaning of men taking leave somewhat differently. Both women and men in this study reported that gendered assumptions that men were breadwinners and not family caretakers created informal workplace norms that men should not take all the family leave to which they were entitled. For example, in one respondent's workplace, it was unthinkable that a new father would take more than a week or two of leave.

> Our office was small so I would say they were more understanding with the women having a baby. I know that men are able to take off time too, my husband worked there also, we worked together.
>
> Interviewer: Can you tell me more about that?
>
> [T]here was another guy who was having a baby and I think that they got more pressure to come back to work, okay, "It's okay for you to take a week off and maybe a week and a half off, but let's not go crazy here." And that wasn't, I don't think they would have been open for the FMLA for the men. At least the men I knew just took their vacation and didn't take, didn't use the FMLA when they could've. Because they were pressured to come back to work, like "Hey, *you* didn't have a baby."
>
> Interviewer: And there wasn't the same kind of pressure on women?
>
> No. [Interview 1020]

Whereas most women in this study found that their employers expected them to take leave to care for others, all the male respondents reported that their employers and co-workers were incredulous and even hostile when they decided to take family leave. In other words, the same cultural schema of the family wage ideal constructed different meanings for respondents' leaves depending upon their gender.

These deeply entrenched conceptions of work and gender shape not only workers' experiences, but also their legal consciousness. For example, some men who took unpaid family leave struggled to reconcile leave rights with taken-for-granted expectations that they are the breadwinner for their families and should make work a priority over family needs. For example, one respondent who took leave intermittently to care for his terminally ill wife found that the leave caused problems for him at work. His employer sent him a disciplinary letter telling him to keep his leave use to a minimum, and his co-workers questioned his time away from work. This respondent resisted the message that he was a "bad" worker by pointing to other evidence of his ability, including offers of promotion. At the same time, however, he believed he should not seek to advance at work while he might need family leave.

> [T]here has been plenty of opportunities for me to move up and stuff, but I didn't pursue them because ... I'm not ready to give 100% responsibility. My responsibility deals with my wife and family at this time. And I've known how sick she is so I didn't pursue any of those advancements for that reason. It was that my priorities are with my family and not

moving up at this time … [W]e are pretty middle class. I mean there is nothing we are deprived of. We probably have more things than what most people got, but that has never been a priority to me, like having more or whatever. You know, my priority is my family and that's how I'd like to keep it. [Interview 1012]

Family wage discourse helps construct this respondent's understanding of his situation. Even though he is aware of his legal rights and takes leave, he understands leave and advancement at work to be an either/or choice – one cannot both pursue a career and also care for sick family members. He interprets the right to leave in a way that reflects the family wage norm in which the ideal worker is not needed to care for others. In addition, his statement that his family is "pretty middle class" despite his choice to put family first implicitly references cultural expectations about the male breadwinner role and justifies his choice against those norms.

This respondent also draws on legal discourse to interpret the meaning of his leave, however. When his co-workers, his employer, and even his wife question his time away from work, he responds by pointing to the law:

I always made them understand that I'm under Family Leave … and that allows me the right [to take leave] … [M]y wife a lot of times, says "Babe, you can't miss this much work," this and that, and I'd say "Honey, you know, I'm not missing work to miss work. You're sick or whatever and if you need me, I'm here and that's what Family Leave is, that's why I'm under it, and that's why we fill out the Certification papers with your medical provider to protect me in these times of need." [Interview 1012]

By referencing his legal rights, this respondent constructs missing work as legitimate, both to himself and to others who question his absence from work. That his choice to care for his wife requires justification, however, reflects how these rights are embedded within other systems of meaning that shape his legal consciousness. He reconciles legal schemas with these other cultural schemas by simultaneously asserting his rights and voluntarily compromising his advancement at work.

This respondent's perceptions both reproduce and are shaped by deeply entrenched understandings of what work and being a good worker mean. For example, when he justifies his decision to care for his wife by arguing he has passed up opportunities for advancement, he both accepts and reinforces the norm that ideal workers should have no responsibility to care for others. At the same time, he draws on legal discourse to resist this norm. He insists he is not a "bad" worker "missing work to miss work"; instead, he is claiming his legal right to care for his spouse. The fact that he references law does not mean, however, that no other cultural schemas contribute to his legal consciousness. Rather, he draws on law to legitimate taking leave as *resistance* to family wage discourse, not in its absence.

Women who took maternity leave, or who took leave to care for their children, navigated a different web of institutionalized meanings about work and family: the conflict between what it means to be a good worker and what it means to be a good mother. For many women in this study, claiming legal rights to leave, particularly the right to return to work, conflicted with cultural discourses about the traditional role of women in caring for others. They struggled to reconcile legal discourse about their entitlement to return to work with cultural discourses that constructed care for others, and in particular motherhood, as incompatible with work.

Let me use one respondent's experience to illustrate this subjective process. When this respondent tried to return to work after her maternity leave she discovered that her employer had filled her position. She was angry, and when friends suggested that she contact a lawyer about pursuing her rights, she did. At the same time, she worried that she was to blame for her situation, and that she had violated norms about being a good worker.

> I was speaking with a lawyer all that time, trying to get back my job and see if they would offer me anything else, but they just wanted to put me in housekeeping. They couldn't find anything for me. At least that's what they were saying. Other situations they were hiring for, other things like sales. And I was like, "Well I can learn sales, anything." A lot of my friends tell me that it's not my fault, that people are just like that. I felt like I was to blame. I even talked to my boss about it. I said, "Didn't I do a good job ?" … [Interview 1013]

Her boss assured her that she had done a good job, but still demoted her from human resources assistant to hotel housekeeper. She continued to work as a housekeeper for several months while her lawyer negotiated to get her job back.

While negotiating her rights, she struggled to reconcile contradictory expectations about mothers and workers. She worried about failing to meet her obligations as a mother, saying "I just felt that no one else would take care of [my child] like a mother would." In her view, she had been undermined as both mother and worker: she no longer had the job she loved, and she had to leave her child with another caretaker to work as a housekeeper for less pay.

> I felt bad in my own way and I was very sad. And I think a lot of it was because I knew my child was with this other person. I couldn't do anything about it. My job went to another woman and what was I going to do? All I could do is cry. [Interview 1013]

From her perspective, by demoting her and lowering her pay, her employer labeled her as a bad worker, and also made continuing to work less desirable and rewarding. Although some of her friends thought she should continue to fight, others suggested a different solution:

> I have one friend, she was always telling me, "[Maria] if you feel this way why don't you just quit your job and just take care of your son?" Then my husband got a better job offer so that's when I said, I think I will do that. [Interview 1013]

Eventually, she gave up her negotiations with her employer and quit her job.

This respondent negotiated her rights within three overlapping and contradictory frames: legal entitlements to leave, institutionalized expectations about what it means to be a good worker, and deeply entrenched norms about what it means to be a good mother. The conflict among these schemas made claiming her rights psychologically taxing. Although she hired a lawyer to fight for her job, she also felt less sure of her claim to being a good worker after taking leave. She wondered what she had done wrong, saying "I felt like I was to blame." At the same time, she worried about not meeting an idealized norm of a mother-child relationship of intense and personal care (Hays 1996). This respondent's comments reveal the contradictory legal and cultural schemas about the meaning of caretaking and leave that shape her legal consciousness.

Although this respondent decided to quit, it is too simplistic to interpret her choice as simply the result of immutable gendered "preferences" without considering the material conditions and cultural meanings that form the context of her decision. Preferences are shaped by norms and by structural opportunities. Perhaps her choice would have been different had she been able to return to work without resistance. Also, her interactions with others, including her employer and her friends, shaped her understanding of her situation and options. For example, by suggesting that she should quit and care for her son, her friend frames her situation as a choice between work and motherhood, rather than as a legal violation. Family wage discourse about the mutually exclusive roles of mother and worker raises doubts in her mind about pursuing her legal rights, and constructs a culturally acceptable solution for resolving her stress. Her choice, channeled in part by taken-for-granted understandings of what it means to be a good worker and a good mother, then helps recreate those understandings despite the protections of the law.

Note that whereas the male respondent discussed above resisted the idea that taking leave undermined his status as a breadwinner, this respondent worries that asserting her rights might undermine her role as mother. Together, their experiences suggest that conflicting legal and cultural schemas generate cognitive discomfort that varies with gender because the expectations associated with those schemas also vary with gender. As the responses of their employers, friends, and family suggest, culturally, women are expected to quit work to care for new children, whereas men are expected to make work their first priority. Consequently, actors' legal consciousness about leave is likely to vary with their gender because family wage discourse constructs the meaning of leave in ways that vary with gender.

Competing Discourses and the Social Meaning of "Medical Leave"

Respondents who needed leave for their own serious health condition negotiated leave rights within different set of cultural meanings and expectations. Although the FMLA entitles workers to time off from work for a serious illness, respondents encountered informal workplace norms that interpreted leave taking as slacking. In this discourse, "committed" workers were expected to come to work even when sick. Conversely, workers who were unwilling or unable to work while sick were perceived as less valuable. These informal expectations made respondents wary of taking leave.

> There seemed to be kind of, I forgot the proper way to word this, the company's attitude towards people working when they're ill and working to the point of causing illness, that was sort of a badge of courage. And I had seen other people in the company pretty much be discounted as valuable employees because they wouldn't or couldn't work when they were sick. And I think that's where my fear came from. [Interview 1008]

Even some of respondents' co-workers interpreted taking leave as shirking.

> Well some people consider that you're a slacker or whatever ... because you're off. They don't consider sick at any point. They know I'm very energetic and hyper and all this stuff, but I should just retire or quit or whatever. I'm in the way ... [S]ome people who are real company oriented or upward, yuppy types feel like you're not being a good employee if you're off. Even if you do the job efficiently. [Interview 1003]

Respondents' employers communicated this norm through concrete practices: by passing over leave takers for promotion, by transferring (or refusing to transfer) them, by cutting their hours, or by assigning them undesirable work or shifts. These responses mark those who manage to take leave as poor workers, despite the legal protection for leave.[10]

Everyday workplace practices can help reinforce the understanding that taking leave is a form of shirking. For example, employers who do not replace workers who take leave can encourage hostility toward leave takers.

> Like for instance the, well the FMLA they have to give you. But what they do is some departments and most of the departments actually, they won't replace you when you get sick, so it causes peer pressure and creates hostility ... [a]mongst your own co-workers ... "Well if this person didn't have so much family leave all the time," you know, that type of situation ... You call in and say, "I'm sick, I'm taking a family leave day." But the end result of that is that it creates hostility in the workplace. They're not supportive because the employer doesn't replace the person. [Interview 1006]

This particular workplace practice deflects blame for the extra workload away from the employer by framing workload problems as a conflict among workers, rather than a conflict between workers and the employer. Although the law has changed, this workplace continues to be structured around the always-ready, always-present worker; the employer lacks any contingency plan or substitute staff to cover workers who are on leave. The structure of this workplace thus reinforces the idea that taking leave is illegitimate.

The slacker discourse suggests how systems of meaning other than law can create resistance to rights and discourage workers from using leave. By drawing upon the image of the "slacker," respondents' employers and co-workers reinterpret mandatory leave rights as a form of shirking. The slacker construction is not a spontaneous local norm, however; its roots lie in the historical construction of work in opposition to disability. The image of the slacker reflects deeply held beliefs that work and disability are mutually exclusive and therefore any claim to be both a worker and disabled is illegitimate. In other words, one cannot legitimately be disabled if one also claims to be a worker because of deeply entrenched beliefs that being "really" disabled means not being able to work at all. Accordingly, leave-takers find themselves straddling the cultural line between disability and work, and disrupting the mutually constitutive relationship between the two. The "slacker" image both reflects and polices this line by penalizing workers who claim a disability, however temporary that disability may be.

Law as a Counterhegemonic Discourse

Although competing interpretive frameworks can undermine legal rights, law is also a symbolic resource that workers can draw upon to construct a different meaning for

---

[10] Many of these practices are technically illegal. For example, the FMLA prohibits discrimination against workers who use leave rights, including using the taking of leave as a negative factor in employment actions such as hiring, promotions or disciplinary actions. 29 C.F.R. § 825.220. These kinds of claims can be very difficult to prove, however.

taking leave. For example, this respondent uses legal discourse to create a counter-interpretation of leave:

> [W]hat I've done because of this situation and because I've heard all these things, is I've been meeting with groups of employees and telling them that you don't need to go there. People are entitled to this [leave]. If it was you or your family member you would want this leave too. And you sure wouldn't want to come back to work and find out that your own co-workers are being ugly about it. And if they don't replace you, it's not the employees' fault. It actually has to do with the employer. And trying to appease people. I talk to them and explain to them what the rules are and explain to them that the person who is the sick person, is entitled to this time. And you're just making it worse by doing this to them.
>
> Interviewer: And how has this been received?
>
> Actually pretty good. I've been trying to get them not to fuss with each other … [Interview 1006]

This respondent uses legal discourse to combat the slacker interpretation. First, she explains "what the rules are." She argues to co-workers that leave is a legal entitlement, and therefore not subject to qualification or discussion. Second, she references legal norms of equal treatment by pointing out that all workers can benefit from the FMLA's protections. She undercuts the "slacker" interpretation by pointing out that the employer, not the absent worker, controls workload distribution. In this way, legal discourse helps reveal how the slacker interpretation obscures the employers' role in imposing an increased workload when workers take leave. This example suggests how legal discourse can be used to challenge other systems of meaning that shape workplace perceptions of leave rights.

Even those workers who negotiated their rights on their own said that legal rights were an important resource in these negotiations. Most respondents reported that they felt empowered by the legal entitlement to leave as they negotiated with their employers. For example, many respondents said they felt morally justified in pursuing claims to leave once they knew that their employer acted illegally. As one worker put it, "[Information about FMLA rights] gave me a leg to stand on. And some kind of moral or ethical support knowing that this is what my rights were …" [Interview 1003]. In addition, many respondents described law as a pragmatic resource for confronting employers, even when they did not make a formal legal claim. For example, this worker used legal knowledge to negotiate successfully with her employer:

> [When my employer denied my leave request] I didn't say, "It's not legal," I said, "According to this state statute …" I put the statute number and stuff, so that they know that I know what I'm talking about … [A] lot of people will go, "Are you sure this is legal?" … and then they'll try and like moonshine their way around it. And rather than have people do that to me, I just got to where when stuff comes up, I'll learn the legal statute numbers and it's more effective for me that way … [Information about my rights] gave me knowledge which gave me the power to act on what was going on. [Interview 1021]

Learning about their rights helped these workers frame their experiences in both legal and moral terms, and gave them confidence to press for time off. Some workers also drew on law to interpret time off as an entitlement, rather than a personal problem that interfered with their work. Thus, these data indicate that workers can use law as a symbolic resource both to make sense of their experiences at work, and to negotiate with their employers over time off.

Certainly informal norms about what work and being a good worker mean can create resistance to leave rights in the workplace. Nevertheless, law provides a symbolic resource that workers can use to undermine these institutionalized meanings and to change social practices and expectations. Law can operate as a counter-hegemonic discourse for framing alternative ways to organize work life, assign blame, and understand the meaning of taking leave. And, to the extent that larger social structures are created and recreated through micro-interactions (Sewell 1992), in this way legal discourse may help bring about social change.

Conclusion

Sociolegal scholars have moved beyond understanding legal consciousness as mere attitudes about law or as "false consciousness" that is an epiphenomenon of capitalist production (Silbey 2001). More recent approaches view legal consciousness as a dynamic process of meaning-making that takes place in particular social contexts already structured by law itself, and in which actors construct their consciousness through lived experiences. This study extends this approach by examining how other institutionalized systems of meaning as well as legal discourse shape workers' consciousness in this dynamic process.

Workers in this study articulate how their experiences negotiating family and medical leave shaped their consciousness. As they engaged with those around them – including family, friends, co-workers and employers – they encountered multiple and conflicting discourses about the meaning of taking leave. In these social interactions, other actors deploy interpretive frames that are not idiosyncratic or random, but that are tied to deeply entrenched norms and understandings of work, gender, and disability. By articulating these alternative interpretations, these interactions help shape how workers understand and think about the role of legal rights in the conflict over leave.

One interesting theme in these interviews is that at least for family leave, the meanings deployed in these interactions seem to vary with gender. Because work and the ideal worker have been historically defined in gendered terms, the same act of taking family leave can take on different meanings depending upon the worker's gender. For women, although they may encounter little resistance taking leave, attempting to return to work goes against contrary gendered norms that women with families place caretaking ahead of work. Subjectively, women may consequently worry that pursuing rights undermines their ability to care adequately for their families. Men, on the other hand, encounter much more resistance to taking family leave in the first place because doing so violates gendered norms that men with families place breadwinning ahead of caretaking. Similarly, men often were encouraged by friends and family to take less time off, while women were encouraged to quit their jobs to care for others. The cultural schema – family wage discourse – is the same, but the meaning of that discourse, and how that discourse shapes workers' perceptions of what they normatively *should* do, vary with gender. In other words, not only the gender of the worker, but also the gendered nature of the discourse, helped shape workers' legal consciousness.

Workers' experiences also suggest how non-legal cultural schemas can give different meanings to the same legal right depending upon the social context. For example, note that the act of taking leave is the same whether the reason is care responsibilities or personal illness. Culturally, however, medical leave is interpreted through the "slacker" discourse and the moral obligation to work, whereas family leave evokes gendered norms about work and the division of labor in the family. Meaning and legal consciousness, then, vary in complex ways influenced not only by individual characteristics such as gender, but also by the other cultural schema through which interactions about legal rights unfold.

What does this study suggest about the potential of workplace rights like the FMLA to bring about social change? Respondents' experiences indicate that workplace civil rights may face stiff resistance from deeply entrenched norms, expectations, and practices in the workplace. Institutionalized practices and beliefs about work generate cultural discourses that compete with law, and these alternative interpretive frameworks can undermine legal reforms. Contrary to the arguments of some theorists that the discourse of rights displaces all other discourses in society (Glendon 1991), these non-legal discourses shape workers' legal consciousness and how they think about the role of law in workplace conflicts. To the extent that cultural discourses about work construct not only work, but also gender and disability, these discourses help maintain and recreate inequalities in the workplace by shaping cognition and action to be consistent with existing social structure.

Nevertheless, new civil rights laws give rise to their own cultural meanings, and actors may draw on law as a resource to reinterpret long-standing social relationships. In this way, law provides a counter-hegemonic discourse that both challenges and reveals the mutually constitutive relationships among work, gender, and disability (Hunt 1993). For example, when workers reference rights to refute the slacker discourse and to discourage co-workers from harassing workers on leave, they undermine the implicit constitutive relationship between work and disability. Similarly, when workers draw on law to justify their absence from work to care for family members, they envision a workplace in which the roles of breadwinner and caretaker are not fundamentally incompatible.

Although legal rights may not be the dominant normative system in workplace negotiations over leave, legal entitlements help shape workers' legal consciousness to make the contradictions in their circumstances more visible. They reveal cracks in the hegemonic institution of work, and allow workers to question the idea that penalties for leave are natural and normal. Certainly pervasive practices and norms can constrain social change by creating resistance to rights, and one important question for future research is what factors, such as power, affect which discourses are disseminated and which are silenced. Nevertheless, legal rights provide a source of cultural meaning through which work can be restructured, reinterpreted, and reimagined to be consistent with family and medical leave.

References

Berger, Peter L., and Thomas Luckman (1967) *The Social Construction of Reality*. New York: Anchor Books.

Bourdieu, Pierre (1977) *Outline of a Theory of Practice*. Cambridge: Cambridge University Press.

Commission on Leave (1996) "A Workable Balance: Report to Congress on Family and Medical Leave Policies." Washington DC: Commission on Family and Medical Leave.

Drimmer, Jonathan C. (1993) "Cripples, Overcomers, and Civil Rights: Tracing the Evoluion of Federal Legislation and Social Policy for People with Disabilities." *UCLA Law Review* 40:1341–1410.

Edelman, Lauren B., Howard S. Erlanger, and John Lande (1993) "Internal Dispute Resolution: The Transformation of Civil Rights in the Workplace." *Law & Society Review* 27:497–534.

Ellickson, Robert C. (1991) *Order Without Law: How Neighbors Settle Disputes*. Cambridge: Harvard University Press.

Engel, David M. and Frank W. Munger (1996) "Rights, Remembrance, and the Reconciliation of Difference." *Law and Society Review* 30:7–53.

Engel, David (1998) "How Does Law Matter in the Constitution of Legal Consciousness?" in *How Does Law Matter?*, edited by Bryant G. Garth and Austin Sarat. Chicago: Northwestern University Press/American Bar Foundation.

Ewick, Patricia and Susan Silbey (1992) "Conformity, Contestation, and Resistance: An Account of Legal Consciousness." *New England Law Review* 26:731–749.

Ewick, Patricia, and Susan S. Silbey (1995) "Subversive Stories and Hegemonic Tales: Toward a Sociology of Narrative." *Law and Society Review* 29:197–226.

——. (1998) *The Common Place of Law: Stories from Everyday Life*. Chicago: University of Chicago Press.

Felstiner, William L.F., Richard L. Abel, and Austin Sarat (1981) "The Emergence and Transformation of Disputes: Naming, Blaming, Claiming ..." *Law and Society Review* 15:631–654.

Folbre, Nancy (1991) "The Unproductive Housewife: Her Evolution in Nineteenth-Century Economic Thought." *Signs* 16:463–484.

Foner, Eric (1995) *Free Soil, Free Labor, Free Men: The Ideology of the Republican Party before the Civil War.* New York: Oxford University Press.

Frank, Meryl, and Robyn Lipner (1988) "History of Maternity Leave in Europe and the United States." pp. 3–22 in *The Parental Leave Crisis: Toward a National Policy*, edited by Edward F. Zigler and Meryl Frank. New Haven: Yale University Press.

Fraser, Nancy, and Linda Gordon (1994) "A Genealogy of Dependency: Tracing a Keyword of the U.S. Welfare State." *Signs* 19:309–336.

Fried, Mindy (1998) *Taking Time: Parental Leave Policy and Corporate Culture*. Philadelphia. PA: Temple University Press.

Gerstel, Naomi, and Katherine McGonagle (1999) "Job Leaves and the Limits of the Family and Medical Leave Act: The Effects of Gender, Race and Family." *Work and Occupations* 26:510–534.

Giddens, Anthony (1984) *The Constitution of Society*. Berkeley: Univeristy of California Press.

Glendon, Mary Ann (1991) *Rights Talk: The Impoverishment of Political Discourse*. New York: Free Press.

Glenn, Evelyn Nakano (2002) *Unequal Freedom: How Race and Gender Shaped American Citizenship and Labor.* Cambridge, MA: Harvard University Press.

Heimer, Carol A. (1999) "Competing Institutions: Law, Medicine, and Family in Neonatal Intensive Care." *Law and Society Review* 33:17–66.

Hirsch, Susan F. (1993) "Subjects in Spite of Themselves: Legal Consciousness among Working-Class New Englanders." *Law and Social Inquiry* 17:839–858.

Hochschild, Arlie (1997) *The Time Bind: When Work Becomes Home and Home Becomes Work*. New York: Metropolitan Books.

Hunt, Alan (1993) *Explorations in Law and Society*. New York: Routledge.

Kerber, Linda (1998) *No Constitutional Right to be Ladies: Women and the Obligations of Citizenship*. New York: Hill and Wang.

Krieger, Linda (2000) "Afterword: Socio-Legal Backlash." *Berkeley Journal of Employment and Labor Law* 21:475–519.

Lempert, Richard (1976) "Mobilizing Private Law: An Introductory Essay." *Law and Society Review* 2:173–189.

———. (1998) "A Resource Theory of the Criminal Law: Exploring When it Matters." pp. 227–247 in *How Does Law Matter*, edited by Bryant G. Garth, and Austin Sarat. Evanston, IL: Northwestern University Press.

Lipset, Seymour Martin (1996) *American Exceptionalism: A Double-Edged Sword.* New York: W.W. Norton & Co.

Macaulay, Stewart (1963) "Non-Contractual Relations in Business: A Preliminary Study." *American Sociological Review* 28:55–68.

MacKinnon, Catharine A. (1989) *Toward a Feminist Theory of the State.* Cambridge: Harvard University Press.

McCann, Michael (1994) *Rights at Work: Pay Equity Reform and the Politics of Legal Mobilization.* Chicago: University of Chicago Press.

McEvoy, Arthur (1998) "Freedom of Contract, Labor, and the Administrative State." pp. 198–235 in *The State and Freedom of Contract*, edited by H.N. Scheiber. Stanford: Stanford University Press.

Merry, Sally Engle (1990) *Getting Justice and Getting Even: Legal Consciousness Among Working-Class Americans.* Chicago: Chicago University Press.

Montgomery, David (1987) *The Fall of the House of Labor: The Workplace, The State and American Labor Activism, 1865–1925.* Cambridge: Cambridge University Press.

Nielsen, Laura Beth (2000) "Situating Legal Consciousness: Experiences and Attitudes of Ordinary Citizens about Law and Street Harassment." *Law and Society Review* 34:1055.

Okin, Susan Muller (1989) *Justice, Gender and the Family.* New York: Basic Books, Inc.

Oliver, Michael (1990) *The Politics of Disablement: A Sociological Approach.* New York: St. Martin's Press.

Pateman, Carole (1988) *The Sexual Contract.* Stanford: Stanford University Press.

Sarat, Austin (1990) "The Law is All Over: Power, Resistance and the Legal Consciousness of the Welfare Poor." *Yale Journal of Law and the Humanities* 2:343–379.

Sarat, Austin, and Thomas S. Kearns (1993) "Beyond the Great Divide: Forms of Legal Scholarship and Everyday Life." in *Law in Everyday Life*, edited by Austin Sarat and Thomas R. Kearns. Ann Arbor: University of Michigan Press.

Scheingold, Stuart A. (1974) *The Politics of Rights.* New Haven: Yale University Press.

Schor, Juliet B. (1992) *The Overworked American: The Unexpected Decline of Leisure.* New York: Basic Books.

Scott, W. Richard (1995) *Institutions and Organizations.* Thousand Oaks: Sage Publications.

Sewell, William H. (1992) "A Theory of Structure: Duality, Agency, and Transformation." *American Journal of Sociology* 98:1.

Shklar, Judith (1991) *American Citizenship: The Quest for Inclusion.* Cambridge, MA: Harvard University Press.

Silbey, Susan (2001) "Legal Culture and Legal Consciousness." pp. 8623–8629 in *International Encyclopedia of the Social and Behavioral Sciences*, edited by Neil J. Smelser and Paul B. Bates. Amsterdam: Elsevier.

Stone, Deborah (1984) "Causal Stories and the Formation of Policy Agendas." *Political Science Quarterly* 104:281–300.

Swidler, Ann. (1986) "Culture in Action: Symbols and Strategies." *American Sociological Review* 51:273–286.

Thompson, E.P. (1967) "Time, Work-discipline, and Industrial Capitalism." *Past and Present* 38:56–97.

Weber, Max (1930) *The Protestant Ethic and the Spirit of Capitalism.* London: Unwin Hyman.

Williams, Joan (2000) *Unbending Gender: Why Families and Work Conflict and What to Do About It.* Oxford: Oxford University Press.

Chapter 4

LGBT Family Rights, Legal Consciousness, and the Dilemma of Difference

KIMBERLY D. RICHMAN

In 2003, same-sex relationships in the United States experienced some of the most significant legal changes in recent memory. Following on the heels of Vermont and California's unprecedented creation of civil unions and domestic partnerships to impart marriage-like family rights and responsibilities in same-sex relationships, the Supreme Court in June 2003 overturned the last vestige of criminal law prohibiting same-sex sexual activity in *Lawrence v. Texas*, ruling that such sodomy statutes constituted discrimination against homosexuals. Five months later, relying explicitly on the precedent set in *Lawrence*, the Massachusetts Supreme Court ruled in *Goodridge v. Department of Public Health* that the civil institution of marriage must be made equally available to homosexual and heterosexual couples. *Goodridge* confirmed the worst fears of those who were not supportive of the *Lawrence* decision. But for others, both were long-overdue formal affirmations of families and relationships that they had personally and culturally experienced as "real" for decades.

This cultural-legal "lag" is emblematic of one of the most persistent questions in sociolegal research – what exactly is the relationship between legal and social, cultural, and personal understandings of identity, meaning, and change? After decades of dispute over the utility of legal "rights" (Scheingold 1974; Tushnet 1984) and the plausibility of law as an impetus of social change (Rosenberg 1991), a growing group of scholars have embraced an approach that views social and legal meanings as mutually constitutive, and privileges ordinary peoples' experiences of law in their daily lives (McCann 1994; Kostiner, Nielsen, and Fleury-Steiner, this volume). The constitutive approach bears explicitly on traditional sociolegal scholarship regarding civil rights and marginalized social groups, such as those discussed in this volume, by disrupting the binary between "rights bearer" and "rights giver". This approach is particularly apropos in the context of gay and lesbian family rights, where personal and legal definitions and realities long have been at odds.

This chapter provides a brief legal and social background, summarizing historical and recent developments in gay rights, as they relate specifically to family and family law. I will then begin the analytical section of the chapter with a discussion of lesbian, gay, bisexual and transgender (hereafter LGBT) parents' and advocates' views of law – in general and in the custody context – and its relationship to social change and the family. This will be followed by an exploration of the differences between LGBT families' visions of themselves and how they are defined and portrayed in law. I will then analyze two conflicts emergent in the data. The first is the conflict between legal strategy and ideological purity and the second is the issue of division and debate *among* LGBT parents and activists about their own positions and rights vis-à-vis each other and the law. I conclude with a synthesis of these analytical issues, arguing that the variations in LGBT parents' legal consciousness, rights-based aspirations, and life circumstances revealed here reflect a need for nuanced constitutive analyses of gay family rights, and a return to the feminist jurisprudence concept of the "dilemma of difference".

This chapter is based on a set of 36 interviews with LGBT parents, attorneys and advocates involved in child custody or adoption cases, as well as family court judges, from across the United States.[1] The interviews, ranging from 40 minutes to 2 hours and 15 minutes, were conducted from January to July of 2002. Each of the parents was either currently or previously had been a litigant in a child custody or adoption case, most of which were appealed or are in the process of being appealed. The attorneys, with few exceptions, were either affiliated with a major gay rights organization or in practices specializing in gay rights and family law issues. In addition, many of the attorneys were themselves gay or lesbian parents. Some of the family court judges interviewed had also either previously worked as an attorney representing LGBT parents or were otherwise involved in LGBT issues.

The Legal and Social Backdrop: LGBT Families Within and Without the Law

It is no longer novel, nor disputed, to note that gay and lesbian-headed families have existed long before they were ever formally recognized in law (Benkov 1994; Dalton and Bielby 2000; Stein 1997). As early as the late 1970s, custody and adoption issues were coming to the forefront of the gay rights movement, and legal scholars were taking note (Hunter and Polikoff 1976; Hitchens and Price 1978–79). Not only were lesbian mothers being deprived of custody of their children from former heterosexual marriages, but LGBT-headed families created by adoption and advances in reproductive technology were growing in number – though entirely unprotected or recognized in any legal sense. With the "gayby boom"[2] of the 1980s and 1990s, awareness of how the lack of legal recognition of same sex relationship could affect LGBT-headed families came to a head; and the events of September 11 2001 brought it to an urgent crescendo. The movement for same-sex civil unions, already in place in Vermont, became galvanized by the tragedies endured by surviving same-sex partners in the 9/11 attacks and the infamous "dog mauling" case of Diane Whipple in San Francisco, and similar statutes were soon passed in California – Assembly Bill 25 in 2002 and Assembly Bill 205 in 2003 (Gledhill 2003).

In most jurisdictions the easiest and most sound way to form a family for gay and lesbian parents is through these domestic partnerships which are functionally equivalent to marriage in most ways though not all. And, but for a liberal construction

---

[1] Interviewees were recruited via a combination of snowball and purposive sampling, and came from New York, Illinois, Ohio, Tennessee, Washington DC, and several counties in Northern and Southern California.

[2] The term "gayby boom" is used commonly to refer to the rapid increase in lesbian and gay-headed families, particularly those who conceived via donor insemination or adopted, in the 1980s and 1990s.

by some judges of the states' adoption statutes, domestic partnership would, in the vast majority of states, be the only secure way to assure two members of the same gender legal parental rights.[3] While not uniformly supported even by those within the gay rights movement, as will be discussed further below, such arrangements seemed to best represent public consciousness about the position of lesbians and gay men in American society: deserving of some civil rights and protections, but still separate from the mainstream institutions of marriage and family.

Yet it was the debate over same-sex *marriage* that came to occupy public consciousness about gay rights more than any other issue in the post-*Lawrence* era. First put on the national agenda in the 1990s following the decision of a Hawaii appeals court to legalize same-sex marriage in the case of *Baehr v. Lewin* (1993), the issue seemed to be all but shut down after the Federal government responded with the Defense of Marriage Act, as did several state legislatures with similar statutes defining marriage as consisting only of a man and woman. Though the majority opinion in the *Lawrence* sodomy law decision made no explicit or implicit reference to same-sex marriage, the public attention immediately shifted to this issue was enough to induce whiplash. *Newsweek* wasted no time in turning out an issue displaying a lesbian couple on the front, and emblazoned with the headline: IS GAY MARRIAGE NEXT?

Since then – and particularly in the wake of the Massachusetts Supreme Judicial Court's legalization of same-sex marriage and San Francisco's decision to issue same sex marriage licenses – politicians, activists, and commentators have been put in the position of having to declare themselves for or against, while gay rights organizations have publicly praised the long-overdue formal legal recognition of their already extant families and relationships. Ironically, this dynamic has forced the LGBT community, advocates, and individuals into supporting and defending an institution and accompanying legal trend that has not been uniformly supported within the movement. While few LGBT activists or scholars would vociferously condemn the decision in *Goodridge* or like legal developments, they have been far from unanimous in the desire to achieve entrance into the historically problematic institution of marriage (Ettelbrick 1989; Polikoff 1993; Sherman 1992).

Thus, same-sex marriage is one very visible example not only of how official legal institutions and definitions differ from the lived reality of gay and lesbian partners, parents and family members – but also that variations in legal consciousness and experience of "rights" exist even *within* the LGBT community. What the role of law should be more generally in defining LGBT relationships and families is similarly debated. It is frequently pointed out that gay men and lesbians had been forming

---

[3] In 2002, the California case of *Sharon S. v. Annette F.* (2002) illustrated the importance of such domestic partnership laws when an appeals court nullified the second parent adoption of a lesbian non-biological mother who split from her partner before the adoption was finalized. The ruling suggested that such adoptions were illegal except where the parents had formally registered as domestic partners with the state under AB25. This precedent was later overruled by the California Supreme Court in 2003, but it remains unclear whether such adoptions will remain possible in the future, in the absence of a domestic partnership. Vermont's adoption law is different in that it was decided before the passage of civil unions, and therefore can exist outside of them. Still, because of the complexity and number of family laws related to marriage, domestic partnerships and marriage remain the easiest way to secure all of these rights at once.

families *without* the law for decades before they ever came to the attention of the courts in significant numbers (Nardi 1997; Weston 1991). While understanding the practical and perhaps even symbolic importance of securing legal rights and protections for their families and selves, gay men and lesbians are well aware of the law's historical efforts to not only restrain and exclude them, but to actually do violence to them and their families.

Beginning with the sanction of execution in colonial times for the crime of homosexuality, and more recently with affirmative exclusions such as the proposal of a Constitutional Amendment to permanently exclude same-sex couples from the institution of marriage and some states' policies prohibiting adoption by gay men or lesbians,[4] LGBT parents and others well understand their position "against" or at least "outside of" the law (Ewick and Silbey 1998). Yet this history has done little to slow the progress of demands by the LGBT movement to be included and protected by legal institutions (Eskridge 1999). It has, however, bred some ambivalence with regard to law's position vis-à-vis sexual orientation, politics, culture, and the direction of the movement. Are these recent legal changes indicative of – or even responsible for – an impending shift in the social position of LGBT families, either as a reflection of social fact and change, or a catalyst for this change? Or is law only belatedly reacting to and co-opting what was already culturally present?

Relationships in LGBT Legal Consciousness: A Constitutive Approach

As mentioned previously, sociolegal scholars have long concerned themselves with the chicken-egg question in regard to the relationship between sociocultural and legal consciousness and change (Rosenberg 1991; West 1998). Though the constitutive perspective adopted by this volume makes a point of not assuming a causal or uni-directional answer to this question, many of my respondents found themselves devoting considerable time to it as they considered the role of law in their lives, particularly with regard to gay rights and family. One New York-based attorney, who had previously headed several national gay family rights organizations and is herself a lesbian mother, felt that legal concepts are so deeply embedded in our culture that people think rights exist even when they do not:

> ... the way our law and our culture work together, I think we have such a concept in our culture thanks to the civil rights movement and the women's movement of a quality that it almost never occurs to people that gay and lesbian people wouldn't be in that, whether they like it or not (Interview 24).

Another attorney, activist, and lesbian mother from San Francisco had more of a reciprocal sense of the relationship: "Actually both move together at different points in time, there will be a push from a case, and at another point in time, there'll be a push from some other cultural event." Yet, she also emphasized the extent to which

---

[4] Only Florida, Mississippi and Utah continue to explicitly prohibit gay and lesbian adults from adopting children, but many more either prohibit or have not yet allowed second parent adoptions by the non-biological parent in a same-sex relationship.

legal happenings can affect public (or even personal) consciousness, especially in particularly egregious cases:

I think that there's no doubt that to some degree it is the cases that move public opinion, especially in high-profile cases. I mean, the case of Mary Ward in Florida [*Ward v. Ward* (1996) in which a lesbian mother lost custody of her children to her convicted-murderer ex-husband] I mean, people were just outraged, shocked, they couldn't believe that a convicted murderer could get custody over a lesbian, and that was her only "offense" ... And it provided the perfect example of the perfect way to educate folks around how entrenched homophobia is. And I think there was some movement attitudinally, from folks who were aware of the case, to stop and question their own biases about, wow, this is just going too far (Interview 21).

A very common topic, among parents, attorneys, and judges alike, was the extent to which the law seems to lag behind modern culture, standards of acceptability, and notions of family. One supervising family court judge in Southern California commented, "The courts are very, kind of, behind a little bit in terms of what the social values are that need to be applied to the facts of the case." In specific regard to lesbian-headed families initiated via reproductive technology, she added, "The court system is a couple of steps behind it at every step of the way" (Interview 12).

Many attorneys and activists, in particular, had a perception of this lag by virtue of their lengthy involvement in the issue; one, who litigated some of the first high-profile cases involving the break-up of LGBT-headed families, commented on the early days: I'm not saying gay people weren't having kids, they were ... But the courts were such an unfriendly place to be – it would not have occurred to you to go to the court, the court, which basically said no gay people should have their children (Interview 30). Others, particularly those LGBT parents who had lost custody of their children, felt the lag even presently; one such mother from Ohio exclaimed,

My biggest issue here is that we live in a society that has a legal system that is supposed to give us justice for wrongdoings ... I can't comprehend that we live in America and we're told, there is no remedy for this wrong. There is no way to right this wrong. There is no one that will even listen to it. How can that be? How can we live in a society that has the kind of court system and judicial system that we have and there is not to be somewhere that you can go to have a right remedied? (Interview 27)

Mothers in the Midwest and South were most likely to have similar interpretations of the law's position toward gay parents; one mother from Tennessee commented, "Why should a lesbian mother be able to keep a child, say in California, but I can't keep mine, in Tennessee? We all live in the United States. What's wrong with this picture?!" (Interview 34). Mothers in same-sex parenting dyads were also apt to bring up the court's narrow and antiquated interpretation of how families are comprised:

... [T]he fact that we no longer live in a society of nuclear families, the court system has to change to address that. They have to change to address the fact that there are thousands of children ... that have same-sex parents or that have grandparents raising them. The court system ... has not been willing, uniformly, to look at that as a new standard (Interview 27).

Some parents and attorneys brought cases "precisely to broaden the legal concept of parent", as one attorney stated (Interview 24). Speaking of the first case in which a non-biological mother from a lesbian parenting dyad challenged the biological mother for custody, the attorney who tried the case commented, "... you could hear a pin drop in the court ... It was just so bizarre, nobody was really talking about that then ... not in any public way ... Really, it's more like bringing it out as a little enclave of the lesbian community, such as it was at that point" (Interview 24). One mother, at least, recognized a change in the last ten years as a result of this case and others like it:

> Clearly, all across the nation, courts are looking at families and saying, you know, families don't just consist of a married man and woman who decide to biologically have children. We're into a world where children are brought to fruition in [a number of ways]. We have donor insemination, we have *in vitro* fertilization, we have adoption ... We simply do not live in that narrow, constricted viewpoint of what makes up a family (Interview 27).

Thus, many LGBT parents felt that their long-standing reality would only become "mainstream" after entering the legal realm – thus forcing cultural change and awareness. As one lesbian mother and attorney summed up, "... [T]hose things always go hand in hand, the law almost always follows the culture and in some ways [when] we bring these cases, we try to put the law out in front as a way of forced succession and hopefully forcing of the cultural change or reaction" (Interview 24). Another mother from a same-sex parenting dyad commented on the judiciary's role in "educating our politicians to understand that people's mindset is no longer staid on the fact that a child has to have a mother and a father" (Interview 27).

Parents and advocates also felt that favorable laws and judicial decisions helped to define or increase cultural awareness of their families and their rights by allowing LGBT families and parents to be more visible, or "out". As an attorney and mother from New York commented,

> I think that what happens is the legal rulings have a lot to do with how comfortable lesbians and gay men feel about being out and really structuring their families in ways of really being out about who their families are. I think they make choices that are sometimes different and more visible (Interview 24).

Indeed, a number of parents commented on their position vis-à-vis the courts and the likelihood of their feeling "safe" as families and in custody matters. As one California judge, who is also a lesbian mother and was formerly an attorney for LGBT parents, commented, "It takes a lot of courage and effort on the part of lesbian and gay men to get custody of their kids, you have to really love your kids a lot, because they are put through such hell" (Interview 6). These families and others could be said, as one judge put it, to be "operating in the shadow of the law" – anticipating its power and effects on society and acting accordingly (Interview 12). One mother, in fact, was chastised by the court in her custody trial "for not showing love and affection [with her partner] in front of [her daughter]" – which came as a surprise since she and her partner specifically avoided being affectionate for fear this would be held against her in court (Interview 34).

Ultimately, most interviewees felt that it was not only likely but *necessary* that the law follow from sociocultural changes and understandings of family and sexuality. This reactivity was even more important, they reasoned, in family law as compared to other areas of law because of its fact-intensive nature and its intensely cultural subject matter. As one very experienced judge from California stated, "[There is a] very distinct evolution in the legal process to accommodate changes of view, and it's always occurring" (Interview 2). An attorney and mother from New York asserted, even more adamantly,

> I think in family law it's absolutely needed [a sense of social change] and I think a lot of judges, even if they don't state it, that's the basis on which they're making decisions. I mean … if there's any group of judges who have to be more aware of changes, in, not even in social mores but just in the social structure of the family, it's judges looking at family law cases (Interview 24).

Yet inevitably, this was not uniformly the case. In many situations, parents and attorneys found themselves confronting a system of law that was completely out of synch with their own reality.

A Separate Reality: LGBT Families' Vision versus the Law's Vision

One of the guiding themes in this volume and in the study of legal consciousness more generally is that legal sources, opinions, and official actors may often differ substantially in their depiction of the subjects of civil rights, or citizens, from how the citizens themselves view their personhood, position, and legality (Espeland 1994; Merry 1990). Espeland, for example, discusses how lawmakers acting on behalf of a Native American group would often – in the process of garnering rights for them – depict them in ways that were contrary to their self-image (1994). The same is true in the context of LGBT families – the sexual and parental identities attributed (or denied) to LGBT parents are often contrary to the identities claimed by the individuals themselves (Richman 2002).

In some situations, this departure took the form of emphasizing traits that the parents themselves did not see as dominant to their identity. One mother from Tennessee, whose custody was revoked on the basis of her lesbianism, commented, "I think the court thought they were protecting [her child] from a gay mother – how awful! But, if they had listened to all the facts in the proceedings, the part about being gay was so little compared to all my other qualities" (Interview 34). She went on to say:

> The bond my daughter and I had meant nothing … The fact that my daughter did not want to leave her mother meant nothing. Her father's terrible track record meant nothing. All that mattered was that I was a lesbian and he was straight … [The daughter] was forgotten … The only thing that was important was that I was gay.

In this situation the mother experienced a disconnect between her reality and the law's depiction of her not because the law said she was something that she was not, but because it essentialized one part of her personhood – her homosexuality – in a way that was not true to her experience. This was one example of how individuals' own consciousness could differ markedly from their official position in law.

This tendency was even more pronounced when the individuals in question were part of a family of non-traditional origins (for example, a same-sex couple who had a child via donor insemination). In one such case, two lesbian mothers in New York were challenged by their sperm donor for paternity rights – despite the fact that he had agreed in advance to an arrangement that did not involve any rights or recognition of him as a father, and that he had had virtually nothing to do with the child's life up to that point. The two mothers said they were "shocked" when they heard of the lawsuit (Interview 36). What was more shocking to them was the way that he was presented and interpreted in court as a "divorced father", and how the case was represented as an "old-fashioned father's rights case", since this was completely divergent from the lived day-to-day reality of their family. One attorney who consulted on the case commented:

> [T]he majority [decision in the appellate court] just completely reframed the family. Just saw the family of a child and a mother and a father and a mother's partner whose presence didn't take away at all from the fact that the child had a father ... I think we see that in a lot of the sperm donor cases that courts are so anxious for children to have fathers that they are going to name this guy a father if there is any way they can do it (Interview 26).

At the same time, the non-biological mother was not recognized as a parent during the proceedings and was actually excluded from the courtroom for much of it.

Other cases further exemplified how the non-biological parent in a same-sex couple must struggle to be recognized on the basis of something other than biology or marriage. In several cases, lesbian couples who had conceived via donors and raised a family, then broke up, ended up in court where the non-biological mother sought custody or visitation with the child(ren). In the vast majority of these cases, the non-biological parent had not been allowed by the courts previously to formally adopt the child, leaving them with virtually no legal link to the children they had raised. One lesbian activist and attorney from California who had been involved in several such cases commented that the courts' attitude toward the non-biological parent was:

> [W]e're not even going to hear from you. And it doesn't matter if you've been parenting this child, even as the primary caretaker for five, six, seven years; it doesn't matter if this child looks at his family and says, "I have two moms" and draws the whole picture ... You could cut this person out of his life forever based on these legal formalisms about whether or not she's got an adoption decree and was the biological parent.

A non-biological mother who had experienced this agreed:

> [T]o me, certainly, the definition of parenthood goes way beyond some legal wording or legal documentation. I think if you ask anyone, if you just walked up to anyone on the street and said, "what makes a parent?" They would tell you, "well, it's a person who loves a child, who cares for a child," it doesn't even have to be the person who brought the child into the world (Interview 27).

This mother went so far as to try to make the court issue an order demanding that she pay child support, because, as a parent, she felt "that was an obligation of mine." Previous efforts she had made to provide such support directly to the child were rebuffed by the biological mother, who by the time of the court date had completely cut off contact between the child and the non-biological mother. Such continued efforts were important to this mother on both a symbolic and a practical level: she wanted her son to be well provided for, but it was also a way to legally recognize her as a parental figure.

In general, there was strong support from parents, attorneys, and even several judges that a family should, in fact, be defined legally according to how its members define it – and in particular, the court should honor a child's perception of who his or her parent or parents are. One attorney and lesbian mother from California asserted, "If the child is raised by two people who the child considers his or her parents, then it behooves the law to consider them similarly if they are going to serve the child's best interest ..." (Interview 22). Another attorney and lesbian mother agreed:

> Instead of looking at the legal formulas of did this person have an adoption decree, was this person a biological parent, which is never going to be the case, that both of us are, in a lesbian or gay relationship – you look at the functional life of the family. Does this child think she has two moms? Did they hold this child out as a child of both of theirs? Were they both treated as parents? Did the school treat them both as parents? Did they both act like parents and did they treat their family life as if they were both parents caring for this child? If so, then she is a parent (Interview 21).

In the New York sperm donor case described above, the trial court initially recognized the family as complete without the sperm donor, before being overturned on appeal. An attorney from Washington D.C. who consulted on the case explained,

> [T]he trial court really looked at all of these people and said, "this is a child who has two mothers and a sister. She also has this man in her life who she knows gave sperm for her birth and who she even sometimes refers to as her dad. But she doesn't consider him a father, a parent, you know, the way some other child might. She's really clear. Her family is her two mothers and her sister. This guy is somebody outside that family unit who has some importance to her, but not as a parent" ... I think it was kind of a high-water mark for a judge, being able to grasp the reality of a particularly constructed family for a child (Interview 26).

She added more generally, "[there's a need for] recognition of more complex family structures than what the courts see. To recognize it by not superimposing one idea of family on every child they see, but rather seeing what that family looks like from the child's point of view."

Yet this was not the approach taken in the appeals court in this case. The two mothers explained that they had purposely chosen a donor in a different part of the country and made explicit the fact that the donor would not be recognized as a father – but that this was not recognized in the court proceeding, nor was their family form:

> The kids [the subject of the dispute and her sister by a different donor] were asked to justify their family ... [The court-appointed psychologist asked] "what makes them your mother?"

This is confusing for kids. They hated it, hated him, were frightened that [the child] would be taken away ... It was scary that they [the court] could make him a parent (Interview 36).

The child herself later commented, "It's such a crazy idea because I had parents. I had my mothers and I didn't need another person." The parents commented that generally they "don't want the court manufacturing case by case who is a family and who isn't", as it did in their case. The Washington D.C. attorney added, "The appellate [court] ... said, 'this child just looks like a child of divorce to us. It looks like a mother and a father who weren't married to each other, but have this child together ... They [the child and donor] have a fond relationship. He's a father'." The divergence between the child's perception and lived experience on the one hand, and the court's view of the family on the other, illustrates the stark disjuncture that can exist between the legal and the personal experience of family and rights.

This was also the case for a non-biological mother in California who was denied any access to her daughters after splitting from her partner, the girls' biological mother. Though the elder child was born prior to the relationship, the younger daughter was conceived via donor insemination after a joint decision by the couple to have her, and carried the non-biological mother's last name. The mother commented, "The children call me 'mom'. For [the younger daughter's] entire life she has known me as her mother" (Interview 28). She introduced testimony and evidence at her trial from day care workers, teachers, tax documents and wills, which all positioned her as a mother to the children. During the separation, the children wrote letters to her, in fact, calling her "Mom" and saying they wished they could be back together as a family. Notwithstanding these pleas, the court denied that her relationship with the children was that of a parent, and she was never again permitted to have contact with them.

In some situations, parents' representation in court was not consistent with their own images of their family because a particular contrary portrait was more functionally expedient for the legal purposes at hand. For example, it is common for non-biological parents to seek the right to adopt their children using what is called the "step-parent exception" rule – analogizing them to step-parents even though no marriage can exist between themselves and their partner. The "step-parent exception" rule is a legal rule whereby the statutory assumption that a child can only have one parent of either gender is circumvented by the claim that a parent's second spouse (the step-parent) has acted in significant parenting capacity and deserves the right to adopt. At the time when same-sex second parent adoptions began coming to court, this was the most relevant legal precedent on which to draw. As one of the first attorneys to work in this area of law commented, "In second parent adoptions, I've kind of thought that whatever theory looks like it will be best in terms of how that particular statute is written and the predilection of those judges in other cases ought to fly. If the step-parent analogy works that's fine" (Interview 26).

However, in terms of the families' lived experience, it was a problematic analogy. One attorney and lesbian mom from New York explained that the adoptive parents in these situations,

... were different from stepparents in that they had together decided to have the child in the first place, which seemed like a semantic difference, but ... when you represent people at this level, you want to make sure you are representing the population in the way that you want them understood (Interview 24).

Indeed, this distinction is important not only in the fact that gay parents cannot legally marry each other, but also in that the title "step-parent" assumes a person who entered the family at a later date via marriage – not someone who was involved in the family from the beginning and was part of the affirmative decision to have a child.

In another case, where two men in New Jersey decided to adopt a child together, state law did not allow them to adopt jointly, so the state arbitrarily chose one of the fathers as the "official" adoptive parent. As it happened, the father that the state chose was not the father that the couple decided would act as primary caretaker – and in fact, the other parent, who would have no parental rights under the court's scheme, had already quit his job in order to stay home with the child. The attorney who represented the two men explained,

New Jersey just picked one of the two of them to be the [adoptive] parent and picked [the other father], not the person who was staying home, because [he] doesn't have an income. And so, for their paper work, they wanted the adoptive parent to have an income ... A lot of it was the symbolism of why can't this couple adopt together ... (Interview 23).

While the couple was eventually allowed to jointly adopt after a protracted legal battle, the court's orientation to them as parents stood in stark contrast to their own self-image as a family.

Expediency versus Ideology: Legal Consciousness about Strategy and Truth

These last scenarios represented situations in which an ostensibly positive legal outcome (permitting the adoptions at all) could be attained at the cost of a positive symbolic outcome for LGBT parents – where they were forced into legal roles that did not represent their reality. This tension was raised multiple times with LGBT parents and their attorneys. Is it best to sacrifice their powers of self-definition and self-determination in the name of winning a positive legal outcome, or must they remain true to their ideologies and lived experiences no matter what the legal cost? Often this choice between strategy and being true to oneself came at the moment of deciding whether to pursue a case in court against improbable odds, or whether to appeal an adverse trial court decision at the risk of setting a precedent that could have a negative impact on the LGBT community more broadly. As one mother in Ohio recounted,

I found that most attorneys in [the county] and in the state of Ohio were not even willing to look at the case because they knew that there was no chance of winning. No one had ever done this in the state of Ohio and most of them were not willing to take on a case that they knew they were going to lose ... It was made very clear to me that nothing like this [involving custodial rights for a non-biological lesbian mother] had ever been tried before, that I was going to wind up spending an awful lot of money, an awful lot of time, and an awful lot of tears fighting something that inevitably I would lose anyway. And I told them all, that's not the point, if I don't try, that's the real loss ... [I]n the history of the state of Ohio no one had ever tried to do this before and I found that nauseating, to tell you the truth. I mean, that no one was willing to try and fight this, even if they thought that they were gonna lose (Interview 27).

One attorney from New York, who worked on several such cases during the early years of the "gayby boom", commented, "we were actually sort of having to communicate to people, whoa, hold on ... don't rush to court with this, the court is not a friendly place to go" (Interview 30). Another attorney from Illinois agreed, "I often think that these decisions may be better off outside of an adversarial court process and resolved through alternative dispute resolution" (Interview 29).

Likewise, attorneys often found themselves in the difficult role of encouraging their clients not to appeal such losses because of well-founded fears of setting a negative precedent that would in turn affect future cases. One, who was involved in several high-profile cases over her tenure as legal director of a national gay rights organization, commented on this problem: "They [LGBT parents] don't understand it [the strategy of not pursuing an appeal] and also ... when someone is fighting for custody of their children, you don't feel as comfortable saying, 'don't pursue this for the good of others'." (Interview 30). Another attorney from Washington DC added,

> I've been part of those discussions with clients who have lost, who have to make a decision whether to appeal, who really don't want to make it bad for everybody ... that's a common conversation to have ... [T]he national organizations I think have often wished they could control all of the litigation on all gay rights issues, so that the right cases went to the right places at the right time. But ... nobody really has that control (Interview 26).

One attorney also explained that, in some situations, this strategy of non-pursuance could end up advantaging the individual litigant as well, to some extent:

> ... a lot of times what you were faced with was parents who were like, 'well if I continue the litigation now, that gives the other party a sort of interest in not letting me have visitation'. A lot of times [attorneys] have the feeling that actually stopping the litigation process was more likely to gain some resolution (Interview 30).

There were, of course, a number of other ways in which parents were faced with strategic decisions that were legally expedient but personally damaging or contrary. Often they were forced to settle for lesser contact with their children to avoid the risk of not getting *any* visitation. In many cases, it took the form of sacrificing their own romantic relationships – either remaining celibate or not living with their partner in order to help their custody case. One mother from Tennessee commented early on in the legal process, "I am fighting just to be able to see my child. I may have to deal with never having her in [my hometown]. If I am able to have her here, I might have to change my life to exclude my partner and friends in [my daughter's] presence." After the trial she explained, "Even after we owned a home together [my partner] had to leave every night when [my daughter] was home" (Interview 34). In other cases – particularly those involving non-biological lesbian mothers attempting to gain joint custody or visitation rights after a split with their partner – the mothers were encouraged to adopt a strategy of claiming their former partner was an unfit parent in order to gain sole custody. This did not resonate well with many such mothers whose real goal was to allow their children to maintain a relationship with *both* parents. One such mother from Ohio explained,

... [I]n the court proceedings at one point, one of the judges said to me, "why don't you try for full because we would be able to hear the case if you were trying for sole custody, claiming that she [the biological mother] was not a fit parent." And I said, "well, first of all, that would be a lie, I don't think she's an unfit parent. And I said secondly, I would be doing no better for [her son] if I tried to take him away from her than her trying to take him away from me. That is not the point. I'm trying to what's in the best interest of my son here and that is to allow him access to the people that love him and care about him and brought him into the world" ... (Interview 27).

Attorneys specializing in LGBT custody had some other notions of the types of ideological sacrifices that are made when arguing these cases. One common example was the common use of the "nexus" test, which states that, in order to deprive a lesbian or gay parent custody on the grounds of sexual orientation, it must be proven that some sort of nexus exists between that sexual orientation and harm to the child. This was hailed as a positive development when it was formulated in 1967, and has been cited religiously in the years since.[5] Yet, upon deeper reflection, many gay and lesbian activists, parents and attorneys felt that any legal argument that began with the presumption that homosexuality might cause harm was symbolically and ideologically damaging to the LGBT community. As one lesbian attorney who has been trying these cases since the 1970s stated,

... [W]e shouldn't be advocating the nexus test, we should be advocating a position that a parent's sexual orientation is always irrelevant in a custody dispute. My very short riff on the difference between those two is that as I've read the cases, even the ones who win, if there's any adverse impact on the child, it isn't the parent's sexual orientation that produces the adverse impact. It's something else, which is what it ought to be called so that ... [B]asically I've come to think that any argument that suggests that a parent's sexual orientation could have an adverse impact on a child is missing the point ... [and] that has been the strategy we've considered a success for the last 25 years including me. The cases go down as solid victory if we get that test and if we get a court to apply it ... So, you know, it's hard to abandon something that has brought quite a bit of success ... But you can read a dozen of the best opinions we've ever had where the gay or lesbian parent wins ... and still not get any rhetoric that says, "Hey, gay people are a part of life, like, not a big deal that they raise children" or "gay people have something positive and unique to offer in a culturally pluralistic society." Nothing (Interview 26).

Thus, for attorneys and parents alike, the possibility of sacrificing fidelity to their own ideologies, feelings, and experiences in return for formal legal conferrals of rights was an oft-present dilemma.

Divisions and Debate: Is it about Rights? Is it about Gayness?

Not surprisingly, parents, attorneys and activists in the LGBT community had vastly different takes on these issues of strategy and ideology. Almost everyone in the interviews agreed with the proposition that "it is not in the best interest of children to have winners and losers" when it comes to families and family law (Interview 9). Yet,

---

[5] *Nadler v. Superior Court in and for Sacramento County* (1967).

even when the language of "rights" was invoked, as it often was, there was disagreement as to what constituted "winning" and "losing" per se, and what LGBT family "rights" should look like. This diversity of legal consciousness was exemplified by reactions to the U.S. Supreme Court decision of *Troxel v. Granville* (1999), which dealt specifically with the rights of grandparents, and more generally with the ability of "third parties" or anyone other than legally recognized parents (by birth or adoption) to seek custody or visitation (Polikoff 2001). In many circles of the LGBT community, this was hailed as a victory because it meant that grandparents and other relatives could not win custody of a child over a parent's objection, solely on the basis of the parent's homosexuality (as had happened several times previously, most notably in the high-profile case of *Bottoms v. Bottoms,* 1996). Yet for many others, particularly same-sex parenting dyads, the decision was problematic in its potential to deny non-biological parents, such as those discussed above, any standing to pursue custody or visitation. By strengthening "parents' rights" to the exclusion of others, the decision seemed to reify the traditional family constellation that assumes children are raised by one or two parents related by either biology or formal adoption – an arrangement that some strains of queer theory and politics have been battling against and trying to transform for years (Stacey 1996). So, the decision – though very consequential and closely followed – was by no means a clear "win" or "loss" for all LGBT families.

The diversity of opinion regarding the implications of the *Troxel* decision was indicative of a more general division among LGBT parents, would-be parents, and advocates regarding the proper legal position of *de facto* parents, or those acting in a parental capacity but not legally related to the child by biology or adoption. While second-parent adoptions are increasingly common in states such as California and Vermont, many non-biological partners in lesbian parenting dyads were not able to secure such adoptions to formalize their relationship with the children they had raised.[6] In still other situations, some adopted a queer theory approach to family, specifically flouting the conventions of the one- or two-parent family and opening up the possibility of multiple persons having parental relationships with a child (Stacey 1990, 1996).

Not surprisingly, the interviewees' feelings about such arrangements and the legal theories of family tied to them were largely dictated by their own experience and position vis-à-vis their children. Without exception, those men and women who had been denied the right to adopt and subsequently lost the right to any sort of custody or visitation with the children they raised based on their lack of legal standing as non-biological parents, such as those discussed above in California and Ohio, felt recognition of this sort was crucial to the security of LGBT families and an indispensable gay rights issue. However, those parents who were legally tied to their children by either biology or adoption, who had been challenged for custody by a third party, such as a grandparent (as in the Virginia case of *Bottoms v. Bottoms,* 1996), or a sperm donor (as in the New York case of *Thomas S. v. Robin Y.,* 1994), saw such theories of family law as antithetical to their rights as lesbian and gay

---

[6] As of 2005, 3 states had adoption statutes that specifically allowed second parent adoptions, 7 had case law allowing such adoptions, and there were 15 states in which these adoptions had been allowed by a trial court, without an explicit law in place.

parents. A Washington D.C.-based attorney and lesbian mother advocating the latter position presciently explained,

> Maybe that's because some people are legal strangers and shouldn't be treated as parents. When judges don't want to make those distinctions I don't think they are always crazy ... I mean, there's a stream of thought among feminist family law people that has never been fully supportive of giving non-biological parents visitation rights because they believe that the same theories that support them are the theories that's been used to delete the rights of mothers to raise their children [without] interference from outsiders including battering boyfriends and other people who think they can do it better than mothers can do it. So there has been a group that's been very protective of mothers and has just taken the position that "you want it to be your kid, you adopt the kid. If you don't adopt the kid, it's not your kid. It's the mother's kid, period." They are certainly not anti-gay, their slant is different. They are essentially willing to sacrifice those non-biological mothers and their relationships with their children if that's what it takes to preserve mothers from power play from their battering boyfriends who they are trying to get rid of, who may be going after the kids as a way to control the mother. It's just a different slant on the issues. So, I mean, there was some tension in having to decide how to deal with the *Troxel* case in the Supreme Court that once you let anybody who isn't a legal parent have any rights to a child, you are opening the door for all sorts of problems including grandparents getting custody from lesbian mothers like the *Bottoms* case. And yet, if you define parents really narrowly, then you cut out all those non-bio moms. So that tension is there. It's there among the gay and lesbian lawyers who work in the area. It's certainly there in the different briefs that were written in *Troxel* (Interview 26).

An attorney from Illinois concurred, "I think there [are] some concerns raised ... about whether or not this [allowing non-biological parents custody rights] would open up a sort of Pandora's box in terms of who else would be coming forward to try to adopt children" (Interview 29). The New York mother who fought her daughter's sperm donor in court was also understandably skeptical of such a Pandora's Box, and did not consider such "open" approaches to custody advisable:

> I can't go along with de facto parents [being eligible for custody] – it opens up the floodgates to others who assert rights ... There's a danger that some want it [definitions of parenthood and rights to custody] opened up too much ... [to the extent that] family friends can come in and pursue rights. I find that scary (Interview 36).

Yet another interviewee from Illinois found this position dangerous to LGBT couples and to children, and implored judges and others to accept a broader definition of family and parenthood, in the absence of formal adoption:

> [You have to] educate them specifically about what the child loses by not having a legal parent-child relationship. Yeah, you can appoint somebody guardian. You can put somebody in your will, that is pretty much it. That is pretty much what you can do, and here are the other hundred things, which are really important, that you can't do unless you allow this. We're not asking you to choose or to say that this family situation is better than that. We're saying, this family exists and the only issue here is whether you're gonna secure the family that already exists ... It requires then to think about a particular child in a particular context that they inherited (Interview 25).

Another interviewee described a conversation with this Illinois attorney, where a fundamental difference of opinion on this point was expressed:

> She just basically said, "I understand that's the theory you like, but, I've got to do something else if these people are going to get any contact with these kids." Like "that's not going to work here. The court isn't going to say they are parents. So the only way that I can get them contact is if I have a theory under which some people who aren't parents can have visitation rights to kids." So, you know, we wound up with a difference of opinion. You know, my position might be more theoretically pure and more consistent with how I think you can get out of the conundrum of giving too many people rights. But, what she was saying is valid also, which is "okay, that all these lesbian co-parents in this state and the court has already eliminate the possibility of calling them parents. So that's closed to us. What legal theory do we have to get them rights?" You know, some thing that allows some people who have some function in some specific way to be granted visitation rights under some theory that doesn't require them to prove harm by clear and convincing evidence or something impossible like that. If you are going to open that door, it's going to be wide enough for some people to get in who have bad motives. So there is some inherent tension, and it could be unresolvable in some instances (Interview 26).

While this debate was in part fueled by practical concerns and personal experience, it was also clearly a political issue for those on either side. One biological mother in California, for example, in her successful defeat of her ex-partner's bid for guardianship and visitation rights with their two children by donor insemination, asserted that she "shouldn't be singled out to have to share her children just because she was a lesbian" – clearly characterizing the potential for such guardianship by a non-biological and non-adoptive parent (or would-be parent) as contrary to her notion of gay rights (Interview 28). Yet, the attorney for her ex-partner, also a lesbian, explained that such a finding was in fact homophobic and sexist to her mind:

> [I]f you are straight, this has been going on since *Johnson v. Calvery*, surrogate babies. What we have is a situation that involves homosexuals, not parenting issues and the problem is that it involves homosexuals. It's not an issue of parental rights, parental rights have already been decided. We have it all, all the law that I use is there. It is not even a stretch to apply this to women, it is simply a matter of equal rights. Now, they won't do it and it's not because the law isn't there, the law has been there since medical technology started to be available to create babies. And then it got worse, we have the first cases are donor insemination, then it goes on to surrogacy, it goes on to biological, non-biological, what it means to be a father, we have the law, they simply refuse to apply it to women (Interview 32).

Though the two positions are clearly opposed, and, as the interviewee above posited, unresolvable, advocates of each felt their position to be fundamentally grounded in the same sociopolitical ethic of gay rights.

A similar division in legal consciousness was evident among LGBT parents and advocates in regards to the movements toward legalizing same-sex marriage and domestic partnerships, such as those in California and Vermont.[7] Indeed, the dominant discourse in the national LGBT rights movement has been one of ardent support for

---

[7] At the time of the interviews, the Massachusetts Supreme Court case of *Goodridge v. Department of Public Health* (2003), legalizing same sex marriage in that state, had not been decided.

equal access to the institution of marriage (Sullivan 1997; Wolfson 1996). Without fail, these conversations inevitably include as a major focus the rights to child custody, adoption, and visitation attendant to marriage. One lesbian non-biological mother from Ohio explained, "... I had no legal connection to [her ex-partner] because I had never married her, which, of course, we all know in the United States you cannot do. And because I had no blood relation to either [her or the child], I had no legal standing as a parent" (Interview 27). An attorney and activist from California explained how the inability to marry could impact even a custody decision between a LGBT parent and his or her former spouse from a heterosexual marriage:

> Cohabitation is often used by the courts ... to deny custody on "moral grounds" ... Of course, it becomes much more complicated after a divorce is granted, where the heterosexual cohabitant is now legally married and thereby getting all the cultural support and approval of the relationship, and the lesbian or gay cohabitant will always be a cohabitant because they never will be able to marry in any state in this country right now ... And we've been in situations where we've argued ... "look they would marry if they could, but they can't. So therefore, you can't apply cohabitation law to this person because this is a committed relationship like a marriage and if they could marry they would and then they wouldn't be cohabitating, without the benefit of marriage." And it was a total catch-22 (Interview 21).

Others felt that, while domestic partnerships and civil unions were certainly helpful and a step in the right direction, it was nevertheless imperative to gay rights that full marriage be extended to same-sex couples. As one interviewee exclaimed:

> My problem with these things are, we already went down that road, that's what *Brown v. Board of Education* said, separate is not equal, HELLO! Half a loaf is not better than a full loaf and we don't have equal rights. We have something, we have a little end piece of the loaf that they've put a little butter on. But we don't have equal rights (Interview 32).

Others, however, though equally committed to LGBT family rights, were opposed ideologically to both civil unions and the pursuit of same-sex marriage. One lesbian attorney and long-time activist commented,

> [T]he minute a line is drawn and then you advocate for your population to fall within that line, then you are always going to have a bunch of people who don't fall within the line or who don't move up the line, who are the issue. And that's been my argument around marriage forever. It's like, okay fine, so tomorrow every gay couple got married in every state; what would we do about the gay couples who chose not to marry, you know? I mean, it just makes no sense and so the Vermont court [in custody cases following the civil union law] sort of is, in a way, made my worst nightmare come true (Interview 24).

Another, from Washington D.C., had similar concerns:

> So now, registered domestic partners get to be treated like step-parents. Well, that's a huge problem. My fear would be that then the court would say that nobody else can do it ... And that it's a constricting rather than an expanding of family possibility ... There are certainly other situations where people might be in a situation where they want to make the commitment to raise a child together, but they are not domestic partners and they don't want to be domestic partners. Or maybe they are and could be but they don't want to register ...

So [judges can say], "if you are not registered as domestic partners or married to each other, go home" (Interview 26).

This, like the debate over extending parental rights to non-legal parents, seemed essentially unresolvable in both the philosophical and practical senses.

These sorts of ideological debates illustrate the range of rights consciousness among LGBT parents and advocates – clearly suggesting that all in this community do not speak with one voice. Yet this point was even more bluntly made when interviewees spoke of specific incidents of embattlement and hostility *among* LGBT parents and advocates. The most common site of such hostility was in cases where former lesbian partners opposed each other in court for custody of children they had by donor insemination, but had not formally adopted. In such situations, the most likely scenario, described by interviewees, was that the biological mother retained full custody and denied the non-biological mother – technically a "legal stranger" – any parental rights. Such situations were extremely divisive, as observers and participants were ultimately put in the position of having to decide who was the "good lesbian" and the "bad lesbian" – as opposed to the more typical "LGBT parent versus straight/homophobic parent" binary. Such situations were so contentious that initially, in the late 1980s, the major LGBT legal advocacy organizations refused to represent litigants in such cases. As one activist and mother commented:

[Y]ou know, [it's] just as a community issue, we have to be better to each other. We cannot, we *cannot* bring this cases just because we can. And we can't exercise this power immorally. Which biological moms are doing. I mean, here we are already oppressed to some degree, lesbian and gay people, and now this person becomes the oppressor. You know, this is as old as history and it's the classic thing and it's no better done now and than by anybody else and we need to do a better job of being honorable. And if you made an agreement that you were going to have this child together and raise her together, I don't care if you hate each other now, the fact is, you agreed to have a child together. And she needs both of you and is relying on both of you to be her mom (Interview 21, emphasis in original).

The New York sperm donor paternity case discussed earlier provided another example of how hostility and division could manifest itself within the LGBT community. In this case, the sperm donor challenging the two lesbian mothers happened to also be gay and a very active member of his local gay rights community. As one of the mothers explained, this provided significant tension in the case and within the community:

Our worst enemy in this case was the lesbian and gay "community" itself. They latched on to his "fatherly" rights in the most self-hating way. They wanted to make our family anything and everything but what it is – two moms and two kids. There was this negative party line that we were somehow mirroring the straight world by creating a two-parent family. Rather, we were supposed to move beyond that heterosexist model and create a family that was inclusive of anyone who had "significant contact" with our kids. There were many others who were much further along in line than he [the sperm donor litigant] was who could meet that criteria. Lesbian and gay families were, and are, just not as "real" somehow as straight families … (Interview 36).

She went on to emphasize this division within the LGBT population:

> [T]he most virulent opposition to our lesbian family came from some very powerful segments of the gay community – the sperm donor ... and many others in the community were very vocal in their support of his position and waged a massive bi-coastal campaign to discredit us. They were our worst enemies. The straight media was far more positive about our family. It says something about internalized homophobia, at least back then, and male privilege and identifying with powerful white men.

These latter comments in particular provoke discussion of an issue that came up with multiple interviewees – that is, that classism, racism, and sexism exist within the LGBT community just as in the heterosexual community. The same mother commented in regard to the appellate decision in the case, which ruled in favor of the sperm donor, "I don't think you can read that decision without finding sexism – it wins out over homophobia as the dominant influence in the decision." She also emphasized, "Money played a huge role in the decision ... this was a rich white man, a lawyer, and very charming ... the judge immediately related to this guy." An attorney and lesbian mother from California commented that classism was also to be found in many of the custody cases she worked on, citing specifically the aforementioned case of *Bottoms v. Bottoms* (1994):

> I mean, Sharon Bottoms didn't lose custody ... just because she was a lesbian, she lost because she was a *poor* lesbian. And that decision is every bit as much classist as it is homophobic. And you know it's hard to say whether if she had been a white picket fence surgeon if as a lesbian she would have lost custody, she may have. She may have. But what's absolutely clear is that the fact that she was poor played a huge role (Interview 21).

An attorney who worked on this case agreed,

> [C]lass issues come up a lot in these cases, a *lot*. I mean, these are the cases where gay and lesbian people who might otherwise be in the closet, because of their circumstance, and because of the tough areas in which they live, in terms of homophobia come out because they have to. So, we end with there being a lot of people in family law cases who live in poor neighborhoods, live in trailers, work in minimum wage jobs and class issues come up ... [W]hat seems to happen, you get a hostile judge, the judge takes the indicia of living life on the edge and uses that against the parent that the judge disfavors and that's where class stuff can play out (Interview 23).

Such observations suggest the possibility that the legal losses and difficulty faced by many gay and lesbian parents is not only about their homosexuality – and that not all LGBT parents are equally positioned. Yet even on this point, there was some disagreement. When talking about cases where non-biological parents were denied custody, one lesbian attorney from Washington D.C. said, "When a judge doesn't see it that way, when a judge sees a parent and a legal stranger, is that inherently anti-gay? I am not sure that it is" (Interview 26); yet, another attorney, from California, maintained, "It is not about what's good for children, it's about the lack of equal rights for *homosexuals*" (Interview 32).

Conclusions: LGBT Legal Consciousness and the Dilemma of Difference

It should perhaps come as no surprise that gay and lesbian families and family law advocates are just as diverse in their opinions and ideologies as are their heterosexual counterparts. Yet, what sets them apart in this respect is the extent to which they – and their rights claims – are assumed, by both their foes and allies, to be unitary. While the challenges LGBT parents face in family court are based largely on assumptions of who they are as homosexuals and how "that type" of person may be incompatible with parenthood, there are also assumptions that more "gay rights" will overcome these challenges (Richman 2002). Yet these data show that both of these assumptions are problematic in their failure to account for the full range of situational experiences, beliefs and legal consciousness. Not only do LGBT parents and members of the gay rights community interviewed for this chapter have different ideas about the direction of gay legal rights, their cultural place, and the strategies that should be employed (and at what cost) – but there are significant differences in what their visions of gay family rights look like. Is it reasonable to try to fit LGBT families into the mold provided by straight families in order to gain legal victories, or does this betray the ideological commitments and epistemic realities of their own lives? Should LGBT legal goals move in the direction of expanding the concept of family and its membership beyond biology and formal adoption – "queering the family", as some say – or does this threaten the very families it is meant to protect? Should LGBT parents and advocates work to attain universal same-sex marriage, or will that constitute more of a limitation than a liberation?

Moving beyond these differences of opinion, the variety of situations, responses, and conflicts represented in the data evince a more complicated picture of who the "LGBT community" is – and provoke the question, is there *a* LGBT community? And if not – if LGBT parents are as different from each other as are other parents, and if the same divisions, conflicts, and hegemonic relations exist here as elsewhere – can they really be defined and categorized based on their gayness? A negative answer might lead to the logical corollary that if LGBT parents cannot be defined as a group, they cannot be discriminated against as a group based on this aspect of their identity. As one lesbian mother exhorted, "[T]his is not just a gay issue … let's take the whole gay issue out of the equation and let's look at the children" (Interview 27). Clearly, however, this is not currently the case – every parent and attorney interviewed told of ways in which sexual orientation was made a centerpiece in their custody claim. Thus, despite their differences in legal consciousness, they are held together by a common category of discrimination, both within and without the law. Yet the recognition that their experiences, aspirations, and visions of law and rights vary vastly – and that perhaps there is no one LGBT legal consciousness in regard to family – is an important caveat in the constitutive study of gay family rights.

How the realization of such diversity within LGBT legal consciousness explicitly and concretely affects the ongoing struggle for gay and lesbian legal rights, however, is a question of great import but no easy answer. In one sense, this analysis is reflective of the enormous progress of the gay rights movement in the last twenty years. Whereas gay/lesbian families were once thought to be contradictions in terms – one interviewee noted that to use "gay" and "children" in the same sentence was thought of as child abuse when she first started practicing law in this area – the data in this chapter reveal the expansion of legal, familial, and sociopolitical opportunities and possibilities now available to gay and lesbian parents and potential parents. The proliferation of family forms and differing visions of LGBT family rights offered by the interviewees are indicative of an expanded palette of legal rights and an attendant sense of security on the part of those parents and families. Yet these diverse and often contrary experiences and opinions also call into question the trajectory of the gay rights movement more generally – leading some to wonder whether such ideological differences might cause the movement to splinter or self-destruct. While the data here do not provide an affirmative answer to this question, they do provide insight into the potentialities attendant to such a trajectory.

As the agenda of expanding gay rights in the United States progresses in the 21st century, family law appears positioned at the forefront of the movement and the ensuing legal debates. One is left to wonder, however, whether the divisions within and the lack of a unitary rights consciousness among LGBT parents and advocates may cause this movement to self-destruct. This quandary represents a new take on Martha Minow's (1987, 1990) concept of the "dilemma of difference" – is it best to gloss over differences within a marginalized group for the sake of "equal rights"? Or is the more authentic approach to recognize difference, celebrate it, and (hopefully) respond to it in a meaningful and nuanced way? As Minow observes, "Rights analysis begins with the view that legal rights apply to everyone: the facts of personhood and membership in the polity entitle each individual to rights against the state and rights to be treated by the state in the same way as others are treated" (1987:322). This concept is problematized significantly by the observation that law, rights, and identity are conceived differently not only *by* different groups, but *within* groups. How can "LGBT family rights" materialize legally if the parents and activists themselves cannot agree as to what these rights should look like, how they should be attained, and what types of family arrangements they should protect? One answer, suggested by Majury (1987), is to use the rhetoric of equality as strategy, not theory, in the pursuit of legal rights. Yet, this again raises the dilemma of legal strategy that does not reflect the lived reality and ideological commitments of LGBT parents and families.

Continued research on the range of legal consciousness of LGBT parents and others and the dilemma of difference, adopting a constitutive perspective and focusing on fidelity to lesbian mothers' and gay fathers' own visions of rights, law and family, may come to reveal an essentially irreconcilable tension. However, the tension itself may prove productive. It has been noted in multiple contexts that divisiveness and questioning can often provide an impetus for social change to occur, even in an arena that has undergone significant change already. As one interviewee noted, "Social change never happens just by staying on the side of the road, at some point you have to jump out ..." (Interview 24).

References

Benkov, L. (1994) *Reinventing the Family: The Emerging Story of Lesbian and Gay Parents.* New York: Crown Publishers, Inc.

Dalton, S.E., and Bielby, D.D. (2000) "'That's Our Kind of Constellation: Lesbian Mother Negotiate Institutionalized Understandings of Gender within the Family," 14(1) *Gender & Society* 36.

Eskridge, W.N., Jr. (1999) *Gaylaw: Challenging the Apartheid of the Closet*. Cambridge, MA: Harvard University Press.

Espeland, W. (1994) "Legally Mediated Identity: The National Environmental Policy Act and the Bureaucratic Construction of Interests." 28(5) *Law and Society Review* 1149.

Ettelbrick, P.L. (1989) "Since When is Marriage a Path to Liberation?" *OUT/LOOK National Gay and Lesbian Quarterly* 8.

Ewick, P., and Silbey, S.S. (1998) *The Common Place of Law: Stories from Everyday Life*. Chicago: University of Chicago Press.

Gledhill, Lynda (2003) "Senate OKs Domestic Partners' Benefits" *San Francisco Chronicle* A25.

Hitchens, D., and Price, B. (1978–9) "Trial Strategy in Lesbian Mother Custody Cases: The Use of Expert Testimony," 9 *Golden Gate University Law Review* 451.

Hunter, N., and Polikoff, N. (1976) "Custody Rights of Lesbian Mothers: Legal Theory and Litigation Strategy," 25 *Buffalo Law Review* 691.

McCann, M.W. (1994) *Rights at Work: Pay Equity Reform and the Politics of Legal Mobilization*. Chicago: University of Chicago Press.

Majury, D. (1987) "Strategizing in Equality," 3 *Wisconsin Women's Law Journal* 169.

Merry, S.E. (1990) *Getting Justice and Getting Even: Legal Consciousness Among Working-Class Americans*. Chicago: The University of Chicago Press.

Minow, M. (1987) "When Difference Has Its Home: Group Homes for the Mentally Retarded, Equal Protection and Legal Treatment of Difference," 22 *Harvard Civil Rights–Civil Liberties Law Review* 111.

—— (1990) *Making All the Difference: Inclusion, Exclusion, and American Law*. Ithaca, NY: Cornell University Press.

Nardi, Peter (1997) "Friends, Lovers, and Families: The Impact of AIDS on Gay and Lesbian Relationships" in Levine, Nardi, and Gagnon (eds) *In Changing Times: Gay Men & Lesbians Encounter HIV/AIDS*. Chicago: University of Chicago Press.

Polikoff, N. (1993) "We Will Get What we Ask For: Why Legalizing Gay and Lesbian Marriage Will Not 'Dismantle the Structure of Gender in Every Marriage'." 79 *Virginia Law Review* 1535.

—— (2001) "The Impact of *Troxel v. Granville* on Lesbian and Gay Parents," 32(3) *Rutgers Law Journal* 825.

Richman, K. (2002) "Lovers, Legal Strangers, and Parents: Negotiating Parental and Sexual Identity in Family Law." *Law & Society Review* 36(2): 285.

Rosenberg, G. (1991) *The Hollow Hope: Can Courts Bring About Social Change?* Chicago: University of Chicago Press.

Scheingold, S. (1974) *The Politics of Rights: Lawyers, Public Policy, and Political Change*. New Haven: Yale University Press.

Sherman, S. (1992) *Lesbian and Gay Marriage: Private Commitments, Public Ceremonies*. Philadelphia: Temple University Press.

Stacey, J. (1990) *Brave New Families: Stories of Domestic Upheaval in Late Twentieth Century America*. New York: Basic Books.

—— (1996) *In the Name of the Family: Rethinking Family Values in the Postmodern Age*. Boston, Massachusetts: Beacon Press.

Stein, A. (1997) *Sex and Sensibility: Stories of a Lesbian Generation*. Berkeley: University of California Press.

Sullivan, A. (1997) *Same Sex Marriage: Pro and Con*. New York: Vintage Books.

Tushnet, M. (1984) "An Essay on Rights." 62(8) *Texas Law Review* 1363.

West, C. (1998) "The Role of Law in Progressive Politics," in D. Kairys (ed.) *The Politics of Law: A Progressive Critique* (3rd edn). New York: Basic Books.

Weston, K. (1991) *Families We Choose: Lesbians, Gays, Kinship*. New York: Columbia University Press.

Wolfson, E. (1996) "Why We Should Fight for the Freedom to Marry," 1(1) *Journal of Gay, Lesbian, and Bisexual Identity*.

Cases cited

Baehr v. Lewin, 852 P.2d 44 (1993)
Bottoms v. Bottoms, 249 Va. 410, 457 S.E.2d 102 (1996)
Bowers v. Hardwick, 478 U.S. 186, 106 S.Ct. 2841, 92 L.Ed.2d 140 (1986)
Goodridge v. Department of Public Health, 440 Mass. 309 (2003)
Lawrence v. Texas, 123 S.Ct. (2003)
Nadler v. Superior Court In and For Sacramento County, 255 Cal.App.2d 523 (1967)
Sharon S. v. Annette F., 39 P.3d 512; 116 Cal. Rptr. 2d 496 (2002)
Thomas S. v. Robin Y., 209 A.D.2d 298, 618 N.Y.S.2d 356 (1994)
Troxel v. Granville, 527 U.S. 1069 (1999)
Ward v. Ward, WL 491692 (1996)

Chapter 5

Consciousness in Context: Employees' Views of Sexual Harassment Grievance Procedures

ANNA-MARIA MARSHALL

In 1997, the Supreme Court issued two related decisions that clarified the law surrounding an employer liability in cases of sexual harassment. In *Faragher v. City of Boca Raton* and *Burlington Industries v. Ellerth*, the Court held that an employer can establish an affirmative defense against sexual harassment claims by showing that it had a grievance procedure to handle employee complaints and that the "employee unreasonably failed to take advantage of any preventive or corrective opportunities provided by the employer or to avoid harm otherwise" (*Burlington Industries v. Ellerth* 1997, 765). Thus, the Court gave employers the central responsibility for protecting women's rights against sexual harassment.

Legal commentators have critiqued the Court's rulings in these cases. They have noted that the employers' burden is trivial and easily fulfilled by simply adopting a policy and doing little more (Bisom-Rapp 1999). Others have suggested that requiring women to come forward to complain flies in the face of extensive research which demonstrates that women rarely use grievance procedures to resolve their problems with sexual harassment (Fitzgerald, Swan, and Fischer 1995; Merit Systems Protection Board 1995). Indeed, in the aftermath of *Faragher* and *Ellerth*, courts have looked unfavorably on plaintiffs who did not pursue a grievance. In one analysis of lower court cases following the Supreme Court's decisions, the authors found: "Employees who failed to report were deemed to have acted unreasonably" (Sherwyn, Heise, and Eigen 2001: 1286).[1] These analyses have suggested that the Court's rulings in *Faragher* and *Ellerth* may not adequately protect – and may in fact undermine – women's right to be free from sexual harassment at work.

Rather than focus on judicial decisions, however, the constitutive approach to understanding rights examines ordinary individuals as they navigate an employer's sexual harassment policies. Relying on women's accounts of their experiences, this approach asks how women interpret their encounters with unwanted sexual attention at work, how they choose a strategy for redressing the problem, and what role law and legal institutions play in these social and cultural practices. Thus, rather than

---

[1] According to the authors, employers should derive a mixed message from the courts: "Specifically, employers ... should exercise just enough reasonable care to satisfy a court, but not enough to make it easy or comfortable for employees to complain of workplace harassment" (Sherwyn, Heise, and Eigen 2001:1267).

speculating about the effects of legal doctrines on the workplace, this analysis reveals what these laws and related legal institutions actually mean to their intended beneficiaries (Marshall 2003; Marshall and Barclay 2003) and identifies the role of organizational practices in shaping legal consciousness.

Civil rights laws frame many employment practices in the US workplace by defining the prohibited practices that constitute prohibited discrimination, such as sexual harassment (Edelman, Erlanger, and Lande 1993; Edelman, Uggen, and Erlanger 1999). For example, demanding sexual favors in exchange for a promotion is illegal; occasionally telling sexist jokes is not. Reproduced in employment policies, these legal definitions provide one set of schemas for ordinary men and women trying to understand their working lives. Civil rights schemas can be liberatory, promising equal opportunity in the workplace for members of minority groups. On the other hand, the enforcement mechanisms, embedded in employers' organizational routines, can undermine that promise.

A constitutive approach to civil rights law is uniquely positioned to capture these contradictions because it focuses on both the meaning of the employment rights and the social practices that implement those rights (Marshall and Barclay 2003). The focus on meaning generates important questions about what people know of their rights and how those rights shape the way they understand their experiences. But equally important is how they invoke their rights – not just in courtrooms, but in the everyday locations of workplaces, schools, and neighborhoods (Marshall and Barclay 2003; Ewick and Silbey 1998).[2] Through these social practices, legal schemas derive their continuing power to shape social relations (Ewick and Silbey 1998; Hoffmann 2004). By invoking their rights in novel circumstances – or by declining to invoke their rights when they are entitled to – these social practices may reshape the very meaning of the underlying rights.

Organizations can exert a powerful influence over the reciprocal relationship between meaning and practice in the development of legal consciousness. People rarely learn about the law by reading judicial decisions and legislation. Instead, what they know of their rights comes from their schools, workplaces, families, neighborhoods – all of which are social, political, and cultural institutions that are characterized by hierarchies and imbalances of power and that read their own interests into the legal meanings they circulate to their participants (Edelman, Erlanger, and

---

[2] The emphasis on meaning and practice collapses the rigid distinctions sometimes made between legal consciousness and the earlier tradition of legal mobilization (Marshall and Barclay 2003; Sarat and Kearns 1995; Zemans 1983). More than just formal legal complaints, legal mobilization has been defined as "the process by which legal norms are invoked to regulate behavior" (Lempert 1976, quoted in Zemans 1983, 693). In this intentionally broad definition, legal mobilization does not require courts, lawyers, or other formal trappings of the legal system. Stripped of its formality, then, legal mobilization resembles the social practices enacting legal consciousness (Miller and Sarat 1980–81; Kritzer, Vidmar, and Bogart 1991). Blurring this distinction between legal consciousness and legal mobilization emphasizes that law may be invoked in many everyday social interactions in many locations, and in the process, law is re-created, shaped by the actors and institutions where it gets mobilized. In courts, the re-creation of legality through lawyers and juries, and creates new precedent. In workplaces, schools, and neighborhoods, the changes to law are not enshrined in judicial opinions or verdicts, but they are nevertheless influential on the meaning-making for the participants in these institutions, all of which are areas of inquiry for those studying law in everyday life. This is the essence of a constitutive approach to law.

Lande 1993). Moreover, in these organizations, schemas other than law may be prevalent. For example, management interests in efficiency and employee harmony often compete with civil rights frames protecting employee rights. And in the social practices where management policy gets implemented, those alternative schemas may dominate the law (Edelman, Erlanger, and Lande 1993; Marshall 2005).

New empirical questions emerge from the theoretical implications of the New Civil Rights Research, questions that emphasize specific legal rules and organizational context. How do organizational practices shape the legal meanings, opportunities and choices of ordinary people confronting inequality in their everyday lives? What are the consequences for the laws themselves in those specific contexts? In this chapter, I address these questions by drawing on a study of sexual harassment laws in action in a single workplace. I show that employers are a central source of employees' information about their rights. That information consists not simply of legal rules and written policies. Instead, employees' understandings of the law is shaped in part by management practices implementing sexual harassment policies. Based on these practices, employees come to see law as offering only limited protection against sexual harassment. This view, in turn, shapes their decisions about whether or not to resist harassing behaviors or to try to ignore them. Those decisions affect the quality of rights women enjoy in the workplace.

Data and Methods

The data in this chapter is drawn from a study of women's experiences with unwanted sexual attention in a single workplace. I chose to focus on women's experiences because women remain the predominant targets of sexual harassment at work. In addition, I have limited the study to women working for one employer. Situating the study in one workplace may limit the generalizeability of the findings, but this research design has the countervailing advantage of focusing on one set of employment policies. Both the employees and the managers are bound by the same set of rules and procedures. Using this focus, I can detect patterns in the ways that women understand their rights and the way that managers administer the grievance procedures designed to enforce those rights.

This chapter is based on in-depth interviews and open-ended responses to a survey questionnaire. First, I conducted in-depth interviews with 25 female staff members and administrators at a midwestern university ("the University"). I solicited their participation through a listserv maintained by an organization of female staff members, asking members who had experiences with "unwanted sexual attention" to contact me for an interview. Using a semi-structured battery of questions, I interviewed all 25 women who responded to the e-mail.[3] The interviews lasted from 45 minutes

---

[3] The women interviewed varied in income and occupational status. Five of the women were low-paid clerical workers who administered budgets and performed clerical tasks. The rest were middle-management employees performing a range of administrative tasks, including supervising employees and developing workplace policies. Of course, using a computer-based method of communication, I was only able to contact women who had access to computers and women in pink and white collar occupations – but my sample does reflect variation across occupations. One of the women interviewed was Latina; the remainder were white.

to an hour and a half and covered a range of subjects, including women's experiences with sexual attention at work, their familiarity with the employer's policies, and their decision about whether or not to complain. All the interviews were tape-recorded and transcribed.

I also conducted a survey of women working at the University. Designed to confirm the general patterns found in the in-depth interviews, the survey was distributed to a random sample of 1000 women working at the University.[4] Survey questions asked about women's experiences with sexual harassment and the way that they responded to it. Among the questions was an invitation to offer extended comments on any of the issues covered by the survey. About 20 percent of the survey respondents wrote additional thoughts about their experiences and responses. Those comments are included in this analysis.

I used interpretive methods to analyze the interview transcripts and open-ended survey responses. I reviewed the transcripts for several themes that emerged from the theoretical effort to contextualize legal consciousness. I asked how women understood their rights to be protected from sexual harassment and the organizational milieu in which they acquired that information. Specifically, I examined the management practices women cited when describing their rights. From this review, general patterns emerged, revealing women's legal consciousness documented in this chapter.

The Legal Environment

The Equal Employment Opportunity Commission (EEOC) and the courts have identified two basic types of sexual harassment as forms of sex discrimination. The first type, quid pro quo harassment, occurs when supervisors make compliance with sexual demands a requirement of the job (MacKinnon 1979; *Williams v. Saxbe* 1976; *Barnes v. Costle* 1977). The second form of sexual harassment is the hostile working environment (Schultz 1998; Francke 1997; Saguy 2000). A hostile working environment is one where sexual behaviors interfere in a discriminatory way with an employee's ability to perform his or her job (Saguy 2000; *Oncale v. Sundowner Offshore Services* 1998). Courts have recognized that both quid pro quo and hostile working environment harassment violate Title VII's proscription of sex discrimination (*Barnes v. Costle* 1977; *Meritor Savings Bank v. Vinson* 1986).

The standard for determining whether a working environment is hostile has both objective and subjective components. The objective component requires that the offending behaviors be "sufficiently severe or pervasive" to alter a reasonable person's working conditions (*Meritor Savings Bank v. Vinson* 1986, 67; *Harris v. Forklift Systems* 1993).[5] The subjective component requires that the behaviors

---

[4] The survey had a 35 per cent response rate, an acceptable rate for a survey on a sensitive subject such as sexual harassment (Arvey and Cavanaugh 1995).

[5] The Supreme Court has stated: "Conduct that is not severe or pervasive enough to create an objectively hostile or abusive work environment – an environment that a reasonable person would find hostile or abusive – is beyond Title VII's purview" (*Harris v. Forklift Systems* 1993). To determine whether the conduct was objectively offensive, some courts rely on a "reasonable woman" standard, which the 9th Circuit has argued acknowledges that men and women assign different meanings to sexual harassment at work (*Ellison v. Brady* 1991).

actually interfere with the employee's performance of her job duties. The Supreme Court in *Harris* observed: "If the victim does not subjectively perceive the environment to be abusive, the conduct has not actually altered the conditions of the victim's employment, and there is no Title VII violation. But Title VII comes into play before the harassing conduct leads to a nervous breakdown" (*Harris v. Forklift Systems* 1993).[6]

In the wake of expanding liability for sexual harassment, employers widely adopted grievance procedures to redress workplace problems (Edelman, Uggen, and Erlanger 1999). The University had such a policy (the Written Policy) in place at the time of this study. In the preamble, the University's expansive view of the harms of sexual harassment moved beyond discrimination and espoused a commitment "to the maintenance of an environment free of discrimination and all forms of coercion that impede the academic freedom or *diminish the dignity* of any member of the University committee" (emphasis added). The policy broadly defined prohibited practices:

> Sexual advances, requests for sexual favors, and other verbal or physical conduct of a sexual nature constitute harassment when: (1) submission to such conduct is made or threatened to be made either explicitly or implicitly a term or condition of an individual's employment or education; (2) submission to or rejection of such conduct by an individual is used or threatened to be used as the basis for academic or employment decisions affecting that individual; or (3) such conduct has the purpose or effect of substantially interfering with an individual's academic or professional performance or creating an intimidating, hostile or offensive employment, educational or living environment.

By prohibiting conduct that had the *purpose* of interfering with other employees' working lives, the Written Policy gave managers discretion to intervene before harassers committed a legal violation.

The Written Policy also outlined a flexible process for resolving complaints. First, employees could bypass their supervisors and take their complaints to one of many specified University officials, including the Deans of the colleges, the Human Resources Department, and the Women's Center. In fact, supervisors were not even specified as an option, thus perhaps suggesting that the policy was directed mostly at preventing and punishing harassment by supervisors. It explicitly promised employees that they would not be retaliated against if they complained, and it directed officials receiving complaints to "immediately seek to resolve the matter by informal discussions with the persons involved." The policy therefore anticipated that managers would handle problems before the more formal grievance procedure was ever invoked.

---

[6] The legal definition of sexual harassment continues to be a subject of debate in the courts, in the EEOC, as well as among activists, human resource professionals and academics. For example, critics have argued that the current law places too much emphasis on sexual behavior and consequently leaves unregulated the most problematic aspects of sexual harassment at work. Schultz (1998) argues that the requirement of sexual behaviors ignores many forms of gender harassment that denigrate women's competence on the job and thus push them away from male-dominated occupations and relegate them to low-status employment. She urges the inclusion of non-sexual gender harassment in the legal prohibition (Schultz 1998). Others have argued that the standard for sexual harassment should be grounded in concepts like respect and worker's dignity rather than sexual practices (Bernstein 1994, 1997; Cornell 1995).

Along with its flexible approach to resolving complaints, the Written Policy provided due process protections for both the complainant and the accused. For example, the Written Policy provided that if the informal process did not produce a satisfactory outcome, employees could also file "formal complaints" within the University's formal employment grievance procedure. But the policy also provided due process protections for the accused. For example, an official could initiate an investigation of the employees' charges but only after finding "probable cause" to believe that the policy had been violated. The Written Policy offered very little guidance on the breadth and depth of these investigations except to require the complainant to support the claims with "clear and convincing evidence." Thus, managers and supervisors had wide discretion under the Written Policy to take complaints very seriously or very lightly as circumstances dictated. If a complaint was found to be "substantiated," the University could discipline and even discharge the harasser.

The University made significant efforts to publicize its sexual harassment policies. All employees were given a copy of the policy when they were hired. The University also circulated a copy to all employees every two years and kept the policy posted on its website. In addition, the University offered workshops and training programs to supervisors to provide them with guidance about how to handle complaints.

Like most internal dispute resolution mechanisms, the University's Written Policy promised protection to complaining employees and accused harassers while also preserving a supervisor's flexibility in investigating and resolving sexual harassment complaints. This mix of formal and informal processes created considerable ambiguity in the meaning and operation of the sexual harassment grievance procedure. As I will show in the remainder of this paper, the interpretations and practices of both University supervisors and employees clarified the meaning of the grievance procedure, but in a way that sharply accentuated the adversarial nature of the process and that protected the harasser rather than the complainant.

Perceptions of Law and Policy

To challenge sexual harassment at work, women first have to be familiar with their rights and the processes that protect them. Through various sources of information – particularly the mass media and the University – the women in this study were mostly familiar with the basic definition of sexual harassment and the procedure for filing a complaint. Women also relied on their own experiences by observing the way grievance procedures were implemented by University supervisors. Through their knowledge of the laws and policies on the books, along with their observations of these laws and policies in action, women developed rights consciousness reflecting not just civil rights laws but also their employers' practices.

Law and Policy on the Books

Most women participating in this study were generally familiar with the legal regime surrounding sexual harassment. They had a rough understanding of the legal definitions of harassing behaviors and understood that not all sexual interactions at work amounted to sexual harassment. For example, most women understood that the conduct had to be a relatively severe intrusion, that it had to occur frequently, and that it had to have a detrimental effect on their job performance – criteria that conform to the legal rules governing sexual harassment claims (Marshall 2003).

Three women had read about sexual harassment law by taking law-related classes or attending talks while in college or graduate school. For example, one interviewee, Joanne, was taking a graduate class in human resources laws and chose to write a paper about state laws governing sexual harassment. In these courses, women were introduced to the basic elements of sexual harassment claims through relatively direct contact with legal materials. As a result, they were more familiar with some of the details of the legal regime, such as the differences between quid pro quo harassment and hostile working environments.

Women also got a great deal of information about sexual harassment law from the mass media. Many women were attentive to news stories about prominent lawsuits, such as the EEOC's case against Mitsubishi. The dramatic allegations in that case – of physical assault on the shop floor and company parties staffed by strippers – were much different than the kinds of harassing conduct that they encountered in their working lives. These highly publicized cases sent the message that "real" sexual harassment consisted of extremely intrusive behaviors.

The women were also familiar with mass media reports of allegations of sexual harassment against politicians and other public figures. But rather than learning much about the legal rules governing sexual harassment, the women I interviewed were more attentive to the way that accusers were treated by third parties. Several mentioned Tailhook, Bob Packwood, and Paula Jones' allegations against Bill Clinton which were just starting to be made public at the time of the study. And all of the women interviewed mentioned Anita Hill and her testimony against Clarence Thomas at his confirmation hearings before the Senate. For Dallas, the most striking aspect of the hearings were the Senate Republicans' attacks on Hill's credibility, especially given the delay in Hill's revelations:

> I felt like they're not going to believe you sweetheart; they never do, and especially when you're coming too late. Now they're never going to believe what you're saying to them. They're going to grill you until there's nothing left of you. And sure enough.

Matilda agreed, but emphasized Thomas' powerful friends in the Senate: "I didn't see she had a chance. I mean, the power that the man had, and the old boy's club with him? No way did she have a chance to be heard. But whether it's big names or it's little names. I don't think much has changed." Like other women in the study, Matilda identified with Hill, particularly with Hill's relatively lower status compared to her harasser and the problems that created in telling her story.

The University was a frequently cited source of information on sexual harassment for many women in the study.[7] Some women interviewed knew the details of the procedures: because they were supervisors or members of employee advisory

---

[7] Among the survey respondents who reported experiences with unwanted sexual attention, 50 percent said that they got most of their information about sexual harassment from mass media sources, including newspapers, magazines, and television. The next largest percentage, 14 percent, cited the University as their main source of information.

committees, they themselves handled complaints about sexual harassment and were therefore expected to understand the policy itself. While others may not have had this detailed familiarity with the Written Policy, most women were simply aware that it existed and knew that they could find the details if necessary. One survey respondent, for example, stated: "[The University] has a very good policy for dealing with sexual harassment to my knowledge. The HR office sends info regularly (2–3x/yr) to employees re: policy and what to do it if sexual harassment occurs at work." Another employee who worked with student athletes observed: "I think [the University] does a good job about informing its employees about the issue." Almost all of the women interviewed reported receiving pamphlets and brochures from the University or remembered receiving a copy of the policy at some point during their employment. For example, Nora observed:

> I think I've probably heard about [the procedures for complaining about sexual harassment]. There are these flyers that come out now and then, which I nicely file in my file drawer. It hasn't come up – it comes under the category of things that I don't remember. I put them somewhere so that if I have to, I can go to the file and pull it out, and find out what it is.

Women drew on these materials for their definitions of sexual harassment. For example, Erna stated: "I got a lot of information when I was [working] in human resources. I mean, I had to read a lot of stuff. And then here they do send sexual harassment pamphlets around, and I don't know, I think I just read it because I was just interested." Rose reported that when the coaches and receptionist in her office were exchanging sexual banter: "It was about this time that I think the University came out with their sexual harassment policy. Or at least there was a point in that period when they redistributed the policy with pamphlets, and I can remember reading through it." This pamphlet prompted her to think about the definition of sexual harassment as a form of prohibited conduct.

Like other employers, the University also offered training programs, particularly to employees in management who were among those designated to handle complaints. Some women reported that, in the course of these programs, they learned a great deal about protecting themselves and not just other employees. For example, Abbie said that she attended a management training seminar at the University where she "learned about sexual harassment and what goes into personnel files."

The employer was an important source of women's information about their rights to be protected against sexual harassment. The definitions of harassing conduct found in the Written Policy helped them make sense of confusing or distressing events in the workplace and even provided them with oppositional interpretations that expose such conduct to challenge. But being familiar with one's rights is different than invoking those rights. Messages from the media provided warnings about the dangers of asserting rights. Moreover, the conflicts in the workplace had to be channeled into grievance mechanisms, and the implementation of those grievance procedures is itself a source of information about the meaning and value of rights.

Law and Policy in Action

Women also became familiar with the Written Policy through interactions with supervisors who administered the procedure. But in these interactions, women believed that the University's commitment to preventing sexual harassment was limited to circulating a policy. Women in the study suggested that the University made little effort to ensure that employees understood the policy and knew how to use it. Moreover, women believed that when complaints arose, the University would take the side of the more important employee, who was usually the harasser. Thus, through their observations of the policy in action, women became skeptical of the University's willingness to protect their rights.

While the University trained supervisors about what to do when they received a complaint about sexual harassment, ordinary employees did not receive training about what sexual harassment was or what to do about it. As a result, even women familiar with the Written Policy felt unsure about their options when confronting harassing behaviors. One survey respondent was the frequent target of crude sexual remarks and discussions of her sex life. Although she knew there was a special procedure for handling sexual harassment complaints, she nevertheless felt she needed additional guidance:

> Women need workshops on what actions constitute harassment and the action we can take. The circumstances for me were the most horrible of my life. It was the lowest point I've ever had regarding self-esteem. We need education because throughout the whole process (verbal only) I was in self-denial that it was actually happening (a definite coping strategy) and the men aware of the situation intimidated me every time I brought it up.

Similarly, Erna believed that circulating a statement was not enough to communicate the University's anti-harassment policy to employees. She observed:

> I think sometimes there's too much to read, and people don't read it, and so maybe it's clear in a certain paragraph, and by that time you're so mixed up ... I mean, I have an office where I can close the door, and I can read it, or I can take it home. But a lot of people don't want to take it home because they find it embarrassing, or they think that they might get a comment, and then reading it out in the open people don't do. And I'm not sure – and I mean, I don't think that I've ever heard of any program here that they teach supervisors at upper levels and then filter it down to what is acceptable and not acceptable. I think they kind of just put this statement out and say, "Okay. That's what you should be doing and we're behind it," but then what do you do?

Even when such training was available, however, many women believed that it did not have its intended effect. One employee working with student athletes complained of "inappropriate comments and touching" by the students. She observed: "They have all been given sensitivity training during orientation, but it doesn't seem to have tempered the aggression shown by a handful of the worst apples."

Women were also generally skeptical of the way the University handled sexual harassment complaints when they arose. Women interviewed thought that highly charged problems like sexual harassment were too complex for the Human Resources Department to untangle. Describing the complaint procedures, Erna noted: "You could go to Human Resources. And that seems to have been a very negative thing because Human Resources doesn't ... has never come through with any *other* problems that people have had. So people don't do that." Observing several times during the interview "I don't trust Human Resources," Dallas reflected critically on advice she herself gave to a young woman sexually propositioned by the chair of a department: "I told her 'Why don't you go to Staff Advisory Council [SAC] or to Human Resources?' But the thing was, okay, SAC is there, but it really isn't a strong arm. Human Resources – that's a joke." To Dallas, women complaining of sexual harassment had very few options for obtaining relief from their problems.

Several women echoed the concerns of legal commentators that the Written Policy and the grievance procedures were created to protect the employer's interests and not the employees. As a manager, Rose felt that the University's primary concern was avoiding lawsuits rather than protecting employees:

> But if you get involved with Employee Relations, invariably everything is colored and tinted by the question of risk management. Everything is colored and tinted by, "Where does this fall in terms of the University's liability, and will we ever come to suit on this?" And so all the information you're given as a manager, at least my experience has been, has been about "CYA." Cover your ass. And "make sure you put it in writing," and all the rest of it that goes along with that – and a much less clear emphasis on the practicality of dealing with the situation.

Siena said, quite simply, "I think the University would have taken the University's side and not the employee's side."

Women also believed that in the course of protecting the University's interests, the Human Resources Department would inevitably side with the person who was most valuable to the University, and that person tended to be the harasser. Matilda observed:

> I think they normally don't stand up for the staff anyhow. If a faculty member wants something, they usually get it. So are you going to go to them with this problem? I don't think so. I don't think they're impartial. I don't at all. I think there's too much interest in "Well, he makes a lot of money for the University, we have to appease him." I see it every day.

Dallas stated it more bluntly: "Staff are peons. [The University] is not going to get much money out of us. He is generating money for the University so whatever he does [they] are going to overlook."

Like many employers, the University adopted a flexible policy designed to prevent sexual harassment before it occurred and to handle problems after they arose. But based on their experiences and the experiences of others, the female employees in this study questioned the value of those policies. In particular, they questioned the loyalties of the staff who implemented the grievance procedures, recognizing that they would almost inevitably choose the employer's interests over those of the employers. Thus, in the view of its intended beneficiaries, the Written Policy was not meant to protect employee rights but to guard the employer against legal liability.

Rights Consciousness in Action: Enacting the Grievance Procedures

In the workplace, employees' rights consciousness is more than their familiarity with their rights or their expectations about how the grievance procedure would work.

Legal consciousness also embraces their efforts to assert their rights. In this study, women's practical knowledge of the grievance procedure shaped their responses to unwanted sexual attention at work. By providing opportunities for women to pursue complaints, the Written Policy did create an arena where women could resist sexual harassment. On the other hand, supervisors administered the Written Policy in an adversarial way that discouraged women's complaints. When women feared the procedure and censored their own grievances, they enact a limited view of rights that re-creates rather than subverts inequality.

Pursuing Complaints and Self-Help

No one in the study actually filed a formal grievance, let alone a lawsuit. A small group of women brought their complaints about unwanted sexual encounters to the attention of third parties. Consisting mostly of extremely explicit sexual overtures or physical contact, these incidents probably met the behavioral tests for sexual harassment, and women turned to the Written Policy in their efforts to resist such treatment. But based on their observations of management practices, women anticipated an adversarial process that would question their credibility and challenge their claims. As a result, women approached the grievance procedures only after trying to substantiate their complaints, or they bypassed the procedure by engaging in self-help.

Women prepared for making complaints as though the grievance procedure was an adversarial process by generating evidence that would support their claims and that would bolster their credibility. For example, some preserved incriminating evidence to substantiate their allegations. Jane worked with a professor from another unit in the University. On an almost daily basis, he sent her e-mails that critiqued her marriage, complained about his sex life, and asked her out on dates. When asked whether she had thought about filing a complaint, she said: "Yeah, I have, but … I kept the messages, and I, you know, made sure I had a backlog of things just in case I had to, but I didn't think that I would do it unless I really had to." She showed the e-mails to her supervisor who was sympathetic but advised her not to mention the incident to anyone else. Although she agreed, she kept hard copies of the messages in case she finally decided to file a complaint.

When there was no incriminating evidence, women tried to create it by documenting the harassing incidents. For example, Siena told a friend working in the office that her co-worker's lingering near her desk making suggestive comments was making her feel uncomfortable. Her friend suggested that she record each event. She said: "I'm pretty thorough at documentation. I wrote down word for word what happened and what I said in response to it as well." She would later produce this document when she went to her supervisor to complain about her co-worker's behavior. Notably, every other woman I interviewed – even the ones who did not complain – had committed the incident to writing.

Other women combined complaints and direct confrontations with harassers as part of a multi-strategy effort to get the harassment to stop. Using the Written Policy, women reported "educating" their harassers about the limits of appropriate behavior in the workplace. Supervisors sometimes reinforced these lessons by having informal discussions with the harassers about their conduct. One survey respondent reported:

There were a few faculty members who made inappropriate, sexually harassing comments. One left. The other has been educated – partly by me, partly by a firmer dean. This person thought jokes and cartoons of a sexual nature were appropriate for work but now knows they are not and has been "rehabilitated."

Thus, both employees and University supervisors invoked the Written Policy as a basis to encourage harassers to adapt to their working environments even without pursuing formal complaints.

Directly confronting the harasser was sometimes a last resort when the grievance procedure failed. When supervisors failed to act to protect employees with complaints of unwanted sexual attention, those employees directly invoked their rights by telling the harasser that the behavior had to stop. Rose concluded the receptionist's sexual conversations with the coaching staff were sexual harassment after reading the University's sexual harassment policy. But none of the designated complaint handlers was willing to intervene because the accused harasser was a woman and a co-worker. Finally, Rose decided to take matters into her own hands:

So basically I finally said, "Screw the system." Because I went through the system. And I said, "I'm going to confront her on my own." And all four of us, all four of the secretary staff got together, and I just said it right to her face. I said, "I'm completely uncomfortable with the way you behave around the office. I think you're inappropriate in your behavior with the coaches. I don't need to be told that I'm a prude, or that I'm being irrational, but I've talked to some of the staff about it; they see it as well. If nothing else, you need to do your job. And you're not doing your job. I'm doing your job for you. I've had enough of it, and I'm not going to do it anymore."

In these cases, the Written Policy offered the potential to undermine sexual employment practices that interfered with women's equality in the workplace. But that potential was undermined by supervisory behavior that created an adversarial process. In the face of this process, most women chose not to pursue a complaint.

Lumping It

Most women in the study did not complain to supervisors about their experiences with unwanted sexual attention at work. This decision was sometimes based on a judgment that the conduct was not sufficiently serious to merit a complaint. Other women, however, experienced incidents that were disruptive and distracting to their job performance and would have liked some assistance in resolving the problem. When considering whether to make a complaint, however, they anticipated their supervisors' response. Many believed that this response would be adversarial and hostile to their complaints; some believed that their supervisors would be ineffectual in solving the problem; others were concerned about retaliation, and so they decided not to complain. Thus, they anticipated an adversarial complaint process, which provided a serious disincentive to pursuing a grievance.

Women often expected their supervisors to take the side of the harasser. As the harasser's representative, the supervisor might wonder whether the woman had done something to attract the harasser's attention or suggest that the problem was not particularly serious. For example, Erna worked in an office with a middle-aged man relentlessly made sexual comments to his mostly female colleagues. Erna described him as:

> ... always making sexual innuendos; and with every word you said, he found something to make an innuendo about it ... To me, it is almost worse than having somebody come up and *grab* you. Because it's a constant barrage of innuendo. And it just gets really annoying. And then you don't know how to handle it. And if you would say, "Look, you're always making this innuendo," then he would start to say, "Are you one of those dykes too?" or whatever the case was. That sort of thing. He just didn't understand that that was not appropriate.

Although her contact with the harasser was a daily irritant, Erna did not complain about his conduct to her supervisor. She anticipated that her supervisor would suggest that she was at fault for failing to handle the harasser in an appropriate manner. She said: "I think when you go to tell your supervisor, it always comes back: 'Well, what did you do?' You know, 'Just tell him no ...,' 'Well, I haven't heard this from anybody else,' type of thing."

Women were also skeptical of their supervisors' power to handle any kind of personnel problems, let alone an issue as sensitive as an allegation of sexual harassment. Erna observed:

> The procedures here don't work ... If I had wanted to complain about [the harasser] I really had two choices. I could have gone to my boss. Or I could have gone to the office manager. And my boss ... might have told me to go to the office manager, or he might have said to me "Why don't you just leave it?" And that was the whole chain of this process that was going on [with a different personnel problem], and people trying to take it up the chain of command, and it didn't work. In our particular case, our office manager just doesn't deal with this stuff. And I don't know if she doesn't deal with it, or if she just gets no reinforcement from her point of view ... And then you have another choice: you could go to Human Resources. And that seems to have been a very negative thing because Human Resources ... has never come through with any other problems that people have had. So people don't do that.

In the course of her employment, Erna had watched the supervisors and human resources professionals as they tried to settle employee conflict with very little success. Their ineffectual responses to employee problems undermined Erna's confidence that they would ever be able to get the harasser to stop his behavior.

Finally, although the University's sexual harassment policy specially promised to protect employees from retaliation, women still feared the effects of a complaint. While they acknowledged that their jobs might not have been in danger, they feared that by coming forward, their more powerful harassers would make subtle but consequential changes in the working environment. At a previous job, Joanne had noticed such changes when she complained about a high-ranking company official. When she entered a room, he would either stop talking or loudly comment on her humorlessness to colleagues. This experience made her reluctant to complain at the University when her female supervisor grabbed her breast: "If I didn't lose my job, it would make for a more hostile environment than it was working with her, being how she is."

Conclusion

This chapter suggests that employment policies and grievance procedures may not be fulfilling their promise to protect women from sexual harassment. Indeed, the policies provide expansive definitions of sexual harassment that not only prohibit discrimination but also protect women's dignity. These are important messages of equality, but the policies only represent the organization's aspirations. The effectiveness of those policies depends on supervisors who may be more concerned with defending the employer from a potential lawsuit than with vindicating the rights of women. In fact, managerial behavior may turn a grievance procedure into an adversarial system fraught with risks and obstacles often associated with the formal legal system. In this view, it is hardly surprising that many women decline to pursue a complaint in favor of engaging in self-help or doing nothing at all.

Yet sexual harassment policies may be revitalized to better serve the employees who need them. Employers may invest more resources in familiarizing all their employees about their rights and responsibilities with respect to sexual behavior at work. In addition, supervisors may be specifically encouraged to intervene more often, in informal ways, to diffuse unpleasant working environments before they turn into potential lawsuits. Some employers have hired an ombudsperson, outside of the ordinary managerial structure and highly visible, who can address problems with sexual harassment with flexibility.

This case also illustrates both the promise of civil rights laws and the perils of entrusting them with the mission of dismantling inequality. Laws like those prohibiting sexual harassment create opportunities for resistance and empower individuals to challenge inequality in their daily working lives. But those opportunities are often in the hands of organizations that can be hostile to employee interests. By emphasizing both legal knowledge and cultural practice, the constitutive approach to law in everyday life reveals the way organizations can shape the legal consciousness of ordinary people. That consciousness can be empowering and can undermine structural disadvantage, or it can simply lead people to be resigned to injustice.

References

Arvey, R.D., and Cavanagh, M.A. (1995) "Using Surveys to Assess the Prevalence of Sexual Harassment: Some Methodological Problems." *Journal of Social Issues* 51:39–52.

Bernstein, A. (1994). "Law, Culture, and Harassment." *University of Pennsylvania Law Review* 142:1227–1311.

——. (1997) "Treating Sexual Harassment with Respect." *Harvard Law Review* 111:445–527.

Bisom-Rapp, S. (1999) "Bulletproofing the Workplace: Symbol and Substance in Employment Discrimination Law Practice." *Florida State University Law Review* 26:959.

Cornell, D. (1995) *The Imaginary Domain: Abortion, Pornography, and Sexual Harassment.* New York: Routledge.

Edelman, L.B., Erlanger, H.S., and Lande, J. (1993) "Internal Dispute Resolution: The Transformation of Civil Rights in the Workplace." *Law and Society Review* 27:497–534.

——, Uggen, C., and Erlanger, H.S. (1999) "The Endogeneity of Legal Regulation: Grievance Procedures as Rational Myth." *American Journal of Sociology* 105:406–454.

Ewick, P., and Silbey, S.S. (1998) *The Common Place of Law: Stories from Everyday Life*. Chicago: University of Chicago Press.

Fitzgerald, L., Swan, S., and Fischer, K. (1995) "Why Didn't She Just Report Him? The Psychological and Legal Implications of Women's Responses to Sexual Harassment." *Journal of Social Issues* 51:117–138.

Francke, K. (1997) "What's Wrong With Sexual Harassment?" *Stanford Law Review* 691–772.

Hoffmann, E.A. (2004) "Selective Sexual Harassment: How the Labeling of Token Workers Can Produce Different Workplace Environments for Similar Groups of Women" *Law and Human Behavior* 28:24–45.

Kritzer, H.M., Vidmar, N., and W.A. Bogart. (1991). "To Confront Or Not To Confront: Measuring Claiming Rates In Discrimination Grievances." *Law and Society Review* 25:875–87.

MacKinnon, C.A. (1979) *The Sexual Harassment of Working Women*. New Haven: Yale University Press.

Marshall, A.-M. (2001) "A Spectrum in Oppositional Consciousness: Sexual Harassment Plaintiffs and Their Lawyers" in J.J. Mansbridge and A. Morris (eds) *Oppositional Consciousness: The Subjective Roots of Social Protest*. Chicago: University of Chicago Press.

—— (2003) "Injustice Frames, Legality, and the Everyday Construction of Sexual Harassment." *Law and Social Inquiry* 28(3) 617–628.

Marshall, A.-M. (2005). "Idle Rights: Employees' Rights Consciousness and the Construction of Sexual Harassment." *Law and Society Review* 39:83–123.

Marshall, A.-M., and Barclay S. (2003). "In Their Own Words: How Ordinary People Construct the Legal World." *Law and Social Inquiry* 28:617–28.

Merit Systems Protection Board (1995) *Sexual Harassment in the Federal Workplace: Trends, Progress and Continuing Challenges*. Washington DC: US Merit Systems Protection Board.

Merry, S.E. (1990) *Getting Justice and Getting Even: Legal Consciousness Among Working-Class Americans*. Chicago: University of Chicago Press.

Miller, R.E., and Sarat, A. (1980–81) "Grievances, Claims and Disputes: Assessing the Adversary Culture." *Law and Society Review* 15:525.

Nielsen, L.B. (2000) "Situating Legal Consciousness: Experiences and Attitudes of Ordinary Citizens About Law and Street Harassment." *Law and Society Review* 34:1055–1090.

Saguy, A.C. (2000) "Employment Discrimination or Sexual Violence? Defining Sexual Harassment in American and French Law." *Law and Society Review* 34:1091–1128.

Sarat, A.and Kearns. T.R. (1995). "Beyond the Great Divide: Forms of Legal Scholarship and Everyday Life." In *Law and Everyday Life*, eds. Austin Sarat and Thomas R. Kearns. Ann Arbor: University of Michigan Press.

Schultz, V. (1998) "Reconceptualizing Sexual Harassment." *Yale Law Journal* 107:1732–1805.

Sewell, W.H. (1992) "A Theory of Structure: Duality, Agency and Transformation." *American Journal of Sociology* 98:1–29.

Sherwyn, D., Heise, M., and Eigen, Z.J. (2001) "Don't Train Your Employees and Cancel Your '1–800' Harassment Hotline: An Empirical Examination and Correction of the Flaws in the Affirmative Defense to Sexual Harassment Charges." *Fordham Law Review* 69:1265–1304.

Zemans, F.K. (1983) "Legal Mobilization: The Neglected Role of the Law in the Political System." *American Political Science Review* 77:690–703.

Cases cited

Barnes v. Train, 13 FEP Cases 123 (D. DC 1974), rev'd sub nom *Barnes v. Costle*, 561 F.2d 983 (DC Cir. 1977)
Burlington Industries v. Ellerth, 524 U.S. 742 (1998)
Ellison v. Brady, 924 F.2d 872 (9th Cir. 1991)
Faragher v. City of Boca Raton, 524 U.S. 775 (1998)
Harris v. Forklift Systems, Inc., 510 U.S. 17 (1993)
Oncale v. Sundowner Offshore Services, Inc., 523 U.S. 75 (1998)
Vinson v. Meritor Savings Bank, 23 FEP Cases 37 (D. DC 1980), rev'd 753 F.2d 141 (DC Cir 1985), aff'd sub nom *Meritor Savings Bank v. Vinson*, 477 U.S. 57 (1986)
Williams v. Saxbe, 413 F.Supp. 654 (D. DC 1976), rev'd on procedural grounds 587 F.2d 1240 (DC Cir. 1978), on remand sub nom *Williams v. Bell*, 487 F.Supp. 1387 (D. DC 1980)

PART II
CONTESTED RIGHTS

Chapter 6

On-the-Job Sexual Harassment:
How Labels Enable Men to Discriminate
through Sexual Harassment and Exclusion

ELIZABETH A. HOFFMANN[1]

This chapter explores legal consciousness in a traditionally male, blue-collar occupation – taxicab driving – at a company I call "Coop Cab."[2] It examines how the men at this cab company understood – and misunderstood – sexual harassment prohibitions. Informally, they assigned their women co-workers different labels, treating each woman differently based on which label she had. Specifically, some women were labeled "heterosexual" and were sexually harassed while others were labeled "lesbian" and were left alone. At this worksite, the men's legal consciousness, reflecting their differential use of labels, greatly affected the nature of the interactions between men and women within the company and created radically different workplace experiences for each group of differently labeled women. The labels they assigned were "lesbian" and "heterosexual." These labels did not necessarily correspond with the reality of these women's lives, but were simply the way that their male co-workers categorized them. Because men constituted a greater percentage (84 percent) of the workers at the cab company, their labels had greater power in affecting the dynamics of their workplace.

The men at Coop Cab understood sexual harassment law as prohibiting "unwanted" sexual advances. These men believed their lesbian-labeled co-workers to not be interested in any type of sexual relationship with them and so did not engage them in sexual talk. However, the men failed to understand that many of their actions toward those women they labeled as heterosexual also were unwanted and might have constituted sexual harassment.

This disparate treatment of different groups of women employees may be particularly problematic when women account for a small percentage of the workers at a given site. Kanter's research on token women demonstrates that women whose numbers compose approximately 15 percent of a company's workforce are often "labeled" and divided into differently treated subgroups by their numerically dominant male co-workers and supervisors (1977). Male co-workers ascribe specific female stereotypes to each label and, subsequently, have different types of interactions with female co-workers of each label. These labels allow male co-workers both to

[1] This research was supported by a National Science Foundation grant (SBR–9801948).
[2] The name of the company, Coop Cab, is an alias, as are all interviewees' names.

treat women as different from men and also to categorically treat some women differently from other women on the job (Kanter 1977).

The focus of the chapter is on men's behaviors and their labeling of female co-workers, not merely on the women's perceptions of their male co-workers' actions or attitudes. This is an important distinction. I interviewed various groups of workers at the company I studied: women who were labeled heterosexual, women who were labeled lesbian, men workers and men managers, recent and long-time employees, and workers who had left the company. Well-triangulated data in this study strongly indicate that the dynamics at this company were the result of the men treating different groups of women differently based on labels, rather than of women who had been labeled in different ways interpreting men's actions differently.

I begin by examining theories on token women and sexual harassment. I follow this with a discussion of extant legal consciousness literature. Next, I turn to the data and explore how the use of labels divided women employees in a harassed group and an ignored group. I explore how these different labels result in different experiences with regard to sexual harassment. Finally, I discuss how these labels informed the male co-workers' framing of the male-female interactions and the results for their sexual harassment legal consciousness.

Token Women and Sexual Harassment

Numerous scholars have documented gender segregation in the workforce and the correlation between jobs being less desirable and being held by women[3] (for example: England 1979; Miller 1992; Miller-Loessi 1992; Roos and Reskin 1992; Swerdlow 1989; Wharton 1991). Not only have women historically been employed in different jobs from those held by men, but they have held the lower-status, less flexible, and less financially rewarding jobs (England 1979; Miller 1992). However, increasingly women are entering occupations that had been held exclusively by men.

When gender desegregation of traditionally male occupations began, both men and women workers had difficulty adjusting to the new work environments. The men in these jobs had to contend not only with the physical changes and new policies that were implemented as women entered "their" fields, but also with the social changes in the workplace as it grew away from being a homosocial, male environment. Rather than blurring the gender line between what are considered acceptable male jobs and acceptable female jobs, the presence of women in traditionally male jobs often heightened gender differences (Swerdlow 1989). The handful of women in these occupations also had to adapt to a sometimes unwelcoming, sometimes hostile, workplace environment. No longer having access to a supportive social group of all-

---

[3] Some researchers argue that jobs are based less on what tasks are actually performed and are more socially constructed by the perceptions and expectations of employers and the capability of workers to negotiate roles (Miller 1992). Miller found that gender, more so than other variables, significantly and systematically differentiates the organization of work (1992). Gender is an important aspect of this interactional construction because men and women continually reproduce gender inequalities in their daily interactions at work (and elsewhere). One implication of the pervasive belief in the gendered nature of work is that "essential natures" of men and women in the workplace are reinforced (Miller-Loessi 1992).

women co-workers, these women often experienced isolation in the workplace (Hoffmann 2005; Kanter 1982). While some men reacted positively to the entrance of women, many reacted with physical and verbal hostility (Swerdlow 1989). Many researchers contest whether the new environments created by the slowly growing numbers of women in traditionally male jobs were any easier for these token women than when their percentages were minuscule.

Kanter's work on women in large business settings demonstrates that women who constitute a small percentage of the employees at their workplace face numerous impediments to success. Kanter differentiates between small groups of women by the ratio of these women to their male co-workers. She defines "tokens" as those who belong to the sex that comprises 15 percent or less of the workforce, with the other 85 percent being the "dominants"(Kanter 1977:208–9).[4] Dworkin and others add to this conceptualization by arguing that the term "token" refers not simply to any numerically rare workers, but more specifically to those who also have lower status than those who comprise the majority of the workplace populace. In this way, their marginality is "dual" because the token group includes few members in the workplace and also possesses little status and power in the greater society (Dworkin, Chafetz, and Dworkin 1986:402).

Kanter found that male colleagues rarely saw token women as individuals, but rather as personifications of stereotypes about their gender or as symbols to reinforce the dominant masculine subculture. She found that part of the male subculture's reaction to the presence of tokens was to create boundaries that served to exclude these tokens from informal relations and networks. Facing such boundaries, tokens had to choose to either "assimilate" or maintain a separate identity and be labeled as "troublemakers" (Kanter 1977).[5]

Not only are token workers viewed differently, but the attitudes and actions of male co-workers strongly affect token women's performance and well-being (Kanter 1977). Tokens were treated as "strangers, not accepted as welcome colleagues" (Dworkin, Chafetz, and Dworkin 1986:403). For example, Swerdlow's research on token women working in a mass transit system found that men's "deeply held belief in male superiority" was challenged by the presence of these women (1989). These men responded by creating collective re-interpretations of women's success at the job that allowed them to preserve their beliefs in male supremacy while accepting the entrance of women (Swerdlow 1989). Kanter found that token women often experience "role encapsulation" which places labels on token workers based on stereotypes and assumptions. By being seen as fulfilling the stereotypes of all the women within one's imposed category, individual differences and personality of the labeled woman are not seen by her male co-workers and supervisors.

In her study of token women in a corporate work setting, Kanter described four categories of labels for token workers: "mother," "seductress," "pet," and "iron maiden." The labels discussed in this chapter are not the same as those labels described by Kanter (1977), but are particular to this workplace. Other worksites

---

[4] When the ratio reaches 35:65, Kanter refers to the smaller groups as "minorities" and the larger groups as "majorities" (Kanter 1977:208–9).

[5] Kanter assumed that tokens are aware of both their token status and any negative treatment (1977). Other researchers, however, question these assumptions (Dworkin, Chafetz, and Dworkin 1986).

might have different labels. However, the specific labels are not what is important, but rather the different treatment of groups of women workers based on their labels.

Scant research exists on sexual harassment of token workers specifically (see Hoffmann 2004 for further discussion). Some researchers suggest that sexual harassment occurs because of gender-role expectations within the job itself and is especially strong in workplaces with strong gender skews. Traditionally male jobs become masculinized and are linked with male gender-role behaviors (Konrad and Gutek 1986). Konrad and Gutek suggest that these jobs are likely to have expectations whereby males are supposed to initiate sexual contact and women are supposed to respond. When women work in these nontraditional jobs, surrounded by men, they are treated differently because they violate sex-role expectations (1986). Marshall explains that "[p]olitical debates about women's role in society offer varying interpretations for the everyday experience of sexual interactions at work" (Marshall 2003:667). Because women in traditionally male jobs challenge the sex-role expectation, they may be sexually harassed (Konrad and Gutek 1986).

Sexual harassment of women in blue-collar, non-traditional jobs, such as taxicab driving, might be more prevalent than in other occupations. Ragins and Scandura found that "women in male-typed, blue-collar occupations (e.g., firefighters, police officers) reported greater sexual harassment than women in male-typed, white-collar occupations (e.g., engineers, attorneys, managers)" (Ragins and Scandura 1995:444). Also, women in blue-collar jobs who experienced greater sexual harassment were also *less* likely to bring harassment-based legal action (Ragins and Scandura 1995). Instead, women workers in traditionally male occupations are more likely to leave their jobs than are other similar women employees in jobs categorized as traditionally female (Schultz 1990).

This chapter describes how the labeling used by men at Coop Cab determined which women they sexually harassed and which they, instead, avoided. By examining legal consciousness in the workplace rather than in dispute-processing institutions such as courts or neighborhood mediators' offices, I investigate perceptions of harm and blame without the biases possibly imposed by drawing from subjects already present in dispute-processing settings. Because much of the legal consciousness research is conducted within dispute-processing institutions (Merry 1990; Sarat 1990), many interview subjects have already had their legal consciousness prompted and focused by their contact with these institutions before they become part of legal consciousness research (Marshall and Barclay 2003). Additionally, subjects who sought out certain forms of dispute resolution prior to participating in research studies and who, thus, self-selected into the studies, might experience legal consciousness that is less characteristic of the general population.

This research circumvents these methodological difficulties by interviewing people in their workplace and asking them about a wide range of workplace issues. The interview topics included the culture of the company, previous positions held, interpersonal dynamics, positive and negative aspects of the job, gender dynamics at work, and comparisons to previous jobs. The workplace, a familiar place for the interview subjects, is not associated specifically with dispute resolution or other legalistic procedures. Thus, in the same spirit as the work by Ewick and Silbey (1998), this study located interview subjects who had not self-selected into the category of "grievants" and simply invited the interview subjects to share their "everyday" legal consciousness without focusing them on specific forums or events.

The wide, loosely structured focus of the interviews attempted to avoid prompting subjects or suggesting responses about legal consciousness. I explain my specific methodology in the following section.

Methods

Sample and Interviews

To study workplace sexual harassment and legal consciousness, I drew on both interview and observational data. I selected a taxicab company, "Coop Cab," which employs about 150 workers, 16 percent of whom are women – approximating the 15 percent given by Kanter as her definition of "token women." The company's location in a university town, Jefferson City, affects whom it employs: Coop Cab is known as having well-educated drivers, many with advanced degrees and often ideologically progressive (Hoffmann 2003).

I interviewed 20 workers at Coop Cab: ten women and ten men, two of the interviewees were no longer working at the company at the time of the interview. I was careful to sample a diverse mix of interviewees in order to capture a range of perspectives. Each interview was open-ended and lasted approximately two and one-half hours. I used a set of questions as initial probes on a wide variety of work-related topics. I based follow-up questions on each interviewee's response. In each interview, I encouraged the informants to tell me "anything they thought applied" to each set of questions. Most of the interviews were conducted in public places, such as coffee houses and restaurants, and at the companies themselves, in the parking lots and the breakrooms. All of the interviews were taped and transcribed, so the quotes included in this chapter are direct quotes rather than paraphrases.[6] I asked for the permission of each interviewee before I began taping, and explained that even if they would not let me tape them I still would be interested in conducting the interview. No one objected to my taping.

I also observed meetings, attended formal grievance meetings, simply spent time in the breakroom. Additionally, I read several years of back issues of the company newsletter. Although neither my observations nor the company newsletters are specifically cited in this chapter, they contributed to my knowledge of this cab company.

Sexual Harassment

Officially, the company took a firm stance against workplace sexual harassment. In addition to being regulated by the laws that affect workplaces, such as sexual harassment laws, the cab company also had a handbook of rules and procedures. The handbook was given to all new members. Among other rules, sexual harassment was explicitly forbidden at the company.

---

[6] The quotations presented in this chapter have been edited for confidentiality and readability. Great care was taken to maintain the substance and tone of interviewees' remarks, while eliminating some of the more awkward constructions of impromptu responses.

Coop Cab had a two-prong formal grievance system. To appeal discipline decisions, workers came before the Workers' Council, a randomly selected, rotating committee of members. To initiate discipline against another member, workers brought grievances before the elected Board of Directors. Workers were more likely to have brought grievances before the Workers' Council than the Board.

Instead of using my own understanding of sexual harassment law or offering the interviewees exact legal wording, I wanted *their* definitions because *that* is what informs their legal consciousness. I gave examples along a broad spectrum, if they asked me for clarification of the term, although few did. In many interviews, the term sexual harassment was brought up by the interviewees themselves before I had a chance to raise it as a question. I deliberately chose not to provide the legal definition of harassment on the basis of sex as defined in Sec 703 of Title VII of the Civil Rights Act (1964), because I feared this official definition would inhibit the interviewees from using their own definitions of "sexual harassment."

The women in this study often began certain anecdotes by categorizing the behavior as sexual harassment, although some would occasionally begin a story not using the label of harassment and then affix this label towards the story's end or during their discussion of the story. Men were less likely to label their own behavior as "sexual harassment," although three men, when describing the behaviors of other men, categorized the other men's behaviors as sexual harassment. More commonly, in describing similar behavior as that labeled by the women as harassment – sometimes even in describing the very same stories – the men used words like "teasing," "having some fun with," "messing with," and other terms which implied that they saw little harm in their behavior.

Because I am interested in men's treatment of their women co-workers, I was careful to triangulate my data on this phenomenon. "Triangulation" refers to collecting stories of the same phenomena from interviewees with very different perspectives. This allows the researcher to explore a given phenomenon – such as sexual harassment – from a variety of standpoints, thus substantiating that the researcher's evolving understanding of the phenomenon is accurate and not simply reflecting the bias of an insular group of friends. By triangulating, I was able to confirm the dynamics the interviewees described, thus heightening the validity of the data. To gather this information, I asked about men's accounts of themselves, men's accounts of other men's behavior, and women's accounts of men's behavior. Each way of gathering this data produced similarly accurate accounts.

The women at Coop Cab were aware of which label the men had attached to the individual women. During the interviews, the women discussed what label they believed they and others had; they were well aware of whom the men perceived as heterosexuals or lesbians. Even though the men's labels sometimes did not match the women's own self-definitions, the women could discern that one particular woman was labeled "heterosexual" while another particular woman was labeled "lesbian." The women's actual sexual orientation was sometimes correlated with the men's labels. Often, women who did self-define as heterosexual were labeled "heterosexual" and women who self-defined as lesbian were labeled as "lesbian." However, the labels did completely match the self-labeling. Sometimes self-defined heterosexual women were labeled as "lesbian" and vice versa. Moreover, women who defined as bisexual were always categorized as either "heterosexual" or "lesbian."

I also spoke in-depth with some men about how they labeled and who had which label; the men, in their own interviews, confirmed the women's understandings of the labels' applications. Also, during these discussions, although usually at separate times during the interview, the men talked about how they interacted with various women co-workers. Thus, although I learned a great deal about the impact of labeling from the women, I confirmed this information with the men's reports. In the following sections, I do not provide each woman's assessments and the confirmation of these by her male co-workers. Since this would be lengthy and cumbersome without adding sufficiently to the discussion, I generally provide only the most illustrative quotations.

Because this sample is small and non-random, these findings may not represent all workers in all businesses, or even all cab drivers. However, I believe that the depth and richness of information that this data achieved balances the lack of generalizability that would have been possible with a more quantitative study. Rather than produce widely generalizable statistics, this study offers a nuanced examination of legal consciousness in one company.

Results

The men at Coop Cab stated that they were quite aware that sexual harassment was prohibited both by law and by company rules. As one male driver explained the importance of these rules in the company handbook: "It's written in our bible that sexual harassment is one of the easiest ways to get fired out of the place." Nevertheless, these men did harass some women co-workers, while leaving the other women free of this harassment.

At the worksite studied here, men divided their women co-workers into two groups and assigned different labels to each group. Based on these labels, men sexually harassed some women, but left others alone. The label each woman received did not necessarily reflect the woman's self-identity, but rather reflected how her male co-workers chose to treat her and how they understood the sexual harassment laws.

Although the use of labels at Coop Cab was similar to the behavior reported by Kanter in terms of the labels' bright lines and powerful divisions, the men at the cab company did not use the same labels described by Kanter (mother, seductress, pet, iron maiden). The labels that were used to subcategorize and divide token women at Coop Cab were labels that referred to how the men perceived the sexual orientation of their women co-workers: heterosexual or lesbian. Sometimes the labels reflected the woman's self-identification, but other times the labels did not mirror the woman's own perceptions. The labels the men at Coop Cab used were not random or meaningless terms. The labels "heterosexual" and "lesbian" implied certain types or stereotypes of women to these men. All interviewees – heterosexual, bisexual, and lesbian women and heterosexual men[7] – explained that men treated different groups of women differently, based on which label (lesbian or heterosexual) a woman had – lesbian or heterosexual. This produced dissimilar workplace experiences for these two groups of women: men rarely harassed women labeled lesbian, but often targeted women labeled heterosexual.

---

[7] All of the men I interviewed self-identified as heterosexual.

Harassment of Heterosexual-Labeled Women

Men subcategorized the women at Coop Cab based on their perceptions or assumptions about these women's sexual orientation. Each woman was placed into one of two categories: heterosexual or lesbian. The labels were distinct from women's own identities – sometimes the labels correlated with the woman's own self-identification, but other times they did not. Yet, in either situation, the labels had powerful effects on how the men treated their women co-workers and how these women experienced their workplace environment. Thus, the labels are important because they constitute an essential first step in engaging in differential treatment.

Importantly, the labels had nothing to do with sexual orientation per se; the phenomena of selective sexual harassment could have occurred with any other labels. Nevertheless, the labels were not random or meaningless classifications. The labels "heterosexual" and "lesbian" implied certain types or stereotypes of women. Women whom the men labeled "heterosexual" were perceived by the men as inherently and always interested in romantic or sexual relationships with them. In contrast, the women whom the men labeled "lesbian" were seen as not only disinterested in intimate relations with the men co-workers, but as disdainful of all male contact. The perceptions of these labels greatly affected the nature of interactions between men and women within the company and, specifically, the likelihood of sexual harassment of individual women. While the particular names of the labels have importance and meaning outside their use for differential treatment, this chapter focuses specifically on how the labels were used to harass some women while others were not harassed.

All interviewed workers – heterosexual, bisexual, and lesbian women and heterosexual men – described the company as having a workplace culture in which (heterosexual) men would treat different groups of women differently, based on which label a woman had – "lesbian" or "heterosexual." Men's statements support this assessment that their labeling was binary. This labeling produced dissimilar workplace experiences for these two groups of women: men often targeted women labeled "heterosexual," but rarely harassed women labeled "lesbian," as is discussed further below.

One woman who was labeled heterosexual by her male co-workers was Nancy. She had dated several men at Coop Cab. She described her experience when she initially tried to train for a dispatcher position, one of the positions in the cab company with more responsibility and status. She recounted being driven out of the dispatcher office, forfeiting her opportunity to gain the necessary training:

> If you go and sit in the [dispatch] office when it's slow, that's called "slumming." So I kind of got in this habit. There would be other people slumming in there and people would be sitting around joking because it was pretty slow; dispatcher's not stressed out.
> I started to notice that these three guys in particular in the office sort of had these inside jokes going on while I was there. It took me awhile to figure out that they decided that I was hanging out there because I had a crush on the dispatcher. When I got there, [one day] one of the other guys who was in there said, "Jake's not here today, he's in New York." Jake was the dispatcher. I don't remember what I said to them, but I remember I was pissed. I said something real nasty to him though, and he said, "Well just tell me. Don't you like Jake?" I said, "Yeah, I think Jake's a great guy. I think he's really smart and I think he's really witty. How come you don't think Frank has a thing for Jake. Frank is in the office all the time." And he said "Frank who? The only Frank I know is a guy." I go, "Exactly."

I got really mad and I stopped hanging out in the dispatch office; I stopped slumming. What I didn't realize at the time was that this was the way that you started to work in the dispatch office. There was no training. When you were slumming in the office, if it got busy, you picked up the phone. Then the dispatcher would tell you what you were doing wrong, what other information they needed on the call, and you learned to answer the phones. Then when a shift became available, you became the phone answerer. And then a dispatcher.

Essentially, although they were just "joking," it was really harassing me out of this opportunity. [It turns out, the person] who was hired two weeks after I was, was dispatching within the year, because he kept on slumming in the office.

While Nancy described her experience with sexual harassment as one which drove her out of the dispatch office and prevented her from receiving the necessary training to become a dispatcher, Laura discussed how her fear of harassment forced her to curtail her after-hours activities. Specifically, she described her reluctance to go out with male co-workers after work in order to avoid sending a message that some would read as availability. Laura later expressed her belief that these precautions and concerns would not be necessary if she were labeled "lesbian." She put it in this way:

I did feel intimidated, sometimes. There was one situation that I thought was really out of hand. In that, one of the dispatchers [wouldn't stop harassing her]. Well, a lot of times if you're just nice, and you're thought of as straight, you open yourself up to being harassed. Sometimes I'm very reluctant to [go out with male co-workers after work], because I don't want it to be interpreted the wrong way.

Thus, in order to avoid sexual harassment, Laura would seldom go out after work with her male co-workers.

Helen, who was also labeled heterosexual, described the debate she repeatedly had with herself over how to respond to sexual harassment at Coop Cab. In the first quote, she described men whom she felt portrayed themselves as pro-feminist, yet failed to fulfill this ideology with their actions, using offensive actions or sexual comments. She said:

I think, a lot of men still feel that [cab driving's] a traditional male area, and women, it's not their place to cross it. And no one's going to be direct about that. I mean no one's going to say, "You shouldn't be here." That's not what this cooperative is all about. They talk about "equality." You know? Say that in quotations. But it's hard to get behind that mentality … And sometimes there are other drivers who you just don't know whether you want to take it seriously.

You just don't know what the repercussions are going to be if someone is joking around and saying something sexual, or whatever, toward you. You don't know whether: is it just like I don't have a sense of humor, or what if I file a grievance about this? Or should I just be taking this? Should I just be verbally strong back at this person? Is that how I should deal with it?

In a later quote, she explained that some behaviors that may have seemed like sexual harassment were, to her, part of the milieu of the job, while other actions constituted sexual harassment of a more menacing nature:

There are policies involving harassment, especially sexual harassment. Because things have come up in the past ... Sometimes (harassment's) so subtle, and you're working in a cab company and cab companies tend to be bawdy, people spit, talk, swear a lot. And tell a lot of bawdy jokes. I mean, if you're really ultra-sensitive you probably shouldn't be working at a cab company because that's just the atmosphere ... You know? So it's a fine line. [A particular dispatcher] has a real bawdy sense of humor. He just likes to be that way and doesn't hurt anybody because of it. He just likes to tell these jokes.

But it's a different feeling than you'd get from other people, from somebody else who is closing in on you. And trying to change your behavior and trying to intimidate you, through jokes or through use of certain types of harassment that might be subtle and might be *not* so subtle.

While Helen tried to not be "oversensitive," she, nevertheless, believed that some men's behavior toward her was offensive and intimidating.

Mimi described an incident in which she stood up to her harasser who had labeled her "heterosexual." On this occasion, a male co-worker, in front of other drivers, asked her to meet him at the airport to have sex with him:

I've had a couple of guys hit on me, harass me [make sexual, inappropriate inquiries] ... I can remember one of the guys was telling me, like, we're in the office in the afternoon. A bunch of us were getting ready to go and drive and this one guy had gotten the van, which is 59. You know, big deal, Cab 59. It's a van and we all know that. He was saying, "Mimi, why don't you meet me out at the airport, I got 59." "I'm like, what's up with that?" He says, "You know, it's so romantic, wouldn't it be fun if we could get in the back of the cab." And all this stuff. The other drivers kind of look at me and I said, "Dude, you'd better shut up now while you're ahead because you're coming close." You know? I kind of pointed my finger at him and told him, "You're really coming close to harassing me," and he said, "Well wouldn't you like it, blah-blah-blah?" and I'm like, "Stop, stop while you're ahead or there's gonna be a problem." ... I think he didn't realize at that point that he was pushing it. That's what he was doing. And being rude at the same time. It's just the whole difference between men and women that a lot of times men just don't get it.

In contrast, she later added:

The men that work there (Coop Cab) that I chose to come out to right away when I first started working I think definitely had a lot of respect for me. And they knew better than to hit on me *after* that. Then the guys I ended up saying, "You'd better shut up" to were people that I had not come out to and they did not know that I was a lesbian.

Thus, Mimi specifically found harassment to be a problem from those men who labeled her heterosexual. Supporting Mimi's alternate experiences based on her "multiple labelings," the other women who reported sexual harassment as an ongoing problem believed themselves to be labeled as heterosexual.

Helen, who identified herself as bisexual but was labeled heterosexual, felt that the harassing behavior could at times be quite aggressive. She viewed this behavior as an ongoing dynamic of the company culture:

When I first started working at Coop Cab, I'll tell you, I kind of felt like meat on the hoof. We had a lot[8] of women working for us but still it's a very much male-dominated profession and women put up with a lot of shit on the job and off ... So I had these guys really pressing on me hard ... These guys are dogging us constantly. I see it happen every time a cute, new woman comes to work at the cab company. The women are not the same way. (They're) just like, I want to make some real money, screw this. No, that's not necessarily true. It's not that there aren't women who aren't wild sexually who've worked at Coop Cab. They're very aggressive about their sexuality. It's not the same kind, like, bordering on sexual harassment.

Helen distinguished between people being "wildly sexual" and sexually harassing other co-workers. To her, the former was fine, but sexual harassment was part of "a lot of shit on the job" that she resented.

In stark contrast to their women co-workers, men at the cab company often asserted that sexual harassment did not occur at the company. To support this, they often cited the fact the company was a cooperative, implying that its workers were necessarily progressive and beyond such behavior. For example, David – whom several women had mentioned as one who occasionally harassed heterosexual-labeled women workers – discussed how he would embrace the law and rules of the cooperative and confront someone engaged in sexual harassment:

> If it was proven that it actually happened, there would be a lot of backlash against that driver by the other drivers, because we're all pretty intelligent about the way life is supposed to be and things like that. If I found out somebody was sexually harassing somebody I worked with, male or female, if a guy was harassing a woman, or if a woman was harassing a guy, or a woman was harassing a woman, vice versa, or any other combinations, I'd be one of the first people to walk up and say, hey look, you can't be doing that. That's not cool.

David then responded to my question "Have you ever seen that happen?" by describing an incident of "possible" sexual harassment. Although he found the language used in the incident he described as so offensive he did not know how to repeat it, he nevertheless concluded that the incident was not sexual harassment – an opinion not held by his women co-workers. He added:

> No. Not to my knowledge. Not to my direct knowledge anyway. We had an incident a couple of years ago where there was an argument between [a male and a female co-worker] and [the man] turned around as he was leaving at the end of the argument, and – well, God, how do I want to say this? – he told the other dispatcher to suck on his dick. Sorry, that's a direct quote. And she filed a complaint against him ... It was prosecuted in the disciplinary letter as a sexually harassing remark.

This story was repeated to me by several of those I interviewed at Coop Cab. Bruce's analysis of the account asserted that the behavior was not sexual harassment, and,

---

[8] "A lot" is a comparative term. Jo is referring to a period when the women at Coop Cab comprised less than 20 percent of the workers at the cab company; at the time of the interview, the women at Coop Cab comprised 16.3 percent.

moreover, that the motivation for the woman to invoke the company rules was to vindictively bring the power of the cooperative against the man involved:

> Management actually suspended him for awhile ... He appealed it and the Workers' Council overturned the decision with a letter saying, "Look, sexual harassment will not be tolerated here, but it is our opinion that this was not sexual harassment." That is not to say that the event was excusable, but it was not sexual harassment. I don't think he intended it as a sexist remark. I don't find it to be a sexist remark. She was just upset with him and decided to punish him.
>
> [Interviewer: Why do you think?]
>
> Because she's a vindictive woman. Same reason she yelled at me at the coop and then wanted to speak in front of witnesses. She's a paranoid vindictive woman.

Bruce believed that it was so easy to bring a sexual harassment claim, or various other grievances, against a co-worker, that he felt he had to be especially careful not to inadvertently offend others.

Less Harassment of, but also Less Contact with, Lesbian-Labeled Workers

In contrast to the heterosexual-labeled women discussed above, the women who were labeled as lesbian did not perceive sexual harassment as an issue at Coop Cab.[9] The quotes from Sarah and Ursula, who were both labeled lesbian, provide good examples.

> [Sarah]: I mostly feel that there's pretty much respect for women at Coop Cab. My experience for the most part has been fine. People showed me respect, were courteous. Stuff like that ... I feel we have a good place in terms of harassment and discrimination. It depends on the person and the events ... I think the incidents are few and far between and I think the incidents are dealt with very quickly and fairly. Men and women get along pretty ok, I mean, we're not working in a utopia.
>
> [Ursula] I mostly feel that the level of harassment at work is pretty low ... I mean, for the most part I don't mind the way I'm treated by the men at work. I mean, aside from the fact that there are bits and pieces about the men's brains that I don't necessarily enjoy, I'm sure there are bits and pieces about the women's brains that I wouldn't enjoy either.

Like the other lesbian-labeled women, Sarah and Ursula did not feel that they had been targets of sexual harassment.

---

[9] Possibly the only study to examine sexual harassment with a focus on sexual orientation found the exact opposite of the situation at Coop Cab. Schneider found that lesbian-identified workers reported much *more* sexual harassment at their workplaces than were the heterosexual workers she studied (1982). Schneider explained this in two ways. First, she found that, on average, lesbians scored higher on a scale of feminist beliefs than did heterosexual women. Secondly, she hypothesized that, "while heterosexual intimacy at work may or may not be wanted by individual heterosexual women, gestures suggesting intimacy are an expected feature of their lives. They may have great difficulty determining what is unwanted and in drawing boundaries between their work and emotional activities. On the other hand, for the lesbians, sexual interactions with men at work are for the most part not desired. There is less emotional confusion about the meaning of these interactions" (1982: 84).

Some women explicitly explained that lesbian workers did not get the same level of harassment that heterosexual women drivers did. Jo asserted that being labeled lesbian was an effective way to avoid harassment. She had been at the coop for approximately seven years at the time of the interview. Jo self-identified as bisexual; however, she preferred for men to label her as a lesbian because she felt she was treated better by the men in the coop when thus defined:

> Sometimes I get treated like a lesbian, sometimes I get treated like a straight woman. I don't like being treated like a straight woman. I actually think there is [a difference in treatment]. Generally speaking, I prefer people think of me as a lesbian ... I find people approach me with just a lot more ease if they perceive that I'm straight. The men have learned their lessons with the lesbians, to be a little more stand-offish. If they're single men, they treat the straight women like potential dates, someone to fuck, and that *is* different.

This "strategy" for avoiding sexual harassment by actively trying to be labeled lesbian is a strategy that several other women discussed.

Further confirming this description of Coop Cab's dynamics, several women whose labels changed – either through 'coming out' or by switching from a female to a male partner – reported that how they were treated changed when their labels changed. For example, Mimi, who had only come out to some of her co-workers at the time of the interview, discussed how men's labeling of, and interactions with, her changed as she came out to more and more people at the cab company. She quoted others at the company who advised her that coming out would be an easy way to end the sexual harassment from some men that made her so angry:

> It was interesting because I had some other people say, "Well you should just tell these guys that you're a lesbian, then they'll leave you alone." I'm like, that has nothing to do with it, but it was interesting to see, then again, I started thinking about the people I came out to right away and how they treated me. And then the people who assumed I was straight and how they treated me, and there was a difference.

As an interesting "testing" of her colleague's reports of the men's selective harassment of those co-workers they labeled heterosexual, Mimi was able to observe how men's reactions to her changed as she gradually came out to them – she found that the sexual harassment dropped as more men labeled her as lesbian.

Melody related experiences in which she felt that sometimes men labeled her as heterosexual and treated her one way, and other times categorized her as lesbian and treated her another way. When labeled as heterosexual by the men, these co-workers interacted with Melody more regularly, although the interactions were not always pleasant. However, when she was labeled as lesbian, she had significantly less interaction with the men at work but avoided sexual harassment. For example, Melody observed different behaviors from male co-workers depending on the sex of her current partner – and, hence, the label ascribed to her:

> When I just started working here I was going out with a woman and then I started seeing a man ... It's kind of like, if you're kind of established as a lesbian you don't get harassed by the men at work. Once it got out [that I then was dating a man], it's kind of open for question, some of them will try and make passes. I just don't like it. It's like if I was

looking, believe me you'd know. It's not like you have to find it out. I don't like doing that kind of thing at work, so I guess it's almost like a protective thing.

Interviewer: But you can be a lesbian and be left alone pretty much?

Yeah, you got left alone by everybody. Not by everybody, you just get left alone by the men ... It's not like it's really bad, it's just a little bit like they kind of "queer out."

Melody concluded that when she first joined the coop she received much less harassment and less attention from men at the cab company because they labeled her as lesbian. Melody's experience is particularly illustrative when juxtaposed with the comments from Jo and Laura earlier in this chapter, which stated that new women employees receive especially trenchant sexual harassment.

In addition to the consensus on the lower rate of sexual harassment toward lesbian-labeled workers, all women interviewed indicated that men had noticeably less contact with those women they labeled lesbian. For example, Shirley, who was labeled lesbian, believed that merely deciding on how to relate to their lesbian-labeled co-workers was difficult for many men:

A lot of times [men treat me differently], they don't necessarily venture as far as to think that I'm a lesbian, but some of them do and some of them don't. Some of them think that it's none of their business to even wonder, and they think it would be really offensive to me if they asked. Or something. Which it wouldn't. But it's just kind of like one of those things that happens a lot of times with straight people: they think that they'll be offensive to you if they ask you if you're gay.

I think it's a challenge for a lot of the men at work to figure out how to interact with me. I would imagine that the way that they feel weird about it is a little less exhausting to them than it was to me when I started working there and I was trying figure out how to deal with being with all these men.

As a result of this difficulty, many men at the cab company opted to avoid contact with their lesbian-labeled co-workers.

The men's discussions of their interactions with the co-workers they labeled as lesbian agreed with the women's assessment – the men described treating those co-workers differently from the co-workers they thought of as heterosexual. Generally, this involved simply having very limited contact with lesbian-labeled co-workers. Some of the men's comments merely alluded to a gender split in the socializing at the cab company, such as Bob's comment that socializing at the cab company seemed to be informally sex-segregated except for some of the straight women who were dating male co-workers: "In general, I guess they (women) hang around with members of their own sex."

However, other men, such as Tom, below, expressed more homophobic sentiments. He explained that, while he was fully supportive of his female co-workers' right to date whomever they wished, he tried to avoid women he labeled lesbian. Like all but two men in this study, Tom expressed fear of inadvertently offending others at the Coop Cab. He believed that by avoiding lesbian-labeled women altogether he could avoid the risk of giving offense. He put it thus:

Well, so many women [here] are lesbians that you really have to be careful. Like, if you're not used to dealing with lesbians, you have to watch yourself. Sort of keep your distance. 'Cause you don't want to get them all upset with you, you know? I mean, who they are is OK and everything, and so you don't want to do something that would be misunderstood.

Tom's "solution" of simply avoiding lesbian-labeled co-workers was shared by many men at the company.

Discussion

This chapter addresses two key workplace dynamics at a cooperative cab company. First, men at Coop Cab interacted more with women they labeled as heterosexual and tended to have less contact with women labeled as lesbian. Second, the interactions with heterosexual-labeled women often involved sexual harassment, while the lesbian-labeled women reported no harassment.[10] This means that, based on which label was attached to each woman – lesbian or heterosexual – she either experienced very little interaction with her male co-workers, or she faced unwanted sexual harassment (see Hoffmann 2004 for a discussion of the legal implications of this behavior). This type of "hostile environment" sexual harassment more often occurs at predominantly male workplaces, such as cab companies. Female employees are subject to sexual comments and other behavior from male co-workers or other employees that create a hostile and uncomfortable work environment for these women (Yoder 1991).

Understanding Labels

This study examines men's behaviors and their labeling of female co-workers, not merely the women's perceptions of their male co-workers' actions. This is an important distinction. The data demonstrate that the dynamics at Coop Cab were a result of the men treating different groups of women differently based on labels, rather than of differently labeled women having different interpretations of men's actions.

The discussion of these data is not simply to explore the sexual harassment, or the lack of harassment, of heterosexual or lesbian women per se. Indeed, the fact that the labels used were "lesbian" and "heterosexual" are not important; the labels could have been "striped" and "starred" and be as meaningful. Rather, these data illustrate how similar women in the same company with the same co-workers have very different experiences with regard to sexual harassment – depending on how they were labeled by their male co-workers.[11]

---

[10] The statements by lesbian-labeled workers that they were not sexually harassed is surprising given how problematic sexual harassment can be for women in male-dominated occupations (Ragins and Scandura 1995) This lack of harassment of lesbian-labeled co-workers is particularly interesting given Schneider's earlier findings that lesbian working women were more likely to define behavior as sexual harassment compared to heterosexual women (Schneider 1982).

[11] For a discussion on the impact of selective sexual harassment on employer defenses and legal claims of sexual harassment see Hoffmann 2004.

While these labels determine how men will interact with each category of female co-worker, they are not merely blue-collar parallels of those labels described by Kanter in her work on white-collar employees in a large corporation (mother, seductress, pet, and iron maiden) (Kanter 1977). Unlike the situation at Coop Cab, Kanter's categories were a unique part of the work culture in that the categories were not tied to any physical "falsifiable" evidence. Her categories, therefore, only had meaning within the workplace. Not only would Kanter's labels lack meaning outside of work, but the labels for each token worker could be difficult to anticipate based only on observations of each woman when away from the worksite. For example, one might guess that a certain token woman might receive the label of "pet" based on watching how others perceived and interacted with her in the workplace and by observing, at the worksite, her own behavior toward others and her personal presentation. However, observations of the same token woman away from the workplace would most likely not predict how she would be labeled by her male co-workers.

The labels used by the men at Coop Cab were not workplace-specific in the way that that the labels described by Kanter were. At the cab company, the men categorized women into two labels: lesbian and heterosexual, but these categories were often embraced by the women themselves and, also, are commonly used in the larger society. In addition, if one were to observe these token women in their lives away from Coop Cab, one might possibly be able to discern – although not perfectly – which label might be designated to each woman, unlike the labels in Kanter's study. In this way, the categories used by the men at Coop Cab had some basis in a life outside the workplace and at times mirrored the women's own self-perception.

However, the men's categorization did not perfectly reflect women's self-identification and still involved forcing token women into labels which some of them might not identify with independently. While the men in this study classified women as either lesbian or heterosexual, the women themselves usually distinguished between three categories, more representative of reality: lesbian, heterosexual, and bisexual. Thus, by placing these token women at Coop Cab into binary categories, the men did, in fact, create labels that did not accurately correspond to reality outside of the company. Additionally, it is possible that women who self-defined as heterosexual were labeled as lesbian, and vice versa. In fact, men at the company did label one woman in this study, who self-identified as lesbian, as heterosexual.

Labeling, Framing, and Legal Consciousness

This study demonstrates how men's labeling of their female co-workers affected the framing of their interactions with these women and the subsequent impact this framing had on their legal consciousness of sexually harassing behavior. Men at Coop Cab understood the work rules and laws against sexual harassment as prohibiting "unwanted sexual attention." They did not recognize their sexually harassing behavior as being unwanted, and so did not see it as prohibited.

Most of these men considered themselves "liberal," "leftist," or "progressive." Part of this self-identification included perceiving their treatment of women, including their women co-workers, as being respectful or "politically correct." In contrast to the women's reports, the men did not see their behavior as constituting sexual harassment.

Drawing on the legal consciousness orientations enumerated by Ewick and Silbey, these men often expressed the orientation of being "against the law" (1998:165). They felt caught up in the various laws and rules and perceived themselves as having adjusted their conduct at work so as to avoid violating these. They did not seek to use the rules to their advantage (being "with the law") nor were they in awe of some separate, reified law (being "before the law") (Ewick and Silbey 1998); they simply wanted to avoid contact with the rules and laws if at all possible.

The men labeled their female co-workers as either "lesbian" or "heterosexual." They used these labels to frame the contacts with their women co-workers in order to interact with these groups of women in a manner consistent with their perception that the anti-harassment laws and workplace rules prohibited specifically "unwanted" sexual advances. Based on the labels they applied to their women co-workers (lesbian/heterosexual), they concluded that some women, the heterosexual-labeled co-workers, would or should welcome their sexual talk, while others, their lesbian-labeled co-workers, would not.

Using these labels, they framed their interactions with different groups of women differently. Sexual bantering, propositions, and other sexual talk with the heterosexual-labeled co-workers were framed as appropriate male-female interactions and, therefore, not in violation of sexual harassment prohibitions. Similar behavior with lesbian-labeled co-workers was framed as inappropriate, constituting sexual harassment.

Thus, they used their framing of their interactions with female co-workers as either "appropriate" or "inappropriate" to inform how they should act in order to avoid crossing the sexual harassment laws and work rules. This framing by the men at Coop Cab was sufficiently powerful to inhibit incorporation or internalization of the women's' reactions. Despite many instances in which heterosexual-labeled women resisted their sexual harassment or directly condemned such behavior, most men did not digest this feedback in ways that altered how they framed these interactions.

However, their understanding of their interactions with their lesbian-labeled co-workers – for whom sexual advances were framed as "unwanted" – mandated a strategy of avoidance. Their legal consciousness focused on their fears of how the law and workplace rules could be used against them if they were found harassing someone for whom their attention was clearly unwanted. Many men in this study expressed a fear of inadvertently offending others at the Coop Cab – most especially their lesbian-labeled co-workers. They not only understood that sexual advances would be unwelcome (and thus prohibited), but they also were concerned that even non-sexualized interactions might be unwanted; therefore, these were avoided as well. This strategy meant that one portion of the female workforce at the cab company, those women labeled lesbian, had less interaction with the majority group of the coop: the men.

These two dynamics – harassment of one group and avoidance of the other – could greatly disadvantage the women because all but one of the managers and dispatchers were men. With limited contact with their male co-workers, these lesbian-labeled women had minimal access to the most powerful workers at Coop Cab. They also had less contact with men who could mentor them into other positions, such as that of dispatcher. However, the other group of women workers, those women labeled heterosexual, also did not have easy access to the men at the company. The men at

Coop Cab framed their encounters with the women they labeled as heterosexual as constituting "fair game;" therefore, subjected them to various types of sexual harassment. Thus, these women were not avoided by their male co-workers the way the lesbian-labeled workers were, but instead were sexually harassed. This harassment caused these (heterosexual-labeled) women, themselves, to deliberately avoid some or all of the men at the company and may have strained the interactions between these women and their male co-workers, including the more powerful group of workers at the company, the male managers.

Conclusion

By intensely examining a small group of workers' understandings of a single legal issue, workplace sexual harassment, this study attempts to provide important insights into how workers' legal consciousness develops and affects their workplace behavior. Both men and women workers at the company agreed that the right to work in an environment that is free of harassment is an important civil right. Yet, the legal consciousness of the men framed their interactions with their women co-workers so that only one group worked free of harassment. Because the men comprised the majority of the workforce at the cab company, it was their legal consciousness that shaped the culture of sexual harassment at Coop Cab.

Despite embracing rights talk that supports their co-workers' civil rights, the men at Coop Cab sexually harass one group of their women co-workers and ignore the other group. Thus, the gendered power hierarchy is maintained in this predominantly male workplace. By closing out the lesbian-labeled women and harassing the heterosexual-labeled women, the men enjoy more exclusive contact to the powerful members of the company – the male managers and male dispatchers who control the workings of the business.

The effects found here might be more indicative of gender-skewed workplaces with only token numbers of women, such as Coop Cab. Subsequent studies might explore these effects in workplaces with even gender balances. Additionally, future research might build on this study by exploring legal consciousness around less gender-identified legal issues.

References

Dworkin, A.G., Chafetz, J.S., and Dworkin, R.J. (1986) "The Effects of Tokenism on Work Alienation Among Urban Public School Teachers." *Work and Occupations* 13:399–420.

England, P. (1979) "Women and Occupational Prestige: A Case of Vacuous Sex Equality." *Signs* 5:252–365.

Ewick, P., and Silbey, S.S. (1992) "Conformity, Contestation, and Resistance: An Account of Legal Consciousness." *New England Law Review* 26:731–749.

—— (1998) *The Common Place of Law: Stories from Everyday Life*. Chicago: University of Chicago Press.

Felstiner, W.L. F., Abel, R.L., and Sarat, A. (1980–81) "The Emergence and Transformation of Disputes: Naming, Blaming, Claiming ..." *Law and Society Review* 15:631–654.

Hoffmann, E.A. (2003) "Legal Consciousness and Dispute Resolution: Different Disputing Behavior at Two Similar Taxicab Companies." *Law & Social Inquiry* 28:691–715.

—— (2004) "Selective Sexual Harassment: How the Labeling of Token Workers Can Produce Different Workplace Environments for Similar Groups of Women." *Law and Human Behavior* 28:29–45.

—— (2005) "Gender Differences in Dispute Resolution Strategies: Procedural Justice at a Worker Cooperative." *Law & Society Review* 39:51–82.

Kanter, R.M. (1977) *Men and Women of the Corporation.* New York: Basic Books.

—— (1982) "The Impact of Hierarchical Structures on the Work Behavior of Women and Men" in R. Kahn-Hut, A.K. Daniels and R. Colvard (eds) *Women and Work: Problems and Perspectives.* New York: Oxford University Press.

Konrad, A.M., and Gutek, B.A. (1986) "Impact of Work Experiences on Attitudes Towards Sexual Harassment." *Administrative Science Quarterly* 31:422–438.

Marshall, A.-M. (2003) "Injustice Frames, Legality, and the Everyday Construction of Sexual Harassment." *Law & Social Inquiry* 28:659–689.

—— and Barclay, S. (2003) "Introduction: In Their Own Words: How Ordinary People Construct the Legal World." *Law & Social Inquiry* 28:617–628.

Merry, S.E. (1990) "The Discourses of Mediation and the Power of Naming." *Yale Journal of Law and the Humanities* 2:1–36.

Miller, J. (1992) "Gender and Supervision: The Legitimation of Authority in Relationship to Task." *Sociological Perspectives* 35:137–162.

Miller-Loessi, K. (1992) "Toward Gender Integration in the Workplace: Issues at Multiple Levels." *Sociological Perspectives* 35:1–15.

Nielsen, L.B. (2000) "Situating Legal Consciousness: Experiences and Attitudes of Ordinary Citizens About Law and Street Harassment." *Law and Society Review* 34:1056–1090.

Ragins, B.R., and Scandura, T.A. (1995) "Antecedents and Work-Related Correlates of Reported Sexual Harassment: An Empirical Investigation of Competing Hypotheses." *Sex Roles* 32:429–455.

Roos, P.A., and Reskin, B.R. (1992) "Occupational Desegregation in the 1970s: Integration and Economic Equity?" *Sociological Perspectives* 35:69–91.

Sarat, A. (1990) "'… The Law is All Over': Power, Resistance and the Legal Consciousness of the Welfare Poor." *Yale Journal of Law and the Humanities* 2:343–379.

—— and Kearns, T.R. (1995) "Beyond the Great Divide: Forms of Legal Scholarship and Everyday Life." in A. Sarat and T.R. Kearns (eds) *Law in Everyday Life.* Ann Arbor: University of Michigan Press.

Schneider, B.E. (1982) "Consciousness About Sexual Harassment Among Heterosexual and Lesbian Women Workers." *Journal of Social Issues* 38:75–98.

Schultz, V. (1990) "Telling Stories About Women and Work: Judicial Interpretations of Sex Segregation in the Work Place in Title VII Cases Raising the Lack of Interest Argument." *Harvard Law Review* 103:1750–1843.

Swerdlow, M. (1989) "Men's Accommodations to Women Entering a Nontraditional Occupation: A Case of Rapid Transit Operatives." *Gender and Society* 3:373–387.

Wharton, A.S. (1991) "Satisfaction? The Psychological Impact of Gender Segregation on Women at Work." *The Sociology Quarterly* 32:365–387.

Yoder, J.D. (1991) "Rethinking Tokenism: Looking Beyond Numbers." *Gender and Society* 5:178–192.

Chapter 7

The "Seesaw Effect" from Racial Profiling to Depolicing: Toward a Critical Cultural Theory

FRANK RUDY COOPER[1]

It is well known that the United States' Constitution prohibits unreasonable seizures and searches and requires a showing of probable cause before a warrant may be issued pre-justifying a seizure or search. Less well known is the fact that at the end of 1967 Supreme Court jurisprudence applied the probable cause test, rather than the less stringent reasonableness test, to all seizures and searches made for criminal purposes. That would change.

In its 1968 *Terry v. Ohio* decision the Court considers whether a police officer's brief "stop" of a suspect for questioning and "frisk" of the suspect's outer clothing for weapons triggers Fourth Amendment analysis. The Court holds the stop is a seizure because it restrains a person's liberty and the frisk a search because it invades a person's privacy. The Court also holds it will no longer determine whether to apply the probable cause test or reasonableness test based on whether or not the seizure and search are made for criminal purposes. Instead, it will apply the probable cause or reasonableness tests depending on the scope of the intrusion. Finding an officer's stop and frisk to be intrusions of limited scope, the *Terry* Court decides it will only apply the less strict reasonableness test to those activities.

During the arguments preceding the *Terry* decision, civil rights organizations contended that allowing police officers to seize and search people under a reasonableness test would lead to harassment of racial minorities. The *Terry* Court rejects that argument on grounds that only a few rogue officers will take such action and that rogue cops cannot be deterred by constitutional rulings. In 1968, therefore, the Court entertains a belief that race-based uses of the *Terry* doctrine will not be so extensive as to challenge the value of the rule.

Skip ahead to 1993. Mainstream residents of New York City are feeling overrun by crime. That opinion is reflected in frequent news reports arguing that not enough is being done to stop crime. Mayoral candidate Rudolph Giuliani taps into that sentiment by campaigning on an anti-crime theme. Giuliani implicitly blames racial minorities for crime by running advertisements about the riots by blacks in the Crown Heights neighborhood. Once elected, Mayor Giuliani embarks on an anti-crime

[1] © 2006. I dedicate this Chapter to my sister, Sarah Lynne Cooper. I welcome comments on this Chapter at fcooper@suffolk.edu.

campaign spearheaded by his Street Crimes Unit (SCU). The SCU engages in an experiment in maximum use of *Terry* stops and frisks as a means of fighting crime.

Consider now the scene in New York City circa 1999. People accuse the New York City Police Department (NYPD) of using *Terry* stops to "racial profile." That is, there appears to be an unjustifiably high rate of police stops of racial minorities, seemingly on the basis of race rather than an individual's level of suspiciousness. Further, it appears that racial profiling has created an environment that encouraged several incidents of police brutality against racial minority men. Suddenly, mainstream New Yorkers become critical of racial profiling. That sentiment is reflected in news stories calling for police reform.

That anti-police environment helps explain the events at the 2000 Puerto Rican Day Parade. Rampaging groups of men, most of whom were from racial minorities, harass and sexually assault at least 57 women. Police officers initially refuse to intervene in the sexual assaults. By way of explaining their inaction, some officers claim they were afraid to assert themselves against racial minority men because of the criticism of their racial profiling. In other words, officers "depoliced" racial minority men at the Parade as a response to public criticism of racial profiling. Consequently, our story brings us full circle: officers swung from over-policing racial minorities to under-policing racial minorities based on the public's shift against aggressive policing.

I tell the story of the swing from racial profiling to depolicing in New York City to demonstrate that *Terry* doctrine can have a "seesaw effect." A seesaw is a playground toy. It balances a plank on a fulcrum. Two children sit one on each end of the plank. They take turns swinging all the way up and all the way down.

Terry doctrine creates the potential for a seesaw effect by giving police officers discretion to stop and frisk people with relative ease. We can imagine an "enforcement practices continuum" between maximum use of *Terry* stops with little justification and minimum use of *Terry* stops despite their being justified. That continuum represents the plank in *Terry*'s seesaw. The fulcrum is the "cultural context continuum" between public opinion that supports or condemns aggressive policing against particular social groups. When public opinion called for anti-crime measures by any means necessary, NYPD officers over-used their *Terry* stop powers to racial profile. When public opinion swung against racial profiling, officers under-used their *Terry* stop powers as part of depolicing racial minorities at the Parade. New York City thus demonstrates *Terry* doctrine's potential for a seesaw effect from racial profiling to depolicing.

Terry's seesaw effect in New York City teaches us that we cannot understand the practical meaning of a legal doctrine without understanding the cultural context in which it will operate. For that reason, scholars seeking to understand doctrines as they are experienced need methodological tools capable of tracing changes in cultural context. I propose solving this problem by synthesizing critical race theory's analyses of the effects of cultural identity norms and law and cultural studies' analyses of the interplay between legal and cultural discourses into a critical cultural theory approach. Specifically, we should focus on how the particular meanings of identities are socially constructed at a given moment and then create slippages between how courts imagine doctrines and how they are applied in practice.

In the first part of this chapter, I describe how *Terry* doctrine creates a scope continuum approach to the Fourth Amendment and why that approach enables racial profiling. In the second part, I identify the components of *Terry*'s seesaw effect in New York City. In the third part I outline a critical cultural theory methodology and draw theoretical insights from *Terry*'s seesaw effect in New York City. Conclusions are then drawn.

Why *Terry* Doctrine Encourages Racial Profiling

We first need to conduct a close reading of the *Terry* decision in order to reveal some inherent problems in the opinion that led to *Terry*'s seesaw effect in New York City. Specifically, the opinion ignores the possibility that a racially neutral legal doctrine will be applied in a racially disparate manner. I argue the decision makes that mistake because of the way it fundamentally restructures Fourth Amendment law.

The Story Told by the Terry Decision

In the *Terry v. Ohio* (1968) decision, the Court considers a situation where a police officer, McFadden, is patrolling his regular area (5). His attention is "drawn to" two men, Terry and Chilton.[2] McFadden observes one of the men walk down a block, peer into a particular store window, keep walking, turn, peer into the same store window, return to, and confer with the other man (6). Each man repeats that process approximately a half dozen times. A third man, Katz, then joins Terry and Chilton, confers with them, and walks away.[3] Terry and Chilton continue their peering and conferring approximately a half dozen times each. Terry and Chilton then walk in the direction of Katz. McFadden, fearing the men are planning a robbery, follows them. McFadden comes upon Terry and Chilton as they are conferring with Katz a block away. McFadden asks the men to identify themselves (7).

When the three men only mumble a reply, McFadden grabs Terry, spins him around and pats the outside of his overcoat. Feeling a gun, McFadden seeks to retrieve it, but cannot do so. McFadden then orders the three men into a store, removing Terry's overcoat and retrieving the gun as they enter. McFadden orders the three men to face a wall and begins patting Chilton's outer clothing. Feeling a gun, McFadden retrieves it. Feeling no gun on Katz, McFadden does not reach inside Katz's outer clothing.

The question presented was whether McFadden's actions triggered Fourth Amendment scrutiny. According to the *Terry* decision, a "stop" occurs when an officer's questioning of someone he suspects of crime falls between a mere consensual encounter and an arrest (22). A "frisk" occurs when an officer's patting down of a suspect's outer clothing in search of weapons falls between a mere consensual

---

[2] In the interest of fluid reading, I have skipped duplicative citations. When multiple citations can be found on the same page, I cite the first reference and then skip references until the page or citation changes.

[3] Here, we can highlight the way a racially neutral "Statement of the Facts" is always itself an articulation of the meaning of the underlying elements. The unlikelihood that a white man, Katz, would confer with two black men, Terry and Chilton, for innocent reasons played a crucial, but unacknowledged, role in the Court's validation of McFadden's suspiciousness (Thompson 1999:964–8). Past and ongoing demonization of black men means that police officers are often primed to suspect us of crime (Cooper 2006).

encounter and a "full blown" search (24–25). As an example of a frisk, the Court quotes a police manual suggesting an officer "feel with sensitive fingers ... the groin and area about the testicles ... (17 n.13)." The Court holds stops and frisks are more than mere "petty indignities" and are thereby subject to Fourth Amendment scrutiny as seizures and searches (16–17). The Court also holds that stops and frisks are not subject to the probable cause requirement in the second half of the Fourth Amendment, but only the general reasonableness requirement in the first half of the Fourth Amendment (20).

Citing its newly minted *Camara v. Municipal Court* (1967) "balancing test," the *Terry v. Ohio* (1968) Court creates the "reasonable suspicion" tests for stops and frisks (20–21). The *Terry* Court holds that a stop is warranted when:

- a "man of reasonable caution" (22)
- would find facts specific to the suspect (21)
- that he could articulate
- which, taken together with rational inferences, justify suspecting the person is committing a crime or is about to do so (22).

The Court holds a frisk requires that:

- the stop itself is valid (32) and
- a "reasonably prudent man" (27)
- granting "due weight" to "specific reasonable inferences" based on the officer's experience
- would be warranted in believing the suspect is armed and dangerous.

Based on its new reasonable suspicion tests, the Court upholds Terry's conviction. The Court finds McFadden's stop valid because suspects passing in front of one store window 24 times reasonably warrant further investigation (28). The Court finds McFadden's frisks valid because the facts suggest a daylight robbery, making it reasonable to suspect the men would be armed. In the Court's own words, the upshot of the *Terry* decision is that officers may "accost" (16) people on the street and pat down their groins (17 n.13) whenever they can articulate a reasonable suspicion a crime might be afoot.

How the "Scope Continuum" Model Enables Racial Profiling

Prior to the *Terry* decision, the Fourth Amendment required probable cause in order for a criminally-oriented seizure or search to be reasonable. As of 1966, the Court's decisions suggest that any activity constituting a seizure or search must satisfy the Fourth Amendment's probable cause requirement. In its groundbreaking *Camara v. Municipal Court* (1967) decision, the Court declares that some searches need only satisfy the Fourth Amendment's reasonableness requirement. Such searches are judged by means of the "balancing test" – weighing the government's law enforcement interests against the individual's privacy interest (536–537). According to the *Camara* Court, the balancing test applies to administrative searches – those conducted for health and safety reasons pursuant to a regulatory code (535). For instance, a fire department's entry of an apartment building for purposes of inspecting fire extinguishers is subject to the balancing test. Notably, the *Camara* Court explicitly forbids application of the balancing test to criminal investigations. Those investigations are subject to the tougher probable cause test. In light of the *Camara* decision, the *Terry* Court's application of the balancing test to criminal investigations is a fundamental rearticulation of Fourth Amendment jurisprudence.

There was an alternative way to decide the *Terry* case. The court below had ruled that the Fourth Amendment does not apply to stops and frisks, but that when it does apply "probable cause is essential" (*Terry v. Ohio* (1968), 16). The Supreme Court could have rejected the idea that stops and frisks do not warrant Fourth Amendment scrutiny while accepting probable cause as the test for criminal seizures and searches. Since McFadden's observations arguably would have supported a finding of probable cause, the result might have been the same.[4]

The *Terry* Court rejects the alternative rationale's "all-or-nothing" application of probable cause to seizures and searches (17). "In our view," declares the Court, "the sounder course is to recognize that the Fourth Amendment governs all intrusions by agents of the public upon personal security, and to make *the scope* of the particular intrusion, in light of all the exigencies of the case, a central element in the analysis of reasonableness" (18 (emphasis added)). That approach enshrines what I call the "scope continuum" approach to the Fourth Amendment and prevents courts from seeing the effects of cultural context upon actual enforcement practices (Cooper 2003:852–54).

The reason the scope continuum approach eventually leads to racial profiling is that it enlarges the number of people police officers have the discretion to stop. Under the *Camara* approach, officers would not be able to stop a suspect as part of a criminal investigation without probable cause. Under *Terry* doctrine, an officer may stop people as part of criminal investigations at an earlier point in their fact-gathering process – at the point where he only has reasonable suspicion. As a consequence, the *Terry* decision expands police officer discretion.

If we do not believe that people should be stopped based principally upon their race, we should be concerned about the amount of discretion the *Terry* doctrine affords. That police officers are members of this society requires us to question the discernment of those who claim officers never racial profile (Cooper 2002a:869–76; Goldberg 1999:51). Scholars argue that nearly everyone in our society, be they black, white, brown, yellow, or red, has some degree of prejudice against racial minorities (Armour 1997:135; Nelson 2003). Take for example the Reverend Jesse Jackson, Sr., who admitted, "There is nothing more painful to me at this stage in my life than to walk down the street and hear footsteps and start thinking about robbery – then look around and see somebody white and feel relieved" (Armour 1997:35). If one of the most prominent black civil rights activists has been affected by stereotypes of who is dangerous, how could a police officer of any race escape at least that initial instinct to assume racial minorities are more suspicious than racial majorities? The answer is that he could not. Background social norms of prejudice against racial minorities are too pervasive and too strong for any of us to escape them without effort (ibid., 134–36). In short, "unless a low-prejudiced person consciously monitors and inhibits

---

[4] For a somewhat contrary view, see Tracey Maclin's analysis of why the Court chose not to find probable cause (Maclin 1998:1303).

the activation of a stereotype in the presence of a member (or symbolic equivalent) of a stereotyped group, she may unconsciously fall into the discrimination habit" (ibid., 137).

Given the ability of stereotypes to continue without an individual's conscious awareness of their existence, we should ask where prejudiced desires exist. I argue stereotypes exist at the meta-level of "cultural identity norms" that influence how people perceive the world (Cooper 2003:866–68). Cultural identity norms are the prevailing assumptions about the implications of someone's status as a member of a particular identity group that exist in a given cultural context at a given time. In the Jesse Jackson, Sr. example, a nationwide norm of assuming black people are crime threats influences his reaction. Such cultural identity norms are the source of the assumptions considered "common sense"; they are the perspectives on identity that are taken to be "just the way things are" (Slack 1996:117). We take those "scripts" about identity to be true because they are background social norms of what to expect from people (Carbado and Gulati 2000:1261). At least when we are the privileged group, we do not question those norms, for they are as taken-for-granted as the air we breathe (Flagg 1998:2). As a result, we can subconsciously believe a person's racial characteristics are telling us something objectively relevant about the facts to which we are applying the facially neutral standard (ibid., 49).

One way in which people who are not consciously prejudiced can produce a racially disparate result is by following majority norms. For instance, the general social norm might be that people should not wear oversized and extremely loose fitting jeans (Gilbert 1999:14–15). The very small portion of the black population that sells drugs may have a greater tendency to wear baggy jeans (*Bivens v. Albuquerque Pub. Sch.* (1995), 561). But wearing baggy jeans may also be a subcultural norm among young black males even though practically all of them are not criminals (560–561). Those facts could lead a police officer to produce a racially disparate result, the disproportionate *Terry*-stopping of innocent young black males, while consciously intending only to apply a facially neutral criterion, whether an individual is wearing baggy jeans. Since whites are the majority, however, their norms will constitute the general norm (Audain 1995:720; Flagg 1998:4). If whites tend to act differently than racial minorities, the general norm will be race-specific (Audain 1995:720–721; Flagg 1998:2–8). *Terry*-stopping people based on their violation of the general norms will thus constitute both a facially neutral, majoritarian principle and a racially disparate form of reasoning with invidious effects.

The *Terry v. Ohio* (1968) Court's rearticulation of the Fourth Amendment as indifferent to police harassment that does not produce evidence (14–15) rests on a flawed principle. The Fourth Amendment's ban on unjustified invasions of privacy exists not only to free suspects caught by unfair means, but also to deter law enforcement from even trying to unjustifiably infringe upon anyone's security (Sklansky 2000:1740). To protect people from unjustified invasions, the *Terry* Court should have denied or clearly limited the reasonable suspicion rationale for stops and frisks. While *Terry* stops and frisks are not the only aspect of the criminal justice process that is infected with racial prejudice, the *Terry* decision's grant of broad discretion is especially enabling of race-based harassment. The Court's failure to limit stop and frisk discretion creates the possibility for the seesaw effect I will now investigate.

Terry's Seesaw Effect in New York City

I have argued that the *Terry v. Ohio* (1968) decision lays the groundwork for extensive racial profiling. That is so because the case enlarged the number of situations in which officers may stop people. Moreover, analysis of the operation of cultural identity norms suggests we should expect discretion to be exercised in racially disparate ways. For those reasons, I argued the *Terry* decision opened the door to racial profiling. I will now argue that certain cultural contexts can not only activate *Terry* doctrine's potential for racial profiling, but also lead to eventual depolicing of racial minority communities.

The likelihood of a swing from extreme racial profiling to depolicing is not merely speculative. In the early 1990s, Rudolph Giuliani was able to convince New Yorkers to adopt aggressive, implicitly race-based policing policies. In the late 1990s, the weight of racial profiling inspired police brutality became too much to bear and the media shifted against racial profiling. In response, the NYPD depoliced the mass sexual assaults at the 2000 Puerto Rican Day Parade. This Part of the Chapter details that seesaw effect from extreme racial profiling to depolicing.

Supporting Extreme Racial Profiling

Terry doctrine's seesaw effect begins with the development of public support for extreme racial profiling. In New York City, this stage began with Rudolph Giuliani's 1993 mayoral campaign. Giuliani argued the NYPD should be granted greater powers in order to control crime. "Crown Heights" became Giuliani's battle cry, the prime example of Mayor David Dinkins' "soft on crime" approach (Roberts 1993:4). The Crown Heights neighborhood had seen massive violent riots by racial minorities in response to a Jewish man's hit-and-run killing of a black child. Rioters murdered a Jewish student, and the mayhem created massive negative publicity for Dinkins. Giuliani contended the four-day riot would have been quelled sooner if he had been Mayor.

The media noted the race-based nature of Giuliani's anti-crime appeal. In an article titled "A Race About Race," *New York Newsday* declared that Giuliani was consciously cultivating a "silent majority" (Cottman 1993:27). Giuliani wanted the majority to associate Dinkins, who is black, with favoritism towards blacks. With about $1 million more in cash than Dinkins, Giuliani flooded the airwaves with images of homelessness and crime (Mitchell 1993:B-3). The rhetorical power of Giuliani's crime theme is suggested by the fact that it was effective even though crime actually went down during Dinkins' term (*New York Times* 1993).

Nonetheless, Giuliani's funding advantage does not adequately explain how he won in a city where Democrats outnumber Republicans by five to one. What does explain Giuliani's victory is that some liberal whites switched from having voted for Dinkins to voting for Giuliani. Why would this presumably non-prejudiced group of whites vote for Giuliani despite Giuliani's having foreshadowed that he would rule in a racially disparate manner? The answer is that those liberal whites could not see the prejudice in Giuliani's policies.

We can consider the failure to predict that Giuliani's administration would racial profile in light of the theory of background social norms described in the last part of this chapter. Background social norms for thinking about identity lead whites (1) not to think of themselves as having a race (Flagg 1998:1–8), (2) to think of perspectives they share with other whites but not with racial minorities as being race-neutral, and (3) not to think of problems primarily faced by racial minorities as part of their own world. Here, even though overall crime dropped during Dinkins' term as Mayor, many whites perceived crime as having recently risen. Either of two things could explain that disconnection: (1) the media tricked liberal whites into believing overall crime had risen, or (2) crime had only recently moved from racial minority communities to white communities, causing an actual rise in the crime rate in white communities. While the media certainly assisted Giuliani's campaign by overstating the comparative prevalence of crime during Dinkins' term, that does not fully explain why Giuliani's anti-crime theme had traction with liberal whites.

I argue background social norms had allowed New York City's liberal whites to ignore late 1980s crime because it was portrayed as concentrated in racial minority communities (Brownstein 1995:51). When the early 1990s media began suggesting there was a crime epidemic, liberal whites suddenly became aware of the problem. If that is so, liberal whites could honestly believe crime was increasing overall during the Dinkins era even though, at worst, crime rose in white neighborhoods while falling by a greater percentage in racial minority neighborhoods. As a consequence of believing crime was a new phenomenon, liberal whites supported Giuliani's call for aggressive policing.

Predictably, racial minorities bore the brunt of the Giuliani administration's aggressive policing tactics. A report by New York's Attorney General found that NYPD officers used their *Terry* stops in a racially disparate manner (Rayman 1999, A3). In areas where blacks comprised 26 percent of the population, they accounted for 50 percent of the *Terry* stops. Hispanics, comprising 24 percent of the population, accounted for 33 percent of the stops. Whites, who were 43 percent of the population, accounted for just 13 percent of stops. Giuliani's pet project, the SCU, stopped blacks 63 percent of the time. In short, the NYPD was using *Terry* stops to racial profile.

The Media Shifts against Racial Profiling

The second stage in *Terry* doctrine's seesaw effect begins when excessive racial profiling itself spawns a popular movement against aggressive policing. The NYPD got its first serious taste of hostility after the Abner Louima incident. After that incident, reports of police brutality against racial minorities began to snowball. To make matters worse for the Giuliani administration, four officers shot and killed unarmed African immigrant Amadou Diallo. Throughout all of this, Giuliani remained a staunch supporter of the department.

You may recall that Louima, a night security guard from Jamaica, Queens, was arrested after a scuffle between police and revelers at a Flatbush Avenue nightclub (Barry 1997:1). Officers Volpe and Schwartz took Louima into the jailhouse bathroom and beat him. Officer Volpe anally raped Louima with the wooden handle of a toilet plunger. Volpe then chained Louima in a holding cell. Investigators said the precinct called for an ambulance for Louima over an hour after the suspect was booked. Although the ambulance arrived at 6:25 a.m., it did not leave the station house until 7:58 a.m., as paramedics waited for police officers to escort them to the hospital.

You may also recall that Diallo, an unarmed West African immigrant with no criminal record, was shot to death in the doorway of his apartment building by four NYPD officers (Cooper 1999). The officers spotted Diallo and thought he matched the description of a serial rapist. After observing Diallo's behavior, the four officers felt he was "suspicious." The officers shot at Diallo 41 times, hitting him with 19 bullets. When the body was recovered, investigators found Diallo had only a beeper and a wallet on his person. The four officers involved in the shooting (Sean Carroll, Edward McMellon, Kenneth Boss, and Richard Murphy) were part of the aggressive SCU that Giuliani had touted as part of his anti-crime program.

While the Louima and Diallo incidents were extreme cases, New Yorkers linked them to the NYPD's use of *Terry* stops and frisks to racial profile. A *New York Times* poll following the Diallo shooting showed New York City's racial minorities were sharply critical of Giuliani and his police department (Barry and Connelly 1999). The survey found that three quarters of the black population and half of the Hispanic population disapproved of the way Giuliani was doing his job. Most blacks and Hispanics felt the NYPD were doing a poor or fair job. Forty-seven percent of all New Yorkers said the policies of the Giuliani administration had caused police brutality to increase. In addition, 70 percent of all those polled, including whites, said the police "often engage in brutality" against blacks.

The final straw in the unraveling of Giuliani's ability to convince people to support aggressive policing occurred during his aborted senatorial campaign (Robbins 2000:45). Senate opponent Hilary Clinton was able to exploit the popular shift against the NYPD. She contended "the Louima and Diallo cases were symptomatic of problems in the city's overall approach to policing" (Herbert 2000). Clinton's attacks made NYPD practices an embarrassment to their greatest ally, and may have led officers to avoid any further potential racial controversies.

The NYPD's Response: Depolicing the Parade Sexual Assaults

With the public turned against racial profiling, New York City was primed for the third stage of *Terry* doctrine's seesaw effect: depolicing of racial minorities. That is what occurred at the Parade. There is substantial evidence that police officers refused to act while groups of men harassed and physically assaulted women following the Parade. For instance, a man running laps around Central Park stated that on three separate occasions he alerted officers that groups of men were spraying water on women's shirts to expose their breasts and making lewd comments to women (Barstow and Chivers 2000). Officers never moved to intervene. A woman who was stripped and groped stated that police officers ignored her request for assistance (*New York Times* 2000). The mother of a teenaged victim claimed that officers responded to her daughter's cries for help by merely pointing toward a nearby ambulance.

Officers have told reporters they refused to act at the Parade to avoid any potential for racial controversy. Essentially, the officers claimed they were suffering from "motivational distress." As one officer put it, "You're never going to get in trouble by not doing anything" (Purnick 2000, B1). That thinking appears to be rooted in conflict avoidance: "Are you the one who is going to precipitate a riot? The political fallout would be a career-ender. You'd be doing midnights in the Bronx." Perhaps, then, the police officers' non-response to post-Parade sexual assaults was simply a matter of individuals seeking to "keep their heads low."

In fact, officers' claims of motivational distress cover for race-based reasoning. One officer stated that police decisions during the Parade assaults were affected by tensions between the NYPD and racial minority communities. A further reason officers did not intervene after the Parade is because it occurred in the wake of criticism of Mayor Giuliani's administration for racial profiling and police brutality. Police officers had recently been tried on charges in the slaying of Diallo. Puerto Ricans have been "African-Americanized" in New York City (Grosfoguel and Georas 2000:14), so police action against Puerto Ricans at the Parade would be associated with prior police actions against African-Americans. As I noted, Giuliani had consciously tied his political future to the performance of the New York City Police Department (Robbins 2000:45). As a group, officers considered themselves to have a personal stake in the perception of the Giuliani administration. The officers' statements about their need to "lay off" racial minorities during the Parade mass sexual assaults are grounded in that political context (Smolowe et al. 2000). Consequently, the Parade depolicing should be viewed as a reaction to the public's shift against racial profiling.

In considering police practices in New York City, therefore, we are returned to the problem of extreme racial profiling's ability to morph into the equally insidious practice of depolicing. This part of the chapter has detailed that seesaw effect. The next part of the chapter argues that the existence of phenomena such as *Terry*'s seesaw effect requires a rethinking of our methods for analyzing the effects of legal doctrines.

A Method for Analyzing Seesaw Effects: Critical Cultural Theory

While it is certainly possible to do so otherwise, I believe a certain perspective best leads us to see phenomena such as *Terry*'s seesaw effect. That perspective is the constitutive approach advocated by this volume. The particular constitutive approach I advocate is Critical Cultural Theory (CCT). Critical cultural theory synthesizes Critical Race Theory (CRT) and Law and Cultural Studies (L&CS) methodologies and applies them to the question of how doctrines are translated into particular enforcement practices. Critical race theory understands identities to be simultaneously false, in being social constructions of appearance characteristics that do not connote personality difference, and materially consequential, in that they both structure the broad distribution of goods and influence the ways people interact. Law and cultural studies provides tools for understanding how popular discourses influence, and are influenced by, legal discourses.

Critical Race Theory

Critical race theory is the field that identifies and draws insights from the following conundrum: "any identity is simultaneously socially constructed and materially crucial" (Hutchinson 2004:1190). That race is a social construct is shown by the fact that the meanings of race have changed over time. For example, the racial inferiority of blacks has been asserted based on God's will, biological deficiencies, cultural abnormalities, and so on. The very fact that the bases of assertions of racial difference have changed over time shows that the meaning of race is "formed" rather than naturally given (Omi and Winant 1994). That assertions of racial difference have material consequences is demonstrated by the fact they have justified whole social systems, such as slavery, Jim Crow, and so on. On the basis of race's simultaneous unreality and real consequences, CRT insists on a substantive version of equality: do not allow racially disparate treatment of similarly situated individuals, but do treat differently situated people differently.

Critical race theory is valuable for the productive tension by which it generates several areas of study that are relevant to this project:

- How has law itself constructed society's cultural identity norms? (Crenshaw et al. 1995:xxv)
- How has law been shaped by society's cultural identity norms?
- How have subordinated social groups utilized law to remake their own and others' senses of the meanings of their identities? (ibid., xiii–iv)
- How have battles over the meanings of legal terms served as sites for battles over the social meanings of identity? (ibid., xxviii).[5]

This chapter's analysis of *Terry*'s seesaw effect in New York City serves as an extended example of the ways the meanings of identities are socially constructed. In the first part of this chapter, I showed how the *Terry* decision rearticulates the meaning of the Fourth Amendment based on an assumption that racial harassment is rare. I also posited that prejudice lives on at the level of cultural identity norms and is then instantiated as background social norms that cause facially neutral doctrines to have racially disparate impacts. In the second part, I showed how Rudolph Giuliani manipulated the meaning of racial identity in order to gain support for aggressive policing practices. I also showed how a race-based critique of the NYPD changed policing practices. The Chapter's second Part further showed how the NYPD's depolicing of the Parade sexual assaults was tied to its new understanding of racial minorities as people to be avoided.

Nonetheless, I also challenge CRT to extend the scope of its analysis. As commonly utilized, CRT is better at explaining why law is organized and enforced against the interests of certain groups than it is at explaining how the very meanings of categories of identity are constructed. To expand its explanatory power, CRT must attend to the discursive struggles between competing social groups to articulate the meanings of specific categories of identity in ways that support their interests. That is why I call for a synthesis of CRT and L&CS methods. To that end, the next section of the chapter introduces tools for a discourse analysis of the relationship between identity, law, and culture.

---

[5] I am noting the CRT questions most relevant to criminal procedure. Critical race theory also requires us to recognize the intersectionality/multidimensionality of identity and the dangers of thinking only within the black/white binary paradigm (Hutchinson 2004:1197–1203).

Law and Cultural Studies

The second method I recommend using is L&CS analysis. Law and cultural studies has its roots in the interdisciplinary field of cultural studies. Cultural studies is concerned with analyzing the effects of large-scale sets of representations, known as "discourses." The reason we should analyze discourses is because a discourse

> constructs the topic ... It governs the way that a topic can be meaningfully talked about and reasoned about. It also influences how ideas are put into practice and used to regulate the conduct of others. Just as a discourse "rules in" certain ways of talking about a topic, defining an acceptable and intelligible way to talk, write, or conduct oneself, so also, by definition, it "rules out", limits and restricts other ways of talking, of conducting ourselves in relation to the topic or constructing knowledge about it (Hall 1997:44).

Discourses are important because they seek to become the exclusive means of thinking about a set of objects, people, and/or events by "ruling in" and "ruling out" particular viewpoints. For example, the dominant late nineteenth century discourse of inherent difference between races created the context in which the *Plessy v. Ferguson* (1896) Court could conceive of the legitimacy of separate-but-equal doctrine.

Scholars interested in why the law is constituted in a certain way at a certain time must study discourses. This will be especially important for understanding the translation of doctrines into particular enforcement practices since "what we think we 'know' in a particular period about, say, crime has a bearing on how we regulate, control and punish criminals" (Hall 1997:49). Hence, in my analysis of the *Terry* opinion, I revealed how the decision turned on a shift in the very way of thinking about the Fourth Amendment. Likewise, failure to recognize the likelihood the *Terry* decision would result in racial profiling turned on a worldview in which officers are not subject to the prejudice infecting the rest of society. Both the *Terry* Court's version of the Fourth Amendment and its denial of racial harassment rely on underlying discourses about how the world ought to or does operate.

Discourses are important not only because they lead to specific practices, but also because they are a means by which social groups struggle. A social group's successful promotion of its discourse as the commonsense way of thinking about a topic helps it achieve hegemony, ideological influence, over other groups. For that reason, the study of which discourses are currently dominant is necessarily the study of which groups have social power. Consider the fact that Justice Harlan's dissent challenged the discourse supporting the *Plessy v. Ferguson* (1896) Court's separate-but-equal-doctrine with an alternative discourse under which the Constitution required social equality. The latter discourse was untenable in its time, but would be developed by the nascent black civil rights movement and eventually adopted by the *Brown v. Board* (1954) Court.

The focus on discourse analysis from the field of cultural studies serves as the backdrop for L&CS analysis. Law and cultural studies uses discourse analysis tools to analyze the interplay between law and culture. Cultures manifest themselves through objects such as newspaper stories, clothing, films, manners of expression, and so on. There is an ongoing tug of war that occurs both within large and small cultures and between them. The predominant cultural norms for the group, its traditions, hold sway over our very way of seeing the world. Nonetheless, individuals define themselves in reaction to what has come before and create new discourses. Noting this dialectic between stasis and change, Amsterdam and Bruner aptly define culture as a constant struggle between what was and what might be (2000:219).

In fact, law *is* culture (Mezey 2003). Law is a set of discourses that hold sway over our very ways of seeing the world. We expect law to provide us with neutral principles that can be used to resolve disputes. As such, law is a repository of values, which are statements we typically think of as expressing our culture. Moreover, common law principles operate in the way culture operates: a consensus is arrived at and becomes the majority rule, but new perspectives are constantly emerging as minority rules that challenge the prevailing way of thinking.

To say law is a form of culture is not to deny that law sometimes influences culture. Take for example the *Brown v. Board of Education* (1954) decision. It changed both where and on what terms racial majorities and racial minorities interacted in civil society. The *Brown* decision and its progeny also spurred the 1960s black civil rights movement. Those are large-scale examples of the ongoing phenomenon of law's influence on culture.

Simultaneously, culture influences law. This is illustrated by the *Grutter v. Bollinger* (2003) decision, which considered the use of racial preferences in higher education. For decades, the Court had been rearticulating the *Brown* decision as barring any consideration of race by public officials. Yet the proponents of affirmative action formed a cultural movement that included schools, businesses, and the military. Seemingly in response to cultural pressure more so than its own precedent, the *Grutter* Court upheld racial preferences in the realm of higher education. The Court also went so far as to enter the cultural debate by proposing in dicta that racial preferences will no longer be necessary in 25 years. Here, then, is an example of culture influencing law and law attempting to reciprocally influence culture.

The recognition of law and culture as embedded in one another suggests an object of inquiry for L&CS analysis: the "slippages" between the meanings law attempts to produce and the uses actually made of the law in popular culture (Mezey 2003:38). Mezey defines slippage as the way law inevitably fails to dictate the terms of culture and culture fails to directly influence the law (ibid., 54–56).

Mezey's idea is compatible with the approach I have taken herein. I have argued the *Terry* Court's decision imagines a world where police harassment of racial minorities is rare. The slippage when that doctrine is translated into practice is that certain cultural contexts can lead to widespread racial profiling. My analysis of public acceptance of the Giuliani administration's aggressive use of *Terry* stops and frisks is an example of how that slippage occurs. Further, we see a slippage between cultural reformists' attempt to reduce racial profiling and the result of depolicing. In New York City, claiming the right to be free from racial profiling indirectly led to the loss of the right to appropriate policing at the Parade. As a whole then, *Terry*'s seesaw effect shows how there are ongoing slippages that occur in the interactions between law and culture.

Critical Cultural Theory Insights from *Terry*'s Seesaw Effect in New York City

The CCT approach I advocate merges insights from both the CRT and L&CS approaches, thereby allowing us to draw theoretical insights from *Terry*'s seesaw effect in New York City. From CRT it takes a focus on how cultural identity norms are socially constructed at a given moment and then influence material consequences. From L&CS it takes a focus on the slippages that occur when law and culture attempt to influence one another. I use a CCT approach to interrogate the ways that failure to consider the effects of cultural identity norms creates slippages between legal doctrine as imagined and actual enforcement practices.

The story of *Terry*'s seesaw effect in New York City reveals many instances of misapprehending the effects of cultural identity norms. First, the *Terry* Court does not acknowledge the role race may have played in officer McFadden's suspicion of the interaction between two black men and a white man. Second, the Court ignores the likelihood that police officers might apply their new powers in a racially disparate manner. Third, liberal white New Yorkers ignore Giuliani's foreshadowing that his anti-crime campaign would be conducted along racial lines. Fourth, a new understanding of racial minorities as victims of profiling affects the popular consensus about what constitutes appropriate policing. Fifth, however, the NYPD misconstrues calls for less profiling as a call for ignoring crime in racial minority communities. In each of those cases, identity plays a role in the translation of doctrine into practice, but with results that were not predicted.

The story of *Terry*'s seesaw effect in New York City also reveals many slippages in the relationship between legal and cultural discourses. First, the *Terry* Court creates a legal doctrine that imagines culture as largely non-prejudiced despite the reality that culture still includes many subtle forms of prejudice. Second, as the baggy jeans example illustrates, legal doctrines turn out to be inherently susceptible to misapplication in race-based ways. Third, we see how law can become a part of the culture, for Giuliani used the discretion created by *Terry* doctrine in order to create an aggressive policing regime. Fourth, the anti-racial profiling movement causes changes in actual enforcement practices. Fifth, culture proves vulnerable to law; the call for less racial profiling yields depolicing because there are no minimal legal requirements preventing officers from refusing to act (Cooper 2002b:359).

Merging CRT and L&CS approaches as applied to *Terry*'s seesaw effect in New York City suggests a general CCT approach for future analyzes of criminal procedure doctrines. I contend that any legal doctrine creates a range of potential enforcement practices. Unless a doctrine dictates a very specific practice on all possible sets of facts, it necessarily affords some discretion to choose among potential actions. The doctrine covers a zone of activities, but some related activities will fall below that zone and others above the zone. Under the doctrine's zone of activities lie activities that are insufficient to trigger the doctrine or that require less justification. Above the zone, another doctrine is triggered or the activity requires greater justification. Even within the zone, some activities take maximum advantage of the doctrine's discretion and others take minimum advantage. For example, officers might *Terry* stop every racial minority member who is even arguably suspicious or avoid *Terry* stopping racial minority members who are definitely suspicious. That range of potential for relatively high or low advantage taking within the doctrine's zone of coverage is its "enforcement practices continuum" (Cooper 2003:846–847).

Since doctrines afford discretion within the enforcement practices continuum, we should consider what might lead to maximum versus minimum enforcement within that continuum. With respect to police officers, we wish to understand why they might investigate people with more or less frequency in a specific community at a particular time. One influence upon that choice is the prevailing set of discourses about the appropriateness of law enforcement methods. Those prevailing discourses might support pervasive policing by any means necessary to reduce crime. Prevailing discourses might instead prioritize civil liberties over crime control. Moreover, officers will draw their background assumptions about the implications of an identity status from the pool of popular representations. Accordingly, their choices of how often and how vigorously to investigate a particular group may vary based on whether prevailing cultural identity norms associate that group with crime. That is, a group could be closely associated with crime or perceived as victims of over-policing. Taken together, general articulations of the appropriateness of aggressive versus deferential policing and specific cultural identity norms associating a social group with crime will constitute a "cultural context continuum (ibid., 847)." Officers' exercises of discretion along the enforcement practices continuum will be influenced by where their community is located on the cultural context continuum at a given time.

Having identified a cultural context continuum as affecting the point at which police officers locate themselves along the enforcement practices continuum, we should now consider the effects of change over time. A cultural shift toward articulating anti-crime measures as more important than civil liberties in conjunction with a shift toward cultural identity norms associating a particular social group with crime would lead to more frequent and vigorous investigation of that group. Similarly, a shift to articulating civil liberties as more important than crime investigation along with a group's decreasing association with crime would lead to less frequent and vigorous investigation of the group. As I have detailed, New York City saw a shift toward anti-crime discourses and associations of racial minorities with crime in 1993, then a swing toward civil liberties discourses and cultural identity norms depicting racial minorities as victims of profiling in the late 1990s. Hence, at Time #1, the cultural context led NYPD practices to be located on the *Terry* stop maximizing end of the enforcement practices continuum, but at Time #2 the cultural context led NYPD practices to be located on the *Terry* stop minimizing end of the continuum. I call that swing from one extreme point along the enforcement practices continuum to another extreme point along that continuum a "seesaw effect" (Cooper 2003:847–48)."

Conclusion

Just as we must sometimes fight fire with fire, we should fight the cultural phenomenon of *Terry*'s seesaw effect in the realm of culture. We should not accept that *Terry*'s seesaw effect requires either solely anti-sexist or solely anti-racist policing. Solely anti-sexist policing would ask for greater policing of events such as the Parade in order to protect women, and thereby endanger over-policing of racial minority men. Solely anti-racist policing would ask for less policing of racial minority men, and thereby endanger depolicing such as that seen at the Parade.

This chapter's mission has been to identify the related problems of over- and under-policing and outline a method for better understanding them. I realize, however, that hope is also a theoretical tool. I wish, therefore, to suggest that we can prevent seesaw effects by creating counter-discourses challenging initial calls for draconian policing. In order to prevent our counter-movement from reestablishing the anti-racism versus anti-sexism divide seen in New York City we must promote discourses that resist either/or thinking. Such a discourse was indeed suggested following the Parade depolicing:

> Police officers have a tough job, but it is not made any easier by a populace that is frightened or resentful of them. To do their jobs better, police should have more selections on their crime-fighting menus than a) excessive force or b) complete indifference (Page 2000:17).

This call for policing that is simultaneously anti-racist and anti-sexist is the type of re-articulation of what constitutes appropriate popular expectations of officers that we need to encourage.

References

Amsterdam, A., and Bruner, J. (2000) *Minding the Law*. Cambridge: Harvard University Press.

Armour, J.D. (1997) *Negrophobia and Reasonable Racism: The Hidden Costs of Being Black in America*. New York: New York University Press.

Audain, L. (1995) "Critical Cultural Law and Economics, The Culture of Deindividuation, the Paradox of Blackness." *Indiana Law Journal* 70:709.

Barry, D. (1997) "2d Police Officer Charged in Attack on Arrested Man." *New York Times*, 16 August.

Barry, D., and Connelly, M. (1999) "Poll in New York Finds Many Think Police Are Biased." *New York Times*, 16 March, A1.

Barstow, D., and Chivers, C.J. (2000) "A Volatile Mixture Exploded Into Rampage in Central Park." *New York Times*, 17 June, A1.

Bivens v. Albuquerque Public Schools 899 F. Supp. 556 (D.N.M. 1995).

Brown v. Board of Education 347 U.S. 483 (1954).

Brownstein, H. (1995) "The Media and the Construction of Random Drug Violence" in J. Ferrell & C. Sanders (eds.) *Cultural Criminology*. Boston: Northeastern University Press.

Camara v. Municipal Court 387 U.S. 523 (1967).

Carbado, D.W., and Gulati, M. (2000) "Working Identity." *Cornell Law Review* 85:1259.

Cooper, F.R. (2002a) "The Un-Balanced Fourth Amendment: A Cultural Study of the Drug War, Racial Profiling and Arvizu." *Villanova Law Review* 47:851.

—— (2002b) "Understanding 'Depolicing': Symbiosis Theory and Critical Cultural Theory." *University Missouri–Kansas City Law Review* 71:355.

—— (2003) "Cultural Context Matters: Terry's 'Seesaw Effect'." *Oklahoma Law Review* 56:833.

—— (2006) "Against Bipolar Black Masculinity: Intersectionality, Assimilation, Anxiety, and Hierarchy." *University California-Davis Law Review* 39:__.

Cooper, M. (1999) "Officers in Bronx Fire 41 Shots." *New York Times*, 5 February, A1.

Cottman, M.H. (1993) "A Race About Race." *New York Newsday*, 30 June.

Crenshaw, K., Gotanda, N., Peller, G., and Thomas, K. (1995) "Introduction" in *Critical Race Theory: The Key Writings That Formed the Movement*. New York: The New Press.

Flagg, B.J. (1998) *Was Blind But Now I See: White Race Consciousness and the Law*. New York: New York University Press.

Gilbert, C. (1999) "We Are What We Wear: Revisiting Student Dress Codes." *Brigham Young University Education & Law Journal* 1999:3.

Goldberg, J. (1999) "The Color of Suspicion." *New York Times*, 20 June.

Grosfoguel, R., and Georas, C. (2000) "'Coloniality of Power' and Racial Dynamics: Notes Towards a Reinterpretation of Latino Caribbeans in New York City." *Identities* 7:1.

Grutter v. Bollinger 539 U.S. 306 (2003).

Hall, S. (1997) "The Work of Representation" in S. Hall (ed.) *Representation: Cultural Representations and Signifying Practices*. London: Sage Publications.

Herbert, B. (2000) "In America; A Delicate Balance." *New York Times*, 9 March, A29.

Hutchinson, D. (2004) "Critical Race Histories: In and Out." *American University Law Review* 53:1187.

Maclin, T. (1998) "Terry v. Ohio's Fourth Amendment Legacy: Black Men and Police Discretion." *St. John's University Law Review* 72:1271.

Mezey, N. (2003) "Law as Culture" in A. Sarat and J. Simon (eds) *Cultural Analysis, Cultural Studies, and the Law: Moving Beyond Legal Realism*. Durham: Duke University Press.

Mitchell, A. (1993) "Giuliani Zeroing in on Crime Issue; New Commercials Are Focusing on Fears of New Yorkers." *New York Times*, 20 September, B3.

Nelson, C. (2003) "Breaking the Camel's Back: A Consideration of Mitigatory Criminal Defenses and Racism-Related Mental Illness." *Michigan Journal of Race & Law* 9:77.

New York Times (1993) "A Broad Plan for Safe Streets." *New York Times*, 7 December, A26.

—— (2000) "The Outrage in Central Park." *New York Times*, 14 June, A26.

Omi, M., and Winant, H. (1994) *Racial Formation in the United States: From the 1960s to the 1990s*. New York: Routledge.

Page, C. (2000) "Critics of Cops Still Need the Cops." *Chicago Tribune*, 18 June.

Plessy v. Ferguson 163 U.S. 567 (1896).

Purnick, J. (2000) "Park Rampage Stirs Anguish on 2 Fronts." *New York Times*, 19 June, B1.

Rayman, G. (1999) "Report Shows Who Cops Stop." *Newsday*, 1 December, A3.

Robbins, T. (2000) "The Con and the Mayor." *Village Voice*, 1 August.

Roberts, S. (1993) "A Tarnishing Report for the Mayor of New York." *New York Times*, 25 July.

Sklansky, D.A. (2000) "The Fourth Amendment and Common Law." *Columbia Law Review* 100:1739.

Slack, J.D. (1996) "The Theory and Method of Articulation in Cultural Studies" in D. Morley and K-H. Chen (eds) *Stuart Hall: Critical Dialogues in Cultural Studies*. New York: Routledge.

Smolowe, J. et al. (2000) "Unanswered Cries: Victims of a Central Park Sexual 'Wilding' Say Police Ignored Their Please For Help." *People Magazine*, 3 July, p.63.

Terry v. Ohio 392 U.S. 1 (1968).

Thompson, A. (1999) "Stopping the Usual Suspects: Race and the Fourth Amendment." *New York University Law Review* 74:956.

Chapter 8

Keeping Rights Alive: The Struggle for HIV-Infected Prisoners

BENJAMIN FLEURY-STEINER AND JESSICA HODGE

Over the past two decades, we have witnessed an alarming explosion in the number of lawsuits filed by State and Federal prisoners ... Prisoners have filed lawsuits claiming such grievances as insufficient storage locker space, being prohibited from attending a wedding anniversary party, and yes, being served creamy peanut butter instead of the chunky variety they had ordered.

— Senator Robert Dole

In this chapter, we explore how the recent retrenchment of a prisoner's right to adequate medical treatment is *experienced* by those who advocate on behalf of HIV-infected prisoners. Unlike most sociolegal research that focuses on the lived effects of *added* rights (for example, McCann 1994, Silverstein 1996, Engel and Munger 2003), we focus on the lived effects of rights being *taken away*. What kinds of experiences have advocates of HIV-infected prisoner rights had in this era of dying prisoner rights? To explore this question, this chapter focuses on the experiences of 25 such advocates from across the US.

Dying Prisoner Rights in the US

For most of American legal history, the concept of "prisoner rights" in practice has largely been a contradiction. Until the 1960s, prisoners were viewed as right-*less* slaves of the state and thus were rarely able to redress unconstitutional harms they experienced frequently behind bars (Barnes 1972; Lewis 1922; Semple 1993). Indeed, not until the Warren Court were prisoners formally recognized as possessing at least some rights under the Constitution (for example, Herman 1998). Beginning in the latter half of the 1960s, the Warren Court lifted the ban on prisoner access to law libraries (*Johnson v. Avery*, 1969). The 1970s signaled an even greater breakthrough period for prisoner rights in the US. The most significant advances included:

- providing prisoners with the right to practice their religion behind bars (*Cruz v. Beto*, 1972);
- the inclusion of a prisoner's right to private correspondence with non-prisoners (*Procunier v. Martinez*, 1974);
- the prisoner's right to due process protections at prison disciplinary hearings (*Wolff v. McDonnell*, 1974).

Perhaps the Supreme Court's most fundamental affirmation of prisoner rights came in its decision in *Estelle v. Gamble* (1976). In *Estelle*, the Supreme Court ruled that when prison officials are deliberately indifferent to the serious medical needs of prisoners, the prisoners' Eighth Amendment right to be free from cruel and unusual punishment is violated. However, more recent Supreme Court decisions have dramatically narrowed the impact of *Estelle*. In both *Wilson v. Seiter* (1991) and *Farmer v. Brennan* (1994),[1] the Supreme Court required prisoners seeking to challenge the conditions of their confinement to demonstrate a *culpable state of mind* on the part of prison officials. This dramatic narrowing of a prisoner's right to adequate healthcare thus excludes the more common occurrences involving prison officials who are "oblivious to an inmate's need for protection, or perhaps even well-intentioned wardens who lacked adequate funding to maintain clean and safe institutions" (Herman 1998:1050).

In addition to the Supreme Court's narrowing of the deliberate indifference standard, many over-populated US prisons attempting to cut costs have begun to increasingly rely on privatized health maintenance organizations (HMOs). As Maddow cogently observes:

> In the 1980s, with rising prison populations already straining state budgets, US prison healthcare costs started to rise at a faster rate than the rest of corrections costs. … To prison officials beset by rising numbers of prisoners, stretched healthcare budgets, the high incidence of expensive illnesses including HIV/AIDS, and the ever-present threat of Eighth Amendment lawsuits private prison healthcare providers offered convenient-sounding solutions to longstanding problems (Maddow 2001:191).

If HMOs are found disproportionately to focus on cost-cutting over quality of care (McDonald 1995; Robbins 1999), then not surprisingly the risk of inadequate treatment is even greater for prisoners:

> Concerns regarding inadequate healthcare are magnified in a prison setting, in which inmates have no choice about healthcare and cannot seek outside advice. They are left to the discretion of the healthcare provider chosen by the county or state. In addition, since prisoners themselves are not usually paying customers, healthcare providers have even less of an incentive to provide quality care (Robbins 1999:198).

Most distressingly, the Supreme Court's recent decision in *Correctional Services Corporation (CSC) v. Malesko* (2001) has ruled that for-profit providers contracted to run health services in federal prisons are protected from suit for violating a prisoner's constitutional right to adequate healthcare. Observing that CSC's failure to provide the plaintiff in this case with proper healthcare was not an isolated incident, Elizabeth Alexander, the Director of the ACLU (American Civil Liberties Union) National Prison Project, writes:

---

[1] While *Wilson* narrowed a prisoner's right to challenge the cruel and unusual conditions of his or her confinement, the Supreme Court in *Farmer v. Brennan* (1994) dramatically narrowed what constitutes a "deliberate indifference" to the harm prisoners experience behind bars. Specifically, the Court in *Farmer* once again invoked its prisoner officials-centered jurisprudence. However, in this case the Court ruled that a deliberate indifference to a prisoner's well-being is established only if prison officials actually *knew* the prisoner faced a specific harm and disregarded it.

[R]eductions in [private prison] labor costs are achieved in two ways: hiring fewer staff and hiring less qualified staff ... CSC, the private corporation that confined Mr. Malesko when he was injured has a history of using both methods to reduce costs at the price of services (2003:71).[2]

Alexander also documents how two other leading for-profit prison healthcare providers, *Corrections Corporation of America (CCA)* and *Wackenhut Corrections Corporation*, have equally dismal records for meeting prisoners' healthcare needs.

Complicating this issue further have been recent legislative reforms passed by Congress. Despite a growing epidemic of *preventable* deaths of HIV and Hepatitis C infected prisoners at the hands of prison healthcare providers,[3] Congress has enacted what many commentators have argued is the most sweeping retrenchment of prisoner rights (such as Herman 1998), *The Prison Litigation and Reform Act of 1996* (PLRA). One of the PLRA's many controversial provisions requires all prisoners – including the most indigent – to pay a mandatory case filing fee. Additionally, the PLRA caps all attorneys' fees. One consequence of this has been that fewer prisoner rights litigations have been filed by increasingly under-funded and under-staffed prison law organizations. Indeed, in some cases, prisoner rights lawyers have been forced to deny even the most meritorious cases post-PLRA.[4]

The Present Study

Data and Methods

To explore the contemporary world of HIV prisoner rights, Fleury-Steiner conducted 25 interviews with advocates who work in prisons from 4 major regions in the US. Given the tremendous cutbacks in prisoner rights advocacy since the PLRA, obtaining a truly representative sample of respondents proved impossible. In the initial attempt

---

[2] In her analysis of the *Malesko* case, Alexander discusses CSC's history of cost-cutting over quality health services at various facilities across the US. Specifically, she describes the preventable death of a boy at a Texas boot camp, and the grossly negligent treatment of a juvenile at a youth correctional center in Florida.

[3] Several reports from around the US have documented this recent trend (Fazlolla and Lin 2002; Guillemette 2003; Highleyman 2003; Hylton 2003; LaFay 2002; Wilson 2003). Most recently the more than 40 preventable deaths of HIV-infected prisoners in Alabama's segregated HIV ward has been well documented in the media (Hodges 2003) and in recent scholarly research (Fleury-Steiner forthcoming).

[4] Margo Schlanger's (2003) recent empirical analysis of data collected by the Administrative Office of the US Courts documents that even the most meritorious individual damage suits brought by federal prisoners pre- and post-PLRA have declined dramatically. Indeed, her analysis attributes such declines in meritorious cases to the PLRA's mandatory filing fee, attorney fee cap, and its provision requiring prisoners to exhaust all prison administrative remedies before being permitted to file suit:

> In particular, the new filing fee makes it uneconomical for inmates to pursue low-stakes cases even when such cases are high in merit, and the new attorneys' fee limits further increase the difficulty for even those inmates with good cases to find counsel and actually litigate successfully. Moreover, the PLRA's exhaustion provision has effected a major liability-reducing change in the legal standards: inmates who experience even grievous loss because of unconstitutional misbehavior by prison and jail authorities will nonetheless lose cases they once would have won, if they fail to comply with technicalities of administrative exhaustion (Schlanger 2003:1694).

to set up interviews, it was discovered that many advocates could not participate – indeed, their dramatically increased workloads left them literally without *any* free time to spare. We also discovered that several of the organizations that we originally planned to contact had run out of funding and thus were forced to shut down.

In addition to these unforeseen logistical impediments, another obstacle towards obtaining a representative sample was the tremendous variation in the treatment protocols for HIV infection in US prisons. Specifically, each of the 50 states and the federal government employ different protocols for treating HIV-infected prisoners.[5] We were thus unable to systematically analyze variations in treatment protocols in the context of advocacy on behalf of HIV-infected prisoners. At the same time, because our main interest was on rights advocacy on behalf of HIV-infected prisoners – instead of an explicit interest in the effectiveness or ineffectiveness of various treatment protocols – this impediment became less of a concern.[6]

These limitations notwithstanding, we do believe the study presents a compelling picture of a diverse array of advocates. One of the advantages of this analysis is that the interviews were conducted with respondents from states with disproportionately high levels of HIV infection among prisoners. In a word, the respondents interviewed were all very *experienced* prisoner rights activists and thus were able to provide detailed accounts of their experiences. Secondly, nearly all of the respondents interviewed had advocated on behalf of prisoners within the last six months and thus experienced few problems recalling important details. Finally, and perhaps most importantly, because interviews were conducted with respondents who approached prisoner rights advocacy from different professional orientations (such as lawyers, ex-prisoners, and activists), we were able to explore how their different roles, and thus the different situations they found themselves in, shaped their views of the PLRA, their experiences as advocates, and their views of law and social change.

The study began with a discussion Fleury-Steiner had with a colleague who was both a former attorney for a state ACLU prison project and a legal academic who is an expert in law, HIV, and public health. This initial discussion led to the first contact with a prisoner rights activist in the South. The use of a snowball sampling strategy[7] continued until the sample achieved a reasonable level of regional diversity.[8]

---

[5] An extreme example of this variation can be seen by comparing Alabama and New York. Alabama is the only state that continues to quarantine HIV-infected prisoners in total isolation (for example, *Onishea v. Hopper* 1999). Quarantined prisoners in Alabama, moreover, receive very substandard care for HIV and receive no treatment for Hepatitis C (Tabet 2003). By contrast, New York state prisons (as of 1998) provide all FDA-approved HIV drugs to infected prisoners as well as a limited treatment for Hepatitis C (Siegal 1998).

[6] Indeed, the questions focused explicitly on respondents' actual experiences. Drawing on the insights of Riessman (1993), the questions presented typically asked respondents to tell a story.

[7] In snowball sampling, one or more key individuals is located and then asked to name others who would be likely candidates for the research project. Specifically, one respondent gives the researcher the name of another respondent, who in turn provides the name of a third, and so on (Vogt 1999). This strategy has been observed as especially useful for overcoming problems associated with sampling concealed or hard-to-reach populations such as ex-prisoners (Faugier and Sargeant 1997).

[8] In all, 10 activists from the Northeast, 6 activists from the South, 3 activists from the Northwest, and 6 activists from the Western United States were interviewed.

Correspondence with potential interviewees occurred several times in order to introduce the research before the phone interviews were conducted. Each interview lasted one to three hours. Interviews were conducted from January 2003 to May 2003 and audio-recorded. Next, a group of four research assistants and Fleury-Steiner transcribed the interviews. The responses we present here are from those transcriptions. Respondents are identified by pseudonyms and we included only information that did not compromise participant confidentiality.

Breaking the Silence of Prison Walls

The interview focused on three main areas:

- the effects of the PLRA on prisoner rights advocacy;
- respondents' experiences with specific prisoners and the challenges they faced as advocates;
- respondents' thoughts on law as an avenue for social and institutional change.

Effects of the PLRA: Creating Obstacles to Effective Advocacy

Early in the interview, respondents were asked to discuss how the PLRA affected their work as prisoner rights advocates. While many of the non-lawyer respondents were unaware of the PLRA, the vast majority of both activists and lawyers had much to say about its direct effects on their work. For economy of presentation, however, we present only a small cross-section of the narratives that best represent the data as a whole. Specifically, respondents describe the effects of the PLRA on organizational resources, litigation strategy, activism, and the willingness of corrections officials to cooperate with their investigations.

Draining Organizational Resources

Len Erickson: "All around the country, little prisoner shops are going out of business"   Len Erickson, a former director of a prisoner legal project on the East coast, describes how the PLRA has led to the shutdown of many prisoner rights projects across the US:

> The PLRA has influenced everything, or at least, it does among those who are still able to stay in business after the PRLA. And there aren't many of them. The PLRA narrowed the causes of action even further and limited the fees that you could recover even if you won. So, now you have fewer meritorious suits, legally meritorious suits, and less money even if you win. All around the country, little prisoner law shops are going out of business. My prisoner shop is still up and running, but that is, if I may say so, thanks to creative leadership. I mean, if you do the equivalent of a Nexis search and look at how many of them there were ten years ago, you know the local prisoner rights projects, they're all gone now.

Alexandra Michaels: "... And that just sort of happens with PLRA"   Alexandra Michaels, a long-time prisoner rights attorney and director of a national organization, begins by describing the impact of the PLRA on her organization:

> When it became apparent that PLRA was going to be passed, the first impact that it had on my office was that the organization decided to cut the budget by about a quarter ... The projects are self-supporting, and we were primarily supporting ourselves with attorney's fees, and because it would be so difficult to win new cases, and because the fee provisions of PLRA drastically cut the availability of attorney's fees, the organization correctly anticipated that we would have substantially less income. So, the first impact was that there were cuts in staff and cuts in programs.

Undermining Effective Litigation and Activism

Next, Michaels describes the impact of the PLRA on her work routine. Specifically, she contrasts her work schedule as a new public interest lawyer with her present schedule post-PLRA:

> The second impact was when it really became just the standard thing to work sixty to seventy hour weeks on a routine basis. I mean that's what you did during trial. When I went into public interest as an aside; one thing that public interest was supposed to be good for was that unlike working for a firm, you got regular time off. Now, my standard week I'm working seven days a week. And that just sort of happens with PLRA. It also happened in the point of my life where my kids were growing up, and I could do it in a way that I couldn't have done it earlier.

Regardless of how many hours she works, fighting the PLRA proves extremely difficult if not impossible:

> In any event, we lost a lot of cases, and we spent huge amounts of time organizing the plan of bargain, getting the standard briefs done, and fighting PLRA to the extent that we could ... It really has made the litigation much more difficult to do. It now literally means that cases that were won once don't necessarily stay won.

Sally Redmond: "I think it takes the steam out of activism too"   Sally Redmond, a long-time prisoner rights and AIDS/HIV activist from a West coast organization, believes that the PLRA – by making it more difficult for lawyers to share important information with activists – has a direct negative effect on activism. Specifically, the PLRA makes it more difficult for lawyers to bring important media attention to activist organizations.

> I always thought that having both lawyers and activists working together is more effective than just focusing on litigation alone. But part of it really is the PRLA. The lawyers try to do what they could within the confines of the federal legislation and stuff, but, because they are so tied up in red tape, they are less able to give you a hook to interest the media, to have demonstrations around.

Lack of Cooperation by Prison Officials: Dying Under the PLRA

The PLRA has had a clearly negative effect on litigation and activism on behalf of HIV-infected prisoners. Perhaps because of what Sally Redmond observes – that is, lawyers being tied up in red tape – that prison officials appear to be far less willing to cooperate with advocates.

Christina Dyer: "... we got around the Prison Litigation Reform Act because she was dead ..." Christina Dyer, a lawyer and activist from a prisoner rights organization on the West coast, tells a chilling story of the powerlessness of prisoner rights lawyers post-PLRA to challenge the inhumane treatment of one prisoner she worked with. Dyer begins by telling a story of the circumstances leading up to the death of this prisoner. This prisoner was herself an important advocate for other HIV-infected prisoners. She was both HIV and Hepatitis C infected, and was apparently retaliated against by prison health officials for contesting the substandard treatment dying prisoners were receiving:

> There was an activist prisoner who I worked with four years who is actually in pretty good health, and she had HIV, but she was non-symptomatic. And her viral load was virtually nonexistent even though she was on medication, and she is basically just fine with her HIV health, but she was also infected with Hepatitis C. She had very pronounced signs of liver disease and was getting sicker and sicker. She argued, and we couldn't prove this element of it, she thought that in response to how she was advocating for other prisoners for their healthcare, the chief medical officer at the prison she was at, wanted to get rid of her and get her out of the institution. So he had her pulled out of her room and sent her across the street to a different prison, allegedly for having tuberculosis.[9] She was put into isolation and given tuberculosis medications which are highly liver toxic. Anyway, she didn't have any signs or symptoms of having TB. She thought, and I would agree that, he probably did this to get her out of the way, but she went into liver failure as a result of these medications and she died. Before she died she was sent back to the other prison, and that chief medical officer then tried to cover up her condition and was trying to say that she wasn't sick when in fact she was sick.

In a perverse ending to her story, Dyer reveals how she was able to circumvent the PLRA and file suit against prison officials who refused to allow this prisoner's family to be present with her as she died:

> The day after she died, we got a letter postmarked and dated after she was already dead telling us that her condition was under control and she was fine from that chief medical officer. He also then, we suspected that she was dying, and we were trying to get her family to have a special permission for bereavement visits to see her quickly and they denied that. So she died without her family being able to say goodbye, and they also tried to cover up the death. But we got around the Prison Litigation Reform Act because she was dead. So obviously she was an okay plaintiff because she was dead. We sued on her family's behalf for negligence and intentional infliction of emotional distress on them, on the doctor's failure to admit that she was near death, so obviously they weren't prisoners.

---

[9] Tuberculosis has been widespread in prisons in both the US and Russia (Farmer 2003) and has been documented to spread beyond prison walls. For documentation of such outbreaks in San Francisco and New York State, see Alexander 2003.

This experience reminds Dyer that this case is not an anomalous occurrence – perhaps less so since the passage of the PLRA – for prisoner rights lawyers such as herself:

> We just see so many of these things on a regular basis that should be lawsuits, where the time limits aren't met, or we just know the exhaustion is never going to be met or there is no way that we can find an attorney who will take a financial risk to take the cases. It is really heartbreaking, and it is just heartbreaking. So it is something that we constantly see.

Terrence Bernstein: "... and nothing happens but you have to go through that system..."   Terrence Bernstein, an attorney with a human rights advocacy group in the South, describes the devastating effects of the PLRA's requirement that HIV-infected prisoners must exhaust all of the prison's administrative remedies before they are able to file a federal suit:[10]

> One of the provisions of the PLRA is that you have to exhaust all of the administrative remedies of the facility. The inmates have to file grievances and allow the facility itself to make the correction before the clients are allowed to get into federal court. So, we had to wait months while inmates wrote – in futility – grievances and raised issues that were happening to them.

Bernstein describes his current litigation involving a boil outbreak caused by the grossly substandard living conditions of a segregated HIV ward:

> We saw these forms that said, "I have these boils, I need to see a doctor." And nothing happens, but you have to go through that system before you are allowed to go into federal court. Before the PLRA we would have been able to just show [that] our letter writing to the department of corrections and raising the issues with them and their reluctance to address the issues. That this alone should allow us to be in federal court and the federal court would be able to provide the clients with relief rather than waiting so long while so many people die during that whole process. That is one of the toughest parts, to wait for the system, for the administrative process that is in the facilities, wait for that to be completed before you can go to federal court and ask for help.

The PLRA fosters a deepening hopelessness among Bernstein's clients:

> The system takes so long and it very rarely ever works. We all know it is not going to work. I mean, the clients know it isn't going to work. They tell me that they will agree to file these papers, but they say right to me, "It's not going to do anything." I tell them that they have to regardless. You know, I tell them, "Unfortunately, that's the law, we have to have these

---

[10] Prior to the PLRA, prisoners were required to use all of the prison's grievance procedures only if a district court required them to. Moreover, if a prisoner failed to exhaust under the original standards the only consequence would be the stay of a district court proceeding, not its dismissal. Under the PLRA, prisoners must make their complaints using whatever administrative grievance procedures exist, even if that system lacks authority to grant the remedy sought. Thus, the exhaustion provision may, at least in the case of Terrence Bernstein's clients, even be fatal. In short, "[t]he exhaustion requirement has teeth because many courts have held that an inmate's failure to comply with the grievance system's rules (time limits, form, and so on) usually *justifies disqualification* [emphasis added] of the inmate's lawsuit" (Schlanger 2003:1628).

filed." During that time, we lost numerous inmates who died of issues that should have been in front of the court, that should have been addressed, that could have been addressed much quicker before my clients died.

The Prison Culture of Inhumanity

As Terrence Bernstein's story makes clear, the PLRA has made effective advocacy on behalf of HIV-infected prisoners more difficult. If the PLRA has hindered effective advocacy, then it is not surprising that prisoners are paying the price, sometimes (as Dyer and Bernstein's stories make clear) with their lives. In this section, we take a closer look at the suffering of HIV-infected prisoners, or what we call the prisons' deepening culture of inhumanity.

All 25 respondents interviewed provided at least one example of the inhumane treatment and conditions HIV-infected prisoners are exposed to. While these examples do not meet the *Farmer* Court's "state of mind" requirement that places much of the burden on prisoners to demonstrate the *deliberate indifference*[11] of prison officials, these accounts present the subtle and often not-so-subtle ways in which the present system fails on many levels to protect the constitutional rights of prisoners, especially those infected with HIV.

Susan Billy: " ... Nobody has a specified regimen ... " Susan Billy, an ex-prisoner, activist, and paralegal with a non-profit prison law project on the East coast, tells a story of a fellow prisoner that elucidates the inability of prison healthcare systems to address the specialized needs of HIV-infected prisoners:

> Let's see, there was one female who was HIV positive. And she, um, had to do what they call wasting. Wasting is when you lose more than ten pounds in a year. And she had lost, oh god, I would guess thirty or forty pounds. And it was because of the fact that the doctors in the prison setting give everybody the same medicine regimen. Nobody has a specified regimen for themselves. They just give everybody the same things and hope that it works. So people were getting sick, and not responding well to the medications that they were receiving because they were all getting the same thing.

Additionally, Susan Billy describes a second prisoner's death as treated in a cold, bureaucratic fashion by prison doctors:

> There was a female who died she was very, very sick, and she went to the infirmary and they told her she was fine. So, she went back to her unit. Well, the inmates ended up carrying her back to the infirmary. And the doctors acted as if nothing was wrong. They locked her in a room in the back. And she died. She died.

Manuel Colon: " ... it is so damaging psychologically" Manuel Colon, an ex-prisoner and activist from the Eastern United States, also describes both the emotionally and physically cruel and unusual conditions experienced by HIV-infected

---

[11] In *Farmer v. Brennan* (1994) the Supreme Court elaborated on its ruling in *Estelle v. Gamble*. Specifically, the *Farmer* Court held that deliberate indifference exists in a case alleging failure to protect prisoners *only if* prison officials actually knew the prisoner faced a substantial risk of harm and ignored that risk.

prisoners. In answering the question, "What are some recent challenges you have faced as a prisoner rights activist?" he described a recent visit to a state prison's new Special Housing Units[12] (SHUs) or what he calls a "high-tech dungeons":

> There are about eight of these self-contained prisons that they built on the grounds of already existing prisons. And they cost twelve million dollars to build. I refer to them as a "high-tech dungeon." There are two people locked in a cell for twenty-three hours. They are so contained that they have a shower in the cell, they have a door that opens in the back of the cell that leads into this little area that they call it a dog kennel.

> Interviewer: Do they put sick prisoners in there? Even HIV-infected prisoners?:

> Oh yeah. First of all, I think it is so damaging psychologically. You know, the mental, emotional, and spiritual damage of the people confined under these conditions. It's horrible.

Heather Michelle Samuels: "... one of the two worst things I saw ..."   Heather Michelle Samuels, an AIDS activist and prison hospice volunteer from a Southern state, describes her first experience as a social worker assigned to a hospital that serves the medical needs of state prisoners. Like the stories of Billy and Colon, Samuels' account is one of a prison system that is largely indifferent to sick prisoners:

> Interviewer: How did you get involved with prisoner rights?

> My first contact was working as a hospital medical social worker at our city hospital. And all inmates are brought here for their healthcare. They are shackled to their beds no matter how sick they are. So, my consciousness really got raised there, and got me involved in working on behalf of the inmates, because I was working with people who couldn't even walk who were shackled to their beds, which is a distinct danger if there was a fire, if they shared a room with an aggressive patient or a psychotic patient.

Samuels tells a story of "one of the two worst things" she saw at the hospital:

> And one of the two worst things I saw was when a shackled inmate, who they needed to resuscitate, and they had to wait for the guard to come and unshackle him, because it was metal. Well, he died. And that was such an absolutely horrifying thing to think that maybe it would've been different. And then I had another patient who had very advanced AIDS and was slowly losing his mental faculties as well as his ability to walk or move his arms in any way. And they insisted that he had to be shackled to the bed; he was totally confused. He did not get better, and the hospital wanted to send him back to the jail, and we tried, my supervisor and I tried to get him released so we could place him, because we thought he was probably terminal, and the jail would not release him.
>   So, he was instead sent back to jail, and we thought that the jail would say, "We can't manage somebody this sick" and release him, which they often do and send him to the hospital, or, if they send him to the hospital, they would then release him there. But he was basically dumped there in the jail. And they kept him for about three weeks, when he came back to the hospital he also died. He was still in custody, and shackled to the bed.

---

[12] A recent report by the *New York State Senate Democratic Task Force on Criminal Justice Reform,* reveals that approximately 5,500 prisoners in New York State are currently being held in SHUs. Once inside, prisoners are held under 23-hour lockdown (Pareti 2003).

Laura Travers: "… horrible stuff, treatment-wise …"   Laura Travers, a colleague of Terrence Bernstein, who is also an attorney, describes an incompetent doctor as "one of the most egregious" things she has seen:

> One of the most egregious things was the HIV doctor in the jail. The doctor was not only prescribing the wrong medication, but was insisting that people didn't need protease inhibitors and was actually taking people off of their drug regiments and starting them on new regiments. She was not ensuring that they actually got their medicine. I mean horrible stuff, treatment-wise.

Terrence Bernstein: "… this warehouse that is literally falling apart around them" Terrence Bernstein describes the deplorable conditions of a segregated HIV ward:

> … [T]hey put all of the HIV inmates into this warehouse and because of the segregation you have a mixture of all the classes of inmates. You have people that are serving life without parole housed with people that are serving a year or two for minor offenses and they are all living in a dorm setting in this warehouse that is literally falling apart around them. The roof has been collapsing and the rain leaks in. There are rats and spiders that bite the inmates. They do all of their cooking and living in this warehouse, because they are not allowed to associate with the rest of the prison population. The warehouse is located on the other side of the prison from the healthcare unit so during emergencies it can take 30 to 40 minutes for inmates to be brought from the warehouse to the healthcare unit and numerous inmates have died on the route. This is what I learned from going there. The conditions have been awful for the last ten, twelve, fifteen years from what I have seen.

After describing the horrors of the "warehouse," Bernstein tells a story of an HIV-infected prisoner – who is also an amputee – and how this man suffered additional harms as a result of the prison's inadequate services:

> The dorm itself doesn't have any kind of railing for people who are disabled in the shower or beds or anything. He was hopping around in the shower and would fall in the shower on numerous occasions. On one occasion, he fell and was injured and was lying in the shower water for thirty minutes until nurses came and were able to assist him. Because of his lack of prosthesis, he was not allowed to go outside and exercise. There were no ramps for wheelchairs to get out of the dorm and to get outside so he was stuck inside.

Because he is trapped inside, he is one of the first prisoners to contract PCP.[13] And because of inadequate medicine, the disease spreads like wildfire through the segregated warehouse, as Bernstein describes:

---

[13] According to the Center for Disease Control and Prevention:

Pneumocystis carinii (NEW-mo-SIS-tis CA-RIN-nee-eye) pneumonia, or PCP, is a severe illness found in people with HIV. It is caused by a germ called *Pneumocystis carinii*. Most people infected with this germ don't get pneumonia because their immune systems are normal. People whose immune systems are badly damaged by HIV can get PCP. People with HIV are less likely to get PCP today than in earlier years. However, PCP is still the most common serious infection among people with AIDS in the United States" (http://www.cdc.gov/hiv/pubs/brochure/pcpb.htm).

Once a person comes down with pneumonia it could spread without taking medication to prevent it. Four to five people got it and the most recent person died just before this last year. That has just been a big problem, not just with the people getting pneumonia but the same problems that that person had because he was an amputee.

Rather than add hand railings for prisoners who have difficulty walking, prison officials – in order, most likely, to escape responsibility under the *Americans With Disabilities Act* (ADA)[14] – have isolated an HIV-infected prisoner who is also an amputee:

There was another amputee inmate that had the same problems, but he is in lockdown in the healthcare unit, so that the prison can try to avoid liability for falling, because he has fell on four occasions.

When HIV-Infected Prisoners Cannot Read or Write

Each of the above stories reveal how the impersonal, "one-size-fits-all" model of the prison bureaucracy breaks down at the expense of HIV-infected prisoners with obvious consequences for their health and, more often than not, their lives. This situation is only made worse when HIV-infected prisoners are unable to read or write. Respondents' stories describe such prisoners as not only subjected to grossly substandard prison healthcare but, because of illiteracy, they are at even greater disadvantage when it comes to understanding their disease and what treatments to demand from prison healthcare staff.

Walter Spence: "... he's not getting any care ..."   Walter Spence, an ex-prisoner and long-time activist from the Northwest US, describes an experience with one such prisoner. In addition to being HIV-infected and unable to read or write this prisoner is also blind:

Well, he had only been diagnosed for two weeks, but he obviously had HIV for a long time. He gets diagnosed, put in the hospital, the orderlies are inmates, they won't even touch him and he's got no pillow, he's lying on this little thing and can't get comfortable. He's like, "I just can't get comfortable." And I'm like, "What are they doing to you?" And he goes, "I know nothing about it." He couldn't read or write, and he didn't have any way to get any information except from what they told him about his disease. They gave him no medications or anything. And the thing is he can't see, so they send him to the optometrist, and the optometrist says, "We haven't seen this in a prisoner with AIDS in ten years." I mean, there's a drug to take care of this kind of stuff. But of course he's not getting any care and he loses his eyesight over it and it's awful, and, on top of that, he's gonna die soon. There are people that do get drugs, I'm not saying they don't, but they are not prescribed by a specialist, they continually discontinue orders, they don't do blood work and regular follow-ups.

At the Intersections of Inhumanity

These stories present HIV-infected prisoners as trapped in a veritable culture of inhumanity. Such a culture is the product of both old and new problems in the nation's

---

[14] See http://www.usdoj.gov/crt/ada/adahom1.htm.

prisons. First, the disproportionate numbers of poor racial and ethnic minorities behind bars (for example, Mauer 1999), the substandard conditions of many prisons that such prisoners continue to experience (for example, Mauer and Chesney-Lind 2002), and the inability of the prison bureaucracy to properly deal with such problems as overcrowding and inhumane living conditions have all been well documented in the scholarly literature (such as, Evans, Baca and Haney 2000; Gordon 2000; Ross and Richards 2002; Wynn 2001). Poor prison healthcare systems generally and the often substandard treatment received by HIV and increasingly Hepatitis C infected prisoners in particular, have also been well documented (for example, Fazlolla and Lin 2002; Guillemette 2003; Highleyman 2003; Hylton 2003; LaFay 2002; Robbins 1999; Wilson 2003). Moreover, illiteracy among prisoners in the US continues at a disproportionately high rate (Watson and DiIulio 1998).[15]

While each of these problems are well understood as serious impediments to prisoners' rights, the stories of activists presented above reveal how structural factors (such as racial and class inequality) and micro-level factors (such as poor living conditions, substandard healthcare, and illiteracy) *intersect* to perpetuate a culture of inhumanity behind prison walls, especially for those prisoners infected with serious illnesses. Furthermore, in the case of Manuel Colon's "high-tech dungeons," we see how the Prison Industrial Complex's[16] focus on warehousing over rehabilitation can further entrench the culture of inhumanity. Given these daunting obstacles, we might expect the world of HIV-infected prisoner rights lawyers to be especially challenging. We explore this issue in the next section.

Lawyers in the Struggle for HIV-Infected Prisoner Rights

Laura Travers: "... pretty much content to let the contractor negotiate this" Throughout her interview, attorney Laura Travers focused on a recent class action lawsuit her organization had brought against a prison for its substandard treatment of HIV-infected prisoners. Here, Travers describes how the state's increased reliance on private healthcare providers created a conflict of interest:

> I mean an interesting aspect of the negotiations, this is going to be true now for almost any jail or prison system that you go to, is that you got a private medical provider contracted with the county. So the county and the sheriff are pretty much content to let the contractor negotiate this, which really makes no sense at all, because the contractor is here today, gone tomorrow. And ultimately, constitutionally, it's the county that is going to have to make sure that care is provided and paid for, whether it is that contractor or another contractor. We proposed these things that we thought were necessary, but we figured that they would disagree with us or would want you know to "neutralize" us a little bit. It was like the

---

[15] According to the *Prison Policy Initiative* adult prisoners in the US are 5 times as likely to be illiterate as compared to the adult population at large (http://www.prisonpolicy.org/graphs/illiteracy.shtml).

[16] Throughout this chapter we use the term "Prison Industrial Complex" to highlight an "American criminal justice system that has been substantially transformed by almost three decades of rapid growth and by the increasing importance of private interests in criminal justice policy" (Wood 2003:16). Specifically, our analysis of prisoner rights advocates' accounts calls attention to the implications of rising prison populations, the HIV/AIDS epidemic behind bars, and the use of private correctional healthcare providers.

medical people actually knew what was needed but also knew they were not doing it. The lawyers would, in trying to lessen the burden ultimately on the county, would try and shut that off. I mean, this our goal as a group here, as lawyers, to actually set up an adequate system.

Travers then describes how this goal became problematic when confronting the county's cost-benefits-driven Prison Industrial Complex:

We're trying to figure out a basic level of case and systems that can ensure that level of care. So, in trying to negotiate without us, there were all kinds of conflicts between the department and the private contractor. We'd ask for something and the government would be like, "No, it takes us ten days to do that kind of evaluation," and the contract medical people are like [whispering], "We should do it faster than that." It is a very interesting dynamic. Instead of guaranteeing services to prisoners, it is this exchange of proposals and bids. And the contractor knows the department really wants the lowest bid. And they can't provide the level of care they told you they can. So, the Department is like literally asking the contractors, "Given that amount of money, can you do that?" And both sets of lawyers are mediating this, or trying to have this negotiation, but it is the medical providers who know what needs to get done. They know they did not get enough money in the contract to begin with to do it. And now everybody's getting exposed, and the county is like, "Well, you signed the contract that you would do it!" So, as far as the department is concerned this is all the fault of the contractor. Part of our job in this litigation is to keep harping on the idea that this is not the contractor's problem solely. This is the government's responsibility. And that they are entitled to contract prisoner healthcare out, but they must ensure that the constitutional level of care can be and is in fact provided.

Beyond the challenges of negotiating with the Prison Industrial Complex, Laura Travers reveals the profound challenges of separating her professional identity as lawyer from her identity as concerned and caring citizen:

There is so much need in this population for support services and there is so little out there that the more engaged you get on an individual level, the more that is obvious and there is just so much time in the day. I personally struggle with not wanting to so depersonalize that I am not human and that I don't appreciate the human aspects of what I am doing. The humanity of the people I am working with, because they are the people who are so dehumanized in their given situation. To be able to hear and listen to them on a human level, but then not get engaged in all of the various things that they need from an outside advocate. I could help that person if that is all that I did for say, the next two weeks, but I can't. And there are not that many people if, anybody, who can and will in terms of other agencies. So it's a very, it's something that I struggle with just about all the time. In a way, I have been doing a lot of prison visits lately, and the more personal visits that you do, the more that I struggle because people's pain and their needs are so undeniable when you are sitting in the room with them and looking them in the eye and saying, "We just can't help you with that."

Barry Eckhart: "… overwhelmed by the real tension …"   Barry Eckhart, a prisoner rights lawyer from an Eastern state, expounds on the tension between the personal and the professional described previously in Laura Travers's story. Specifically, Eckhart describes how both the substandard conditions within the prison and the broader cutbacks in funding for prisoner legal services have served to exacerbate not only the lawyer's ability to help individual prisoners but the ability to file class action lawsuits:

> The mayor really cut back our funding. We felt like we were fortunate when we got funding for a couple of years, but then the sources dried up. So we lost a paralegal and that is a huge impact. We have dealt with literally thousands of inmates and we have been literally overwhelmed by the real tension between helping individuals and moving a class action, and we are really stumbling on that. People call up and want to have direct and immediate needs and that's a real tension when it is totally removed from the class action. We don't have adequate resources to really do both effectively, and so I think that has caused a tremendous amount of delay in our litigation.

Next, Eckhart describes how the inhumanity of prison life only complicates efforts at meaningful advocacy on behalf of sick prisoners:

> People who are incarcerated have a myriad of problems. We are often the only source they have to deal with some of those problems and some of them we can do something about and some of them we can't. How many times have I spent on the phone, but I think it is important, because prisoners have almost no power.

In Eckhart's experience, many prisoners feel so oppressed by the Prison Industrial Complex that they actually sabotage their own health as a form of protest:

> The only power they often have is the refusal power. They are angry because they wouldn't let them see a specialist, so what do they do, "I am going to refuse all of my medication, or I am going to refuse to see the doctor because he is insulting to me." So this refusal of care is sometimes the only power that they have. Constantly, I am confronted with that. Then I do counseling of how this maybe counterproductive. I understand their rage, it is even justified, but is refusal really effective for their own healthcare? So, we are also social workers and counselors. I am dealing with their medical care, but this officer is harassing them, or they are not safe, and so you deal with all those problems. Do you deal with them as a human being? Do you deal with them because often this population has a lot of social needs that they need your representation on? All of those things can be terribly time-consuming. So it is a constant compromise between providing any of those services or all of those services and doing your big class action litigation.

Elizabeth Sawyer: "... the very next day they are out to erode that as much as they can ..." Elizabeth Sawyer, a long-time prisoner rights lawyer and activist from the West Coast, echoes Barry Lawrence's sentiments, but also argues that personal injury damages in prisoner rights cases are typically exceedingly difficult to litigate. Specifically, when telling the story of a mistreated prisoner infected with AIDS, Sawyer describes how she and her fellow litigators decided not to pursue personal injury damages:

> We chose not to go for the damages in her case, and I think we should have, but we chose other cases to move forward. In part, we chose to do this because of the way that personal injury law played out, and the difficulty of selling these cases to personal injury lawyers, who do not want to deal with prisoners. Things like somebody getting Tylenol 3, and they have advanced AIDS and they're in excruciating pain with shingles or something like that. But can it be proved that that is a personal injury case? Well no, what we really need to do

is get immediate relief for the woman, so we may have to choose between the common strategies, or maybe what is really important to her at that point is not so much getting money damages as getting her to the hospital. So it is very, very difficult and painful.

However, even when her organization wins a class action lawsuit:

> There is a tendency to think that if you win a lawsuit, and then it will all go away. But it doesn't. You get corrections to agree to change one thing, and then the very next day they are out to erode that as much as they can.

Sawyer's decades of experience working with women prisoners leads her to this conclusion:

> You will hear it differently from other people who feel they are more balanced about it, but I take it from what I see, and I have interviewed literally thousands of women. I feel like the truth kind of emerges, maybe not from one or two interviews, but if you interview enough people, and they are all saying the same thing, or variations of the same thing, you probably have something there.

Terrence Bernstein: "... the state refused to invite them in!" Terrence Bernstein frames many of his responses around a current litigation on behalf of HIV-infected prisoners quarantined in a segregated HIV ward. As he described in the previous section, the conditions of the ward are, in a word, dreadful. In addition to outbreaks of pneumonia and other infections caused by the poor ventilation and cramped living quarters, a major health problem among the prisoners – which is the focus of the current litigation – has been a widespread outbreak of boils. Here, Bernstein describes the unwillingness of the private healthcare providers to investigate this outbreak in a scientific way and the refusal of the Department of Corrections to bring in the Center for Disease Control (CDC) to help eradicate it:

> The initial response was that the healthcare providers were insisting that the boils were the mosquito bites and that was the only problem that they could have been, but they refused to culture them to really find out the basis of the illness. And we kept insisting that they culture it and bring in someone who is knowledgeable on infectious diseases and would be able to provide assistance or medical treatment to the guys that were infected with boil infection, and we encountered just a lot of resistance. We even called the CDC, because when a similar infection had broken out in another state penitentiary among the HIV inmates, the CDC went in and were able to eradicate the infections, and did it with no charge to the state. And we asked the prison officials here if they would allow the CDC to come in and address this infection and try to get it under control and eradicate it from the population. And the state refused to invite them in! So, there was a lot of resistance on that. I'm not sure why whether it was to try keep things secretive or to try to keep things out of the press.

Beyond the Law: Contesting Barriers between Prison and the Community

Facing bureaucratically entrenched and often uncooperative prison elites, prisoner rights lawyers' stories suggest a deepening cynicism toward the efficacy of law to achieve justice and save the lives of prisoners who are in obvious need of effective medical care. While the analysis of resistance in the study of legal consciousness typically presents respondents' abstract notions of being "against the law,"[17] respondents in this study offer an alternative form of resistance, what we call "beyond the law." Perhaps a similar but, in this case, more instrumental conception of Avram's conscientious objectors' "extra-legal consciousness" (see Chapter 9), respondents describe not merely being cynical of the efficacy of law to produce change, but describe tangible ways that they *acted* on such cynicism.

Christina Dyer: "... tools of oppression against the oppressors ..." Responding to a question about whether she believed law could produce social change for HIV-infected prisoners, Christina Dyer describes both a deep resistance against law and how that resistance becomes an important focus for her organization's interns:

> I have very little confidence in litigation affecting social change, and I'll give an example explaining why. I think that litigation, because it is about using the law – which is an incredibly hierarchical institution to create change – has really only created a band-aid reform at best. And then those reforms can be used to further damage people and one of the things all the interns in our office here are involved in is a sort of history of prisons and a focus on the Prison Industrial Complex, the growth of it and the expansion of it. And that people, who with very good intentions who are trying to improve the plight of prisoners, have actually managed to expand the prison system, and do enormous amounts of harm to the people they were trying to help. So, then what do they do?

To infuse their work "beyond the law," Dyer's organization employs many HIV-infected women who are ex-prisoners. Even though she is a lawyer, her organization focuses on building a support network for HIV-infected women both in and out of the prison. Indeed, for Dyer:

> ... litigation sort of uses the tools of oppression against the oppressors, and does so ineffectively. The law almost always leaves loopholes where the prison system can come back and kick prisoners in the pants and basically punish them for being part of the litigation as well as really worsen the suffering of people that it is supposed to try and help.

But she does believe that when properly integrated with activism, litigation can play an important role in mobilizing a movement:

> What I think could be different is when litigation is combined with social activism and then you get a grassroots base pushing for bigger and broader changes to go along with the litigation.

---

[17] According to Patricia Ewick and Susan Silbey, being against the law means to be cynical or skeptical of the authority of law and mistrustful of its implementation. Nielsen's (2000) observation about the pervasiveness of law in people's conceptions of their lives – even in the formal absence of law – is especially prescient for the analysis of "dying" prisoner rights:

> Legal consciousness also refers to how people do not think about the law; that is to say, it is the body of assumptions people have about the law that are simply taken for granted ... Thus, legal consciousness can be present even when law is seemingly absent from an understanding or construction of life events (Nielsen 2000:1059).

Walter Spence: "... I developed this HIV awareness program"   Some prisoners such as Walter Spence do not wait for the law to become involved with HIV-infected prisoner rights. Perceiving an entrenched unawareness on the dangers of HIV among his fellow prisoners, especially those unable to read or write, Spence describes his decision to create a program while incarcerated:

> I thought, I need to do something. I just saw these guys, even though I had been in the drug culture and everything that I had been through, I saw people that were 20 or 30 and couldn't read. I started working as a tutor for English as a second language tutor in the education department and I really enjoyed it. I saw a lot of things that I had never really thought of before. There were people sharing needles and having sex. All kinds of sex goes on in there: consensual, survival sex, rape, situational, but especially shooting drugs. When I would see people in the phone booth drawing up water out of a mud puddle and taking a hit of dope and only doing half of it, and there is still blood in the rig and then passing it on to their partner, I'm like, "Oh my god!" So I started educating people about HIV and I developed this HIV awareness program in there. I was basically just allowed to have each new prisoner go through. I was able to use a community phone that was monitored to call outside the prison and get information for this project and I ended up getting a lot of good people, the state health department, The American Red Cross, the community information center, I mean people from organizations that are today my very good close friends once I left prison.

Spence, who, since being released from prison many years ago, has become a very active advocate for HIV and Hepatitis C awareness, describes how his role as HIV awareness leader enabled him to forge relationships with activists on the outside: "You know, I would like write letters to different organizations – that's how I met those people ..." However, Spence constantly risked retaliation by the prison administration:

> ... but I had to be very careful and I was told, I was called in and told by the warden, "You are not an activist, okay? This is not about treatment. You are only to educate prisoners on HIV preventing disease transmission." They were down my throat about that because they knew that I was a mouthpiece to the public and it scared them. They tried to shut me up.

Going beyond the law, Spence argues that program was successful precisely because it was "created by and for prisoners":

> But I was very busy doing this and educating people and I knew I made a difference, and not only me, but the program made a difference because the program became about prisoners. I mean the program was created by and for prisoners. It was a true peer education model. You know, when somebody came up and said, "Hey my cellmate came back to the cell last night and I didn't share it with him because of what I learned in your class last time." When that was more motivating then doing that hit of dope, taking care of himself was more motivating because of what he learned, that was powerful. That is just one example. Probably while in the time I was there, a thousand inmates had exposure to the program.

Through his own reading in prisoner, Spence learns about the growing epidemic of Hepatitis C behind bars:

Then I read an article about Hep C, and they did a blind study at intake and that 32 percent of prisoners walking into the prison system were infected with Hep C. And I said, "Jesus Christ, this is something that I have to know about, my program has got to teach about this."

This awareness enables Spence to forge a new and vitally important relationship with a Hepatitis C infected prisoner rights activist Spence describes as a "one-woman show":

So I called – I saw an ad for a support group – and I got a hold of someone finally and that changed my life and their life. She was like, "Oh my god I can't believe you called, I have tried to get into prisons before and they denied me access." She was down at the legislature giving testimony about Hep C and prisoners, and she was this one-woman show.

Unlike prison lawyers, Spence found his relationship with this activist to be extremely important for developing his program and for effective lobbying in the legislature:

So I got her in, I got her in under my program under the guise of just a guest speaker because I was allowed to have public speakers come in and have little events. So she comes in and talks to people and everything, and then she goes back down to the legislature. I mean, a lot of the prison lawyers I contacted about how bad it was in here said, "Well we only take class action lawsuits, but we can investigate, or when you get out we can do more" or those kinds of things.

Since being released, Spence remains frustrated at what he describes as state officials' preference for lip service over action:

And since I've been out I have had meetings with officials in the state and ran down the issues with them, so when they did a report on the thing, those were the issues that would be addressed. But when they take it to specific prisons those people just pay lip service about everything. You know, "I agree they should have condoms, I agree that they should see a specialist and we're doing something about it, I agree that these problems need to be addressed."

Spence wonders why the problem is not seen in terms of the broader community:

Why can't people see that it's a community problem? You know 85–90 percent of these people get released back into the community. If they get released without knowledge, if they get released with communicable diseases, if they get released with life-threatening diseases that become a community expense, where is the responsibility to our people? Who is going to take care of our people when they go back to their communities? And it's ridiculous, but the prison doesn't want to do it. "Oh, don't shove all your sick people on us, and expect us to treat them while they're in prison." They use every excuse in the book not to treat.

Wendy Jackson: "... we all had kind of given up, especially those of us on the litigation side of it ..."   For others, like Wendy Jackson, a legal assistant who works with Alexandra Michaels, the realization of the limits of litigation has transformed her perspective as a prisoner rights advocate:

I think we all had kind of given up, especially those of us on the litigation side of it. And then we did this huge organizing meeting down there, and people were energized again.

And it was sort of like some of the other activists across the country were so appalled at the Clinton administration telling the Supreme Court not to hear the case on segregating HIV-infected prisoners. That really fueled us and gave us a second wind. We realized that we have to do something else besides litigation.

The conference would eventually be held at a Southern prison with activists, lawyers, and correction officials. In preparation for the conference, correction officials, in a rare act of cooperation, allowed Jackson and her colleagues to tour the segregated HIV units:

We actually got the Commissioner to allow us to tour the program areas and both of the HIV units, and there was a whole other struggle regarding that. But, at first, they weren't going to let us talk to prisoners! And it's like how are we going to collect information and write this report, but eventually they allowed us to do that. So we did the tour, and it kind of like all worked. And it became a real PR thing for the department down there, I mean that they actually allowed us to speak with prisoners and staff folks!

Remarkably, the conference results in the addition of new programs for HIV-infected prisoners:

Eventually the corrections people all come around. It was amazing because it took like two years, maybe a year and half to have access to programs, but now they have access to programs. They are still segregated, they still have bad medical care, but now they have access to programs. And it was strictly community, so we were able to set up a task force and we packed it with people. Amazingly, we were able to get some change. It was purely grassroots. And in that case, it was way more effective then litigation.

Renee Morris: "... they are an organization that's willing to make the necessary adaptation to survive in the post-PLRA universe ..." Renee Morris, a long-time prisoner rights activist and one of the leaders of the initiative described by Wendy Jackson, describes how activists were able to convince prisoner rights attorneys from a national organization to see the problem as going beyond the law and to convince them to actually host the conference:

I mean nobody's going to give them legal fees for hosting a conference. They are not going to get attorneys' time for this. The way they do things is to sue people. But getting a just outcome in this case is the more important thing to do. So they were willing buy any means necessary to do this. And we are hell-bent and willing to accept other ideas about how to do this from everybody who cares about this issue. It really shows how they are an organization that's willing to make the necessary adaptation to survive in the post-PLRA universe.

Conclusion: Surviving the "Post-PLRA Universe"

The world of HIV-infected prisoner rights advocates is largely an uphill battle fought against a Prison Industrial Complex that is neither willing nor equipped to address their clients' many needs. This lack of willingness on the part of prison officials is revealed in a number of ways. First, respondents' stories reveal how the PLRA has made advocates' work increasingly difficult. Specifically, the lawyers describe their organizations as being overwhelmed by the strict cap now placed on attorney fees and the overly broad exhaustion requirement that seems only to promote further inaction among prison officials – indeed, sometimes with literally fatal consequences for their HIV-infected clients. In the case of the PLRA's caps on attorney fees, respondents describe their already cash-strapped organizations struggling to make ends meet, however, as Len Erickson put it, "with even less money even if you win." Thus, for Len Erickson, it is not surprising that "all around the country, little prisoner law shops are going out of business."

The inaction of prison officials is given flesh in respondents' stories of both the effects of the PLRA and in respondents' stories of the prison's culture of inhumanity. In the former, the PLRA's requirement that HIV-infected prisoners must exhaust all of the prison's administrative remedies before they are able to file a federal suit, elucidates how the system, in attorney Terrence Bernstein's words, "rarely ever works" and thus he sees "numerous inmates who died of issues that should have been in front of the court, that should have been addressed, that could have been addressed much quicker before my clients died."

The failure of the system is also exemplified in respondents' stories of the prison culture of inhumanity. Here, respondents' stories reveal collectively a system marred by grossly ineffective healthcare, poor living conditions, and a lack of educational programs that have especially grave consequences for sick prisoners who are unable to read or write. As Walter Spence's story of an illiterate prisoner who is also blind revealed, many disabled prisoners are powerless to do anything about their disease because, in short, "he can't see." And thus when this grossly neglected prisoner with AIDS finally does receive attention, Spence recounts the prison's optometrist as stating, "We haven't seen this in a prisoner with AIDS in ten years."

When lawyers do attempt to challenge the Prison Industrial Complex's flawed prisoner services their efforts are often undermined by the system's entrenched diffusion of responsibility. As Laura Travers' story demonstrated, the correctional authority's increasing reliance on private service providers creates "all kinds of conflict." Thus, during meetings with prisoner rights attorneys, correctional officials argue with private service providers over the costs of care rather than ensuring "that the constitutional level of care can be and is in fact provided." Yet even when prisoner rights litigation is successful the struggle is far from over, as Elizabeth Sawyer described:

> There is a tendency to think that if you win a lawsuit, and then it will all go away. But it doesn't. You get corrections to agree to change one thing, and then the very next day they are out to erode that as much as they can.

This recognition that law is limited in its ability to ensure HIV-infected prisoner rights is widely shared among the respondents interviewed. Indeed, most described their work as incorporating beliefs and practices that go "beyond law." That is to say, respondents, as Christina Dyer eloquently remarked, do more than use "tools of oppression against the oppressors." In short, rather than simply complain about the law's limitations to ensure HIV-infected prisoner rights, respondents *act* to subvert a system they see as inherently stacked against them.

HIV-Infected Prisoners' Rights as Beyond – but Ultimately Strengthened by – Law

In the end, these stories support what studies of *added* rights have long observed – namely, that formal rights empower *real* people involved in *real* struggles for equality and justice. While these studies focus on how the addition of new rights matter for historically marginalized groups such as women in the workplace (McCann 1994) and Americans with disabilities (Engel and Munger 2003), the stories presented here demonstrate – even in the face of declining formal prisoner rights-on-the-books – that rights consciousness *endures* in the practices of those struggling to save the lives of HIV-infected prisoners. In short, the prisoner rights revolution started by the Warren Court continues to have a "broad and pervasive impact in our culture" (Engel and Munger 2003:103).

At the same time, the discovery in these data that prisoner rights consciousness is remarkably durable among such advocates, actually *strengthens* the argument for broader and more strictly enforced prisoner rights under law. Indeed, the enactment of stricter laws guaranteeing HIV-infected prisoners the right to medical treatment will provide prisoners with obviously tangible benefits (such as greater access to treatment). At the same time, we might also expect that such broader enforcement of prisoner rights under law would have important cultural effects. Indeed, as the interviews presented here indicate, we would expect that advocates and the prisoners that work with them would benefit from stricter regulations placed on prison healthcare. In this context, prisoner rights provide an extremely important counterweight to the often inhumane culture of prisons. Perhaps most importantly, stronger rights protections for HIV-infected prisoners inside prison walls paves the way for a far smoother transition for such prisoners upon reentering their communities.

References

Alexander, E. (2003) "Private Prisons and Health Care: The HMO From Hell." In Coyle, A., Campbell, A., and Neufeld, R. (eds), *Capitalist Punishment: Prison Privatization and Human Rights*. Atlanta, GA: Calrity Press.

Barnes, H.E. (1972) [1930] *The Story of Punishment: A Record of Man's Inhumanity to Man*. Montclair, NJ: Patterson Smith (publication no. 112).

Burris, S. (1992) "Prisons, Law and Public Health: The Case for a Coordinated Response to Epidemic Disease behind Bars." *University of Miami Law Review*, November, 47:291.

Chandler, C., Patton, G., and Job, J. (1999) "Community-based Alternative Sentencing for HIV-positive Women in the Criminal Justice System." *Berkeley Women's Law Journal*, 66:14.

Engel, D.M., and Munger, F.W. (2003) *Rights of Inclusion: Law and Identity in the Life Stories of Americans with Disabilities*. Chicago: University of Chicago Press.

Evans, J., Baca, J.S., and Haney, C. (2001) *Undoing Time: American Prisoners in Their Own Words*. Boston, MA: Northeastern University Press.

Farmer, Paul (2003) *Pathologies of Power: Health, Human Rights, and the New War on the Poor*. University of California Press.

Faugier, J. and Sargeant, M. (1997) "Sampling hard to reach populations", *Journal of Advanced Nursing*, vol. 26, 790–797.

Fazlollah, Mark and Jennifer Lin (2002). "New Jersey prisons fail to treat an epidemic; with no care, hepatitis C costs more to society." Philadelphia Inquirer. 21 July: A1.

Fleury-Steiner, Benjamin (forthcoming). *Limestone: A Social Autopsy of Preventable Deaths at One Alabama Prison*. Ann Arbor, MI: University of Michigan Press.

Gordon, R.E. (2000) *The Funhouse Mirror: Reflections on Prison*. Pullman, WA: Washington State University Press.

Guillemette, Sean (2003). "The Silent Killer Doing Time." http://www.hcvinprison.org/docs/silent_killer.html.

Herman, S.N. (1998) "Slashing and Burning Prisoners' Rights: Congress and the Supreme Court in Dialogue." *Oregon Law Review*, Winter, 77:1229.

Highleyman, Liz (2003). "CDC Releases Recommendations for Viral Hepatitis in Prison." http://www.hcvadvocate.org/news/newsLetter/advocate0303.html#1.

Hodges, Sam (2003). "Inmate Deaths: A Fact of Life." *Mobile Register*: 11 May: A1.

Hylton, W.S. (2003) "Sick on the Inside: Correctional HMOs and the Coming Prison Plague." Retrieved from http://www.wrongfuldeathinstitute.com/links/sickontheinside.htm.

Lafay, Laura (2002). "Accountable to No One: The Virginia Department of Corrections and Prisoner Medical Care." http://www.hcvinprison.org/docs/aclu_virginia_lafay.pdf.

Lewis, O.F. (1922) *The Development of American Prisons and Prison Customs, 1776–1845*. New York: Prison Association of New York.

McCann, M.W. (1994) *Rights at Work: Pay Equity Reform and the Politics of Legal Mobilization*. Chicago, IL: University of Chicago Press.

McDonald, D.C. (1995) *Managing Prison Health Care and Costs*. National Institute of Justice Report. Washington DC: US Department of Justice, Office of Justice Programs.

Maddow, Rachel (2001) *HIV/AIDS and Health Care Reform in British and American Prisons*. (Ph.D. diss., University of Oxford, 2001).

Mauer, M. (1999) *Race to Incarcerate*. New York: New Press.

Mauer, M., and Chesney-Lind, M. (2002) *Invisible Punishment: The Collateral Consequences of Mass Imprisonment*. New York: New Press.

Parenti, Christian (2003) "Privatized Problems: For-Profit Incarceration in Trouble." In Coyle, Andrew, Allison Campbell, and Rodney Neufeld eds.,*Capitalist Punishment: Prison Privatization and Human Rights*. Atlanta, GA: Calrity Press.

Riessman, C.K. (1993) *Narrative Analysis*. Newbury Park, CA: Sage Publications.

Robbins, I.P. (1999) "Criminal Law: Managed Health Care in Prisons as Cruel and Unusual Punishment." *Journal of Criminal Law & Criminology*, 90:195.

Schlanger, M. (April 2003) "Inmate Litigation." *Harvard Law Review*, 116:1555.

Semple, J. (1993) *Bentham's Prison: A Study of the Panopticon Penitentiary*. Oxford: Clarendon Press.

Siegal, N. (1998) Lethal Lottery. *POZ* (November 1998).

Silverstein, H. (1996) *Unleashing Rights: Law, Meaning, and the Animal Rights Movement*. Ann Arbor, MI: University of Michigan Press.

Vogt, W. P. (1999) *Dictionary of Statistics and Methodology: A Nontechnical Guide for the Social Sciences*, London: Sage.

Watson, B.H., and DiIulio, J.J. (1998) "A New Idea Worth Having: Literacy and Education can Help Criminals Avoid a Return to Crime." *Philadelphia Inquirer*, 19 March.

Wilson, Mark (2003). "America's Prisons Turn a Blind Eye to HCV Epidemic." http://www.hcvinprison.org/docs/blindeye1.doc

Wynn, J. (2001) *Insider Rikers: Stories from the World's Largest Penal Colony*. New York: St. Martin's Press.

Cases cited

Correctional Services Corporation (CSC) v. Malesko 122 S. Ct. 515

Cruz v. Beto 405 U.S. 319, 321 (1972)

Estelle v. Gamble 429 U.S. 97 (1976)

Farmer v. Brennan 511 U.S. 825 (1994)
Johnson v. Avery 393 U.S. 483 (1969)
Onishea v. Hopper F.3d 1289; U.S. (1999)
Procunier v. Martinez 416 U.S. 396 (1974)
Wilson v. Seiter, 501 U.S. 294, 298
Wolff v. McDonnell 418 U.S. 539 (1974)

PART III
THE FUTURE OF
RIGHTS RESEARCH

Chapter 9

When the Saints Go Marching In: Legal Consciousness and Prison Experiences of Conscientious Objectors to Military Service in Israel

HADAR AVIRAM

Conscientious objection has long constituted a popular and interesting case study, particularly within the study of political philosophy, morality and ethics. In philosophical works providing justifications for following personal moralities (Walzer 1967), political theorists have examined conscientious objection in the context of obedience to the law, mainly in liberal regimes, and specifically in Israel, where compulsory military service creates a myriad of social and ethical issues (Gans 1987a; Gans 1987b; Sheleff 1987). Many of these works distinguish conscientious objection from more "ordinary" offenses; in order to fall under the category of conscientious objection, the law violation should be in the open, and the violator must be ready to suffer on his or her own flesh the consequences of protesting the immorality of the disobeyed law. If an act of objection to follow the law fulfills these conditions, it should, according to some of these works, be justified.

Whatever the moral perspective on the issue may be, conscientious objection is, in some countries, a criminal offense; and, as in the case of civil disobedience, accepting the potential punishment for standing for one's beliefs is not a side effect, but a crucial component of the behavior. Nevertheless, in places where it is defined as crime, it is of a unique nature, due to two factors – its ideological basis and the socioeconomic background of the offenders (Dayan 2003).

When studied in criminological context, ideological crime is often approached from conflict and labeling perspectives, questioning its criminal definition and the social reaction to it. Since ideological crime often has no victims, and is, arguably, not morally wrong, it is a natural candidate for theories questioning the very essence of criminalization and response to deviance. Studies such as Balbus' analysis of the criminal justice response to the Black Rebels (1973) and Weisburd's analysis of Jewish settlers' violence (1989) refer to the social climate surrounding the acts as the dominant factor in their construction as criminal offenses. However, some biographical and literary works have addressed the issue of punishment for ideological crime from a somewhat sociological perspective, referring to the experience of imprisonment for ideological activity (Lytton 1988; Solzhenitsyn 1998). The prison experience is particularly unique for these people, since it involves punishing highly individualistic people, who protest against a law by refusing to abide by it, in a manner that subjects them to a highly coercive institution (Goffman 1961) which involves a high degree of conformity and socialization (Clemmer 1970; Sykes and Messinger 1970).

The second interesting issue in conscientious objection is the objectors' social status. High-status offenders have always been of interest; several studies targeted white-collar offenders in different ways, studying the way they justify and neutralize their actions (Cressey 1973), and the criminal justice system's response to these middle-class offenders (Weisburd, Wheeler, and Waring 1991). However, it is interesting to note that new white-collar scholarship no longer ascribes the same importance to status, and refers more to the nature of the offenses themselves (Shapiro 1990). The objectors themselves are not necessarily members of a socioeconomic elite, but they are closely linked to an intellectual and educated milieu, which would distinguish them from other prison inmates.

The situation of conscientious objectors is unique in that it combines these two factors into a peculiar situation: people who are generally thought of as being highly integrated in society, and highly conscious of moral matters involving government and administration, find themselves subjected to a legal system which treats them as offenders, are convicted and imprisoned in it. This peculiarity raises an interesting question: to what extent do conscientious objectors define their situation by, relate to and respond to the law? How does law matter for those who knowingly challenge it, and who are, as a consequence, subjected to its most coercive form?

This project attempts to address this question through interviews with conscientious objectors to military service in Israel who have recently been released from prison. It observes their perceptions, reactions and opinions through the legal consciousness perspective, and particularly through Ewick and Silbey's three-schema model of law in everyday life (2000).

Background

For the reasons stated above, conscientious objectors make fascinating subjects for research; sadly, my opportunity to engage in this project emerged from the escalation of the Israeli-Palestinian conflict since October 2000. From this point in time, the relationship between the State of Israel and the Palestinian Authority drastically deteriorated, leading to the death of numerous Israelis and Palestinians and to the reoccupation of most of the West Bank by the Israel Defense Forces[1] (BBC News, 4 April 2002). As a result, thousands of civilians were called to perform reserve service in the occupied territories, in accord with the Security Service Act of 1986.

Conscientious objection had existed as a phenomenon in earlier times in Israel, most notably during the 1982 war in Lebanon (Sheleff 1987). In fact, the IDF had been handling conscientious objection for a long time, though before the Lebanon war of 1982 there were instances of individual objection rather than collective movements. The "Yesh Gvul" movement, like the "Peace Now" movement, emerged from the Western-secular left-wing social group, and portrayed the war as an optional one, contrary to the "no choice war" dominant narrative of the time (Levy 2003). About 180 objectors were sent to prison for their refusal to serve in the territories, as

---

[1] Subsequently referred to as "IDF".

part of the movement. The 1988 Intifada led to an increase in the size of the "Yesh Gvul" objection movement, and similar numbers of conscientious objectors were sent to prison (Galili 2002a; Levy 2003); Levy (ibid.) points out the emergence of what he calls "gray objection" – large numbers of middle-class Western seculars seeking and obtaining exemption from service, ostensibly for medical reasons, but in fact for political ones, during the Intifada.

Since 1995, the army gave a certain amount of legitimacy to limited forms of conscientious objection.[2] Whereas the army had always been more open to releasing women from service, through a statutory mechanism, in 1995 a special committee was formed which would exempt men from regular and reserve service based on conscientious arguments. The criteria for dismissal involved the type of objection. Total pacifism – an objection to all war and armed conflict per se – was the only ground for exemption.[3] People who thought military action was justified in certain circumstances, and people who opposed government and military policy, did not count as pacifists, and refusal to be drafted, or to participate in certain military activities, were therefore "refusal to obey orders," an offense punishable under the Military Justice Act of 1955. The creation of the committee coincided with a concern of the military justice system personnel with the potential problem of handling right-wing and religious soldiers who would object to participate in the evacuation of settlements in the occupied territories (Levy 2003).

The more recent events leading to the reoccupation of the territories created a somewhat larger movement for objection, whose emphasis was slightly different than previous movement. The new "objection frontier" (Leibovitz-Dar 2000) took the name "The Courage to Refuse". Although the main activists came from very similar social backgrounds to the ones of previous objection movements, such as Yesh Gvul, they emphasized the legitimacy of their position through their past share in military action. Rather than opting out of the compulsive military service model, and calling for de-militarization, they expressed the legitimacy of their position as stemming from their previous combat service as officers and soldiers, thus hoping to build social support on their earned right to speak about, and against, military action (Lavi 2002). This social approach can be easily discernible from the open letter signed by the objectors:

- We, reserve combat officers and soldiers of the Israel Defense Forces, who were raised upon the principles of Zionism, sacrifice and giving to the people of Israel and to the State of Israel, who have always served in the front lines, and who were the first to carry out any mission, light or heavy, in order to protect the State of Israel and strengthen it,
- We, combat officers and soldiers who have served the State of Israel for long weeks every year, in spite of the dear cost to our personal lives, have been on reserve duty all over the Occupied Territories, and were issued commands and directives that had nothing to do with the security of our country, and that had the sole purpose of

---

[2] This information is based partly on an interview with Captain Yaron Kostelitz of the Chief Military Prosecutor's office.

[3] It is of interest to note the dominance of new immigrants from the former USSR, particularly the parts influenced by middle-class Western culture, among those claiming total pacifism. The committee proceedings name many new immigrants among those claiming pacifism based on non-political grounds.

perpetuating our control over the Palestinian people. We, whose eyes have seen the bloody toll this Occupation exacts from both sides,

- We, who sensed how the commands issued to us in the Territories, destroy all the values we had absorbed while growing up in this country,
- We, who understand now that the price of Occupation is the loss of IDF's human character and the corruption of the entire Israeli society,
- We, who know that the Territories are not Israel, and that all settlements are bound to be evacuated in the end,
- We hereby declare that we shall not continue to fight this War of the Settlements.
- We shall not continue to fight beyond the 1967 borders in order to dominate, expel, starve and humiliate an entire people.
- We hereby declare that we shall continue serving in the Israel Defense Forces in any mission that serves Israel's defense.
- The missions of occupation and oppression do not serve this purpose – and we shall take no part in them.[4]

Several things should be noted. The movement's website lists the soldiers signed not only by name, but by military core and social rank; the website graphics, invoking national and patriotic symbols and colors, show the objectors in uniforms. The character of the movement was, therefore, dual; both linked to the academic and intellectual Israeli elites involved in previous movements and aspiring to invoke mainstream militaristic backgrounds, thus trying to avoid being seen as "overly left-wing" in the eyes of the general public (Lavi 2002). It was, thus, very similar to the profiles of previous objection movements (Linn 1996).

Many of the petitioners were called to perform military reserve service; those who refused to enter the territories were charged with Refusal to Obey Orders,[5] tried in a disciplinary hearing before the commander of their unit, and sentenced to short imprisonment sentences ranging between 14 and 35 days, the overwhelming majority sentenced to 28 days (War Resisters' International Website: Alerts 2005). Sentences were served in military prisons.

For several months, the conscientious objection movement appeared often in the headlines of Israeli newspapers: university professors spoke for and against it (Galili 2002c), the army tried to set policies in regard to the trials (Galili 2002b), and some of the objectors petitioned the Israel High Court of Justice to create a legal option of objection. The petition was denied in HC 7622/02 (Segal 2002); the petitioners, and many others, spent weeks in military prisons throughout 2002 (Leibovitz 2002).

Since the petitioners come from affluent and powerful groups in Israeli society, their adjustment to imprisonment and their experiences there raise a series of interesting questions: How do the imprisoned objectors conform to the socialization procedures described in classical prison literature? How do they reconcile their ideological righteousness with their labeling as criminals and prisoners? And how do these experiences reflect their relationship with the law, and their cultural perceptions of it?

---

[4] The number of petitioners is 614 at the time this book goes into print; updates and information are posted daily in the organizations' website, http://www.seruv.org.il.

[5] Article 122 of the Military Justice Act, 1955; maximum punishment is two years imprisonment. As opposed to several military offenses, this offense does not carry a criminal record in civilian life.

The Study

To answer all these interesting questions would require a large-scale study; the present work is a preliminary study, based on in-depth unstructured interviews conducted throughout January 2003 with fifteen conscientious objectors who had spent time in military prison in the previous year. Naturally, this is by no means a sample large enough to prove a hypothesis, but at this stage it sufficed to generate some ideas and to sketch a possible paradigm regarding the complex and ambivalent relationship of the objectors with the law. It should also be noted that, at the time the interviews were conducted, the interviewees were about ten percent of the population of objectors who had served imprisonment sentences.

The interviewees were reached by two methods; some of them were contacted following a newspaper article or a testimonial they published on the Internet, and some were recruited in a "snowball" manner through other interviewees. This sampling method has obvious disadvantages compared with a random sample of interviewees; however, these drawbacks are not as problematic as they may seem considering the nature of the population involved. This study does not attempt to provide a profile of the "average" or "representative" conscientious objectors; it attempts to sketch alternative responses to law and legal institutions by people who are not "average" or "representative" in themselves. Naturally, to be a conscientious objector one has had to think about one's position on political and military questions and consolidate it. These are vocal, opinionated people, and a large number of the interviewees were even more vocal and opinionated.

Naturally, this study was very different, and in many respects easier to conduct, than other legal consciousness projects; the interviewees were told that the study was concerned with their prison experiences and not with their political views. Despite this warning, they were happy to contribute, generous with their time, helpful, and willing to send me additional sources and materials.

The interviewees were between the ages of 24 and 39. Eight of them had families (spouse and young children), and out of the remaining seven, four were living with partners. The interviewees came from different parts of Israel – eight of them lived in either Tel Aviv or Jerusalem, and the rest were living in smaller settlements, Moshavim and Kibbutzim. All except one of the interviewees had academic degrees (the one who did not was an artist), and 12 of them had graduate degrees. Six people had a master's degree, and six either had a PhD or were in advanced stages of pursuing one. Most were engaged in professional, prestigious occupations – medicine, law and journalism. More than half of the interviewees were pursuing an academic career (mostly in humanities and social science), and perhaps this motivated them to assist in an academic project. Though not necessarily economically privileged, the interviewees spoke, and saw themselves, as members of the Israeli intellectual elite; not surprisingly, political opinions were invariably left-wing, and opinions about socioeconomic issues ranged between vague support of social welfare and committed socialism. It is interesting to note that many of the interviewees were associated with the Tel Aviv University; the interesting alliance of the conscientious objection movement with the university faculty, and the latter's support of the conscientious objectors was in itself, in fact, the topic of a newspaper article titled "School of Objection Sciences" (Galili 2002c).

Many of the interviewees referred, half-humorously, to the interviews as "therapeutic"; three of them brought me written memoirs from prison, and all expressed a keen interest in reading the chapter once the research was completed. I asked the interviewees to describe their prison experiences, and I encouraged them to stick to a "story-telling" mode. Contrary to my expectations, none of the interviewees tried to use the interview as a political forum, and all of them were very articulate, expressing not only their experiences, but also how they felt about and analyzed the situations they encountered.

Findings

Conscientious Objectors Reflect on their Imprisonment: "Games", "Experiments" and "Experiences"

The interviewees' descriptions and stories varied from person to person, according to their personalities and professions. Some of them presented themselves as contemptuous of the system; some had a more matter-of-fact personal style. Also, as was expected following the legal consciousness literature, the responses to different situations in prison varied not only between interviewees, but also for every interviewee between situations. Traces of perspectives and activities reflecting the "before", "against", and "with" the law schemas were evident, as suggested by Swidler (1986) and by Ewick and Silbey (2000); however, the interviews exposed clues to an overarching fourth schema, dominating the cultural choices and existing as a default perspective – that of being *above the law*.

By *above the* law I do not wish to crudely imply that the interviewees saw themselves as Raskolnikovs, Louis XIVs or superhumans; the idea is far more subtle. It is a perspective that allows one to observe the legal realm as a separate framework from other experiences, one that can be entered or exited at will: in short, a paradigm very much polarized to the welfare poor's "all-over" presence of law as presented by Sarat (1990), and much more empowering to the individual. I also do not wish to dismiss the useful analysis presented by Ewick and Silbey; as several following examples will show, the interviewees engaged in reactions reflecting the three schemas identified by them. I see the fourth schema as an addition, or an expansion, of the legal consciousness model.

Adopting an "above the law" schema required reframing the prison experience in non-legal, non-oppressive, terms. In the interviewees' stories, I found evidence for three such alternative frameworks:

- prison as a game
- prison as a social experiment
- prison as a personal experience.

The trial and the prison as "games"   Six of the interviewees referred to their disciplinary trial and imprisonment as a "game" being played. Their images of the trial ranged between movie clichés ("did you see *Paths of Glory?* It was just like that"; "My trial? *Catch-22* springs to mind") and a personal, ridiculous interaction with the officer who sentenced them. Many of them knew the officers, and referred to their opinions on the matter of conscientious objection not as different from theirs, but as irrelevant, or on a different plane. This was not a usual resistance technique. They did not "disagree" with the officers; they rendered their opinions foolish and undeserving reply.

> So I come in there and he gives me this speech, you know, moral dilemmas of colonels, what will happen if everyone else does it and democracy and all that shit, you know, the stuff they teach them in professional courses.

> We ended up yelling at each other for like ten minutes, so he yelled the sentence and told me to leave. There was no use talking to him, when I look back it was kind of ridiculous actually.

> So he said, take a couple of weeks and think about it again, and I said, you know, obviously I thought about it [sneer], it wasn't like he'd really opened new horizons for me and there was actually something new to consider.

> It was like he was reading lines from a crappy script.

The experience of a "game" remained, and intensified, within prison walls. The main features of the game – the staff, the rules, the daily routine – were mentioned and acknowledged, but the objectors regarded them as irrelevant, absurd, or unnecessary, whenever possible. Again, when describing prison labor, administrative proceedings and formal issues, Heller's *Catch-22* was often invoked. Advice many interviewees offered to potential future prisoners was "take it lightly" "don't dive in", and "remember you're not from there".

An example of the game-within-walls perspective was the relationship with the prison staff, mostly young soldiers and officers in regular service. Though conflict sometimes arose, generally the interviewees managed to construct their relationship with the staff around the legal definitions – sometimes pitying them, sometimes despairing of them, shifting in and out of the staff-inmate relationship at will:

> One of the things that surprised me is that they [the staff] don't actually rule the prison. They'd come to us at lunch and say, "you know, we have an evaluation tomorrow, please make sure everything goes fine". They needed us as much as we needed them.

> I felt sorry for the kids. That's their military service, can you imagine, I was there for a month and they're there for what, three years?

> [If I had to take pictures of the prison to explain it to others] I'd do the platoon commander, looking so stuffy and silly with his brassy uniform.

> The commander? A girl, nineteen years old, full of herself and army nonsense and this [gesturing to the shoulders to convey officer's ranks].

This perspective of the staff was most salient in one of the interviewees' pithy explanation: "They just didn't count, we didn't count them". "Not counting" others, in Israeli slang, is rendering them irrelevant, not seeing them as a power to be taken into account.

The difference of powers was made more salient by invoking external characteristics, such as age, military rank outside of prison, profession, intelligence and academic education, in which the staff was no match to this unusual group of military prisoners. One of the prisoners was addressed as "the regiment vice commander" – his role before his involvement in the objection movement; another scolded a guard for her rudeness: "you're a young girl, please don't talk to me like that". Another one, warning the prison platoon commander about a dangerous cellmate, told him: "You're an idiot, what a jerk, in civilian life I wouldn't even look at him, you're an idiot, I'm telling you keep him out of the cell for everyone's safety, you're all going to pay for your foolishness."

One event was mentioned by all five interviewees who experienced it: at some point, the prison staff asked them to clean the room every morning, cleaning and arranging their beds using military blankets that are considered as inducing skin-disease, and hiding their towels under the beds. The arguments put by the interviewees were also "extra-game" ones – using logic, reason and age:

> So I told her, cleaning the room, of course, hygiene makes sense, naturally we would clean, you know, so many men in one room, but all this stuff with the beds, it's illogical, it's ridiculous, they don't call them "scabies [skin disease] blankets" for nothing, like, what's more important, our health or this foolishness.

As can be seen, these are resistance strategies, but they are different from the ones invoked by other groups; whereas Sarat's welfare poor resist the law's overpowering prevalence through need and misery, the conscientious objectors did not exactly resist the law; they set it aside, proclaiming it irrelevant, and invoking different cultural realms that empowered them – logic, rationality, respect for age and status.

The prison as an "experiment"   Another prevalent expression of the "above the law" schema was the notion of the prison as an "experiment" or a social laboratory of sorts. All the interviewees, social scientists and others, used scientific and experimental terms when describing their experience, spent long periods of time during and after their incarceration analyzing it, and some even conducted experiments or "quasi experiments" of their own within walls. One of the common expressions of this was the phrase "anthropological experience" which repeated itself in almost every interview, unprompted by me, as a description of the prison experience and population. The prison reality was tested against "hypotheses" formed by prison film and literature, such as the television series *Oz* and the movie *The Shawshank Redemption*. Some of the clichés presented in these works were falsified (such as the low level of violence they observed in prison); some were partly verified (the existence of ethnic "mafias", described in humoristic, Damon Runyonish prose by some interviewees), and some were found to be true: "Just like in the movies, everyone in the prison is innocent, everyone is like, it's not my fault, my lawyer fucked me, us too of course, but in that we were all the same".

Three of the interviewees had lengthy written memoirs, analyzing the feeling and the experience; but even those who did not have such account showed a high level of analysis – of their own situation and of their surroundings. This was reflected in their thoughts – in the memoirs and the interviews – about the other, non-objector prisoners. Meeting these people, essentially different from the regular crowd populating the interviewees' lives, made a strong impact and was socially insightful. Several people described sad tales of their cellmates' lives; they assisted them in writing requests for vacation and clemency; and they organized lectures, most of which were given by them (but a few by other inmates) on miscellaneous subjects. The other inmates were referred to as "folks", "creatures", "kids", "poor kids", and "soldiers". Two long-term prisoners, convicted drug-dealers, were described in the informal "instruction brochure" prepared by and for imprisoned objectors, in quasi-clinical terms: "In the officers' quarters there are two 'long-term patients', mostly docile" (Toker-Maimon and Sade 2002). Others wrote in their memoirs of certain "case studies" – people who seemed to be particularly miserable, or whose life experiences were very alien to the writers. Several interviewees expressed their intention to keep in touch with non-objector prisoners outside the prison, but this eventually did not happen. Even when they bonded with the other inmates, helped them and spoke for them, the feeling was that, whereas the interviewees' brush with prison life was transitory, coincidental and absurd, "a world to which we don't belong", the others, unjust as their imprisonment or oppression may be, seemed more grounded in the prison habitat.

People who were professionals in fields of therapy and social science used their professional insight to observe what was around them. Others went further, and thought of possible quasi experiments. One interviewee thought of the impact of external politics on the prison atmosphere:

> There was no big bombing event when I was inside, I was very interested, you know, of course I didn't want a bombing to happen, but I was interested, I wanted to see, if there would be a bombing when we're inside [representing the left wing in politics], how they would treat us, and there wasn't one.

One of the interviewees actually conducted a little experiment of his own: several weeks after his release from prison, he returned (though not to the same facility), this time in uniform and wearing his officer's ranks, supposedly to visit a soldier from his unit (actually, to visit another conscientious objector). He was interested to see how differently he was treated when he came as a guest, and not as an inmate.[6]

Another interviewee gave a lecture in prison about feminism. This was part of the series of lectures organized by the conscientious objectors, most of which were given by them. The interviewee had seen the inmates watching the fashion channel on TV and objectifying the women models; in order to explain the concept of the Madonna/ whore duality, he did the following experiment during the lecture:

> I thought I'd have some fun with them, show them, and I said, "suppose the woman you were watching on TV yesterday would come here, here to prison, and would say to you, you're the one I want, you're my man, what would you do?" and of course they started saying they'd look after her and protect her and build walls around her, which proved my point.

When asked, why he had chosen feminism as a subject for the lecture, the interviewee replied "I just saw the way they were behaving, with the TV, and I thought, this is what is necessary here first of all".

---

[6] Incidentally, this interviewee was treated with great respect when he reappeared in the prison wearing his uniform.

The prison as a non-legal "experience"   The third "above the law" perspective consisted of seeing the imprisonment period as an enriching experience. All but three of the interviewees said they enjoyed their experience.

> One of the things I learned is that in every place you can ... I mean, the prison can be the most fun place in the world and the shittiest place in the world, a lot of this depends upon the person's choice ... I managed to make it a positive experience.

Many referred to it as "rest", a retreat, a break from their daily lives ("all of a sudden you have time to read all the books you'd never get to"). Two interviewees mentioned they had had difficulty returning to their calendars and telephones after being released from prison. Even the books read by the interviewees had some common features – many of them read books by Jose Saramago and J.K. Rowling's *Harry Potter* series. Others read meditative, spiritual books. The prison was an experience of personal growth; following their imprisonment, one interviewee decided to move out and live in a different place and another started playing the guitar and started taking classes in history and political science. Some constructed their imprisonment as an opportunity to help others – a theme which, by the way, can also be found in accounts of the Suffragettes' imprisonments at the beginning of the century (Lytton 1988). Some interviewees accomplished this through their lectures; others assisted by using their professional (medical, psychological, journalistic and other) skills to serve the prison community. Several activities chosen by the conscientious objectors transformed the essence of the prison to one of contemplation and personal growth: writing, studying, yoga, and meditation were among the favorite activities. One of the interviewees compared the experience to the one he went through when attending Vipassana meditation retreats. Another interviewee assigned himself a special spot for reading and studying, on a mattress outside, which came to be labeled as "the beach". And one of the interviewees reconstructed the prison as punishment, not for his breaking the law, but rather for his participation in the occupation in the territories ("I cleaned my conscience a bit from the sins I did in my service"), thus not only reconstructing, but reversing, the legal purpose of the experience. Another, in an article published online, compared his prison sentence to that of a Palestinian "administrative" prisoner.

As to the "official" legal purpose of the experience, it was rendered a failure, and the interviewees ridiculed it, invoking once again clichés from popular culture descriptions of prison:

> If the purpose is to punish, they are not punishing. If the purpose is to rehabilitate, make better citizens out of us, that didn't work either.

> Actually, I came out fortified in the justness of my path; you know they say prison is like a school for offenders, I for one came out a bigger delinquent than when I came in.

The interpretation of the experience outside the legal "box", not as punishment but as a personal experience elected out of free choice, repeated itself when the interviewees were asked what would happen next time they were called to serve in the territories. Responses varied; some said they would refuse again and go to prison, some said they would fly abroad, and some said they would attempt to obtain permanent release on medical grounds. However, all answers regarded the choice of service – obeying the law, breaking the law, avoiding the law – as a personal choice, and moreover – an extra-legal one:

> Now that I've seen what it's about, and that it's no biggie, there's no barrier, I can do this again. I could use another vacation next year, I don't mind.

> You know, it's a learning experience, me, what I needed to learn from this I already learned, I grew from it, I don't need it again.

Conscientious Objectors Enter the Realm of Law

Though the perspective of "above the law", in its manifestations as "game" "experiment" and "experience", was the prevalent one, it was certainly not the only one. On many occasions, the inmates chose to re-enter the boundaries of the prison experience as such. Sometimes they chose to play "before the law" – when filling in requests for clemency, thus acting as "clients" of the clemency-granting authorities. Sometimes they played the rules to their advantage and chose to stand "with the law", as when participating in talks with the warden and making recommendations, or when obtaining (medically unfounded) special permission from military doctors not to wear military shoes, to ease the terrible heat in the cells. Sometimes, interestingly, they were involved in "against the law" resistance. One of the interviewees told of two classical "against the law" situations:

> I was amused with the whole hat business. In every count you're supposed to wear a hat. After three days [I said] ok, I lost my hat. [They answered] so go sign for [getting] a new one. Next count, where are the hats, [we repeat] we lost our hats. Ok. Go and sign. We don't sign. Three days pass until they get us the hats, then they bring the hats, we sign for hats, and next count [we say] I lost my hat. Cool. Like what are you going to do to me, I'm already in prison.

> Interviewer: You're a big boy, why did you care so much about the hat thing?

> I reached a conclusion, there is something about maintaining freedom within the prison, it was a very important thing. Like I am in prison, but maintaining the feeling of freedom. So these little rebellions, doing things you're not supposed to, it was lots of fun.
>   On one occasion, I knew that on Saturday there was going to be a demonstration [in support of the conscientious objectors] on the mountain [facing the prison] and they were going to fly kites. So we were guarding the roof, there's a balcony there, so clandestinely I took a sewing thread and built a kite, from local supplies [laughing], a couple of branches and newspapers and stuff, and I hid it, and when there was the demonstration I flew the kite from inside the prison, which was really dangerous, and I, I really wanted to do it. It was so exciting, like a kid, it was big fun to do something that was forbidden.

The duality of the external-internal perspectives on the legal aspects of their confinement was prevalent in all interviews. The general opinion seemed to be that it was best to be an external observer of the prison whenever possible, and that getting involved in the "game", or regarding the situation seriously, was a good strategy only when discomfort and annoyance dictated a dialogue with prison authorities ("there was just too much stuff [too many right-infringements that had accumulated] so I said, like, that's it, I'll complain"). The need to recur to an internal, participatory role in the prison was still mixed with antagonism towards the army, which some interviewees thought other inmates must have felt, too (Smoocha 2002); but it was deemed to be essential when direct negotiation concerning prisoners' rights and prison terms was necessary. The choice between the external and internal perspectives was not, however, an easy one. One of the interviewees described the absurdity of this duality:

> The officers' bathrooms had regular seats, and the rest just had a hole in the ground. Using the officers' bathroom is allowed for officers, military police and others, based on the will of the dwellers of the officers' room [but only before 8 pm, when the cell doors close] ... so if you want me to be grotesque, one of the things that troubled me the most during that month was how to arrange the times I have to shit so that they don't fall between 8 pm and 5 am so that I won't have to go to the hole in the ground. It's amazing, I'm a thirty-year-old man, and I calculate this, should I eat this, perhaps this bread slice will be the crucial one that will send me to the bathroom after eight, that's the infantilization the place takes you to.

Social and Ideological Resources Enabling an "Above the Law" Schema

What makes the "above the law" schema an option for the interviewees? In their memoirs and interviews, they mention two things that made this schema available: their ideological recognition that the law which put them in prison is essentially wrong, immoral and irrelevant, and their social status, very different from that of the general prison population.

The ideological basis for regarding the legal implications of imprisonment as a realm to be entered and exited at will was evident in all the interviews ("it's easy to see it's a game, because you're there for a reason") and in a booklet produced by the objectors themselves (Toker-Maimon and Sade 2002), that states: "Actually, it's not that bad. As an objector, since your entry to the prison is accompanied by a feeling of mission and contribution to society, the humiliation feeling does not exist, and hence, most of the difficulty [of imprisonment] does not exist."

One of the interviewees explained his imprisonment to his small children as follows:

> I told them all the truth, like, "dad is a hero, he's in prison" [laughing], no, but really, what's important is the concept of choice, I didn't do anything wrong, the opposite, I did something good, but it is not according to ... to the laws of the country. It's a matter of choice".

The strong conviction that their actions were not crimes, but were committed out of a superior moral ground, kept the legal and correctional aspects of the prison less real, and made the objectors see beyond it.

Another factor which highlighted the external, non-participatory aspect of experiencing prison, was the notable, visible difference between the objectors and the other prisoners.

> I came into the cell and walked in, and half the room was lying around the television, brain-dead, smoking cigarettes and playing backgammon, and I caught sight of one of the folks in the back, with hairs like this you know (gestures to show long hair), like someone from

Berkeley, reading a book, dunno, something like Noam Chomsky or Kafka or something intellectual, like, it was so obvious, and he gestured to me "come, come".

I remember a nice anecdote, in the families' visit, that … just that my parents are sitting there and looking there and they see exactly the families of the conscientious objectors and the other families. It was so obvious, it was like this [snaps fingers] to locate the families that were more, socio-economical differences so obvious, screaming, you can't ignore it.

The objectors had been described above as a group of very specific demographic qualities; though not necessarily economically affluent, they were strongly affiliated with academia, many were active figures in the political debates, and were seen, by scholars and the media, as an elite group. They saw themselves as such, as:

… high middle class, Ashkenazi, free occupations, a higher percentage of academic background. The majority from the center of the country, the center in Tel Aviv University, high percentage of social sciences, doctoral students, I know the ones that are active in the movement, but wouldn't be surprised if this is the general profile.

Several of the interviewees, notably not the ones with degrees in social sciences, defined themselves in a distinctive way, using terms that differentiated them from the rest of the prison population, prisoners and guards alike, such as "the ok people". Naturally, interviewees who spent their prison time with others were more likely to make that differentiation, whereas those who were there on their own were more likely to search for "ok people" among the non-objector prisoners. In fact, the two facilitators – ideology and social resources – did not work as well for interviewees who spent their imprisonment time with no other objectors. Two of these "isolated" objectors felt more often that they were integral participants in the prison experience, and attributed it not only to lesser ideological discussion within walls, but to the need to socialize more intensely with non-objector, regular prisoners, for whom the external perspective on prison was less relevant. For the others, who spent their weeks in prison with like-minded individuals (ideologically and socially), the facilitating factors eased the external, "above the law" perspective. One of the young objectors stated, in an online journal, how a group of older reservist inmates, objectors as well, saluted him in the prison dining hall. Another one stated that the intellectual debate between the objectors made him feel as if he was in the university, and not in prison.

Discussion: Extra-Legal Consciousness?

The findings suggest the possibility of a supplementary structure to the legal consciousness model developed by Ewick and Silbey (2000). It appears from the interviewees' experiences that the dominant model of relating to the prison experience was, in fact, extra-legal, or even supra-legal. Whereas the interviewees sometimes engaged in behavior that placed them "before", "with", and "against" prison authorities, their preferred attitude reflected a choice to exit the legal framework. This important addition to their "cultural toolkit" (Swidler 1986) enriched their possibilities to adjust to, and be empowered despite, their new circumstances.

Ironically, this perspective is not dissimilar to the one exhibited by the street women interviewed by Levine and Mellema (2001). Both groups lived their lives in a realm supposedly surrounded by legal symbols and experiences, but their own lives within it were not defined, for the most part, by the law. The difference between the two groups lies in the concept of choice. Levine and Mellema's street women were concerned with immediate strategies of survival, and therefore did not have the leisure or the possibility to engage in dialogue with the less immediate and material aspects of their experience, in our case, the legal ones. The conscientious objectors in this study, however, had the cultural resources to enter and exit the legal realm at will, which stemmed from their ideological conviction and social characteristics.

Several issues should be brought up in connection with this analysis. Firstly, it can be said that its inclusion in the original model is unnecessary, and that ignoring the law, or considering it beneath one's framework of reference, is merely a technique of resistance, that could be included in the original "against the law" schema. Indeed, classifications of human experiences are not inherently "right" or "wrong" – we are not dealing with social facts here, only with their interpretation and categorization. The same argument could be claimed against other typologies of human reactions, such as Merton's typology of responses to anomie (1964) and McCorkie's and Korn analysis responses to the imprisonment experience (1954). In both cases, it would not be methodologically wrong to collapse, for example, the category of "retreatism" and that of "rebellion" into a larger "resistance" category. However, categories are valuable if they provide more insight or information about the subject of study, and I therefore believe there is justification in maintaining the "above the law" category separate from that of resistance within the legal realm. The uniqueness of the possibility to exit the legal framework altogether merits a category of its own – one that complements, and does not conceptually overlap, resistance from within the law, of which several examples were mentioned.

Secondly, this addition to the model does not contradict or disprove Ewick and Silbey's insightful categorization; it supplements it by including the possibility of extra-legal experiences. In fact, it enhances the legal consciousness perspective which seeks to free the legal experience from spatial/institutional location, and to account for its separate existence in culture. Through previous research regarding the role of law in everyday life (Ellickson 1991; Engel 1993) we already know that it is possible to experience something in a legal way outside the physical boundaries of the legal realm. This project suggests that this freedom from spatial boundaries works in the opposite way, too. It is also possible to be within a legal institution, or a legally defined situation, and to experience it through non-legal cultural lenses.

One of the difficulties with the model is the fact that it generates an "above the law" schema based on a short-term prison sentence. Can a month in a military prison count as "law", for the purposes of examining if one situates oneself "above the law"? In what ways can this be seen as a "legal" setting when the alternative to imprisonment would be to do military reserve service – not an entirely free experience in itself? The answer to these questions is in the very nature of the situation in which the interviewees were. Despite the fact that the prison sentence was relatively short, it was a dramatic event – in the legal sense – because the interviewees arrived to prison following a hearing in which they were tried for a conscious breach of the law. The offense for which they were imprisoned was not ordinary; it consisted in acting against the law because of a deep conviction that the law was wrong. Therefore, the interviewees were engaged in a dialogue with the law from the time they chose to sign the petition proclaiming their explicit intention to break it for ideological reasons, throughout the trial, into the prison – the "price" prescribed by law for their actions, and necessary to prove their commitment to the superiority of their morality over the law. In this respect, not only was prison an ultra-legal experience because of its nature as a total institution, but because of its direct linkage to a deliberate act of violating the law as such. Under these circumstances, the choice to reframe the prison experience as a non-legal one is rather remarkable.

It is clear, though, that the value of the special population in this study is not in its representation of a more general population, but specifically in its peculiar and unusual circumstances. As such, it has access to a unique "toolkit" of cultural resources that may not be accessible to other populations. As described above, interviewees ascribed their perspectives on prison to their distinctive characteristics – their ideological and social resources, which enabled them access to a supra-legal approach. It is hard to say which of the two factors – the ideological conviction or the social status – was of more influence; it appears that the former should be credited with stronger influential power. Many different groups of people who violate the law for ideological purposes have reconstructed the social control imposed on them by downplaying, or negating, the legal violation involved in their actions, and by accentuating moral, nationalistic or other alternative frameworks (Lytton 1988; Weisburd 1989). However, the social factor must not be entirely discredited; the visible social differences between the interviewees and the other prisoners enabled them to differentiate themselves from what they saw as a "normal" prison experience, as presented to them by popular culture. This conclusion is also strengthened by the fact that the "above the law" schema was easier to live and implement by those of the interviewees who were incarcerated with other conscientious objectors. It may be that the ability to draw on external sources of empowerment – academic education, a supportive, activist political milieu, respectable professional occupations, a common interest in intellectual pursuit – was also helpful in the process of divorcing oneself from the legal aspects of one's experience. In any case, the "above the law" schema seems to be available to certain groups, and not to others; the fact that different groups have access to different tool kits is hardly surprising. Actually, it draws on a myriad of criminological research stemming from Sykes and Matza's work on neutralization techniques (also see Costello 2000; 1957). In the original work, Sykes and Matza hypothesized that justifications for criminal activity may be differ across criminal or delinquent populations; and several studies have shown "specialized" rationalizations presented by different groups. This is not unique to criminal behavior – the literature on "sociology of accounts" refers to justifications and accounts for any behavior as indicators of value systems and social standards (Orbuch 1997; Scott and Lyman 1968). There is no reason to assume these do not differentiate across populations. Whether we conceptualize the imprisoned objectors' perspectives as "toolkits", "neutralization techniques" or "accounts", they have much to do with who these people are and what had brought them into prison.

One of the most important points to elaborate on would be the pragmatic aspect of adopting a certain schema; how does perceiving oneself "above the law" in prison assist one in adjusting to the experience? As seen in the interviews, this perspective was more helpful in certain cases than in others. The default pattern for coping with prison was dissociating from it; the "above the law" perspective enabled detachment from the reality of prison life. This perspective has parallels in the classical prison literature, though there it is exhibited in much longer imprisonment sentences (Korn and McCorkle 1970; Sykes and Messinger 1970). However, when immediate issues of prison terms and prisoners rights come up, a more active, internal perspective was called into action, and the interviewees chose to situate themselves before the law, against it, or with it.

The direct approach of fighting for one's rights and conditions in prison does not always help, particularly not in the microcosmos of prison; two enlightening examples are related to the very same prison system in which my interviewees served their sentences. In 1997, several regular-service soldiers, imprisoned for long periods of time in the same facility as the one described in this study, took over a section of the prison and took several guards as hostages. In their letter of demands, they requested an improvement in their daily conditions (regarding the use of violence, discipline procedure and daily counts), a more compassionate review of sentencing, and clemency for all those involved in the takeover. Several military officials signed their letter of demands, bringing the uprising to an end, but the instigators were immediately arrested despite the promises not to prosecute them. Their appeal to the Israel High Court of Justice failed; the judges ruled that, under special circumstances, the state is entitled to free itself from the contract signed with the prisoners (High Court of Justice 5319, 5706, 5707/97 *Kogan v. the Military Attorney General*). For the prisoners involved, this decision led to a considerable increase of their prison sentences; however, two years later, a military committee examined the terms of imprisonment and sought to improve prison conditions. The aftermath of the uprising was not encouraging to the specific protagonists of the story, but it brought to general attention and criticism the imprisonment conditions (Okon 1998).

More recently, direct resistance did not help a group of young objectors, either. In January 2004, a year after the completion of this study, five young conscientious objectors were convicted for their absolute refusal to serve in the army (they did not limit their refusal to the occupied territories), and were sentenced to a year-long imprisonment sentence. A month later, they were transferred to a civilian facility (210 Committee Hearings, 18 February 2004); although this was not an unlikely decision, considering the long sentence they had received and the lack of resources for long-time sentences in military facilities, it was nevertheless an unlikely decision considering this specific population, whose adjustment to a regular, civilian prison would be far more difficult than that of other prisoners. The hearing proceedings reveal that the decision to transfer the objectors was reached because of their activism within prison walls; a letter written by the objectors' legal representative reveals that the conflict might have been related to the prison authorities' intention to "present the objectors with a moral dilemma" and send them to do prison labor in the territories. Whether this is true or not, it certainly indicates that direct resistance to the law has its advantages and disadvantages in the battle for prisoners' rights. The "above the law" schema, though not optimal for achieving rights in specific situations, might work better as a default schema in the long run, by improving the prisoner's personal experience rather than his or her external conditions.

Finally, this project suggests the need to broaden the spectrum of populations for legal consciousness research. The importance of seminal legal consciousness work was, partly, in "giving a voice" to those whose voices were not heard in the shaping of the legal order and in the system: the "have-nots"(Galanter 1974), the welfare poor (Sarat 1990), working-class New Englanders (Merry 1990, 1995) and more. Although this is an extremely important endeavor, this project suggests that the prevalence of law in people's everyday life may differ for a radically different population, under different circumstances. Rather than attempting to reflect large groups of people, the agenda of legal consciousness might be enriched through the pursuit of varied aspects of law in people's lives, and of the cultural meanings ascribed to them by those living them.

References

War Resisters' International (2005) "Updates on Imprisoned Conscientious Objectors." *Alerts*, http://www.wri-irg.org/news/alerts/, last accessed Oct. 23, 2005.

Balbus, Isaac D. 1973. *The Dialectics of Legal Repression: Black Rebels before the American Criminal Courts*. New York: Russell Sage Foundation.

Clemmer, Donald (1970) "Prisonization." in *The Sociology of Punishment and Correction*, edited by N.B. Johnston, L.D. Savitz, and M.E. Wolfgang. New York: Wiley.

Costello, Barbara (2000) "Techniques of Neutralization and Self-esteem: A Critical Test of Social Control and Neutralization Theory." *Deviant Behavior: An Interdisciplinary Journal* 21:307–329.

Cressey, Donald R. (1973) *Other People's Money: A Study in the Social Psychology of Embezzlement*: Patterson Smith.

Dayan, Arye (2003) "Refusing for the Sixth Time? You'll be Court-Martialled." in *Ha'aretz*. Tel Aviv.

Ellickson, Robert C. (1991) *Order Without Law: How Neighbors Settle Disputes*. Cambridge: Harvard University Press.

Engel, David M. (1993) "Law in the Domains of Everyday Life: The Construction of Community and Difference." pp. 123–170 in *Law in Everyday Life*, edited by A. Sarat and T.R. Kearns. Ann Arbor: Michigan.

Ewick, Patricia and Susan S. Silbey (2000) *The Common Place of Law: Stories from Everyday Life*. Chicago: University of Chicago Press.

Galanter, Marc (1974) "Why the 'Haves' Come Out Ahead: Speculations on the Limits of Legal Change." *Law and Society Review* 8:95–160.

Galili, Lily (2002a) "Every Objector Has His Own Red Line." in *Ha'aretz*. Tel Aviv.

———. (2002b) "The Minister of Security will Form a Stand as to Recurring Calls of Conscientious Objectors to Perform Reserve Service." in *Ha'aretz*. Tel Aviv.

———. (2002c) "Professors from Hebrew University will Assist Conscientious Objecting Students." in *Ha'aretz*. Tel Aviv.

Gans, Chaim (1987a) "Basing the Duty to Obey the law (Heb.)." *Mishpatim* 17:353.

———. (1987b) "The Concept of a Duty to Obey the Law (Heb.)." *Mishpatim* 17:507.

Goffman, Erving (1961) *Asylums; essays on the social situation of mental patients and other inmates*. Garden City: Anchor Books.

Korn, Richard R., and Lloyd W. McCorkle (1970) "Resocialization Within Walls." in *The Sociology of Punishment and Corrections*, edited by N.B. Johnston, L.D. Savitz, and M.E. Wolfgang. New York: Wiley.

Lavi, Aviv. 2002. "We Have Sobered Up." in *Ha'aretz*. Tel Aviv.

Leibovitz-Dar, Sarah. 2000. "The New Frontier of Objection." in *Ha'aretz*. Tel Aviv.

Leibovitz, Shamai. 2002. "New Record: 83 Conscientious Objectors Imprisoned." in *Ha'aretz*. Tel Aviv.

Levine, Kay and Virginia Mellema (2001) "Strategizing the Street: How Law Matters in the Lives of Women in the Street-Level Drug Economy." *Law and Social Inquiry* 26:169.

Levy, Yagil (2003) *The Other Army of Israel: Materialist Militarism in Israel*, edited by R. Tal. Tel Aviv: Yediot Aharonot-Hemed Books.

Linn, Ruth (1996) "When the Individual Soldier Says 'No' to War: A Look at Selective Refusal during the Intifada." *Journal of Peace Research* 33:421–431.

Lytton, Constance (1988) *Prisons and Prisoners: The Stirring Testimony of a Suffragette.* London: Virago Press.

McCorkie, Lloyd and Richard Korn (1954) "Resocialization Within Walls." *The Annal of the American Academy of Political and Social Sciences* 293:88–98.

Merry, Sally Engel (1990) *Getting Justice and Getting Even: Legal Consciousness among Working Class Americans.* Chicago: University of Chicago Press.

Merry, Sally Engle (1995) "Going to Court: Strategies of Dispute Management in an American Urban Neighborhood." in *Law and Society Reader*, edited by R.L. Abel. New York and London: New York University Press.

Merton, Robert (1964) *Social Theory and Social Structure.* New York: Free Press.

Okon, Boaz (1998) "The Military Prison no. 6 Affair." *Ha'mishpat* 4:53–60.

Orbuch, Terri L. (1997) "People's Accounts Count: The Sociology of Accounts." *Annual Review of Sociology* 23:455–478.

Sarat, Austin (1990) "The Law is All over: Power, Resistance and the Legal Consciousness of the Welfare Poor." *Yale Journal of Law and the Humanities* 2:343.

Scott, Marvin B. and Stanford M. Lyman (1968) "Accounts." *American Sociological Review* 33:46–62.

Segal, Ze'ev (2002) "Selective Conscientious Objection Does Not Justify an Exemption to Serve in the Territories." in *Ha'aretz.* Tel Aviv.

Shapiro, Susan P. (1990) "Collaring the Crime, not the Criminal: Reconsidering the Concept of White-Collar Crime." *American Sociological Review* 55:346–365.

Sheleff, Leon (1987) *The Voice of Honor – Conscientious Objection out of Civic Loyalty (Heb.).* Tel Aviv: Ramot.

Smoocha, Shahar (2002) "Twenty Eight Days Inside." in *Ha'aretz.* Tel Aviv.

Solzhenitsyn, Alexander (1998) *One Day in the Life of Ivan Denisovich*: Signet Classics.

Swidler, Ann (1986) "Culture in Action: Symbols and Strategies." *American Sociological Review* 51:273–286.

Sykes, Gresham M. and David Matza (1957) "Techniques of Neutralization: A Theory of Delinquency." *American Sociological Review* 22:664–670.

Sykes, Gresham and Sheldon L. Messinger (1970) "The Inmates' Social Code." in *The Sociology of Punishment and Correction*, edited by N.B. Johnston, L.D. Savitz, and M.E. Wolfgang. New York: Wiley.

Toker-Maimon, Ori and Shuki Sade (2002) "Guide for the Beginner Objector Before Entering Prison 4 or 6 (The Dry Season)." Booklet prepared by two conscientious objectors, distributed by email or hard-copy to those beginning their prison term.

Walzer, Michael (1967) "The Obligation to Disobey." *Ethics* 77:163–175.

Weisburd, David (1989) *Jewish Settler Violence: Deviance As Social Reaction.* Philadelphia: Pennsylvania State University Press.

Weisburd, David, Stanton Wheeler, and Elin Waring (1991) *Crimes of the Middle Classes: White-Collar Offenders in the Federal Courts.* New Haven: Yale University Press.

Chapter 10

Time, Legal Consciousness, and Power: The Case of France's 35-Hour Workweek Laws

JÉRÔME PÉLISSE

In this chapter, I examine France's "35-hour law," a workweek reduction effort developed by the French socialist government in order to fight unemployment, in 1997–98.[1] I do not investigate the minute details of this legislation here – which is implemented through collective bargaining and exchanges between worktime reduction, flexibility, wage moderation or freeze and work reorganization (see Pélisse 2004). Moreover, since 2002, the new right-wing government has decided a new law which maintains the accrued flexibility of the original but freezes the process of worktime reduction. Drawing on an empirical study of the law between 1998 and 2003, I explore the means by which a single law can or cannot modify legal consciousness among employees who have experienced the legal reduction of their worktime.

This chapter focuses on workers who reduced their worktime after the passage of the 35-hour law. I do not examine their opinions and their discourses about the law nor the collective agreements that transposed it in their company, but the changes, or lack thereof, which they had experienced in their daily lives. I explore how these changes in the law affected respondents both inside and outside of work. More precisely, the analysis centers on the means by which they spoke of the time "freed up" by the working time reduction, on what they decided to do – or not do – with their free time, and on the means by which they managed and used it. First, then, I shall analyze time consciousness rather than legal consciousness.

Both time and legal consciousness are related in a general sense as Greenhouse (1989) has demonstrated.[2] In this case, the law's implementation has in fact prompted the negotiation of business agreements for the transposing of the law, the invention of modalities of RTT (for *réduction du temps de travail* or reduction of worktime) and the redefinition of numerous rules relating to time management. These experiences, temporal as well as legal, permit us then to render what appears to be

---

[1] Previous legislation had established (since 1982) the legal working time at 39 hours a week. Like in the 35-hour regime resulting from the *Aubry Laws* (from the name of the Labor Minister between 1997 and 2001, Martine Aubry), overtime is possible above the legal threshold but it is limited and costly. In France, average effective working time has been around 40 hours a week since the middle of the 1980s.

[2] As C.J. Greenhouse writes, "western conceptions of temporality and the ways in which the law (in broad senses of the term) organizes and reproduces an essentially temporal myth" are connected.

invisible *visible*. That is to say, this inquiry "is not reducible to traditional objects of analysis such as individual actors, social groups, or organizations, and therefore it cannot be directly observed" (Kostiner 2003). However, I argue that attention to how time is represented in respondents' stories elucidates the subtle ways social inequalities and forms of domination are reproduced:

> In order to understand how legal consciousness is structured and actualized, one cannot dismiss the individual and collective power relations in which workers are enmeshed in their workplaces. If the identified schemas, categories, vocabularies of motives, and orders are common to a specific group of actors, then we might expect that attending to how power relations are situated is critical. Prior research in the French contexts demonstrates how the strength and power relations concerning the possibility to refer to this or that orders of justification are important to understand the social world (Boltanski and Chiapello 1999).

The resources, structures, and power relations are at the foundation of the practical actualization of this or that form of consciousness in respondents' narratives. These narratives produce subversive stories as well as hegemonic tales (Ewick and Silbey 1995); but in both cases, power relations are brought into play. This has been found to be *especially* the case in the studies of workers' legal consciousness (Hoffman 2003; Trautner and Smith 2003). Together, underlying systems of management, allocated organizational roles, and intertwining power relations, contribute powerfully in structuring individuals' different forms of legal consciousness and their unequal access to the law (McCann 1994; Marshall and Barclay 2003; Edelman and Suchman 1997[3]).

Overview of Chapter

In the first part of the chapter, I discuss the data and methods utilized. Specifically, I conducted both primary and secondary analysis of relevant data sources. In the former, I conducted interviews with employees from five firms that, starting in 1998, had implemented the 35-hour week. The analysis focuses in particular on the manner in which the employees speak of their time "freed up" from work. My secondary analysis involved investigating materials that were relevant to understanding workplace operations. The second part of this chapter presents results from both lines of inquiry. The social construction of the legality of the 35-hour week is studied through the lens of respondents' time consciousness as it is expressed by the employees and identified by the researcher. Furthermore, I show alternatively how various types of legal consciousness are not unrelated to the unequal resources and the more or less restrictive power relations. In the conclusion, I discuss how attention to time is important for the future study of legal consciousness.

---

[3] In what Edelman and Suchman call "the cultural perspectives on the constitutive environment of organizations," "law plays a central role in 'the social construction of reality', with legal definitons often becoming reified and institutionalized as taken-for-granted components of the 'way the world works'. The central task, then, becomes understanding how these consciousness-framing legal schemas construct – and are constructed by – organizational activity" (Edelman and Suchman 1997:503).

Data

The sample was culled from a larger research program undertaken in 1998 on behalf of the Department of the Ministry of Employment (Pélisse 2000). It was based on 12 monographs concerning companies which had adopted the 35-hour workweek according to the *Aubry Law* adopted in 1998. Interviews were conducted with all negotiators involved in the passage of the law, including managerial, trade union, and workers' representatives. Further in-depth studies were pursued between 1999 and 2003 in five companies (Pélisse 2002). In addition to extended interviews with management and workers' representatives, interviews were conducted with 45 additional employees.

Each of the five firms signed an agreement linking working time reduction and hiring and, moreover, each agreed to a follow-up investigation by the Ministry of Employment.[4]

The monographic study of these firms and the modalities that they adopted in order to proceed to the 35-hour week was invaluable for selecting a sample and for conducting the interviews with the salaried employees. Collective and social elements could be taken into account during the individual interviews with the employees. Specifically, employees spoke of the organization of work, the influence of time restrictions, the social climate of the enterprise, and the nature of the working time agreement. I met between 4 and 13 workers in each firm following a short mailed survey. This survey permitted me to obtain information about these employees (such as social characteristics, opinions towards the RTT agreement and its implementation, and so on) and thus enabled me to obtain a sufficiently diversified sample. It also served, above all, as a means to contact directly the employees who agreed to be interviewed without having to contend with the administrative hierarchy or the trade unions. All told, 1,360 questionnaires were distributed; 520 employees responded and 108 agreed to be interviewed in regard to their RTT experiences; however, time restrictions only enabled me to interview 45 workers in total. Interviews were most often conducted at their homes and lasted one and one-half to three hours. Three university students assisted in conducting ten interviews each and every interview was then transcribed in its entirety.

---

[4] First, in a big firm (4,000 employees) in the electrical components sector, two sites were investigated: (1) a plant in a rural environment employing 140 workers – most of them female with no union protection – and (2) the quality control department, with 140 male technicians and white-collar workers, one of whom is an activist of the main powerful union in the company (CGT). A second firm is a subcontracting packaging company which employs 360 people, 65 percent of whom are unskilled female workers and, in addition, approximately 300 temporary workers are employed. Three plants were specifically studied in this firm, where employees are extremely under-represented by unions, even though two representatives are present. The third firm is an intercity passenger transit company (370 employees) in the Normandy region. Most of the workers are male drivers and there are three unions which enjoy some power. The fourth company is an accounting firm with 250 employees which specializes in the agriculture sector. Employees are well represented by a union (CFDT) and an active employees' committee. Finally, the last firm is an agricultural processing plant (70 permanent male employees with only one union representative of the FO's union).

Methods

What Do Employees Talk About?

Prior studies of the implementation of the law and employees' perceptions of the working time reduction process have primarily involved closed-ended opinion polls (see for example Boulin et al. 1998; Crenner 1999; Doisneau 2000; Estrade et al. 2001). On the contrary, my inquiry is based on monographs, numerous meetings with companies' actors, and in-depth interviews with employees. This methodology is justified for two reasons: first, the worktime reduction modalities built by opinion surveys (for example, daily or weekly reduction, "long" weeks alternated with "short" weeks, days off, "time-saving account", and so on) often do not account for the significance of the working time process from the employees' standpoint. The second point is that opinion surveys evaluate the employees' perceptions through questions such as: "On the whole, are you satisfied with the working time reduction?" In other words, these surveys consider the relationship toward working time reduction and the legal process as "attitudes" and individual opinions, which "flatten the way people understand and use the law ... This approach assumes that each individual has, rather than a series of interpretations of different facets of law, an overall stance toward law as a thing" (Merry 1990:5). In such an individualistic framework, studying employees' representations, judgments, and legal consciousness vis-à-vis the working time reduction process is to evaluate the arbitration between individual preferences such as free time, wages, and employment. These three terms would be the variables of an equation that permits scholars to understand how employees' *make sense* of the 35-hour law. Nevertheless, this approach is based on a normative and economic vision of working time reduction, which does not fit with the individuals' discourses.

Indeed, when they explain how the 35-hour law changes both their work and lives, employees are sometimes talking about very different things, beyond legal perception, wage negotiations, or the real effects of working time reduction on their professional and personal lives. They are telling stories linked to their everyday life experiences.

Consider an *accountant* (43 years old, in the accounting firm), who describes the pleasure he takes in his recent marriage, his new house, and the imminent birth of his baby. The implementation of the law, combined with these important biographical events, transformed his time consciousness, his motivations, and the significance of work: "You know, one half day off per week, that is a lot, it is necessary to be busy with that time, one says to oneself there is more to life than work." He thus works differently. He now pays close attention to the timetable without seeking any promotions.

Next, a *bus driver* in the intercity passenger transportation company criticizes the "archaic" management and "backward" working conditions, "like in the Middle Ages." The 35-hour law provoked no changes for him, especially concerning his daily presence in the firm (frequently between 11 and 14 hours a day). Consequently, days off attributable to the new law do not satisfy him, nor the majority of drivers in this company; they dispute the effectiveness of the law.

A *packaging company worker*, unemployed for three years before being hired as a temporary worker, indicates how the new law changed his life: it prompted his definitive hiring thus leading to a secure wage, even if he lost access to the bonus he would receive as a temporary worker. He settled into a new house, bought a car, and his wife gained employment with a temporary job in the same plant, and so on. The law is responsible for his new situation, which, for him, is more important than its effectiveness in worktime reduction.[5]

I focus on a specific theme present in all of the narratives: the manner in which employees spoke of their time "freed up" by the legal working time reduction. The point was to start with the changes (or lack thereof) experienced in their daily lives based on the newly gained – or, in some cases, imposed – free time. The problematic situations revealed by the implementation of the 35-hour law can thus be applied to Ewick and Silbey's (1998) framework.

Results: Accounting for Legal Consciousness Through Time Consciousness

A systematic and comprehensive examination of the vocabulary, categories, and ways in which the employees speak of their newfound "free time" allows an examination of how time consciousness reveals, in turn, legal consciousness. Time consciousness is an ever-present structure within which the salaried employees operate. While some of the individuals interviewed have even developed certain "relationships" with time, others have not.

"The 35-Hour Law, That Hasn't Changed Anything"

Certain employees did not speak of time "freed up" from work. They did not have the impression of having any free time or they did not feel concerned as such. Almost all, at one moment or another during the interview, spoke of the importance of the new legislation and its consequences on their daily lives. Several employees, although they had accepted an interview about their experiences with the work-reduction laws, even began by saying "the 35-hour law hasn't changed anything for me." This perception was often contradicted later in the interview; for example, one female worker from the large firm wanted to say that the legislation did not bring her any new free time because the daily time reduction had been applied to her mornings. She found herself sleeping an extra hour thereby reducing fatigue, but, according to her, "that doesn't change anything." The point was that she could not use the time for personal activities as she *really* wished. Other employees, who experienced the RTT as lengthened lunch breaks, provided similar accounts (for example, "more time doesn't matter").

For these respondents, the 35-hour law was present but had no appreciable impact on their daily lives. They consider, for example, the legal procedure that shortened their workday instead of adding vacation days as legitimate. Given the constraints of business, they describe no appreciable fairness or unfairness with this arrangement. At the same time, some go on to describe its advantages, as one female worker thought that it would be possible to leave an hour earlier rather than begin an hour

---

[5] In a prior study of these data, several couples, who worked in the same enterprise, likewise explained the consequences of the law for their domestic temporal arrangements and for their different relationships with work (see Lurol and Pélisse 2002).

later. These employees were generally not part of the negotiations about the RTT and the administrative hierarchy imposed upon them its form, frequently a daily reduction of worktime.

Some employees complained, but after a period of adaptation, discovered advantages: grocery shopping during a long lunch hour or cleaning house in the morning frees up time elsewhere in the week or, notably, the weekend. In summary, the law remained an externality for the workers, applied without their input, their commentaries reserved for a passing researcher. Admittedly, the modalities of the law's application do not always suit them and change little in their lives, but these modalities are imposed "legitimately" by the enterprise and the work organization.

"The 35-Hour is Not for Me"

Some employees also indicated that the 35-hour law did not concern them or, indeed, it caused them problems (increased burden, organizational complications, and so on). Most of them have fairly skilled positions with responsibilities and they do not count their hours because they have "missions" to accomplish and "responsibilities" to assume. All the same, certain individuals take some extra days off throughout the year (I name them "RTT flex-days"), but rarely use all to which they are entitled.

In all of these cases, the employees spoke of the new law as one which more concerned others than themselves. With its legality having been conceived as an autonomous sphere whose "application" came to disturb their missions, values, self-motivation, and even their ability to do their work, the legal reduction of worktime remains largely external to their lives. Rather than being regarded as sacred, the law is contested. The 35-hour "requires effort because over the period May–June, where we have several 3- or 4-day workweeks [because of RTT], in terms of motivation, it is not always easy to go back to work," explained a manager in the accounting firm. The rules of the agreement express above all the bureaucracy involved, since the administrative hierarchy seeks to respect them but via complex time management control systems like in the large enterprise.

Extra Paid Vacation: The Routinization of 35 Hours

When the employees speak of their free time, several terms stand out. In all of the companies, certain employees often compared RTT flex-days to paid vacation, whereas in reality, this legal definition does not exist in any of the agreements. In fact, this legal categorization results from a routinized extension of paid holiday entitlements, because the practical rules governing the taking of flex-days have been incorporated in practice into the taking of paid vacation.

Take the case of a middle manager who explains to us that "the 35-hour law doubles my vacation;" of a supervisor in the passenger transportation company who describes the "extended week-end resulting from 35 hours;" of an account manager who insists on "the 54 paid holidays I can now spare." These employees localize, plan, and organize these extra flex-days as vacation days, thereby assimilating the routine manner of RTT days and vacation days thanks to the incorporation of the modalities of the new legislation in old categories.

Interviewer: How is your working time organized?

My working time comes down to 37 hours, that is to say, in the context of the 35 hours agreement, we work 37 hours and are entitled to 12 extra days off that are put into a sort of time account …

Interviewer: So how do you go about taking these 12 days?

There has been no change: we do as before. Certain clauses have been defined through the negotiating process with the industrial partners, but when employees wish to take days, or things like that, they submit a request, as they always did for their "legal holidays", but since the banked days are also legal holidays they ask, "Can I have this or that week," they filled in the form, which I then validated, and that's all. (Interview with a middle manager in quality control in the large company.)

But if the legal novelty of the 35 hours is relative (the change is above all interpreted in terms of quantity – "we have more vacation time"), and conceived as external to the individuals, the novelty is not necessarily sacred, transcendent, and impartial. It is, rather, a practical incorporation into the employees' daily life which occurs. The law does matter as the more powerfully it is considered as "taken for granted."

"RTT Days," "Flex-Days," "Absent Days"… To Negotiate

On the other hand, employees distinguish clearly between RTT and paid vacation days, especially when the utilization of the first is more restricted than the latter. "This was conceived in terms of free time, of supplemental flex days … taken regularly. That is to say, not extra vacation but periodic flex-days," said one female accountant. A variable part of these days is fixed to the employees' initiative and the other part by the management, with the rules varying from company to company.

Mastering the scheduling and predictability of these days is always at stake. Arrangements with colleagues and management aid in this mastery. The legality and the rules of the agreements are conceived as partially legitimate and employees mobilize the legal rules in function of their interests, even if the results are seen as indefinite and contingent, in function of workloads, the availability of others, and relations with supervisors and colleagues.

Individual and collective resources, positions and integration in the workplace also explain the different ways to mobilize and implement legal rules. For example, in all interviews with rank and file employees, mothers of young children have legitimate priority Wednesdays, the day French children do not have school. Having children and being a mother play as a resource for taking convenient flex-days, but these factors can also act as a constraint: women are assigned Wednesdays off even when they have other preferences.[6]

Conversely, not reducing one's working time (for example, in systematically exceeding the required number of hours) can constitute a resource with other interests in mind. A worker employed in the packaging company, thanks to the RTT agreements, indicated his unconditional investment in his work and in the company. As this

---

[6] This is the case in the accounting firm where in the RTT agreement Wednesdays are "reserved" for part-time workers; that is, for women who comprise 42 of the 43 part-timers. On the issue of gender in the application of the 35-hour law in this field study, see Lurol and Pélisse (2002).

example illustrates, the 35-hour arrangement is not just about free time, but also the amount of worktime available:

> 35 hours means that I had more time.
>
> Interviewer: What does this mean, concretely, to have more time?
>
> Concretely, given that we are sub-contractors, it is manifested by the fact that we work in waves: there will be periods when there will more work, so the company needs me and I respond "here" ...

This availability, confirmed several times, distinguishes him from those who count their hours and complain about not being recognized in their work. This investment and availability act as a resource in getting noticed by supervisors and to reinforce his position and integration into the enterprise. Two years after his hiring, he was promised a promotion to supervisor "soon." In these examples, the rules of the time reduction laws are experienced simultaneously with daily life instead of being external and transcendent. Employees view them as part of their resources for advancing their own interests. As we saw in the two examples discussed previously, the employees' interests are multiple and can or cannot lead to the privileging of the RTT as an element to improve their "personal temporal equations" (Grossin 1994). Other interests enter into play, based on diverse means of mobilizing the law. In these forms of legal consciousness, legality is seen, above all, as an arena and the rules as instruments for advancing interests.

From "Rootootoo" to "Démodulation": Signs of Resistance

The flex-days or the time "freed up" by the RTT can also be categorized by different forms of resistance "against the law." During the interviews, the ways of pronouncing these "RTT days" often marked their unequal appropriation. One female employee in the transport company, for whom these days are imposed by her supervisors, views the RTT days with detached irony. Seeking to symbolically overturn the RTT days' imposition according to management's whims, she pronounces them in a childish manner: "rootootoo" ["reuteuteu"]. For their part, several female workers in the packaging firm spoke of "the boss's days." A feeling of being caught by the law is expressed by these employees and in the perceived impossibility of appropriating the "35 hours". Taken from an interview with a male worker at the agricultural processing plant, the following excerpt is enlightening:

> Interviewer: So, what has the 35-hour law changed for you?
>
> What was difficult at first was to find a modulation to be able to ... [hesitation], to be able to continue to do the same work because the problem is that it [the plant] opens early and closes late in the evening; so for us, it was not clear. Not at all clear. One runs over a little, that's the problem. OK, one has the right to 90 hours of overtime [in a year] ... But it isn't for that one must do them; it is not an obligation.

This worker responded to our question about the "35 hours" in speaking of modulation, a legal device permitting the varying of the weekly worktime.[7] He perceives the RTT only as a "problem." He indicates how he puts up with the law, which, here, has transformed working overtime into a duty, much more than how he has appropriated the law by taking advantage of days where he does not work.

The case of the packaging company is even clearer. No one talks about "RTT days," "days off," or "flex-days," despite the fact that they are the most frequent form of the working time reduction. All employees used an indigenous, critical term: "demodulation."

Interviewer: And for the 35 hours, how do you go about deciding on your days?

Demodulation. It's always the workshop supervisor who decides. It depends on the orders and how many hours of work we have. One evening, if there's less work, the next day she looks at those who have the most hours and says "you, you and you! You 'demodule' tomorrow." Even if that's Wednesday and they don't have children. And then, sometimes, we can work it out between us [...].

Interviewer: And what do you think about 35 hours and the ways it has been implemented?

Well, when we can take a day off, we are satisfied, of course, but one day, that's not enough. Nothing is possible. And there is no way we can plan ahead to organize our lives. Never. (Interview with an employee in a packing plant.)

These people described how they feel "caught by law," like the welfare poor described by Austin Sarat (1990). Here, time consciousness is directly connected to legal consciousness. The term used to describe time "freed up" by the RTT is built on a word of legal provenance (modulation). "Demodulation" describes how the business and supervisory hierarchy dominate the possibility of getting free of work. Here, legality colonizes everyday life because employees are always available for work between 6 a.m. to 10 p.m. (there is sometimes teamwork), and on Saturday morning, "without planning ahead to organize our lives." Law is thus considered as power for supervisors. Might is right: "she says you, you, you! You 'demodule' tomorrow." Constraints are seen as arbitrary – "even if that's Wednesday and they don't have children" – and their only choice is making do: "sometimes we can work it out between us." This form of legal consciousness "against the law" is linked up with forms of "disqualified integration," that is to say, with job instability, dissatisfaction in the workplace, and a lack of recognition from managers and society. This is the case when employees consider their status to be that of temporary workers insofar as they never know when they are going to be called on to work. "Since we went over to the 35 hours, I can tell you the difference no longer exists, we're just temporary workers now," said a female worker of the same packaging plant. "We've got a green work coat that we have to wear, that's the only difference," added a colleague. If the feeling you are considered as just a proletarian and if the

---

[7] Modulation is a device meant to make working hours more flexible for employers – not to reduce them. More specifically, working time could vary between 0 and 48 hours a week without paying overtime. But the yearly average of working time week must not exceed the legal threshold (35 hours a week). Marginal in 1994 (3 percent of companies had implemented it), this legal device has been adopted in more than half of the RTT agreements between 1998 and 2000.

only link with the company is the color of a coat, then, potential resistance strategies at workplace are feeble. They can only make do, turn away from legal categories ("rootootoo," "demodulation") and seek to resist through daily or stronger tactics like absenteeism or resigning.

One tactic, which is observed in many companies where modulation was implemented, is to follow carefully the number of hours worked every day in order to forecast a minimum. The objective is to have "hours ahead of schedule" (that is to say, credit), in order "to have a cushion of hours," and to have the possibility of refusing imposed hours of work. Nevertheless, these tactics "against the law" strengthen sometimes paradoxically the rationalization of time and the submission of people's time to company time. These types of individual arrangements can prevent any form of collective action. And some employees are even accustomed to administering their time as a "bank account", as they say.

Legal Consciousness and Power Relations

Through categorizations of time "freed up" by a 35-hour workweek, various forms of time consciousness and constructions of worktime legality have been analyzed. These types of legal consciousness are open, punctual, indeterminate and contingent, as emphasized by McCann (1994) and Ewick and Silbey (1998). They are contextualized by the legal frameworks specific to each firm. But they are also connected with different types of integrations, work organizations and social relations in the workplaces. The employees put up with various constraints and dispose of diverse resources that have structural dimensions inscribed in unequal power relations. The rules of the RTT agreements and the opportunity structure that they open determine these constraints and resources in certain contexts. But individual characteristics (such as age, sex, family situation, skills, wage level, and so on) also play an important role, as do collective factors like distribution of resources or types of "professional integration," which depend on job stability and job satisfaction (Paugam 2000). Presence or absence of unions, skill levels, types of management, and so on, give structure to power relations, possible arrangements, individual and collective workers' resistance (Roscigno and Hodson 2004), which allow us to understand the types of legal consciousness and legal mobilization in the workplace (Marshall and Barclay 2003; Hoffman 2003).

Ewick's and Silbey's approach is recorded in the branch of legal consciousness studies that is concerned with the law's capacity to structure the categories, meanings, and practices always evident in power relations (Engel 1998). But their analytical framework has been criticized. In a recent review, McCann (1999), for example, criticizes Ewick and Silbey's refusal to study how the types of legal consciousness are distributed between various social groups in the population. Similarly critical, Garcia-Villegas (2003) explains how Ewick and Silbey's three-schema model of legal consciousness (see Introduction to this volume).

> ... does not appear to give a sufficient weight to the power of certain material factors to restrict pluralism, contingency and legal practices. Ewick and Silbey do not seem interested in investigating why some types of legal consciousness appear to prevail over others and

what relationship exist between this tendency and the existence of a hierarchically divided society (Garcia-Villegas 2003:155).[8]

Perhaps Garcia-Villegas' most profound critique is the way that legal consciousness studies explain both the concept of "legal consciousness" and the symbolic vision of law as fitting better in constructivist theoretical models, particularly ethno-methodological theories, than in those developed by Bourdieu, Giddens or Touraine, where the symbolic is treated not only as "symbolic vision" but also especially – due to its affinity to conflict theory – as "symbolic strategy" or "symbolic uses" (Garcia-Villegas 2003:160). For Garcia-Villegas, the definitions of legal consciousness adopted by Ewick and Silbey are congruent with studies which develop symbolic *visions* more than they develop symbolic *strategies* for the law in bringing about social change. That is to say, they focus more on a problem of social knowledge than on a problem of social domination. Other scholars such as Nielsen (2000) have integrated legal consciousness studies where social characteristics of individuals, power relations, and domination are important. In this perspective, fruitful research would connect legal consciousnesses and legal mobilization studies (Marshall and Barclay 2003). The theoretical framework developed by Edelman (2003) vis-à-vis the forms of endogeneization of the law by organizations could be another means of integrating these preoccupations. In these perspectives, empirical studies on the construction of legality at the workplace and on the legal consciousness of actors embedded in organizations could be particularly interesting.

My inquiry, along with the other chapters presented in *The New Civil Rights Research,* suggests numerous hypotheses about the connections between different types of legal consciousness and the distribution of power, resources, and constraints at the workplace. For example, employees who talk of "vacation days" to describe time "freed up" by working time reduction are not just anyone. They are, in most companies, professional and managerial staff or supervisors, who all share the same categorization of flex-days. Most of these employees benefit from resources linked to their skills, status and work (autonomy, ability to manage their work and working time, and so on). These resources are based on an "assured integration" (Paugam 2000) with their company and society, because they are satisfied with their work, enjoy job stability, and because management supports, in various ways, this form of social integration in the company. This is especially the case for certain accountants in the accounting company and for a large majority of technicians in the quality control department of the big electrical firm. Freedom and power over legal rules are grounded in the personal and collective ability to choose and organize work and work schedules. For example, in the accounting firm, 22 days off per year result from the working time reduction. They are fixed by the accountants in September for the entire year and cannot, in theory, be moved to another day during the year. But practices

---

[8] In fact, Ewick and Silbey are sensitive to the difference of power between individuals. For example, they emphasize in their case study of Millie Simpson, a black woman who works for white employers as a housekeeper, that "in this telling of the story, Millie Simpson is reinscribed in a system of domination from which the law provides no exit. Her engagement with law confirmed her subordination elsewhere" (Ewick and Silbey 1998:11). It seems to me that the critique of M. Garcia-Villegas is more external than internal to the theoretical framework of Ewick and Silbey, contrary to his discussion of the latter's vision of the symbolic.

show how certain accountants in certain settings[9] adapt the rule: to couple two days off in the same week, to move the date, and so on. Daily repertoires of vacation days become available again for these employees to manage their flex-days. Working time legality is incorporated and routinized by these employees, thanks to old schemas (that of vacation days), to positions in the organization, and to social resources, which can be actualized in the workplace. But to speak of "vacation days" – and not flex-days – presupposes social position and resources that all employees do not share. In these cases, where legality is incorporated in the daily working life, working time reduction is particularly favorable for employees, and legal consciousness is more routinized than before the law.

Other employees, who have less capacity, resources and power at the workplace, experience modalities of RTT, which are imposed upon them and do not change their daily lives. In these cases, legal working time reduction stays exterior to their lives. Legality of working time is thought of as a coherent and transcendent discourse, which bears only on their timetables and is subject to the company's constraints. Employers are legitimate in imposing daily working time reduction or flex-days that employees do not plan, because there is a new legal norm and work can not be disorganized. These employees stay before the law. They do not imagine ways of contesting how their supervisors or managers have implemented the law, nor how to use the plurality permitted by it.

On the other hand, law can be considered as a game, with its own rules and playing field, inscribed in the workplace. This legal consciousness presupposes a collection of resources and a capacity to act in order to disrupt the constraints and distribution of power. These resources and capacities are both individual and collective – and they necessitate a sense of entitlement, existence of organizational and social relations based on common interests, solidarity, work culture, and so on, as those described in the case of pay equity reform (McCann 1994). This is why legal consciousness "with the law" takes places in strategic places where resources and the capacity to negotiate are necessary or where the risks are weighed in terms of the diverse interests sought by the employees.

The employees' interests could thus justify forms of resistance to the law as in the case of some managers and supervisors who contested the 35-hour legislation in terms of their personal situations ("that's not possible for me;" "that complicates my job"). Identifying themselves with their firm, their duties, and their responsibilities, these employees refused the law's application to them. They resisted it by not counting their hours, by not taking RTT days, and by denouncing the "rigidity" and uniformity of the law. These forms of resistance, however, were not those of the impotent: because these employees often satisfied management's interests, they could afford not to implement the work reduction.

Indeed, for other employees, working life can paradoxically colonize their private life through the implementation of the 35-hour set-up. Their availability for work and their subordination towards supervisors and towards the time of production are accentuated, especially for female unskilled workers, thus grounding another type of consciousness "against the law". Criticized for having put their work *and* free time in a state of constant flux, the 35-hour legislation has become the object of individual

---

[9] The firm is organized in 11 "offices" scattered throughout a western French département.

acts of resistance, such as absenteism or foot-dragging.[10] Often linguistic in nature ("rootootoo", "boss's day", "demodulation"), these acts of resistance are seldom expressed in terms of collective action. Indeed, the employees demonstrating this type of legal consciousness do not use the resources that would allow them to negotiate the rules of the agreements to make arrangements with their colleagues and, moreover, their bosses. Furthermore, these forms of legal consciousness can also contribute to the structuring of a workplace through resistance to the managerial hierarchy. This is the case in the packaging company, where, for the first time in its history, a strike linked to 35 hours was recently staged at one of its sites.

Conclusion

Two conclusions can be drawn from our study. The first is to show that studies of the implementation of new legislation can be combined with an analysis of legal consciousness. In particular, the social structures affected by the legislation can be an entry point for studying how law and society are formed mutually. Here, for example, the social structures concerning the mastery of time – spent at, or not at, work – in the context of the 35-hour law.

Echoing McCann (1994) and akin to the perspective recently advanced by Marshall and Barclay (2003) and a symposium of articles that they introduce, the second conclusion is that the different forms of legal consciousness and unequal mobilizations of law appear as two connected fields of study. It is thus necessary to take into account the individual and collective power relations and structures in which individuals are enmeshed, as Hoffmann (2003) proposed. Judging from the research proposed by Gray (2002), we are thus headed towards a sociolegal ethnography taking into consideration the meaning and use of rules regulating worktime in order to link the study of legal consciousness and the study of the formal and informal mobilizations of law.

After all, it is rarely the rules of law that are more directly mobilized than the social rules constructed in the shadow of the law. This dimension emerges in the comments of a female employee in the accounting firm and it highlights the tensions existing between the three forms of legal consciousness:

> Me, I believe that to offer resistance against laws like that, clearly and stiffly, in saying there's a rule and I cannot escape it, well, it is the best means for the rule to get you ... but it's always the same because it is accepted in the place where I work, too. I mean, not even 15 days ago, I went to work on a Wednesday morning [while, as a part-time worker, she is not supposed to work Wednesdays].

To be "before the law" could thus consist of saying: "it's like that, there's a rule and I cannot escape it." But the rule could "get you", that is, seize you like an arbitrary power that is used against you. That is why one must not offer "clear and stiff" resistance "against law like that" but negotiate the application of rules with one's interests in mind. This remains possible for this accountant because she is "accepted"

---

[10] See Ewick and Silbey (1998:215–17) on this form of resistance – "taking time" – against the law.

and recognized in the firm where she works. In this case, the negotiation prevails over the systematic recourse to the formalism of the law. To invoke this formalism would effectively disrupt the set of tacit rules governing integration into the firm, which in the end would risk turning against the "resister" who explicitly emphasizes the formal rule. In a way, the explicit recourse to the law and to the rule is not justified except in the case of disregard for other unwritten social rules transmitted particularly by the recognition of one's work and one's social integration in the firm. This is why, if types of legal consciousness are really social structures constructed from schemas, categories, and orders of justification covering the social space, they are not available and obtainable for all the employees: the power relations and the unequal distribution of resources also contribute to form the legality present in everyday life.

References

Avril C. (2000) *L'application des 35 heures dans une entreprise de transport interurbain, règles juridiques et intégration sociale.* Mémoire de DEA de sociologie. Paris: ENS-Ulm.
Boltanski L., and Chiapello E. (1999) *Le nouvel esprit du capitalisme.* Paris: Gallimard.
Boulin, J.Y., Cette, G., and Verger D. (1998) "Les arbitrages entre temps libre et salaire, les enseignements d'une enquête réalisée auprès des salariés de la chimie." *Travail et Emploi* 77.
Crenner, E. (1999) "Les opinions des salariés sur la réduction du temps de travail," *Economie et Statistique* 321/322.
Doisneau, L. (2000) "Les accords Robien un an après: l'expérience des salaries." *Travail et Emploi* 83.
Edelman, M. (2003) "Law at Work: An Institutional Approach to Civil Rights", unpublished draft. Stanford. 37p.
—— and Suchman, M. (1997) "The Legal Environments of Organizations." *Annual Review of Sociology* 23:479–515.
Engel, D. (1998) "How Does Law Matter in the Constitution of Legal Consciousness?" in A. Sarat and B.G. Garth (eds) *How Does Law Matter?* (Fundamental Issues in Law and Society Research vol. 3). Evanston IL: Northwestern University Press and American Bar Foundation.
Estrade, M.O., Méda, D., and Orain, R. (2001) "Les effets de la RTT sur les modes de vie: qu'en pensent les salariés un an après?" *Premières Synthèses* 21.1, DARES.
Ewick, P., and Silbey, S. (1995) "Subversive Stories and Hegemonic Tales: Toward a Sociology of Narrative." *Law and Society Review* 29(2):197–226.
—— (1998) *The Common Place of Law: Stories From Everyday Life.* Chicago: University of Chicago Press.
—— (2002) "The Structure of Legality: The Cultural Contradictions of Social Institutions" in R.A. Kagan, M. Krygier, and K. Winston (eds) *The Study of Legality: Essays in Honor of Philip Selznick.* Berkeley, University of California Press.
Garcia-Villegas, M. (2003) "Symbolic Power without Symbolic Violence? Critical Comments on Legal Consciousness Studies in USA." *Droit et Société* 53:137–162.
Gray, G.C. (2002) "A Socio-Legal Ethnography of the Right to Refuse Dangerous Work." *Studies in Law, Politics and Society* 24:133–169.
Greenhouse, C.J. (1989) "Just in Time: Temporality and the Cultural Legitimation of Law." *Yale Law Journal* 98(8):1631–1653.
Grossin, W. (1994) "Les temps de travail," in A. Coster and F. Pichault (eds) *Traité de sociologie du travail.* Bruxelles: De Boeck Université.

Hoffman, E.A. (2003) "Legal Consciousness and Dispute Resolution: Different Disputing Behavior at Two Similar Taxicab Companies." *Law and Social Inquiry* 28(3):691–718.

Kostiner, I. (2003) "Exploring the Invisible: On the Empirical Study of Legal Consciousness." Paper for Law and Society Association's Annual Meeting, Pittsburgh, unpublished.

Lurol, M., and Pélisse, J. (2002) "Les 35 heures des hommes et des femmes." *Travail, Genre et Société* 8:167–192.

McCann, W.M. (1994) *Rights at Work: Pay Equity Reform and the Politics of Legal Mobilization.* Chicago: University of Chicago Press.

Marshall, A.-M., and Barclay, S. (2003) "Introduction: In Their Own Words: How Ordinary People Construct the Legal World." *Law and Social Inquiry* 28(3):617–628.

Merry, S.E. (1990) *Getting Justice and Getting Even: The Legal Consciousness among Working-Class Americans.* Chicago: University of Chicago Press.

Nielsen, L.B., (2000) "Situating Legal Consciousness: Experiences and Attitudes of Ordinary Citizens about Law and Street Harassment," *Law and Society Review* 34(4):1055–1090.

Paugam S. (2000) *Le salarié de la précarité.* Paris: PUF.

Pélisse, J. (2000) "Le temps des négociations, étude monographique de douze accords de réduction du temps de travail." *Travail et Emploi* 82.

—— (2002) "A la recherche du temps gagné. Les 35 heures entre perceptions, régulations et intégrations professionnelles." *Travail et Emploi* 90.

—— (2003) "Consciences du temps et consciences du droit chez des salariés à 35 heures." *Droit et Société* 53:163–184.

—— (2004) "From Negotiation to Implementation. A Study of the Reduction of Working Time in France (1998–2000)." *Time and Society* 12(2):13, vol. 2–3.

Roscigno, V.J., and Hodson, R. (2004) "The Organizational and Social Foundations of Worker Resistance." *Annual Review of Sociology* 69(1).

Sarat, A. (1990) "'...The Law is All Over': Power, Resistance and the Legal Consciousness of the Welfare Poor." *Yale Journal of Law and Humanities* 2:343–379.

Sarat, A., and Kearns, T. (eds) (1993) *Law in Everyday Life.* Ann Arbor: University of Michigan Press.

Trautner, M.N., and Smith, K.E. (2003) "Legal Consciousness among Homeless Day Laborers." Paper for Annual Law and Society's Meeting, Pittsburgh, unpublished.

Chapter 11

The Power of "Place": Public Space and Rights Consciousness

LAURA BETH NIELSEN

Introduction

American legal and popular culture hold dear the concept of public space. We learn in our civics classes that the public sphere is shared by everyone and can be entered without reservation for purposes of civic participation. In the real world, being in public means something else entirely. Public space and interactions between strangers in public places are embedded in the locations in which they occur, the identities of the individuals involved, and the nature of the interactions.

Social scientists and sociologists, in particular, often study the effect of different types of space on social interaction, individuals' perceptions of those interactions and how different places affect expectations about "proper" behavior. Although there is no formal "sociology of place," sociologists long have recognized the importance of location in how people understand and interpret events (Gieryn 2000; Goffman 1963, 1971; Nielsen 2001, 2002). Put simply, behavioral norms vary depending on location, which is itself a constructed concept.

This chapter utilizes evidence from a study of street harassment to explore the concepts of space, identity, and rights consciousness. In it, I attempt to move beyond a conceptualization of space merely as a physical location or even as a constructed concept. Like the other chapters in this volume and consistent with the emerging tradition of interpretive or constitutive sociolegal research, my analysis here is premised on the rejection of the notion that law and society are separate. Rather, this study fundamentally is premised on the ideas that meanings, ideologies, rights, conceptions of rights, law, and social relationships are not static categories, but are continually being constructed, negotiated, altered, and resisted (Ewick and Silbey 1992, 1998; Harrington and Yngvesson 1990); practice, structure, and ideology are interrelated (Bourdieu 1977). This critical empirical approach (Harrington and Yngvesson 1990) seeks not to make generalizations as much as to embrace the complexity of law and legal rights as locations of power. In this view, law is as much constituted by society as law constitutes society. In so doing, I attempt to expand theories of situated legal consciousness (Nielsen 2000, 2004) in such a way that attends to factors beyond location for understanding rights consciousness. Moreover, the data presented in this chapter demonstrate that it is not just space, but also identity and law which help to create individuals' expectations about, understandings of, and reactions to interactions.

In this chapter, I employ my ongoing research on street harassment, hierarchy, and legal consciousness, to explore rights consciousness. My prior work on street harassment primarily has focused on how offensive public speech maintains, reinforces, and creates hierarchies of race, gender, and class as well as the role of law in buttressing those processes (Nielsen 2000, 2001, 2004). This previous work treated identity categories largely as static. By doing so, I was able to demonstrate that that white women and people of color were more likely to reject the terms the law defines even as they accept the reality the law imposes (Nielsen 2004).

This chapter is somewhat different. Here, I build on the work of sociolegal scholars who have begun to recognize and explore the complexities not only of location and identity, but also of how conceptions about space, identity, and law interact to create expectations about their rights. This chapter demonstrates that in addition to the organizational and institutional factors that affect rights consciousness, a variety of relational factors create multiple (and often contradictory) understandings of law at different times and in different places. In the conclusion of this chapter, I begin to speculate about the implications of this destabilization of the liberal legal model of rights as inhering in the individual.

Law, Speech and Space

As a matter of formal law, free speech reigns in public places in the US. Public places enjoy the highest degree of First Amendment speech protection (*Hague v. CIO*). The traditional commitment to First Amendment principles means that all sorts of problematic speech are allowed to go on in public places unregulated, from racist speech including cross-burning (*R.A.V. v. City of St. Paul*; but see *Virginia v. Black*), to offensive speech (*Tinker v. Des Moines School District*), to religious proselytizing (*Village of Schaumberg v. Citizens for Better Environment*), to begging (*Young v. New York City Transit Authority; Loper v. New York City Police Department*, 999 F2d 699.2d.Cir.N.Y. 1993). When considering First Amendment questions of speech in public space, the formal law recognizes that the totality of the circumstances should be considered when analyzing whether speech is protected or crosses the line into threatening.

Consider cross-burning, for example. In *R.A.V. v. City of St Paul*, the Supreme Court determined that cross-burning was protected free speech. In 2002, however, the Supreme Court recognized that, when done *with the intent to intimidate*, cross-burning is transformed from protected free speech to threatening criminal activity (*Virginia v. Black*). The court agreed in a 7–2 opinion that intent was the most important factor for determining when cross-burning could be legally regulated.

In *Black*, the Court reversed a conviction for cross-burning when done as part of a "political" (KKK) rally but affirmed a cross-burning conviction when done in the front yard of an African-American's home in the context of a series of neighborhood disputes. Why? Because the latter was obviously a threat and when determining threat, a hostile action conducted in a front yard may be more troubling than a hostile action taken in a large crowded place. *Black* thus affirmed what most ordinary citizens already knew: place matters when considering the offensiveness, threat, and legality of public speech.

Ordinary citizens, for a variety of reasons, believe that offensive public speech is a serious personal and social problem. That said, ordinary citizens (perhaps not surprisingly), are not really thinking about the intricacies of First Amendment doctrine when they enter the public sphere and suffer street harassment. The First Amendment, along with other ideas about law's proper role in addressing social problems, provides a powerful rationale of which even those untrained in law are aware, for allowing even very troubling speech to remain outside the bounds of law (Nielsen 2004). And one of the primary reasons that the majority of people disfavor the legal regulation of offensive public speech is based on how they understand place. There may be nearly universal agreement that offensive racist or sexist speech need not be tolerated in a private setting (such as one's home), and there is increasing agreement that such speech should not be tolerated by disadvantaged minorities (white women, people of color) in workplace settings (Volokh 1992), but little agreement about the regulation of offensive speech in public places.

Judges and policymakers are attentive to space when considering the regulation of offensive public speech. Space itself most often is not a category of consideration that is made explicit in judicial analysis, but it is implicated in discussion of what people are doing (working, protesting), their options for exiting a particular space (see abortion protest cases and NYC Transit Authority), among other things. Thus, space is an important factor in their analysis even with the recognition that "place" itself is a constructed and contested concept (Gieryn 2000).

Location, Identity, and Speech

Although location constitutes expectations of norms and behavior, place itself does not tell the whole story. Identity, relationships, and the substance of speech interact to construct how an interaction is understood by those who are in it. In different contexts, different factors may be thought of as definitive as to how an interaction is understood. Perhaps a more accurate way of conceiving of the relationship between speech, space, and identity is to think of them as interacting variables. Space, identity, relationships, and law's definition of these factors matter differently depending on circumstances.[1]

Consider how location matters in an individual's understanding of an interaction by considering the comment "hey baby, looking good," made to a woman by someone she does not know. Her feelings about the comment likely will be very different in different locations. If she is in a bar that she went to for the purpose of meeting a suitor, the comment may be welcome. If she is in a public park during the day, the

---

[1] In describing space, identity, and consciousness as interactive, I am thinking of the excellent work on theories of rights by, among others, Catherine Albiston, Lauren Edelman, Carol Heimer, Anna-Marie Marshall, Michael McCann, and Idit Kostiner, which explore the power of rights in relationship to various normative orders, organizational imperatives, and institutional forces. All of these authors powerfully demonstrate that when formal law is implicated in various situations, its implementation, indeed how ordinary citizens understand it, is in relationship to various complementing and competing imperatives from established social norms (such as the norm that parents take care of their children), organizational demands (including management's preference for managerialized versions of law in the workplace), and institutional factors (including the social institutions of "work" and "family", for example).

comment may be troubling but not frightening. If she is walking alone at night on an otherwise deserted street, it may be terrifying and even criminally threatening depending on the entire circumstances. If she is in her place of work, it is an impediment to full workplace equality.

Identities of and relationships between individuals in spaces are at once being constructed and constituting the space itself. For example, the very same public park might be "home" for a homeless person, a place of leisure for families playing, and "work" for a city employee who is pruning the shrubs. All will likely agree that it is a park, but its meaning as a place is constructed by the individuals' identities (homeless, family member, or worker) and relationships (none, familial relationship, or employment relationship) to others in the park. "Hey baby, looking good," when said to a mother in the park, it is perhaps offensive but not actionable. When said to the city employee by her boss in the park, the remark takes on new significance as, perhaps, part of the creation of a legally actionable hostile work environment. Thus, it is not *just* space that determines the significance of everyday encounters any more than it is "merely" the content of the speech.

Still other factors are important for understanding the nature of an offensive comment. Consider time of day, for example. Imagine no relationship between a speaker and target and the same comment made during the day in a public place versus at night in the dark. The subjective feeling of threat that the woman feels might be very different in those different circumstances.

These examples shows us that space can be meaningless in the face of relationships, determinative in the context of threat and just one of many factors required to assess the harm of and legal liability for speech. Not only are all of these factors present in any analysis of speech, be it from a personal or legal analysis of a particular interaction, law fundamentally defines and constructs these factors in the interactions.

Space, Identity, and Narrativity

That law and space are mutually constitutive is recognized by a growing number of sociolegal scholars whose work considers the importance of place on how ordinary citizens understand law and what they are entitled to by law (Shields 1991; Silbey and Ewick 2003). Studies of legal consciousness, always are embedded in particular locations, be they neighborhoods (Ewick and Silbey 1998); jury rooms (Fleury-Steiner 2002); the workplace (Albiston 2001; Marshall 2003; McCann 1994); prisons (Aviram, this volume); or public interest organizations (Kostiner, this volume). Researchers may be more or less attentive to the constraints imposed by location, and may make it an explicit or implicit part of their analysis but, fundamentally, all studies of law and rights include the study of locations.

However, as shown above, it is not just locations and people's understandings of them that affect how ordinary citizens understand their interactions with one another. Given the complexity of the relationship between space, identity, time, and consciousness explored in the previous section of this chapter, it is useful to explore a set of theoretical and methodological tools for understanding these admittedly somewhat amorphous and contingent concepts.

"Identity" as a subject for study has a long history in sociolegal studies and is important in the work of traditional law and society scholars (Bell 2002; Crowe 1998; Engel and Munger 1996; Ewick and Silbey 1992; Fleury-Steiner 2002; Sarat 1990; Scott 1990; West 1987; Yngvesson 1985), critical race theorists (Harris 1990; Spelman 1988), and political philosophers (Waldron 1995; West 1987; Young 1990), to name just a few. And, while there long has been a notion of identity that rejects an essentialist view of an individual as embodying only one identity characteristic (such as "woman" or "African-American" or "parent"), instead preferring a model of identity that embodies the multiple intersecting aspects of identities (African-American mother, for example) (Harris 1990), there is only now emerging an exploration of the contingency of identity. That is to say, when do particular aspects of one's identity become more or less salient? This empirical question is no easy endeavor. Recent scholarship by three scholars may help to elaborate how I will begin to think about identity as transient.

Fleury-Steiner argues that the subtleties of the effects of identity on legal consciousness are best understood "by elucidating both the stories that give meaning to actors' identities *and in turn* how such identities give meaning to law" (Fleury-Steiner 2002). This theory of legal narrativity is "embedded in stories told by ... [respondents], demonstrates that identity is fluid and is influenced by location and past history." In his book about jurors on capital cases, Fleury-Steiner demonstrates that a middle-class African-American juror can be the lone "expert" on a jury of whites to speak for the life situation of African-American youth living in poverty. Or that juror can distance himself from the defendant by clinging to the shared characteristics of the jury.

Somewhat similar is the approach demonstrated through research that explores individuals' life stories. In *Rights of Inclusion*, Engel and Munger (2003) show how identity is transient; it changes as people change. Assuming that the "distributed self" continually evolves with experience, incorporating along the way multiple and sometimes contradictory elements and perspectives, Engel and Munger study how people living with disabilities understand themselves and their legal entitlements over many years (2003:12).

Engel and Munger and Fleury-Steiner show in dramatic fashion that static identity categories oversimplify identity and that through rigorous qualitative methods, a more complex picture of the contingency of identity can be allowed to emerge. In what follows, I attempt to use the insights by these scholars to examine offensive public speech and how ordinary citizens understand the relationship between law, place, and speech to better understand how place and law work together to construct and affect legal consciousness.

As elaborated in this volume (Fleury-Steiner and Nielsen's introductory chapter) and elsewhere (Engel and Yngvesson 1984; Ewick and Silbey 1992, 1998; Hoffman 2003; Marshall 2003; Nielsen 2000, 2004), legal consciousness is a fluid process. It is culturally produced, constructed and reconstructed continuously as different problems are at issue, as different areas of law are implicated. In other words, this essay is intended to uncover how location and identity affect legal consciousness and to speculate about the implications this has for our understanding of "rights" as a legal concept.

Method

The empirical study of legal consciousness and its relationship to public space presents several methodological challenges described in the introduction to this volume. Legal consciousness is complex and difficult to inquire about without inventing it for the subject or, at the very least, biasing the subjects' responses. Only through in-depth interviews can legal consciousness emerge, leaving the researcher the daunting task of figuring out how to gauge variation in legal consciousness and how it relates to broader social structures from lengthy interview transcripts.

The methodology employed in the study on which I base this chapter is detailed elsewhere (Nielsen 2000, 2004). In brief, I systematically sampled subjects from public places knowing that the subjects were consumers of public space, and thus constituted a set of potential targets for offensive public speech. In addition, I observed different public locations at different times of day as well as various days of the week, giving me an appreciation for the kinds of speech acts experienced by targets. By approaching subjects in person, I established rapport that was necessary given the nature of the questions I was going to ask them about. There was a good deal of offensive speech in the interview schedule itself. My methodology included systematic procedures to construct a sample that, while not a probability sample, included different types of people and minimized the possibility of researcher-biased selections due to my personal predilections and characteristics. I conducted a detailed assessment of data sites with the objective of maximizing variation in the socioeconomic status of potential subjects and guarding against idiosyncratic factors that might bias the results (Lofland and Lofland 1995) in a variety of ways. The field sites I selected were public places, such as sidewalks, public transportation terminals, and bus stops. I devised a system whereby each person in my field sites had an equal chance of being selected in order to introduce controls on who I failed to approach.

This chapter is drawn from the section of the interview during which I used closed-ended questions to probe whether or not respondents believe that certain behavior should be legal or illegal. I asked about a series of increasingly offensive hypothetical scenarios that address begging, sexually suggestive speech, and racist speech. After each hypothetical situation was read to the respondent he or she indicated if that behavior should be legal or illegal. All of the hypothetical situations involved interactions between strangers in public places, but at the very end, in order to probe how much the location of the comment mattered to the respondents' determination about the legality of such remarks, I inquired about the same interactions, should they happen in the workplace. Finally, I inquired how respondents thought about the question of location.

Data

Subjective assessment of fear when one is targeted for offensive public speech dramatically affects whether the individual target believes that they have been the victim of a crime. Subjective assessment of fear, is, of course related to location, time of day, identity (or perceived identity) of speaker and target, as well as other relational factors. When a target feels threatened in a particular interaction, she is more likely to believe that an illegal act has occurred than when she is "merely" offended. This assessment by laypeople mirrors the explicit logic of the law: a "threat" can be criminal while "merely offensive comments" are not. But, the circumstances under which people perceive such comments to be threatening is highly subjective. Location obviously plays a tremendous role in whether or not people experience offensive public speech as "threatening" as the following respondent's remarks indicate:

> Yes, I think [that sexually suggestive or explicit comments are a social problem]. But again, it depends ... and ... I think that the settings can be really scary. You know, like late at night if I was walking down the street and somebody said something sexual to me, that would scare me, but if it was in the afternoon, and I was going to get a cup of coffee, I would look at it as, you know, a weird guy. But I think part of it is living in San Francisco, and if you live there, or any big city, where you have people that say things out of the blue, I think the older you get, the more used to it you get (53-year-old white woman, property manager, interview 21).

This woman/target indicates that there is a proper amount of fear to feel in any given circumstance, but the appropriate level of fear (when properly calculated) depends on any number of factors including identity (she mentions that she is more comfortable as she ages), location (in the city), purpose of being in public (going to get coffee), and time of day (night versus day). Like many other respondents in the research, this woman has a "detailed calculus" for assessing the appropriate level of fear (Nielsen 2004). The detailed calculus exists in the minds of many women and there is remarkable similarity across women (Nielsen 2004), but the substantive decision about under what circumstances one should feel fear depends on the interaction of a host of factors.

This extremely contextual, detailed calculus involves an analysis of location, but, location is not determinative and can serve to confuse the analysis. When asked if sexually suggestive remarks between strangers in public places currently are legally prohibited, one respondent was confused about how location affects legality. She said, "I don't know. I don't know about that. I know it's not [legal] in the workplace. But I don't know about on the street" (24-year-old white woman, student, interview #10). Despite being unclear about the official legal status of such speech, she has an intuition that location is significant for determining the legal status of such speech.

When asked if the comment, "Hey white bitch, come suck my dick", should be illegal, one respondent was careful to note that she thought such remarks were tolerable in the street, but that "in the workplace it is a completely different story as far as I'm concerned" (60-year-old white woman, real estate agent, interview #25). Location was important (the workplace versus public), but the relationship employer/employee is significant in how people understand the harm of offensive speech as well. Consider this woman's remarks which focus both on the relationship of the parties in the interaction as well as the setting of the interaction.

> If people are ... in an office setting or work setting, or a recreational setting, you're with someone you know really well, you can take things pretty far, depending on their sense of humor and your relationship. I think that – in a professional setting, when I'm with clients or in the office ... it is not necessarily appropriate. And therefore, when I hear it from somebody else, I go "ooh, that's not what I would have done" (45-year-old white man, project manager/construction, interview #33).

For him, workplace sexual banter is off-limits simply because of the location (the workplace) but he recognizes that other people in his workplace make this decision based more upon the relationship of speaker to target. Despite the general agreement with law's construction as some places being "open" for such comments including public places (meaning that laws prohibiting such speech are impermissible – like the street) and other places being "closed" to such forms of speech (meaning that laws prohibiting such speech are permissible – like the workplace), there were respondents who felt that the law should protect them from offensive speech in public places. The people who felt that it would be permissible to enact laws designed to prohibit offensive public speech had a very different view of the instrumentality of public spaces. In short, since they have to enter public places to live their daily lives, they should be protected from such insults while traveling through them. For these respondents, it is the instrumental use of public space, meaning that they must be consumers of public space simply to conduct their daily business, and this means that they should be protected from such comments. In other words, simply being in public should carry with it the presumption of equality.

> I just think it's very disrespectful ... Especially when it's coming from somebody you don't know, and you just feel very uncomfortable. And especially in a public place, you feel like you should be protected somehow and somebody's kind of violating [your] privacy ... [and] your ability to go out in a public place. You have that right, and it's kind of like an infringement of your right, to hear something like that (22-year-old Hispanic woman, human resources professional, interview 36).

Having the "right to be left alone" while in public places was a common theme discussed by women for whom sexually explicit remarks were considered a serious affront. When asked, "Do you think that there should be any kind of legal limitations on sexually explicit speech in public places?", she also said:

> Yes ... it's the same as in the work place. You have to watch what you say ... the sexual harassment thing. It should be the same thing in a public place ... you have a right to go out and ... not [feel] uncomfortable ... I feel really insulted, and I am insulted in that I don't have a right to be talked to in that tone. And you feel like you can't do anything about it (22-year-old Hispanic woman, human resources professional, interview #36).

A few women, like the one quoted above, recognized that equality is guaranteed, if not realized, in the workplace and feminists address household inequality, but the public sphere has not received much attention from feminists as a site to struggle for equality. One respondent vacillated in her opinion about whether offensive public speech should be limited. The place that such speech is happening was an important distinction in her mind. She said:

> Like you don't go to a courtroom cussing and going off, but then again, if somebody try to break into your car – so I mean, it's like – there's a time for everything, and a person should know when is the right time. But I don't think somebody should like tell you – "no, you can't say that." Because I mean, some people are different. I don't know. But that shouldn't be outright painful comments and hurtful words and stuff like that (23-year-old African–American man, unemployed/artist, interview #41).

In his determination that no form of sexually explicit public speech ought to be criminalized, one man explicitly stated that it is tough when "[w]e get into that whole sexual harassment thing. But that's usually at work. [laugh] Oh, that's a difficult one (40-year-old white woman, computer specialist, interview #41).

One concern raised by respondents is that when people are in a public place, they may wish to be perceived of as "open" to such encounters. Goffman explained this phenomenon as an acceptable breach of the norm of "civil inattention" (the practice of politely ignoring one another in public places). But a "legitimate" breach of civil inattention depends on whether the target actually is open to teasing or flirting. Is that line different in a bar, in a workplace? Consider this man; when I asked, "Do you think there should be any kind of legal limitations on sexually explicit speech between strangers in public places?", he replied:

> Definitely ... [but] you get really sticky because you say, well what about bars, and you're trying to pick up on somebody, but then again that would be sort of uh – I don't know what the legal term is – a mutual consent type of thing – you're in a bar! ... I don't know if this is a legally plausible thing, but the [standard should be the] willingness of the other person to be listening to it (30-year-old white man, teacher, interview #53).

Sexually suggestive speech is more difficult to think about than race-related or racist speech in public places. As this man indicates, a variety of factors signal to him that a woman may be "open" to such comments. The most obvious is that she is in a particular location (a bar), but the underlying thrust of the comment is that when all signs point to the fact that a woman is "open" to such comments, men should be able to test the waters. And, there should be room for men to get it wrong – that is to say, there should not be a penalty for men who are unable to successfully analyze the clues provided by women. The arguments seem familiar because they are very similar to those made by opponents of the legal regulation of sexual harassment in the workplace (Schultz 1998).

Analysis/Implications

These data show that there is a range of acceptable interactions between strangers in public places. And while what type of interaction falls outside that spectrum is subjectively determined and individualized, it is determined by a variety of factors that are commonly shared. The various factors are analyzed as part of a complex process that is more than just a rank-ordering of importance. The factors include the targets' assessment of the location in which the speech occurs, the relational status of the speaker and the target, the identities of the involved parties, and the law, which constitutes how citizens understand all of the foregoing. Individuals disagree about whether a particular word or comment is or is not acceptable, but they generally agree on the factors that go into the process of determining whether or not a comment is offensive or threatening and whether it should be subject to legal regulation. Although this interview did not include questions about the home, it is likely that a very high proportion of, if not all, people would find such remarks objectionable in the home. Indeed the vast majority of respondents say sexually suggestive comments are *never* appropriate in the workplace and should be legally actionable. And, although they find them objectionable, only a small minority of respondents say that offensive speech should be legally limited in public places.

But it is not just the location, or even the social construction of the activities in the location of the place that affects individuals' assessments of the legal ramifications of such speech. Law plays an important role not just in terms of how the formal law defines such interactions (although that is part of the analysis), but also in how the other categories of location, identity, and relationships are constituted. For the most part, ordinary citizens have a generally accurate understanding of the law. Ordinary citizens may not understand the intricacies of First Amendment jurisprudence, but they understand the lived consequences of it. They understand the First Amendment requires them to tolerate such speech. People understand that such remarks are not legally allowed in the workplace, but they must be tolerated in public places. Thus, the formal law is reflected in the views of ordinary citizens in a general way but law itself remains a part of the other variables as well. Such interactions fundamentally implicate the most personal characteristics of personal identity: gender, race, sexual orientation, and the like.

When ordinary people talk about the distinction between offensive speech in public places versus offensive speech in a workplace, they talk about law. They do not say that offensive speech in a workplace should not be tolerated because it is offensive or because it perpetuates workplace inequality or even because it is unproductive. They say that sexually suggestive speech in the workplace setting should not be tolerated because the law does not tolerate it. A tautology to be sure, but it makes apparent that the law is the fundamental source of authority for how individuals understand offensive public speech. Law is part of a broad range of institutional forces that construct identity categories broadly conceived. When ordinary people talk about location, they talk about law. Law itself constructs the meaning of location – as public or private, as a place of work or of leisure, and so on. As these respondents demonstrate, location, law, and identity come together in the mind of the individual as a process. Ordinary people construct an analysis of events that takes account of location, situation, relationships, and identities of involved parties when offensive public speech occurs.

As these respondents demonstrate, ordinary citizens do not understand sexually harassing speech independent of or solely with relationship to location. The location can be determinative in whether one understands the speech as problematic or legally actionable. In other words, one of the things that makes sexually suggestive speech problematic is location, but the nature of the relationship is important in this analysis as well. When sexually harassed by a direct supervisor, it is both the location (work) and the relationship (employer/employee) that makes it a problem. However, sexual harassment by a non-employee or non-supervisor remains troubling because of the location in part. It remains a problem to be sexually harassed by those in the workplace who are not employed by the same organization because of the purpose of the space. What is supposed to be happening is work and if the sexually suggestive comments of someone nearby (say, a security guard or regular delivery person) are interfering with a woman's ability to do her job or to enter a place where we believe that equality should reign (the workplace), then it remains a problem, despite the different relational statuses of the parties involved.

Conclusions: Implications for Theories and Studies of Rights

That a variety of factors make up how an individual understands any particular social interaction is perhaps not surprising. However, the way that law, space, and identity are implicated in ordinary citizens' assessment of these interactions is important. If ordinary citizens believe they must accept humiliating or threatening public speech, the law is working to normalize or justify such interactions. And, insofar as the current state of the law is one of the many forces that normalizes such interactions, it is part of the construction of these acts of subordination as something that one does not have a "right" to be free from.

"Rights," of course, are social constructions (Tushnet 1984). That is to say, a right is only what we make of it. Understanding even the most basic functions of rights (be they actual legal rights or more diffuse notions of rights that lead individuals to feel entitled even in the face of no formal legal right) requires understanding how law is implicated in everyday situations that implicate inequality such as offensive public speech. This empirical research demonstrates that how individuals make sense of the unexpected comments by strangers about their race or sex are intimately tied to law itself (both a version of formal First Amendment law and a more diffuse notion of a "right" to be left alone or to enter public space without impediment), to space (there are safe and unsafe places, places where such speech should or should not be tolerated), and to identity. In addition to myriad other factors that affect the capacity of rights (Albiston 2000; Edelman 1992; Edelman, Erlanger, and Lande 1993; Edelman and Suchman 1997; Heimer 1996; Rosenberg 1991), this research demonstrates that space and identity also are important considerations.

Legal theorists long have recognized that legal rights, indeed law itself, work differently for those differently situated (Bumiller 1988; Delgado 1993; Ewick and Silbey 1992, 1998; MacKinnon 1987, 1989; McGuire 1995; Nielsen 2000; Yngvesson 1988; Young 1990). Similarly, this research on offensive public speech demonstrates that simply being in public is also different for those differently situated and that law is implicated in that difference insofar as law plays a role in constructing space, relationships, organizations, and institutions (Albiston 2000, 2001; Nielsen 2001, 2002; Silbey and Ewick 2003). This emerging picture of rights is one that becomes tremendously subjective.

Traditionally, "rights" are thought of as inhering in natural persons by virtue of birth or citizenship. But to be meaningful, a right must be understood and asserted by the rights bearer (Felstiner, Abel, and Sarat 1980). The assertion of a right need not be through a formal legal mechanism, however. In fact, much recent sociolegal scholarship on rights demonstrates the unintended and sometimes very effective ways that conceiving of oneself as being a rights holder affects individual actions (Albiston 2000; Heyer 2001; McCann 1994; McCann and March 1996). Conceiving of oneself as a rights holder is the first step in a process of making a claim for equality, be it formal or informal. If location, identity, and interaction are differently implicated in all of these interactions, how can we understand the circumstances under which ordinary citizen think of themselves as rights holders?

Popular and scholarly accounts of American's rights consciousness claim that Americans are very willing to construct everyday problems as something that they enjoy a "right" to be protected from (Glendon 1991) and they (Americans) are overly litigious in the extreme (Olson 1991, 1997, 2003). Despite this, sociolegal scholars have repeatedly demonstrated that individuals are unlikely to understand when they have been legally harmed (Major and Kaiser 2003; Marshall 2003) and are unlikely to claim harms even when they believe they have been harmed (Bumiller 1988; Curran 1977; Nielsen and Nelson forthcoming). The fallacy of the litigation explosion in civil courts has been demonstrated again and again (Galanter 1983, 1986; McCann, Haltom and Bloom 2001; McCann 1993; Nielsen and Beim 2004). Nevertheless, the myth of the litigation explosion prevails in popular culture. As such, it is important that sociolegal scholars continue to practice the kind of empirical social science that uncovers the factors that go into individuals' decisions/opinions as to whether they are in fact, rights holders.

Rights consciousness is necessarily subjective. Whether an individual thinks of herself as having a right depends on her identity characteristics, the nature of the problem, the relationship that the parties involved enjoy, the organizational setting in which the incident occurs, and the institutional and cultural factors that make up the people and place where interactions occur.

Sociolegal scholars have begun to embrace this subjective (interpretivist) conception of rights and to examine the factors that lead individuals to think of themselves as rights holders and about decisions regarding invoking rights. Where claims of rights lead not to systemic change, but to successful outcomes for individuals, scholars debate if this is a positive outcome or a successful reassertion by those in power to placate one individual but fails to provide what is legally entitled to all of those similarly situated (particularly in employment).

What has not received as much attention, however, is how this subjective and fluid conception of rights affects the liberal legal model of rights as omnipresent and static. If you have a right, you always have that right. In the case of offensive racist and sexist speech, however, we have seen that any number of factors are important for determining if an individual enjoys the right to be free from such speech. Can it be said that an individual possess a right if the circumstances under which it is meaningful varies so dramatically?

Because rights are meaningful only insofar as the rights bearer has a sense that she is entitled to something (protection from the state, a level of treatment from an employer), the kind of critical empirical approaches that bring together a sophisticated understanding of the factors that affect how ordinary citizens understand their rights are crucial. We are beginning to understand the ways that organizational and institutional factors affect rights consciousness, but this chapter (and the one preceeding it) demonstrates that other organizing factors (including time and space) may also have an important role to play in our understanding of naming, blaming, and claiming. The subjectivity of rights requires it.

References

Albiston, C.R. (2000) "Legal Consciousness and the Mobilization of Civil Rights: Negotiating Family and Medical Leave Rights in the Workplace." Paper presented at the Law and Society Association's Annual Meeting. Miami, FL.

—— (2001) "The Struggle to Care: Negotiating Family and Medical Leave in the Workplace." CWF Working Paper 26 for the Center for Working Families. Berkeley: University of California.

Bell, J. (2002) "Deciding When Hate is a Crime: The First Amendment, Police Detectives, and the Identification of Hate Crime." *Rutgers Race and Law Review* 4:33–75.

Bourdieu, P. (1977) *Outline of a Theory of Practice*. Cambridge: Cambridge University Press.

Bumiller, K. (1988) *The Civil Rights Society: The Social Construction of Victims*. Baltimore: Johns Hopkins University Press.

Crowe, N. (1998) "Diversity on the Federal Bench: The Effect of Judges Sex and Race on Judicial Decision Making." in *Law & Society Association Annual Meeting*. Aspen, CO.

Curran, B.A. (1977) *The Legal Needs of the Public: The Final Report of a National Survey*. Chicago: American Bar Foundation.

Delgado, R. (1993) "Words That Wound: A Tort Action for Racial Insults, Epithets, and Name Calling" in C.R. Lawrence, M.J. Matsuda, R. Delgado, and K.W. Crenshaw (eds) *Words That Wound: Critical Race Theory, Assaultive Speech, and the First Amendment*. Boulder CO: Westview Press.

Edelman, L.B., Erlanger, H.S., and Abraham, S.E. (1992) "Professional Construction of Law: The Inflated Threat of Wrongful Discharge." *Law and Society Review* 26:47–83.

Edelman, L.B., Erlanger, H.S., and Lande, J. (1993) "Internal Dispute Resolution: The Transformation of Civil Rights in the Workplace." *Law & Society Review* 27:497–534.

Edelman, L.B., and Suchman, M.C. (1997) "The Legal Environments of Organizations." *Annual Review of Sociology* 23:479.

Engel, D.M., and Munger, F.W. (1996) "Rights, Remembrance, and the Reconciliation of Difference." *Law and Society Review* 30:7–53.

Engel, D.M., and Yngvesson, B. (1984) "Mapping the Terrain: 'Legal Culture,' 'Legal Consciousness,' and Other Hazards for the Intrepid Explorer." *Law and Policy* 6:299–307.

Ewick, P., and Silbey, S. (1992) "Conformity, Contestation, and Resistance: An Account of Legal Consciousness." *New England Law Review* 26:731–749.

—— (1998) *The Common Place of Law: Stories From Everyday Life*. Chicago: University of Chicago Press.

Felstiner, W., Abel, R., and Sarat, A. (1980) "The Emergence and Transformation of Disputes: Naming, Blaming, and Claiming." *Law and Society Review* 15:631–655.

Fleury-Steiner, B. (2002) "Narratives of the Death Sentence: Toward a Theory of Legal Narrativity." *Law and Society Review* 36:549–576.

—— (2004) *Jurors' Stories of Death: How American's Death Penalty Invests in Inequality*. Ann Arbor: University of Michigan Press.

Galanter, M. (1983) "Reading the Landscape of Disputes: What We Know and Don't Know (and Think We Know) About Our Allegedly Contentious and Litigious Society." *UCLA Law Review* 31.

—— (1986) "The Day After the Litigation Explosion." *University of Maryland Law Review* 46:3.

Gieryn, T.F. (2000) "A Space for Place in Sociology." *Annual Review of Sociology* 26:463–496.

Glendon, M.A. (1991) *Rights Talk: The Impoverishment of Political Discourse*. New York: The Free Press.

Goffman, E. (1963) *Behavior in Public Places*. Glencoe, IL: Free Press.

—— (1971) *Relations In Public*. New York: Basic Books.

Harrington, C.B., and Yngvesson, B. (1990) "Interpretive Sociolegal Research." *Law and Social Inquiry* 15:135–148.

Harris, A.P. (1990) "Race and Essentialism in Feminist Legal Theory." *Stanford Law Review* 42:581–616.

Heimer, C.A. (1996) "Explaining Variation in the Impact of Law: Organizations, Institutions, and Professions." *Studies in Law, Politics and Society* 15:29–59.

Heyer, K. (2001) "Rights on the Road: Disability Politics in Japan and Germany." Ph.D. thesis. Manoa: University of Hawai'i.

Hoffman, E.A. (2003) "Legal Consciousness and Dispute Resolution: Different Disputing Behavior at Two Similar Taxicab Companies." *Law & Social Inquiry* 27.

Lofland, J., and Lofland, L.H. (1995) *Analyzing Social Settings: A Guide to Qualitative Research and Analysis*. Belmont, CA: Wadsworth.

MacKinnon, C. (1987) *Feminism Unmodified: Discourses on Life and Law*. Cambridge, MA: Harvard University Press.

—— (1989) *Toward a Feminist Theory of the State*. Cambridge, MA: Harvard University Press.

McCann, M.W. (1993) "Reform Litigation on Trial." *Law and Social Inquiry* 17:715–743.

—— (1994) *Rights at Work: Pay Equity Reform and the Politics of Legal Mobilizations*. Chicago: University of Chicago Press.

McCann, M.W., Haltom, W., and Bloom, A. (2001) "Java Jive: Genealogy of a Judicial Icon." *University of Miami Law Review* 56:113.

McCann, M.W., and March, T. (1996) "Law and Everyday Forms of Resistance: A Socio-Political Assessment." *Studies in Law, Politics, and Society* 15.

McGuire, K.T. (1995) "Repeat Players in Supreme Court: The Role of Experienced Lawyers in Litigation." *The Journal of Politics* 57:187–196.

Major, B., and Kaiser, C.R. (2003) "Perceiving and Claiming Discrimination." Paper presented at the conference "Rights and Realities: Legal and Social Scientific Approaches to Employment Legislation," sponsored by Stanford Law School and the American Bar Foundation.

Marshall, A-M. (2003) "Injustice Frames, Legality, and the Everyday Construction of Sexual Harassment." *Law and Social Inquiry* 28(3):659–690.

Nielsen, L.B. (2000) "Situating Legal Consciousness: Experiences and Attitudes of Ordinary Citizens about Law and Street Harassment." *Law and Society Review* 34:201–236.

—— (2001) "Power in Public: Reactions, Responses, and Resistance to Offensive Racist and Sexually Suggestive Speech." *American Bar Foundation Working Paper Series* 2001.

—— (2002) "Subtle, Pervasive, Harmful: Racist and Sexist Remarks in Public as Hate Speech." *Journal of Social Issues* 58:265–280.

—— (2004) *License to Harass: Law, Hierarchy, and Offensive Public Speech*. Princeton: Princeton University Press.

Nielsen, L.B., and Beim, A. (2004) "Media Misrepresentation: Title VII, Print Media, and Public Perceptions of Discrimination Litigation." *Stanford Law and Policy Review*.

Nielsen, L.B., and Nelson, R.L. (2005) "Scaling the Pyramid: A Sociolegal Model of Employment Discrimination Litigation" in L.B. Nielsen and R.L. Nelson (eds) *Legal and Social Scientific Perspectives on Employment Discrimination*. Amsterdam: Kluwer Academic Publishers.

Olson, W.K. (1991) *The Litigation Explosion: What Happened When America Unleashed the Lawsuit*. New York: Dutton.

—— (1997) *The Excuse Factory: How Employment Law is Paralyzing the American Workplace*. New York: Martin Kessler Books.

—— (2003) *The Rule of Lawyers: How the New Litigation Elite Threatens America's Rule of Law*. Truman Talley Books.

Rosenberg, G.N. (1991) *The Hollow Hope: Can Courts Bring About Social Change?* Chicago: University of Chicago Press.

Sarat, Austin (1990) "The Law is All Over: Power, Resistance, and the Legal Consciousness of the Welfare Poor." *Yale Journal of Law and Humanities* 2.

Schultz, V. (1998) "Reconceptualizing Sexual Harassment." *Yale Law Journal* 107:1683–1805.

Scott, J.C. (1990) *Domination and the Arts of Resistance: Hidden Transcripts*. New Haven: Yale University Press.

Shields, R. (1991) *Places on the Margin: Alternative Geographies of Modernity*. London: Routledge.

Silbey, S.S., and Ewick, P. (2003) "The Architecture of Authority: The Place of Law in the Space of Science" in A. Sarat, L. Douglas, and M. Umphrey (eds) *The Place of Law*. Ann Arbor: University of Michigan Press.

Spelman, E.V. (1988) *Inessential Woman: Problems of Exclusion in Feminist Thought.* Boston: Beacon Press.

Tushnet, M. (1984) "An Essay on Rights." *Texas Law Review* 62:1363.

Volokh, E. (1992) "Freedom of Speech and Workplace Harassment." *University of California Law Review* 39:1791.

Waldron, J. (1995) "Rights." in *A Companion to Contemporary Political Philosophy*, edited by R.E. Goodin and P. Pettit. Oxford: Blackwell.

West, R. (1987) "The Differences in Women's Hedonic Lives." *Wisconsin Women's Law Journal* 3.

Yngvesson, B. (1988) "Making Law at the Doorway: The Clerk, the Court, and the Construction of Community in a New England Town." *Law and Society Review* 22:409–448.

Young, I.M. (1990) *Justice and the Politics of Difference.* Princeton: Princeton University Press.

Index

www.ingramcontent.com/pod-product-compliance
Ingram Content Group UK Ltd.
Pitfield, Milton Keynes, MK11 3LW, UK
UKHW020357010325
455677UK00021B/499